Stability and Change in German Elections

Stability and Change in German Elections

How Electorates Merge, Converge, or Collide

**Edited by
Christopher J. Anderson
and Carsten Zelle**

**Westport, Connecticut
London**

JN
3971
.A95
S696
1998

Library of Congress Cataloging-in-Publication Data

Stability and change in German elections : how electorates merge,
    converge, or collide / edited by Christopher J. Anderson and Carsten
    Zelle.
        p.   cm.
    Includes bibliographical references and index.
    ISBN 0–275–96254–7 (alk. paper)
    1. Elections—Germany.   2. Germany—Politics and government—1990–
I. Anderson, Christopher, 1966–   . II. Zelle, Carsten.
JN3971.A95S696   1998
324.943′087—dc21   98–15651

British Library Cataloguing in Publication Data is available.

Library of Congress Catalog Card Number: 98–15651
ISBN: 0–275–96254–7

First published in 1998

Praeger Publishers, 88 Post Road West, Westport, CT 06881
An imprint of Greenwood Publishing Group, Inc.

Printed in the United States of America

The paper used in this book complies with the
Permanent Paper Standard issued by the National
Information Standards Organization (Z39.48–1984).

10 9 8 7 6 5 4 3 2 1

To Carsten

scholar, collaborator, friend

CONTENTS

ACKNOWLEDGMENTS

Carsten died unexpectedly as we were finishing work on the volume. On his behalf I thank his colleagues at the University of Potsdam and the Konrad Adenauer Foundation for their help and his family for their encouragement, love, and support. Carsten was an outstanding scholar of German politics and political behavior as well as a dear friend. We continue to miss him.

I would like to thank Ron Gelleny for creating the index and Katie Chase and Marcia Goldstein for guiding the book through the editorial process. The Political Science Department at Binghamton University (SUNY) provided a wonderful home while working on the completion of the manuscript.

Finally, I am grateful to Kathleen O'Connor for all the things she does.

ABBREVIATIONS

BP: Bavarian Party

BHE: Federation of Expellees

BverfG: Federal Constitutional Court

B90/Greens or Alliance90/Greens: The Greens

CDU: Christian Democratic Union

CNEP: Comparative National Elections Project

CSU: Christian Social Union

DP: German Party

DSU: German Social Union

FDP: Free Democratic Party

FGW: Forschungsgruppe Wahlen

FRG: Federal Republic of Germany

GB/BHE: All-German Bloc/Alliance of Expellees

GDR: German Democratic Republic

GVP: All-German People's Party

KPD: Communist Party of Germany

KSPW: Research Commission on the Social, Political, and Economic
           Development in the New States

LDPD: Liberal Democratic Party of Germany

NPD: National Democratic Party

PDS: Party of Democratic Socialism

SED: Socialist Unity Party

SPD: Social Democratic Party of Germany

WV: Wählervereinigung (nonparty local citizens ticket)

Z: Center Party

Stability and Change
in German Elections

Introduction: German Elections After Modernization and Unification

Christopher J. Anderson and Carsten Zelle

This volume presents analyses of electoral trends in Germany–the only democracy in the world that saw its electorate enlarged by compatriots who had experienced over four decades of Communist rule. The chapters provide those interested in Germany, the postsocialist states, or democratic politics and elections more generally with research that examines the dynamics of an electorate where ongoing trends of Western modernization merge, or collide with, the transformation of a postsocialist society. Against this backdrop, most contributions to this volume focus on those factors that have long been known to affect electoral choice in West Germany as well as elsewhere in the Western world. Moreover, the individual chapters examine long-term electoral changes resulting from processes of modernization, short-term electoral dynamics caused by the process of German unification, or both.

In advanced industrial democracies, long-term electoral change can result from an erosion of social cleavages along which parties organize, from changes in citizens' values and ideology, or from a weakening of partisan ties, to name just a few (Dalton 1996). German unification may have affected these trends in the Länder (states) of the old West Germany. Moreover, it also may have drastically altered electoral politics in Germany as a whole if the voters in the new Länder (the former East Germany) exhibit voting behavior significantly different from the West. This volume therefore examines the factors we know to be of importance for voting behavior in the West (e.g., social class, values, and party identification) in both parts of the newly unified country. Because some electoral conditions are the result of the peculiar situation of transformation in the new Länder (e.g., the case of the electoral fortunes of the Communist party, PDS or Party of Democratic Socialism), a few chapters are devoted to East Germany specifically. Finally, several chapters attempt to stretch the boundaries of traditional electoral research by focusing on variables such as political institutions, which are not commonly considered in electoral analyses. In this introductory chapter, we elaborate the common theme, present the questions that guide the analyses, and lay out how these are addressed by the contributions to this volume.

MODERNIZATION AND UNIFICATION: CONSEQUENCES FOR ELECTORAL BEHAVIOR

Electoral behavior is influenced by both long-term and short-term factors. Starting with the classic voting studies by Berelson et al. (1954), social scientists have demonstrated how relatively stable traits such as an individual's social background (class, education, gender, age, and the like) "predispose" certain electoral decisions. About a decade later, Campbell et al. (1960) showed that long-term psychological attachments to a political party, termed "party identification," also exert a strong influence on vote choice. Subsequent research added value orientations and ideology to the list of potential long-term determinants of partisan orientations, although the long-term impact of these factors remains subject to intense scholarly debate. In addition to these long-standing influences on electoral behavior, several short-term factors have been shown to influence voting decisions: the issues of an election, the candidates, and possibly the current image of a political party. Although initially developed to understand voter behavior in the United States, these concepts have proven useful in the study of other electorates, particularly of voting behavior in the West German case.

Although it is a truism to say that German elections and electoral behavior have changed, the contours of what has changed and why remain vague. As in most other mature democracies, the modernization of society over the course of the past decades (particularly the growth of the new middle class and the rise in educational attainment) is said to have brought about a number of changes in the structures of German electoral politics. Though numerous variants exist, researchers have pointed to a decrease in the influence of long-term factors on electoral behavior all the while voters' decisions became more attuned to politics of the day. Social class in particular is said to have become less important because the new middle class has not been integrated into the cleavage structure of advanced Western societies. As a consequence, so the argument goes, party identification has become less important as well. This latter development was accelerated by the rising levels of education, which make lasting party attachments dispensable as a cue for electoral choice. Simultaneously, value patterns have become more complex as postmaterialism is on the rise, thus adding even greater complexity to contemporary electoral politics. These new values intrude on the traditional political contrast between "left" and "right" and alter the meanings of these ideological poles for voters.

It would be more than worthwhile to devote a book solely to these developments, monitoring the degree of change in these various dimensions and documenting the effects they have on electoral choice. And although much research has been conducted on individual aspects, it has been more than one and a half decades since a comprehensive study traced trends of this sort in order to paint a comprehensive picture of German electoral behavior (Baker, Dalton and Hildebrandt 1981). The importance of a new attempt to offer an encompassing account of electoral dynamics in Germany is underscored by the fact that the above-mentioned trends of modernization not only have continued but have assumed new shapes as well.

Yet, this already colorful mosaic of electoral developments was complicated even further by the advent of German unification. In 1989, the Communist regime of eastern Germany was shaken by civil unrest. As a result of the rapid transformation of the German Democratic Republic (GDR), as East Germany was officially known, eastern Germans for the first time had the opportunity to express a free choice in the parliamentary elections of March 1990. In October of that year, the unification of Germany created a new electorate, which turned out to be roughly one-fifth larger than that of the old West Germany. Finally, the first all-German elections since the Weimar Republic were held in December of 1990. And although empirical study of the enlarged electorate began immediately after the first elections, the tremendous intellectual challenge to understand what drives voters in Germany after unification and modernization remains.

While there are a number of ways in which unification may have affected electoral dynamics in Germany, several key questions remain: For example, how different is voting behavior in the East and the West? Moreover, how do these differences fit into the trends of modernization experienced by West Germans? These differences may result in different relationships between long-term and short-term determinants of electoral choice. Yet it also is possible that some factors work in a different way, that some concepts are of no use at all, or that additional concepts will have to be employed to capture what is happening to voters' decisions. These differences might accelerate changes observed in Western Germany, they might slow them down, they might alter their course, or they might instigate trends not observed before. This volume seeks to investigate these questions in greater detail than has been the case to date.

A NEW TYPE OF VOTER? THE BALANCE BETWEEN SHORT-TERM AND LONG-TERM FACTORS

What are the influences on electoral behavior? How did they change during the course of several decades? How are they different between East and West? These are some of the questions that guide the contributions to this volume. Contributions to the first section are variations on the questions of whether a new type of voter has resulted from either unification or social modernization. Change could have occurred in three different ways, all of which constitute dealignment phenomena. First, the *size* of the groups exposed to long-term influences could be changing, leading to a shrinking of the core electorates traditionally mobilized by political parties. Second, the intragroup *coherence* of these core electorates could be diminishing because the intensity of the long-term influence has lessened. This would make even these core electorates less reliable for parties. Third, *individual attachments* to the parties could be in a process of weakening, leading to an increase in volatility at the aggregate level.

Peter Gluchowski and Ulrich von Wilamowitz-Moellendorff examine the first two of these propositions. They first document that the very groups that cleavage theory has identified as being closely linked with a major party have been shrinking, indicating a dealignment of the first kind. What is more, they demonstrate convincingly that there are signs of erosion even within these groups: Even union members who identify as belonging to the working class stand less firmly behind the Social Democrats, while the Christian Democrats continuously lose ground among those affiliated with a church. Thus, dealignment of the second type is occurring in western Germany as well.

Did these effects of modernization accelerate as a result of unification? At first glance, this appears highly likely because the explanatory value of concepts such as social structure appears dubious in the East. After all, the Communist regime defined society as having overcome class divisions. At the same time, it systematically restricted church activity and membership. As a consequence, the early studies of eastern German voters claimed that there were few if any long-term influences on electoral choice (Roth 1990). According to this interpretation, unification appeared to accelerate trends associated with social modernization, and the eastern voter assumed the role of a radically modernized individual: a voter purely oriented toward short-term factors—that is, not exposed to any long-term forces such as social background and party identification.

It soon became apparent that this position was overstated. Bluck and Kreikenbom (1991), for example, detected attachments to western political parties that had developed throughout most of eastern Germany during the Communist era via exposure to western TV. In his chapter, Karl Schmitt investigates whether and to what extent social background plays a role for eastern Germans. He presents convincing evidence that class divisions existed in Communist Germany as well, and that they continue to influence voting behavior—though in patterns very different from the western ones. Moreover, eastern Germans are exposed to the influence of religiosity as well, although there are differences to the West. Long-term influences thus do exist in eastern Germany, but they function differently than in the West. Rather than merely accelerating the process of dealignment among traditional cleavages, unification actually enlarged the cleavage structure in the new Germany.

Given these findings, individual-level analyses of voting behavior can indicate whether the third type of dealignment plays a role as well. Reviewing hypotheses and evidence that have been proposed by researchers in this field, Carsten Zelle argues that the dealignment view is less than a sure bet on a theoretical level, even though the vast majority of electoral researchers supports it. As for the empirical evidence, it is contradictory. To be sure: data from various sources do indicate a decline in partisanship after unification. There also is little doubt that party identification is weaker in eastern Germany. Yet the matter is less clear when viewed from a long-term perspective. While some trends indicate a decline in partisanship in the old Länder before 1990, a large number of trends does not. Moreover, the results from cross-sectional analyses frequently run counter to the expectations of the dealignment view. In sum, the empirical evidence is not sufficiently clear to discriminate between rivaling hypotheses. Thus, Zelle argues that two interpretations can claim empirical support: Some findings support the hypothesis of a gradual dealignment that has taken place during the process of social modernization. Yet it is also possible to interpret the recent decline as resulting from public dissatisfaction that has reached record levels in the early 1990s and thus may be associated with the problems produced by the unification process.

Angelika Vetter and Oscar W. Gabriel investigate a different aspect of the relative importance of long-term and short-term influences on electoral choice. When considering the balance between long-term and short-term factors, it is frequently claimed that short-term factors have become more important as psychological attachments to parties or social ties have weakened. One implication of this dealignment view is the hypothesis that person- (or candidate-) oriented voting is on the rise. This perspective has gained popularity with electoral analysts who have proposed both social modernization and unification as mechanisms underlying this development. Vetter and Gabriel investigate this question for the 1972-94 period and find little evidence for an increased role of the chancellor candidate in voting decisions. Hence, if electoral behavior became more reliant on short-term factors, this trend did not assume the shape of an increased role of candidate-orientations in the German case. Given that a large portion of political analysts and an even larger percentage of political practitioners apparently think the opposite, this finding is most remarkable. Note, however, that even this finding is not sufficient to reject the more general hypothesis. After all, although a rise in candidate-orientedness is a possible, and maybe even likely, consequence of eroding partisan ties, it is by no means a necessary one. In fact, Vetter and Gabriel propose to interpret the evidence as a dealignment that did not lead to an increase in candidate-orientedness. The authors also compare the relative influence of candidate images between East and West. After all, if long-term factors were indeed less influential in the eastern part of the country, short-term factors should be carrying more weight there. Yet, consistent with the findings for the West, the pull of the candidates is not dramatically stronger in the East.

Much in the same vein, the chapter by Hans Rattinger and Jürgen Krämer tests the plausible notion that voting behavior in the East is more closely connected to the current state of the economy. This would constitute evidence for the interpretation that eastern voters are more issue-oriented. Yet results show that this is the case only to a limited extent. To begin with, the effects of economic evaluations are rather weak. Moreover, they are not generally more pronounced in the East. "Our results show once more," Rattinger and Krämer conclude, "that the differences between East and West are gradual rather than categorical." Apparently, unification has complicated the structure of political conflict in Germany more than it has led to the influx of a new type of voter.

While the analyses presented here supported the first two dealignment hypotheses, they were less favorable to the third one. Possibly, the weakening of social cleavages does not imply that individual voting behavior is devoid of long-term influences. A possible candidate for lasting orientations may be political schema. Indeed, Wolfgang Jagodzinski and Steffen M. Kühnel, who compare the meaning of "left" and "right" in 1976 and 1990, find "more stability than change" in this respect. Partisan attachments and the dominant cleavages continue to define the content of these terms. Thus, it is not the case that the political discourse became more open as a consequence of social modernization. Instead, there are signs of considerable stability in voters' orientations.

Yet, while it did not become more open on the old dimension of "left" and "right," perhaps it was partially transferred onto another dimension of political conflict. This is an implication of the claim that a new cleavage emerged over the course of the past decades that did not necessarily erode, but added onto the traditional cleavage structure. If this was the case, the ideological space would have widened, while producing more possibilities and increasing ambiguity at the same time. Markus Klein examines this widely accepted notion for the case of a new postmaterialist cleavage and finds remarkably little evidence to support it. In fact, contrary to expectations, the materialist-postmaterialist dimension as developed by Ronald Inglehart (1977, 1990) is hardly related to partisan preferences at all. In fact, by the 1990s, it is no longer true that the Greens are predominantly the party of the postmaterialists. Klein also raises serious doubts with regard to whether a postmaterialist value change actually occurred, by pointing to the close connection of the proportions of materialists and postmaterialists with objective economic conditions. While scholars such as Dieter Fuchs and Robert Rohrschneider (1998) argue that it may be conceivable to integrate this connection into Inglehart's theory at least for the time after unification, Klein emphasizes that this dimension fails to detect the changes that truly are occurring in Germany; changes, which he suspects are taking place within the category of the mixed materialist/postmaterialist types. In sum, while Klein's findings once more show that Inglehart introduced a tremendously interesting and challenging concept into the debate on political and electoral change, they also caution once more against making hasty connections between postmaterialism and electoral change.

The final contribution to this first section turns the search for a "new type of voter" into the quest for a "new type of nonvoter," thus investigating factors that may explain the conspicuous decline in electoral turnout in Germany. Thomas Kleinhenz finds that social change cannot account for the decline in turnout in Germany. His analysis reveals that this trend occurred largely independently of the changing composition of the electorate. In fact, it is impossible to pinpoint nonvoters as representing particular social groups. Though the factors causing the decline thus remain unidentified, Kleinhenz interprets these findings as indicating the advent of a new type of nonvoter. Due to the changes in the electorate, and due to the fact that those factors that had been of some help in explaining nonvoting lost the little clout they have had, the nonvoters became more middle class and more average in outlook.

When viewed together, these first contributions confirmed the aggregate aspects of the dealignment perspective but also shed serious doubts on several widely accepted common wisdoms regarding individual level dealignment. In particular, popular claims to the effect that electoral behavior became less tied to long-term forces as a consequence of modernization, unification, or both, did not fare overly well in these analyses.

COLLISIONS BETWEEN EAST AND WEST? REGIONAL DIFFERENCES IN PARTY SYSTEMS

The research presented so far has examined whether East and West are converging, or possibly even merging altogether, with respect to the different trends produced by modernization and unification. Yet there also are instances of open collision between the two electorates (or parts of them). These are most obvious when it comes to the electoral fortunes of the post-Communist party (Party of Democratic Socialism). The electoral showings of this party led to striking differences between the party systems of the old and new Länder. Thus, while Social Democrats and Christian Democrats are the main players in what qualifies as a bipolar party system in the West, the PDS constitutes a third pole in the East. Moreover, the small parties (Greens and Free Democrats) are essentially absent in the East (except for the Land legislature of Saxony-Anhalt, where the Greens obtained 5.1 percent of the vote).

In an innovative approach to the study of electoral politics, Ulrich Eith examines these differences more closely. His database is election returns at the local level. For one, he finds that local election results follow much the same pattern as do elections at the national or state levels, unless there are particular legal regulations. In the present context, a second finding is even more relevant: The constellation of conflict is indeed different in the eastern Länder. Unlike the situation in the old Länder, where CDU (Christian Democratic Union) and SPD (Social Democratic Party) are the antipodes, the CDU confronts the PDS as the major foe in the East. This has tremendous implications for the understanding of partisan dynamics in East and West, as it does for the campaign strategies of the major parties.

If the PDS is at the heart of this dramatic difference between East and West, what are the factors that drive support for this party? The importance of this question is underscored by the fact that the electoral share of the PDS almost doubled between 1990 and 1994, rising from 11 to 20 percent of the eastern electorate. Carsten Zelle examines the factors underlying this development. He finds that the increase in PDS support is only marginally related to the parallel increase in unemployment in East Germany. Instead, the newly found adherence to socialism and political dissatisfaction—that is, issues and ideology—fare much better as explanations of PDS support. In addition to these factors, a third type of variable not commonly considered in electoral research plays a role: regional identifications. In line with the notion that unification produced a regional cleavage in Germany, PDS support is to a considerable degree rooted in a sense of belonging to eastern Germany.

NEW DIRECTIONS: THE IMPACT OF POLITICAL FACTORS ON GERMAN ELECTIONS

In a democracy, the behavior of the electorate influences how politics is conducted. Yet there also are effects of politics on electoral behavior. Therefore, it is important to study how politics is presented to voters and how the resulting perceptions affect vote choice. The study of media effects played a dominant role in the early period of electoral research (e.g., Berelson et al. 1954). Media effects are of particular importance in the case of unified Germany because mass communication followed an entirely different logic in the Communist state. Hence, the dynamics of these effects might be expected to undergo change if new patterns developed in the East. In their chapter, Frank Brettschneider and Peter R. Schrott compare East and West Germans' use of mass media and political communication. In particular, they examine whether potential differences between the two groups have diminished between 1990 and 1995. They find that mass media are used more extensively in the eastern German Länder than in the former West Germany. They attribute this to the greater need for a new political orientation in the East during times of momentous change. However, there appears to be a convergence in media exposure over time. Television is the main information source, and there are few differences between East and West regarding interpersonal communication. For half of all Germans, politics is not a topic for discussion, and about 25 percent not only talk politics frequently, but also try to persuade their communication partners. Moreover, consistent with earlier research on the topic, those who pay more attention to politics and obtain more information also are more likely to vote.

The causal factors identified by this type of research are located at the macro level, but the analysis remains faithful to the individualistic approach. Because of tremendous theoretical and methodological difficulties, electoral research only rarely ventures beyond this strategy. Yet at times this may the only way to empirically assess the effects of the options presented to the electorate. Ulrich Eith's study is unusual because of this: His research design allows an assessment of the effects of electoral laws on electoral outcomes (see above). Thomas D. Lancaster's contribution is similar in this regard. He examines how the characteristics of candidates for the Bundestag at the district level affect electoral outcomes. Remarkably, he finds that incumbency influences district outcomes even in Germany's party-dominated system. Moreover, candidates' gender and age affect the distribution of votes in the district. Candidate effects thus are present not only in the case of the candidates for the top office, but also in the races for parliament. In light of this finding, German voters' increasing tendency to "split the ticket" should not be interpreted in terms of partisan strategy exclusively. Lancaster's conclusion thus adds substantially to our knowledge of German politics: "While individual district candidates clearly ride the electoral fortunes of their political parties, the type of candidate also affects German electoral dynamics."

These findings indicate that it is as important to study the range of options presented to voters as it is to study the agent of the decision–that is, the voter. Reflecting our conviction that it is important for electoral researchers–particularly in the German case–to move beyond the level of individual voters, the final contribution to this volume constitutes an investigation of how the options that are presented to voters emerge as a function of institutional arrangements. Susan E. Scarrow analyzes how political parties compete (or fail to compete) in the structuring of the competition itself. She finds that electoral change may be strongly influenced by the struggle over institutions. Her conclusion that "German parties often cooperate in cartel fashion to promote common structural interests" means that there are political domains–in this case legislation governing party finance–that are beyond the control of electoral politics. These phenomena may help us understand the decline in political satisfaction that has occurred. This would be important in the present context: since political dissatisfaction appears as an explanatory factor for phenomena of electoral change (for instance for turnout decline in the case of Kleinhenz and for the decline in party identification in the case of Zelle), this links the macro level of politics and the micro level of electoral behavior. If future research is successful in establishing connections of this kind, we may find that the way politics is conducted is causally connected to electoral developments. More specifically, this may be true for the details of the design of the framework for electoral competition that Scarrow analyzes. Her analysis shows that changes in voters' behavior may be accelerated or dampened by institutional design. This may occur purposefully–as was the case when certain parties were excluded from the electoral competition in the early years of the Federal Republic through the design of electoral laws, or unwillingly–when the very same regulations made it possible for new parties to enter the system (as was the case for the PDS). Consequences that were both unexpected and undesired appear likely in the case of the regulations of party finance as well. Possibly, the electoral showings of the right-wing parties in the 1980s and 1990s, which are frequently considered an indication of dealignment, might not have been as impressive had it not been for the visibility these parties could afford with the help of public money.

ELECTIONS IN UNITED GERMANY: MORE STABILITY THAN CHANGE?

The individual contributions to this volume offer a wealth of analyses on electoral dynamics in Germany, substantially expanding our knowledge of this part of the political process. Naturally, not all of the pieces of evidence fit together perfectly, and a clear account of what electoral politics in united Germany is about does not, and possibly cannot be expected to, easily emerge. Yet, despite a number of frictions and even some contradictions, a large area of common ground became visible from different angles. Though we certainly cannot do justice to all the contributions, it tempting to identify the major trends:

1. The modernization of German society has changed the balance of long-term forces in the electorate. However, it has not led to a general loss of long-term

predispositions (such as party identification, values, or ideology) for individual voters.

2. Unification has accelerated some of the trends associated with modernization, but long-term influences on electoral behavior are present in eastern Germany as well.

3. Unification has added a new set of conditions to German electoral dynamics. Some long-term forces, such as social class, function differently in East and West; while others, such as region, appear of unique relevance to eastern Germany.

4. Politics, politicians and institutions matter. Yet much too little is known about how they matter, making the connection between the macropolitics and micropolitics an important avenue for future research. These variables should be incorporated as potential causes of electoral change rather than merely being portrayed as having to bear their consequences.

We hope that the findings reported here–be they within this common ground as we perceive it or outside of it–stimulate discussion and further research and thus make this book useful as a starting point for further inquiries into the politics of German electoral change.

Part I

A NEW TYPE OF VOTER?
THE BALANCE BETWEEN SHORT-TERM
AND LONG-TERM FACTORS

2

The Erosion of Social Cleavages in Western Germany, 1971-97

Peter M. Gluchowski
and Ulrich von Wilamowitz-Moellendorff

The relationship between social structure and voting behavior ranks among the most frequently and empirically best-researched topics of party competition and voter behavior. Early election studies conducted in the United States in the 1940s and 1950s (the so-called Columbia and Michigan schools) examined individual voting decisions on the basis of social group influences, albeit clearly coming to different conclusions (Berelson et al. 1954; Campbell et al. 1960). The first German studies of voting behavior continued this tradition (Blücher 1962), and almost all subsequent scholarly volumes on German elections, appearing regularly after a federal election, contain chapters on the impact of social structure on voting behavior and election outcomes (representative are Klingemann and Kaase [1994] and respective interim volumes; Oberndörfer [1978]; Veen and Noelle-Neumann [1991]). Similarly, a description of the voting behavior of different social groups by now has become an integral part of the continuous election reporting of the leading polling institutes such as the Forschungsgruppe Wahlen and Infas (Forschungsgruppe Wahlen 1994a; Infas 1994).

Under these circumstances another examination of the sociostructural bases of party competition may not sound particularly worthwhile were it not for conflicting conclusions scholars and commentators have drawn about the declining influence of social structure on voting behavior in West Germany. These differences merit a new analysis of whether and how the relationship between social structure and party preference has changed over time. Our analysis is based on a cumulative data set that has not previously been used. It contains representative opinion surveys conducted by the Department of Political Research of the Konrad Adenauer Foundation since 1971 and thus constitutes a data set that allows an investigation of how individual behavior has changed over time.

THEORETICAL FOUNDATIONS: CLEAVAGE THEORY AND THE THEORY OF SOCIAL MILIEUS

At the macro level, the connection between social structure and party preference was described in two similar ways. Both the theory of social cleavages proposed by Lipset and Rokkan (1967), as well as Lepsius' (1966) theory of social milieus trace the development of party systems, and above all their stability and durability, to sociostructurally consolidated, opposing interests in a society. Lipset and Rokkan employ a dynamic explanatory model, which interprets the emergence of party systems as the translation of conflicting social interests into party alternatives. According to this model, fundamental dissimilarities in interests characterize societal cleavages. Group interests organize themselves along these cleavages and find ultimate expression in the establishment of parties as "alliances in conflicts over politics and value commitments within the larger body politic" (Lipset and Rokkan 1967: 5). These parties bind themselves to their clientele through continuous political articulation of the respective group interests, and thus organize themselves rather durably along the main cleavages of the society. A transformation of the societal conflict system on the level of the party system ensues, resulting in an association of sociostructural groups and party system that is extraordinarily stable. Based on their comparative analysis of party systems, Lipset and Rokkan (1967: 50) conclude that "the party systems of the 1960s reflect, with few but significant exceptions, the cleavage structures of the 1920s."

For Lepsius (1973), the party system also constitutes the expression of basic political orientations that have been molded by sociostructural context, and which reflect constitutive social conflicts within a society. However, according to his conception, parties are not only shaped by the conflicts which predominated at their formation, but also from dissimilarities in societal interests which arise later. Circumstances permitting, the structure of social conflict in society is expressed in multiple ways. Lepsius uses the expression "social milieus" to describe basic social and political orientations (synonyms are "sociomoral milieus," "sociocultural milieus," and the more general "attitudinal communities"). He employs this expression as a term for social units that are created by the coincidence of multiple structural dimensions such as religion, regional tradition, economic situation, cultural orientation, and the class-specific composition of intermediate groups. A milieu is a sociocultural creation, defined by the specific attachment of such dimensions to a distinct sector of the population.

As Lepsius sees it, social conflicts lead to the formation of these social milieus through a process of reciprocal fortification of shared experiences and contacts among persons with identical or similar interests. The recognition of similarities is ultimately experienced by individuals as membership in a group of people who live in similar circumstances and hold corresponding attitudes and political preferences. It leads to a "we-feeling" that is central to the formation of a social milieu. Lepsius views this social milieu as an attitudinal community that gradually consolidates itself organizationally: "Each one of these attitude communities is linked to pre-political visions of order, social strata and religious communities, and develops its own political-social subculture" (1973: 61, authors' translation).

One further characteristic of a social milieu is that the individuals who identify themselves with it consider it a reference group (Naßmacher 1979). In its capacity as reference group the social milieu cultivates group standards—that is, more or less binding perceptions, norms and codes of conduct, according to which committed group members as well as the party linked to the group orient themselves. Seen from this perspective, the concept of social milieus fulfills an important function: to wit, the cleavage theory with its concept of (self-) interest cannot answer the question as to how sociostructurally mediated norms of political behavior operate between individuals of a specific conflict group and the parties which represent them (Klingemann and Steinwede 1993). As intervening institutions, social milieus depict the connecting link between individual interests and their institutional representation. In this context, Pappi and Laumann (1974:160) emphasize the important function of societal value orientation: "As a rule, the serious interest disparities in a society are fought out with recourse to societal value orientations. Only through endowment with cultural significance do they become relevant for political action" (authors' translation). According to this conception, the ties between voting groups and respective parties must be constantly renewed. This is aided by the positions parties take in contemporary political controversies that fall along traditional cleavage lines.

According to the cleavage and social milieu approaches, a reciprocal effect exists between sociostructurally relevant groups, defined by dimensions of conflict, and the parties which represent them. The former vote for parties to assert the interests, norms, and values particular to their group; the latter actively shape political conflicts in order to mobilize their typical groups of voters at election time and thus maximize their proportion of the votes. The translation of societal conflicts into the realm of politics is thus greatly dependent on the mobilizing effect of parties. This way, a politicized social structure is a decisive contributing determinant of party competition.

THE LINKAGE OF SOCIAL STRUCTURE AND PARTY PREFERENCE IN WEST GERMANY

Above all, two long-term political cleavages were crucial to the German party system: the conflict between labor and capital, as well as the conflict between church and state.[1] The origins of the German Social Democratic Party lie in the class conflict, which can be traced back to the time of the Industrial Revolution. While the SPD developed into the representative of the working classes, conservative parties were established as a counterweight to safeguard the interests of employers (Metje 1994).

The partisan visibility of the denominational cleavage between Catholics and Protestants goes back to the *Kulturkampf* in the German Empire, when Bismarck tried to integrate the Catholic population through violent means. Political Catholicism gained in strength as a result of the *Kulturkampf*, and the Center Party

(*Zentrumspartei*) was constituted as the political representative of Catholics. The Center Party organized and articulated the Catholic protest against a Protestant dominated empire (Pappi 1985). An opposing organization in the form of political representation for Protestants did not originate at this time because there was no need for this group to organize along the denominational cleavage by virtue of the close link between the Protestant church and the Prussian state (Schmitt 1989).

The influence of these historical cleavages on voting behavior proved to be extraordinarily stable during the Empire and the Weimar Republic until the end of the 1920s. After World War II, the reconstituted parties of the Federal Republic latched onto the traditional cleavages in a slightly modified way. While the SPD, in close political cooperation with unions and other labor organizations, resumed its former role of representing the interests of the working classes, the CDU and, in a limited sense the Christian Social Union (CSU), arose as supradenominational parties. On one hand, they continued in the tradition of the Center Party; on the other hand, they also successfully integrated Protestant voters. Thus, the denominational cleavage became a religious one–that is, a cleavage between devout Christians and those members of the population who distanced themselves from Christianity. The intensity of religious commitment superseded the cleavage between Catholics and non-Catholics. Strong ties between the Christian Union parties (CDU/CSU) and the churches, including their organizational networks, were also formed. Moreover, on the strength of its economic policy, the CDU/CSU developed into the party of the bourgeoisie and entrepreneurs, the so-called old middle classes, thus becoming the class-transcending antagonist to the SPD, the representative of labor. Pappi (1977: 196) refers, however, to a peculiarity of the party system in the former Federal Republic: in his view it was "asymmetrical, because a party with the economic ideology of organized labor was up against not a primarily economic conservative party, but rather a religious traditional party" (authors' translation).

In these alliances within the former Federal Republic one can observe significant continuity in the traditional system of conflict. The sociostructurally anchored cleavages between occupational groups and denominational-religious groups still find expression in the West German party system: the SPD finds the most backing among the working classes, whereas the CDU/CSU has its strongest bastions among Catholics and the old middle classes. Regarding party preference, a cleavage has crystallized between Protestants with strong church ties and those lacking such a commitment. Those who feel strongly tied to their denomination lean more toward the CDU/CSU, whereas Protestants without religious attachment tend to prefer the SPD.

As mediating agencies, unions and churches play an important role in mobilizing party preference: in elections the respective party sympathies were constantly highest among union-oriented workers and practicing Christians of both denominations. Typical voter alignments within respective societal groups are strengthened by emotional and organizational ties to the particular intermediary. This suggests that social milieus have a regulative impact on attitudes in the Federal Republic (West) as well. Regarding party competition, this means that the two main parties, CDU/CSU and SPD, can rely on a base of sociostructurally tied core voters. To a large degree, their shares of the vote are thus linked to the sociostructural development of the Federal Republic.

CHANGES IN THE RELATIONSHIP BETWEEN SOCIAL STRUCTURE AND PARTY PREFERENCE IN WEST GERMANY: TWO ASPECTS OF CHANGE

Until the 1980s, the stability of the voter-party-coalitions described above was hardly an issue in election research. Since the beginning of that decade, however, and increasingly in the 1990s, signs of change are emerging in election results. At the aggregate level, changes in voting behavior are unrefutably evidenced by declining voter turnout, by declining electoral returns for the *Volksparteien* (people's parties) CDU/CSU and SPD combined, and in the establishment of the Greens in the party system, among others. These trends suggest changes in the underlying relationships between parties and social groups.

Over time, these relationships between social groups and political parties can come under stress in a number of ways. Of the three types of erosion indicated in the introduction to this volume, we investigate the first two in this chapter. Thus, we will briefly demonstrate that the sizes of the groups integrated into social cleavages decreased over time. While this first type of erosion frequently has been documented previously, our subsequent investigation ventures into an area that has been less well explored: employing a unique database, we examine whether the partisan coherence of the social groups remains intact or whether there are signs of the second type of partisan erosion as well. The third type of dealignment, namely individual party affiliations, are the subject of the discussion by Carsten Zelle in chapter 4 of this volume.

Evolution in Sociostructural Composition: Altered Group Sizes

The far-reaching processes of change in occupational structure and radical secularization that have occurred over the last four decades have changed the size of these groups and thus their impact on election outcomes. Considerable redistribution has taken place since 1950 in the economy. Whereas the proportion of those employed in the primary and secondary sectors (agriculture/forestry and manufacturing, respectively) shrank, the tertiary (service) sector grew. In West Germany the share of employment in the service sector has climbed continuously from 34% in 1950 to 57% in 1993 (Statistisches Bundesamt 1994: 83; authors' own calculations of percentages). Alongside these changes in the economic sphere, modifications in occupational structure could be witnessed as well. Within a context of increased overall employment, there was a proportional reduction within, above all, those occupational groups from which the CDU/CSU and the SPD traditionally drew their strongest support. Between 1950 and 1993 the share of blue-collar workers sank from over 50 percent to 36 percent. The proportion of self-employed (including family members who help out) fell from 29 to 11 percent.

Conversely the white-collar workforce has experienced relative growth. While only 20 percent of the gainfully employed in 1950 were either in salaried employment relationships or the civil service, in 1993 over 50 percent held such jobs (Statistisches Bundesamt 1954, 1994). The generations who grew up as part of this occupational group constitute the "new middle class" (Geiger 1967; Dahrendorf 1957), "which is anchored neither in the economic interests and value perception of the 'old' middle class, nor in the those of the strongly union-influenced working classes" (Brinkmann 1988: 25, authors' translation). By virtue of its rapid growth, a typical class mentality could hardly be passed on from one generation to the next. Pappi (1973) has shown that the steady growth of the electoral share of the SPD in the 1950s and 1960s essentially arose as this group moved from a middle-class position to a working-class position in the articulation of conflict, and Klingemann (1985) traces the stabilization of the CDU/CSU-FDP (Free Democratic Party) coalition to a renewed shift in votes within the new middle classes.[2]

The denominational-religious cleavage has also seen considerable change. Dwindling influence by organized religion is a long-term trend that repeatedly has been observed. Over the past decades, Christian-spiritual norms and religious conceptions have been increasingly replaced by secular systems of orientation and belief (Meulemann 1985). Secularization manifests itself above all in declining church membership and decreasing frequency of church attendance. This indicates that aside from the typical milieu groups of the social classes, the denominational-religious milieus are also shrinking. The decrease in frequency of church attendance was especially drastic among Catholics. Whereas 60 percent regularly attended services in 1953, only 26 percent did the so in 1990. During the same time period, the share of Protestants who regularly attended services dropped from 19 to 7 percent (Metje 1994). Together with declining official church membership, this means that only a small minority of the population is still "regularly confronted with the values and norms of organized religion, whereas the by far largest part of the population is to be viewed as weakly or not at all tied to the church" (Gabriel and Brettschneider 1994: 16-18, authors' translation).

These developments have resulted in an intensification of competition for political parties at election time: the traditional clientele, which comprises their share of loyal core voters, has shrunk, and the portion of voters for which they compete has grown. By winning over other voter groups, the CDU/CSU and SPD were, however, able to at least partially compensate for these losses (Gabriel and Brettschneider 1994).[3] The conditions of party competition have changed as the constituencies of the parties have become more similar over the decades (Veen and Gluchowski 1994; Gluchowski and Veen forthcoming).

Decreasing Partisan Coherence of Social Groups Over Time?

The political relevance of a cleavage alignment stems from both the size of the groups integrated into it and the intensity of the link between social group and party. We have documented above that group sizes are shrinking, which signals a weakening of the traditional cleavages. Below, we investigate whether the link between the remaining groups and the respective parties remain as close as they used to be, or if there are signs of erosion in this respect as well.

Why should such a weakening of the connection between social groups and political parties occur? Put simply, the dealignment thesis assumes that the interpretative help that reference groups provide for political decision-making becomes less and less necessary because voters are increasingly capable of reaching decisions in other ways and consequently feel less closely tied to the traditional group norms. The main causes for this are discernible in the following, partially related developments:

- a differentiation in courses of life and the consequent pluralization and individualization of lifestyles beyond traditional social milieus (Zapf et al. 1987; Gluchowski 1991);
- the evolution of the modern welfare state, which has deprived community-building institutions of these functions by accepting responsibility for a growing number of societal duties (e.g., child care, education), as well as providing security regarding major risks in life (e.g., sickness, age, unemployment) (Elias 1987);
- the shift from material to postmaterial values (Inglehart 1977), or rather from values of duty and acceptance to those of freedom and personal development (Klages 1984), leads to awareness of different problems that parties have not yet taken into consideration (Dalton 1986);
- a rise in the level of education (Dalton 1984), combined with the availability of electronic mass media, has facilitated individual opinion formation and decision-making (Denver 1984).

We hypothesize that processes of this kind have been weakening the electoral relevance of membership in a social group that is covered by a traditional cleavage. This is because the traditional social milieus provided the relevant voting cues to the individuals socialized into them. As the processes listed above take place, these cues may be losing impact as the milieus erode, or they may find themselves in competition with new types of cues that are unrelated to them. Either case implies a loss of electoral relevance of the traditional cleavage groups—that is, a process of dealignment. Thus, we hypothesize that voters within these groups are less reliant on the cues provided by the particular group. This should be reflected in a decline in partisan coherence of these groups over time.

CHANGES AFFECTING VOTER-PARTY LOYALTY IN WEST GERMANY SINCE THE EARLY 1970S: AN EMPIRICAL ANALYSIS

While there is a consensus in the scholarly literature that the traditional clientele of parties has indeed shrunk, it also is true that the alliances between these (albeit smaller) voting groups and their parties appear still basically intact. The typical group-specific behavioral pattern was evident in the federal (national) election of October 1994: 73.9 percent of devout Catholics voted for the CDU/CSU, but only 13.8 percent of this group chose the SPD; and among unionized workers, 59.9 percent voted for the Social Democrats and only 27.2 percent for the Christian Democrats (Forschungsgruppe Wahlen 1994a).

The results of the 1994 federal election thus suggest that the interrelations between political parties and their social core voter groups continue to exist in unaltered form. Longitudinal analyses–that is, surveys utilizing the same measuring instrument over a longer period of time–also suggest stability rather than change. Klingemann and Steinwede (1993: 6) write that it would be misleading to speak of an erosion of traditional ties despite all present displays of societal change. The opinion surveys that form the basis for this conclusion are, however, for the most part, election studies completed shortly before elections and provide no information on developments between elections. In addition, the findings are by no means unequivocal; other analyses have come to different conclusions. Franz Urban Pappi (1990) finds that class differences in voting behavior were smaller in the postwar generations, because workers voted less for the SPD or leftist parties in general, while elites and technical personnel in administration, trade, and services were more prone to vote for such parties than corresponding groups of the prewar generation.

In our view, it is important to go beyond election studies when examining group coherence over time. After all, partisan coalitions, though visible on election day only, are supposed to be in place in the years between the elections as well. Yet, because there is less need for the parties to rely on these links when no election is about, signs of erosion are most likely to be visible during these periods first. Thus, we expect to find a weakening of the partisan coherence of social groups once we study the trends with the years between the elections included. As a consequence of the long-term character of societal change, dealignment of this type should manifest itself not primarily on the occasion of isolated elections, but should be considered a permanent development instead. In our survey we therefore tried to base our inferences regarding variation on the largest possible set of data, drawing upon data collected between elections. We employed a cumulative data set that allowed us to assess the developments of the past 27 years.[4] Due to the long-term focus of this analysis, it has to be limited to western Germany. For an analysis of social cleavages in the united Germany, see chapter 3 by Karl Schmitt in this volume.

The Development of Party Preferences Across West German Cleavage Groups

It is customary to illustrate the cleavage dividing different social strata by means of occupational structure. Most of our surveys allowed for a comparable classification of occupations, which included the occupational groups of workers [Arbeiter], white-collar employees [Angestellte], civil servants [Beamte], the self-employed, and professionals, and farmers. Because there are too few farmers in our representative surveys to be examined as a separate group, and because like the self-employed and professionals, they show a marked preference for the Christian Democrats, we pooled these groups. We also followed Pappi's suggestion and view the combined occupational groups of white-collar employees and civil servants as the "new middle class." In the following sections the so-formed three occupational groupings were employed as indicators of class.[5] The "working class" is thus contrasted to its counterpart, the "old middle class," consisting of self-employed, professionals, and farmers; white-collar employees and civil servants are located somewhere in-between and comprise the "new middle class."[6]

First, we performed our analysis on an annual basis. For most of the years throughout the investigation period, at least two polls were combined, so that we were able to attain statistically adequate numbers of respondents in the examined subgroups.[7] Figure 2.1 shows the findings, ordered according to the three social strata. A familiar picture emerges: the working class favors the SPD, while the old middle class supports the CDU and the CSU. Preferences are less uniform within the new middle class, as party sympathy oscillates between the CDU/CSU and the SPD over time.

Independent of this basic pattern, there are two important developments: first, we see relatively large fluctuations in preferences over time. What at first glance might be suspected to result from sampling error appears more likely to be a systematic phenomenon of cyclical ups and downs of political support upon closer inspection. This becomes plainly visible in several election years: during the 1970s and 1980s several elections clearly polarized the electorate. The 1972 federal election, in which the social-liberal government's policy toward the Soviet Union and East Germany was at issue, saw the hitherto greatest allotment of votes for the SPD and the highest voter turnout ever attained in a federal election. The polarization of the electorate in the election in 1980 was provided by the candidacy of the Christian-Democrat Franz-Josef Strauß for the office of chancellor. In both election years and within individual groups, the pendulum swung in favor of the SPD. This is especially apparent among the core SPD clientele--that is, labor--but also in the new middle class, while the old middle class reacted with a marked decline in support for the Christian Union parties (above all in 1980).

In the federal election that took place between these two, the trend went in the opposite direction: in 1976 the CDU/CSU almost won an absolute majority of seats and received its highest proportion of votes from the old middle class attained over the entire survey period. In the new middle class, the extraordinarily high levels of support for the SPD recorded in 1972 dropped below those for the Christian Union

Figure 2.1. Party Preferences by Social Strata, 1971-97

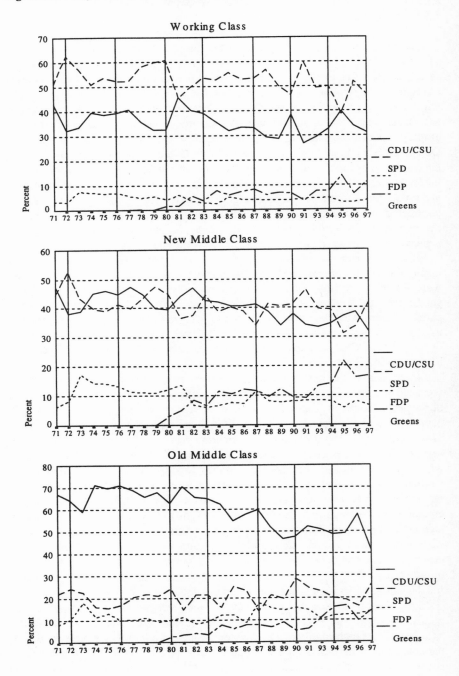

Source: Konrad Adenauer Foundation, Department of Political Research, Cumulative Data File

parties, and support for the SPD decreased visibly even among working-class voters.

A depolarizing effect also is visible in the March 1983 federal election, as the change of government in October of 1982 was confirmed by voters, and preferences shifted simultaneously to the benefit of the CDU/CSU.[8] In this year, the working class supported the SPD to a relatively lesser degree, and in contrast the Christian Union parties to a relatively greater degree, compared to 1980. The old middle class responded once again with a relatively high allotment of votes for the Christian Union parties. Then in 1987 the electorate realigned itself according to the classical cleavage, and the share of blue-collar workers who favored Christian Union parties decreased markedly.

The postunification election of 1990 again is marked by leveling-out tendencies. The differences between votes for the CDU/CSU and SPD among their core groups, the working class and the old middle class, became smaller. By 1994 the partisan preferences of these groups had shifted back to more closely resemble the classical cleavage pattern. The result was a new polarization, though on a lower level of support for either party when compared to the 1970s and 1980s.

This suggests a further development, which clearly is evident in the data: over the course of time, the support that the CDU/CSU and the SPD receive from their core clientele seems to be sinking. This is especially evident in the case of the old middle class, from whom the Christian Union parties usually received approximately 70 percent of the votes during the 1970s and 1980s. Since the end of the 1980s this support is close to 50 percent. A drop in working class support for the SPD is not quite as obvious, although it seems to have taken place to a smaller degree as well. Symptomatic of this trend in the new middle class is the long-term loss in support for both brokerage parties. This can be explained by this group's especially strong predilection for the Greens, whose share of the votes has increased disproportionately since 1980.

The Evolution of Party Preferences of Religious-Denominational Groups

The development of the religious-denominational cleavage is depicted in Figure 2.2. The basic distribution of party preferences in the individual graphs confirms again that these cleavages no longer divide both denominational groups as much; rather, they exist primarily between practicing Christians and nonreligious parts of the population. The difference in preferences for the CDU/CSU and the SPD is especially large among Catholics who regularly attend church.[9] Here the Christian Union parties outstrip the SPD by more than 30 percentage points. In almost all election years, Protestants who go to church regularly also tend to the Christian Democrats, but the distance to the SPD is much smaller. In fact, in some cases, particularly in off-election years, the SPD is stronger than the CDU in this group. Among nonreligious sections of the populace,[10] the percentage allotments for the SPD clearly are greater than those for the CDU/CSU.

The ups and downs of political polarization also are manifested in the interplay

Figure 2.2. Party Preferences by Denomination and Religiosity, 1971-97

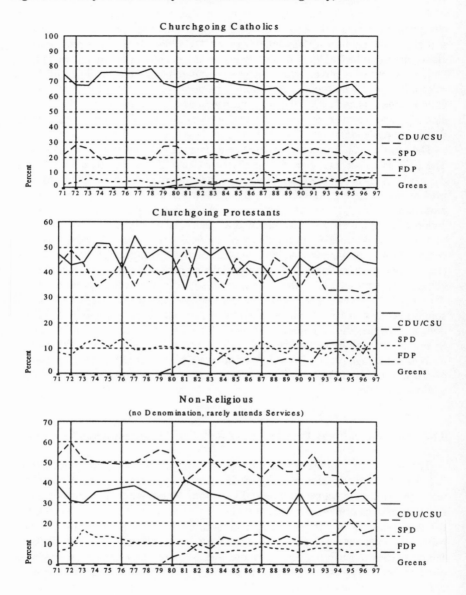

Source: Konrad Adenauer Foundation, Department of Political Research, Cumulative Data File

with religion and denomination, partly to the benefit of the one, partly to the benefit of the other party. In 1972 and 1980 the preference for the Christian Union sank among devout Christians of both denominations, while the preference for the SPD climbed among the nonreligious. The trend reversed itself in 1976 and 1983. In 1987, preferences for both parties had already grown weaker in their respective clienteles, and remained approximately at the same level in 1990 as well as in 1994. This is especially evident in the case of Catholics who regularly attend church. Over the long term, the data suggest a decline in support for the Christian Union among regular churchgoers (both Protestant and Catholic), and a declining trend for the SPD among nonreligious segments of the population. In contrast, the Greens have enjoyed a rapid ascent since the beginning of the 1980s, especially among the nonreligious.

General Long-Term Trends in Party Support Among Client Groups

As a first preliminary conclusion let us suggest that our investigation contains signs of an erosion of partisan ties among the classic client groups of the parties. In reality, the erosion of party ties is most certainly not a constant, linear development. As deviations in party preferences proceed systematically during election years, the preferences of the respective groups will also change because of political short-term trends related to the election situation. Although an investigation into the peaks and valleys of party developments is interesting, our major concern here is with the basic long-term trends behind these deviations. We want to find out whether the traditional party preferences of the relevant societal client groups have essentially remained constant when displayed over a longer term and as most hitherto published analyses claim; or whether they have gradually diminished in accordance with the dealignment thesis. We found the method of linear regression to be particularly suited to this inquiry. This statistical procedure paints a simplified political world, in which developments over time take place in uniform installments, thus neglecting the dynamic ups and downs of political trends. Therefore it allows the general direction of long-term developments to come to light more clearly. Guided by this regression technique, we will examine the trends in our individual polls for the party sympathy allotments of various demographic groups below.[11]

In order to save space, the graphs used to characterize the structures of conflict depicted only the most basic cleavages. Our examination of conflict structure will now go into greater detail. This necessitates, above all, a differentiation of social strata according to union orientation and a combination of class with religious and/or denominational groups. The findings for various societal subgroups, which hitherto have constituted the traditional clientele of parties, are shown in Tables 2.1, 2.2, and 2.3. In addition, we listed the results for the total development of the parties in order to determine whether the evolution of party preferences in the respective groups proceeds above or below the average. For the development of interest to us—that is, party preferences over time—the interpretation of the linear regression coefficient (B) is of importance. As our analysis proceeds from one

Table 2.1. Development of Party Preferences Among Social Strata, 1971-97 (results of regression analysis)

		Total	Workers	Workers with Union Ties	New Middle Class	New Middle Class With Union Ties	Old Middle Class
CDU/CSU	R²	.295	*	*	.278	.274	.548
	B	-.028	*	*	-.029	-.029	-.073
	Beta	-.543	*	*	-.527	-.524	-.740
SPD	R²	.300	.242	.264	.203	.215	*
	B	-.030	-.031	-.041	-.029	-.035	*
	Beta	-.547	-.492	-.514	-.450	-.464	*
FDP	R²	.192	.149	.225	.270	.219	*
	B	-.012	-.008	-.011	-.019	-.020	*
	Beta	-.438	-.386	-.474	-.520	-.468	*
Greens	R²	.861	.755	.716	.846	.797	.766
	B	.056	.038	.040	.064	.075	.049
	Beta	.928	.869	.846	.920	.892	.875

Notes: * not significant (p < .01)
Source: Konrad Adenauer Foundation, Department of Political Research, Cumulative Data File.

Table 2.2. Development of Party Preferences Among Religious-Denominational Groups, 1971-97 (results of regression analysis)

		Total	Catholics	Catholics with Church Ties	Protestants	Protestants with Church Ties	Non religious
CDU/CSU	R^2	.295	.494	.352	.169	*	.184
	B	-.028	-.047	-.039	-.017	*	-.020
	Beta	-.543	-.703	-.593	-.411	*	-.429
SPD	R^2	.300	*	*	.304	.141	.417
	B	-.030	*	*	-.033	-.027	-.042
	Beta	-.547	*	*	-.551	-.376	-.646
FDP	R^2	.192	*	.135	.290	*	.292
	B	-.012	*	.009	-.020	*	-.020
	Beta	-.438	*	.368	-.539	*	-.541
Greens	R^2	.861	.819	.747	.850	.773	.848
	B	.056	.044	.023	.058	.042	.068
	Beta	.928	.905	.864	.922	.879	.921

Notes: * not significant ($p < .01$)
Source: Konrad Adenauer Foundation, Department of Political Research, Cumulative Data File.

Table 2.3. Development of Party Preferences in Social and Religious-Denominational Groups, 1971-97 (results of regression analysis)

		Total	Workers with Church Ties	Workers without Church Ties	New Middle Class with Church Ties	New Middle Class without Church Ties	Old Middle Class with Church Ties	Old Middle Class without Church Ties
CDU/CSU	R^2	.295	*	*	.259	.133	.345	.377
	B	-.028	*	*	-.039	-.020	-.051	-.063
	Beta	-.543	*	*	-.509	-.364	-.587	-.614
SPD	R^2	.300	*	.379	*	.294	*	*
	B	-.030	*	-.046	*	-.042	*	*
	Beta	-.547	*	-.616	*	-.542	*	*
FDP	R^2	.192	*	.202	*	.326	.160	*
	B	-.012	*	-.011	*	-.026	.020	*
	Beta	-.438	*	-.450	*	-.571	.400	*
Greens	R^2	.861	.690	.739	.771	.843	.472	.805
	B	.056	.017	.043	.035	.074	.016	.062
	Beta	.928	.831	.860	.878	.918	.687	.897

Notes: * not significant ($p < .01$)
Source: Konrad Adenauer Foundation, Department of Political Research, Cumulative Data File.

month to the next, it specifies by how many percentage points the support value for a party in a group is changed as time passes by one month.[12]

The overall development during the period investigated here, 1971 to 1997, is marked by the fact that CDU/CSU, SPD, and FDP have lost voters over the long term, while the Greens, in contrast, have made gains. For the Christian Democrats the regression coefficient of -.028 corresponds to an average annual loss of 0.336 percentage points (i.e., 12 x -.028), which over the entire observation period of 27 years amounts to a loss of 9.1 percentage points. The SPD lost an average of 0.36 points per annum, for 9.7 points in all. For the FDP our calculations yielded values of 0.14 percentage points yearly and 3.9 percentage points altogether. By contrast, the Greens gained approximately 12 percentage points overall since 1980, which works out to an average annual growth of 0.7 percentage points.

The regression analysis confirmed the suppositions that were first expressed in the graphic interpretation of party developments. The CDU/CSU and SPD have sustained long-term losses in support from their traditional core groups. The greatest–and well above average–losses of the CDU/CSU are among the old middle class (with or without religious ties) and among Catholics. Over the entire survey period, losses for the party amount to over 17 percentage points among the old middle class with religious ties, more than 20 percentage points among the old middle class without religious ties, and approximately 15 percentage points among Catholics.

The SPD had losses which were clearly above average among union-oriented workers (over 13 percentage points), workers without religious ties (15 percentage points), members of the new middle class without religious ties (circa 14 percentage points) and nonreligious segments of the population (almost 14 percentage points). The FDP also sustained losses within its hereditary clientele, the churchgoing old middle class and several groups within the new middle class.

While the growth of the Greens was apparent in all voter groups, it was nevertheless greatly above average among the union-oriented new middle class, among the new middle class without church ties, and in the nonreligious groups within the populace. This development went chiefly to the disadvantage of the SPD, although the FDP was negatively affected as well.

Our data support the hypothesis of an erosion in group coherence: in West Germany, just as in other Western party democracies, changes have taken place in the relationship between party preference and social structure that are not only traceable to the melting away of social milieus but rather also to weakening party loyalties in the now smaller clientele groups of the parties. Traditional sociostructural associations are indeed now as ever discernible; they operate, however, on a significantly smaller scale than was still the case in the 1970s.

SUMMARY

In this chapter, we investigated two types of long-term electoral change in western Germany. First, we presented recent data on the transformed occupational composition of German society. We demonstrated that the social groups that are viewed as linked to a political party in a social cleavage continuously have been shrinking in size over the past decades. In particular, the core electorate of the SPD, union members in the working class, became smaller. The same is true for the old middle class and for those who are close to a church–that is, groups that used to provide the core electorates of the Christian Union parties CDU and CSU. On the other hand, the new middle class, which is covered by none of the social cleavages as described by Lipset and Rokkan (1967), has expanded over time. This development limits the scope of the traditional voter-party alignments.

We subsequently investigated whether these groups, though smaller in size, stand as firmly as ever behind "their" respective parties. That is, we examined the partisan coherence of the core electorates of the parties over time. While previous research restricted the investigation of this question to election years, we employ a larger database which covers every year since 1971. In our view, it is important to leave the narrow focus on electoral studies behind because signs of erosion are most likely to become visible in off-election years. Indeed, we were able to demonstrate in our regression analyses that the gradual losses sustained by the big parties were most pronounced among the social groups associated with them through a cleavage alignment. Thus, the gradual decline in the Christian Democrats' electoral share was most pronounced in the old middle class and the church-affiliated, while workers abandoned the SPD at above-average frequency. In sum, then, the traditional cleavage alignments have come under stress on two fronts as group sizes and group cohesion have been eroding simultaneously among the German electorate.

NOTES

1. Moreover, in other countries center-periphery and urban-rural cleavages, as well as language conflicts, have occasionally been evident. These cleavages are no longer significant in Germany, or have been integrated into the existing German party system.

2. Yet Metje (1994) recently demonstrated the necessity of differentiating between political generations. In his analysis, those born between 1926 and 1941, who were molded politically around the end of the war and in the rebuilding phase of the Federal Republic, have shown themselves to be a particularly flexible voter group in the new middle class.

3. Their model-based calculations also show that sociostructural change worked to the disadvantage of the CDU/CSU.

4. The database comprises almost all representative opinion polls conducted by the Department for Political Research of the Konrad Adenauer Foundation since 1971. The trend questions contained therein were recoded according to a unified design and then cumulated. The result is a single large data set with 58 individual surveys and approximately 180, 000 respondents. We wish to thank Jutta Graf who worked tirelessly to make this data set available.

5. Based on responses regarding present or past occupation.

6. The differentiation employed by Brinkmann (1988) is more refined and better able to account for changes arising from an overall expansion in education levels. He orders occupational groups on the basis of acquired generation-specific academic qualifications. We have joined the mainstream here, because we would like to compare our results with earlier analyses. Compare, for instance Pappi (1977, 1990); Berger et al. (1977); W.Schulz (1990); Klingemann and Steinwede (1993); Gabriel and Brettschneider (1994).

7. The only gap can be found in 1992, when we collected no data. In the years 1981, 1985, 1988, 1994, 1996, and 1997 we conducted only one survey. 1981 and 1994 had the lowest number of total cases (2,006 and 2,487 respectively). The greatest number of cases was 10,588 (in 1973).

8. The visibly strong shift in voter sympathy in favor of the CDU/CSU and to the disadvantage of the SPD in 1981 could at least partially be related to sampling. This is supported by the fact that we discovered this development in almost all subgroups, and that this year had the lowest number of respondents.

9. We defined as regular church goers those Christians who attended services at least once a month.

10. Persons who do not belong to a religious community, or who attend services less than once a month, were defined as nonreligious.

11. The procedure for our data analysis is as follows: units (n) for the bivariate linear regression are 58 individual West German surveys containing all the relevant variables needed for this analysis. They comprise the aggregate file, ordered chronologically. The allotments of party support in each survey were aggregated to a percent value of support, which in turn constituted the dependent variable for the respective demographic groups to be examined. The independent variable is the survey-month since the beginning of 1971. This was necessitated by the fact that the first available survey in our data set was conducted in June of 1971. The monthly data series thus begins with the value of 6, and ends with the currently last survey from September 1997, which was conducted in the 322th month since the beginning of 1971. The conversion was undertaken to obtain a metric measure of time, which was necessary for the employment of the regression analysis.

12. Statistically speaking, R-square is the explained variance in party support values, defined by the regression line. A low value indicates high error variance. Low R^2 values appear also in our model because corresponding to our assumption of linearity we knowingly masked the aforementioned political cycles which are not statistical errors but reality. Beta is the standardized regression coefficient, which corresponds to the correlation coefficient in the bivariate case. It specifies the strength of the association between time and party sympathy.

3

The Social Bases of Voting Behavior in Unified Germany

Karl Schmitt

Surprises are the result of false expectations. Numerous examples of this simple fact can be found in the developments after the breakdown of the Soviet empire. Contrary to expectations that the change of the political system in Eastern Europe would take place within the framework of the states created after World Wars I and II, the collapse of the Soviet Union, Czechoslovakia, and Yugoslavia, as well as the rapid unification of the two German states, led to the reestablishment of political constellations, which originally had developed in historically distant eras. What was surprising was, on one hand, that these expectations relied on the power of more recently established facts, and, on the other hand, that the durability of historically older forces like ethnic and cultural identities and conflicts were underestimated.

The surprise created by the East German voters was caused by exactly the opposite reason. Before the first free elections in the German Democratic Republic (East Germany)–the Volkskammer (People's Chamber) elections of March 1990–the commonly shared expectation that the Social Democratic Party would be successful at the polls did not anticipate the consequences of the conditions developed under socialist rule. Instead, it relied on the reestablishment of prewar voting patterns. Indeed, the territory which would eventually become the GDR had been a stronghold of left parties during the time of the Weimar Republic. Here, the SPD was supported by 36 percent of the vote during the Reichstag elections of 1928 compared to 27 percent of the vote in the territory of the future Federal Republic of Germany. Taking the results of the SPD and KPD (Communist Party of Germany) together, the left gained 49 percent of the voters (territory of the future Federal Republic of Germany [FRG]: 35 percent). This East-West gradient in favor of the left parties was maintained until the end of the Weimar Republic–even during the emergence of National Socialism. In fact, in the last Reichstag elections of March 1933, the SPD and KPD still won 38.1 percent of the vote in the future GDR territory, compared to only 25.8 percent in the future FRG territory.

Thus, in 1990 it seemed quite plausible that the SPD could resume its prewar successes. For one, past experience in comparable cases supported this assumption. Was it not true that traditional parties and party systems could be reestablished in the western occupation zones of Germany after 1945 (Falter 1981), as well as in countries as different as France, the Netherlands, Spain, or Greece after considerable interruptions of democratic constitutional practice? Moreover, there was a reliable theoretical concept to explain such continuities: the sociostructural model of voting behavior, which regards such developments as an expression of a "politicized social structure" (Pappi 1973). According to this concept, the long-term stability of a party is mainly based upon its close ties to large social groups–"social milieus"–which are able to outlast longer periods of undemocratic regimes even without the parties as their "political action committees" (Lepsius 1973). From this perspective, the expectations of 1990 were well justified. Why shouldn't the same party system that had been formerly erased from this territory in 1946 arise from the ruins of the GDR? And why shouldn't the same kinds of power relations of the individual parties be reestablished according to the realities of an industrial area in a Protestant territory (just like during the Weimar Republic)?

1990: RATIONAL OR GROUP VOTING?

As we know now, things developed quite differently. Instead of the SPD, which was the expected winner of the elections, the "Alliance for Germany" consisting of the Christian Democratic Union, the German Social Union (DSU), and the *Demokratischer Aufbruch* (Democratic Awakening) won the Volkskammer elections, only barely missing the absolute majority. Furthermore, this result not merely resulted from a weak showing of the left in the framework of stable regional patterns. In fact, an almost complete redrawing of the map of the parties' strongholds became apparent. This stood in complete contrast to the 1946 state elections, which had reestablished a prewar political pattern despite all the shifts in the population due to war and postwar conditions (Schmitt 1993).

In the traditional centers of the workers' movement in the industrial south, in Saxony, Thuringia, and Saxony-Anhalt, where the Socialist Unity Party (SED) had been very successful in 1946, the SPD and the PDS (Party of Democratic Socialism–the successor to the SED) received only a small share of the vote. Moreover, this is where the Alliance for Germany reached its best results. The correlations of party shares in the individual urban and rural districts (Table 3.1) documents a landslide that could not have been more dramatic. There does not appear to be any continuity in voting patterns going back to the Weimar Republic or the postwar period. The only exceptions to this rule are the Free Democrats, who were able to gain above-average–but still very modest–results in parts of their former electoral strongholds, and the CDU, which already in 1946 had become the heir of the *Zentrumspartei* in the region of Eichsfeld, the only all-Catholic area of the GDR, and which now repeated its former success there.

Table 3.1. Stability of Party Vote in East Germany Across Areas, 1928-90 (correlation: Pearson's r x 100)

Volks-kammer Election 1990	Landtag Election 1946			Reichstag Election 1928				
	SED	LDP	CDU	KPD	SPD	Liber-als	Zen-trum	DNVP
PDS	0	-12	17	-18	14	-1	-14	44
SPD	-31	4	21	1	1	-7	-8	37
CDU	8	0	-12	-7	-8	-15	25	-32
DSU	35	-4	-17	22	8	28	-13	-45
Liberals	-14	43	-33	40	-28	37	-10	-7
Bündnis 90	-19	31	-12	9	7	40	-8	-2
Greens	-15	27	-14	-5	2	31	-3	0

Notes: Liberals: 1928 = DVP (German People's Party) + DDP (German Democratic Party) + Wirtschaftspartei (Economy Party); 1990 = Bund Freier Demokraten (LDP [Liberal Democratic Party], FDP [Free Democratic Party], Deutsche Forumspartei [German Forum Party]). DNVP: German National People's Party. Data base: 178 units (cities and Landkreise [counties] as of 1946, excluding Berlin).

Since the results of the Volkskammer elections stood in clear contrast to the expectations of reestablishing traditional political power relations on the basis of group voting, it could be concluded that long-term sociostructural ties to parties were unimportant to the vote, but that voters focused on the solution of practical political issues, namely the speed and modalities of German unification. Therefore, the dominant interpretation of the Volkskammer elections was one of mere issue voting (see especially Roth 1990). This interpretation conceives a kind of "ground zero," a tabula-rasa situation in 1990. In this view, forty years of socialism, plus the preceding twelve years of National Socialism, had destroyed all conditions for the survival of sociostructural party ties. On the one hand, this concerns the parties whose competition had been eliminated by a unique party which monopolized political power. On the other hand, it concerns the social basis of the party system, which was flattened by the "Socialist Revolution," even more so since the infrastructure for a free articulation of group-related interests (like unions and associations) had been abolished. According to this view, the voters of March 1990 did not vote as members of social groups, but as individual voters who could choose between offers of a party system "borrowed" from the West (Pappi 1991), which was not and could not have been rooted in their own society. If this interpretation were true, there would be little room for a sociostructural explanation of voting behavior in the territory of the former GDR. The German electoral landscape would be divided into two areas: a western one, where group- oriented voting would still be of importance, and an eastern one, with rational, issue-oriented individuals as the dominant type of voters.

However, there are good reasons to question central assumptions of this interpretation of the Volkskammer elections, especially the underlying tabula-rasa notion, which presents the GDR as a socially as well as politically flattened landscape in 1990. First, this pertains to the assumed lack of social cleavages of the GDR electorate. On one hand, and contrary to the official self-interpretation of the GDR society, interest conflicts between social groups did not disappear after the abolition of the old hierarchy built on private property, just as equality of positions and opportunities could not be forced onto society. On the contrary, a "bureaucratically organized socialist class society" (Meier 1990) developed, which created new conflicts of interests and new social hierarchies, with the party nomenclatura and functionaries of the economic and administrative machinery at the top and the proletariat at the bottom again.

On the other hand, there was a clear opposition between the SED state and the churches during the entire GDR era, although the regime's policy of *Gleichschaltung* (equalization) spared the churches after the power struggle of the 1950s. This made it possible to maintain relatively uncontrolled networks of communication and organizations of interest articulation within the churches, which developed into a reservoir of system opposition through their unique monopoly of autonomy in GDR society.

This means simply that the two most important dimensions of conflict, the class conflict and the church-state conflict, which have been essential for the German party system since its development in the nineteenth century and which remained influential for West Germany after 1945, continued to exist in the GDR as well (Emmert 1991; Eith 1997). Naturally, these cleavage patterns reflected to some extent the specific features of GDR society; moreover, they remained latent in the sense that they could not gain any expression in the party system until 1989.

Thus, under the surface of a one-party-state, neither the political landscape nor the social structure of the GDR resembled a tabula rasa–at least with respect to the political perceptions and orientations among the population. Of course, in contrast to western Germany after 1945, the long-term suppression of free political articulation and organization did not allow leading politicians and the electorates of the former parties to survive beyond the time of the GDR era. But the rapid establishment of the West German party system in the territory of the vanishing GDR can only be explained if it is considered as more than a mere "conquest" by the West German parties.

The assumption that a party system alien to the East had been transplanted to the GDR in 1990 is false for two reasons. First, throughout the entire existence of the GDR, effective all-German mass communication could be maintained. The model of the Federal Republic and with it the West German party system remained almost ever-present through western radio and TV. Therefore, a majority of GDR citizens had the opportunity to mentally participate in all Bundestag elections. This enabled the survival of already existing and the development of new party ties, although these were only of a platonic quality for the time being. Hence, in addition to ties with the SED, people in East Germany developed identifications with parties from West Germany (Bluck and Kreikenbom 1991; Gluchowski and Zelle 1992, 1993). This picture is strengthened by the fact that the images of those parties by the electorate in the East already corresponded to those of the electorate in the West in 1990 (Pappi 1991; Kaase and Klingemann 1994b).

Second this "quasi identification" with parties was not merely related to "foreign parties" (according to the SED), but to the parties which were founded in Berlin in 1945 as the core of the all-German party system after World War II by initiative of the Soviet occupational power, and which continued to exist in western Germany. Elements of this party system survived even within the GDR, if only in the perverted version of the bloc parties CDU and LDPD (Liberal Democratic Party). Therefore the revival of these fossils, the new establishment of the SPD, as well as the connecting of these parties to their West German counterparts, does not simply represent the import of purely western products, but also the reestablishment of the all-German party system in the territory of the GDR, which had been gradually abolished after 1946.

Combining the continued existence of what traditionally had been the most important cleavages in Germany (with specific GDR modifications) and the familiarity of the East German population with the originally all-German party system in its West German version, it becomes clear that there were quite favorable preconditions for new links of social structure to the party system in 1990. The pattern of these new links was determined by two factors. First, by specific cleavage structures handed down from the GDR, which were institutionalized in quite different ways. The state-church conflict had created a clear-cut sociomoral milieu consisting not only of Catholic but also of Protestant church members. Compared to this, interest conflicts related to the position in the social hierarchy did not lead to a comparable development of milieus. Although the working class had common experiences, a clear distinction from other members of society was missing. The suppression of unions and other employees' associations for decades and thus the free articulation and representation of interests prevented common working conditions from creating large social groups whose members would have been distinguished by strong feelings of affiliation and a working-class consciousness. The only group defined by its position in the social hierarchy which can be called a "milieu" is the stratum of leading SED functionaries and cadres who gained their positions through their party careers.

Second, the positioning of the individual parties within the specific constellation of spring 1990 became important for the new linkage of social structure and party system. The demand for loyalty by state and party which had created a polarization between affirmation and rejection of the system as a whole until 1989 now turned into an alternative between being for or against German unification and soon after into an alternative between a rapid or slow process of unification. The party landscape was clearly structured regarding this decisive issue of the Volkskammer elections. One end of the political spectrum was represented by the PDS, which pleaded for a slow unification process and the preservation of as many elements of the old order as possible, together with the civil action groups which propagated a "third way" or wanted to shape the unification into a process of reforms. The opposing view was taken by the Alliance for Germany, which most forcefully demanded a rapid unification and a radical change in the economic and political system of the GDR. The position of the SPD was ambivalent: Willy Brandt pleaded for the unification, Oskar Lafontaine cautioned about its social consequences.

Both factors–the different degrees to which cleavages had become institutionalized in the form of social milieus and the position of the parties toward the dominant decision of the year 1990–can explain not only the outcome of the Volkskammer elections as a whole, but especially the remarkably divergent extent to which the individual social groups opted for the parties (Figure 3.1). The importance of social milieus became evident regarding the religious cleavage.[1] The Catholic part of the religious milieu clearly opted for the Alliance. The Protestant part divided into a majority which supported the Alliance and a minority (especially in Berlin and Brandenburg) which supported the SPD.

The surprising pattern concerning the class cleavage[2] can also be interpreted along these lines. Its core elements are: in comparison with all occupations (except the small group of self-employed), the CDU was most strongly supported by workers; the PDS, on the other hand, gained support from workers far below average and support above average among the already established and the future elite ("intelligentsia," "upper white collar," students). Last, the SPD electorate did not display any marked profile; it received the same modest support from all occupations.

These results suggest that, in contrast to the religious cleavage, where coalitions between milieus or parts of milieus can be found, preconditions for such coalitions of groups defined by their position in the social hierarchy did not exist. Although here, too, the social position was of importance for party preference, it was not mediated by group standards. Instead, it primarily reflected individually perceived interests, which were created by voters' specific occupational experiences with the old regime and by their expectations of the new one. For blue-collar workers, this meant that the unions largely failed to act as the most important mediating body of election standards in favor of the SPD (Weßels 1994). Thus, the majority of members of this group could translate its discontent with the old conditions and their expectations for a radical change into a vote for the clearest alternative–the parties of the Alliance–which also were supposed to be the most competent to bring about the change.

Hence, the most important results of the Volkskammer elections were as follows: First, sociostructural factors proved to be effective in the GDR as the two traditional German cleavages exist here, too. Second, the new linkage of social structure and party system has characteristics that are partly known and, until now, partly unknown. While the proximity of religious voters to the CDU is in line with the

Figure 3.1. Vote by Occupation and Religious Affiliation (Volkskammer Election 1990)

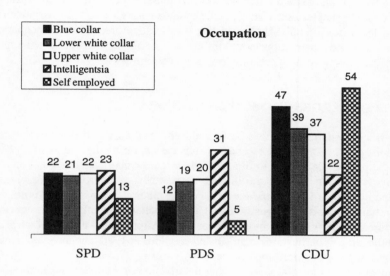

Occupation

- Blue collar
- Lower white collar
- Upper white collar
- Intelligentsia
- Self employed

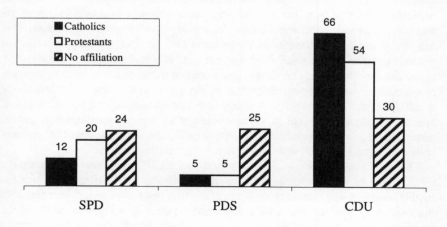

Religious affiliation

- Catholics
- Protestants
- No affiliation

traditional pattern (with two reservations, however: the transformation of denominational cleavage into a religious/secular one, and a drastic quantitative decrease in Christian voters), a clear break with both the historic pattern and the pattern dominant in West Germany can be found regarding the class cleavage. The majority of the workers opted for the CDU; SPD and PDS, the parties which see themselves within the tradition of the working class movement, lack broad support from their classic electorate. Third, in the East the class cleavage resulted much less in the formation of milieus than in the West. Therefore, specific occupational experiences and expectations could influence vote choice according to the model of rational voting without creating long-term coalitions.

1994: CONVERGENCE OF TWO ELECTORATES?

This constellation, which was brought to light during the first democratic elections in the GDR, proved to be basically stable during the course of 1990, the first "super election year" in the East when local elections, state elections, and finally Bundestag elections followed each other in short intervals. Despite continuing and partly intensified regional differentiation, not only the magnitude of party shares, but also the specific East German patterns of linkage between social structure and party system by and large were maintained. This is not surprising since the issue of unification dominated all elections in 1990, and since no decisive changes in party positions took place.

The question was now as to whether the division of the German electorate that had emerged would last beyond 1990. Did the 1990 elections set a new course for the voting behavior of the East German electorate? Or would there be a more or less rapid adjustment of the eastern pattern of voting behavior to that of the common western model during the course of the ensuing years?

The fact that the "socialist class society" of the GDR era would increasingly make room for a sociostructural constellation of western character in the wake of the implementation of a market economy, the emergence of a new occupational structure, and the development of a service society spoke in favor of change. This would also cause basic changes on the political agenda. The polarizing question of political order as well as other GDR specific conflicts connected to the unification issue, like the church-state confrontation, would be things of the past. In their place, new conflicts would appear as results of coping with the economic and social transformation. It was also to be expected that the appropriate procedures of conflict resolution inherent in a free market order would be established and its actors would gain importance. Finally, this would aid the development of western-style coalitions between parties and interest organizations in the East.

The main loser of such a scenario would be the CDU, the main beneficiary the SPD. Changes in the social structure, a shift in the political agenda, and the establishment of free market procedures of conflict resolution would give the SPD the chance to profile itself as *the* employees' party, as a representative of the interests of the working and employees' class, which developed a certain "consciousness as employees" due to the experience of crisis inherent in the transformation. It is an advantage of the SPD that the economic and social problems, caused by coping with executing the unification, brought exactly those issues onto the agenda. This would allow the SPD to rely on traditional political positions that are very close to the sentiments of the eastern German population. Despite the discrediting of "socialism" as a state-planned economy, the "little socialisms" are much more favored in the East than they are in the West. Thus, political preferences of the eastern electorate are closer to the goals of the Social Democrats than they are to any other party in this respect (Pappi 1991: 18ff.).

On one hand, this scenario can rely on the circumstance that in 1990 the cleavage related to the occupational structure was only to a small extent anchored in social milieus. As a consequence, a remarkable latitude for changes existed. On the other hand, however, this scenario relies on circumstances which did not necessarily have to exist. Would the SPD be able to convince the electorate of its superior competence in solving problems of economy and unemployment, and could it present credible leadership personalities? Could the SPD create solid and visible alliances with the trade unions? And could it increase its exceptionally small number of party members, especially among the workers and employees?

The developments since 1990 pointed toward a scenario favorable to the SPD. The severity of the economic and social crisis weakened the confidence in the capability of the governing parties CDU/CSU and FDP. Until 1993 the SPD had surpassed the CDU with regard to competence in problem solving. A clear majority of the East German population believed an SPD-led government to be more capable of solving the economic problems in the East than a Christian-Liberal one. This was reflected by vote intentions shown in public opinions polls. The SPD surpassed the CDU in the electorate's favor in March 1991; with almost 40 percent of support, it consolidated its lead to about 10 percent in 1992 and 1993. The losses of the CDU were not only to the SPD's advantage. The fact that the PDS could almost double its shares to nearly 12 percent from 1991 to 1993,[3] pointed toward support from beyond its milieu core.

Looked at more closely, however, it becomes obvious that the losses of the CDU and the increases in support for the SPD were equally distributed throughout the occupational and confessional groups (Schmitt 1994: 210 ff.). Therefore, the change in the electorates' preferences was not the result of special shifts of certain groups. Neither the workers nor the Protestants swung toward the SPD to a degree out of line with the general trend. Despite the considerable movement in the electorate as a whole, no remarkable changes in the sociostructural patterns of party preferences could be discerned.

The reversed trend in favor of the government in Bonn which had been increasingly obvious since the beginning of 1994 in the wake of the economic recovery, as well as the dynamics of the consecutive elections of the "super election year" of 1994 determined the results of the Bundestag elections in October 1994. The polarization of the election campaign by the formation of a SPD-led minority state government under toleration of the PDS in Saxony-Anhalt played a special role in this development. Compared to 1990, the CDU (which obtained 38.5

percent, a minus of 3.3) of the vote in East-Germany) roughly maintained its position. The SPD improved (with 31.5 percent, a plus of 7.2) and the PDS almost doubled its share of votes (with 19.8 percent, a plus of 8.7). Since all remaining parties stayed below the 5 percent mark, a specific East German party system emerged comprising the three parties CDU, SPD, and PDS (similar to the state elections, with the exception of Saxony-Anhalt), combining 90 percent of the vote (1990: 78 percent).

Considering the support of the parties during the Bundestag elections of 1994 compared to the preceding Bundestag elections, clear shifts–which could have been expected according to the scenario outlined above–did not appear among the individual social groups.[4] Regarding the occupational structure (Figure 3.2), it is first of all remarkable how stable the profile of the CDU remained. Its losses resulted mainly from the decreased support among the new middle classes of the employees and civil servants. In contrast to this, the CDU increased its support among the self-employed, probably partly to the debit of the FDP, whose share among this group dropped from 32 percent in 1990 to 7 percent in 1994. The CDU also maintained its dominant position among blue-collar workers, whereas the SPD achieved only insignificant gains here. The total gain of the SPD is therefore based on its highly improved position among the new middle classes of employees and civil servants. The PDS electorate's profile changed significantly. Its gains were only to a small extent based on increased support from blue-collar workers; in fact, their share still remains below average. The PDS obtained its greatest support from the higher-level employees and civil servants (a third of whom supported the party), and from the self-employed (one in four).

With regard to the denominational groups, the basic patterns of support of the parties remained even more stable than among the occupational groups (Figure 3.3). The gains of the SPD on one hand, and the losses of the CDU on the other–with the exception of the Protestants who supported the CDU more than before–do not show any special developments that went beyond the scope of the general trends. The previous pattern of the PDS remained constant as well: religious voters of both confessions supported it only insignificantly; the party owes its success to the clearly increased support from nonreligious voters.

Thus, religious attachment, a long-standing factor in the West, now has a strong influence on voting behavior in the East as well. In addition, a distinct characteristic of East German voting behavior, which had existed since the Volkskammer elections, became even more evident: party preferences of Catholics and Protestants resemble each other much more than in the West. The more important line does place the denominations in opposition to each other, but divides religious voters as a whole from voters without religious attachments. The extreme positions here are taken by the CDU and the PDS. Consequently, the SPD attracts large parts of the Protestants in the West, since there still is a continuing denominational cleavage, but receives much less support from this group of voters in the East.

During the state elections of 1994, the regional differentiation of voting behavior in East Germany increased as well (see Schmitt 1995). In Brandenburg, the SPD could turn its strong position into an absolute majority. In Saxony, the CDU could

Figure 3.2. Party Vote by Occupation (East Germany)

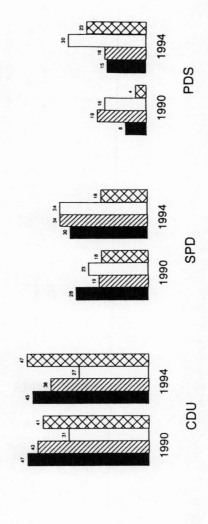

Figure 3.3. Party Vote by Religious Affiliation

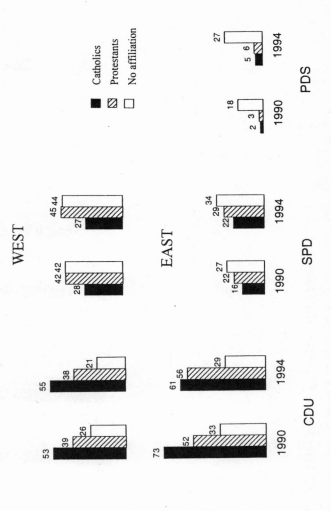

further consolidate the absolute majority it had gained in 1990. These results could not be fully repeated during the Bundestag elections of 1994. Both in Brandenburg (SPD: 45 percent) and in Saxony (CDU: 48 percent) the respective leading parties stayed below the absolute majority. However, the question arises whether these strong regional differences can be traced back to factors that function independently of basic sociostructural patterns of party preferences, or whether they reflect specific regional developments of individual groups of voters.

A comparison of Brandenburg and Berlin (East) on one hand, and of Saxony and Thuringia on the other, yields a different picture for occupational and denominational groups (see Figure 3.4).[5] Although Brandenburg/Berlin and Saxony/Thuringia show very different overall levels of support for the SPD among occupational groups, the general profile of the occupational groups in East Germany was maintained. In contrast, marked differences appear in the denominational pattern of SPD supporters in these states. While the Protestants supported the SPD to an even smaller extent than the Catholics in Saxony and Thuringia, the prevailing majority of Protestants in Brandenburg and Berlin supported the SPD and by doing so surpassed the number of SPD supporters without any religious attachments–the group having the strongest affinity for the SPD in the East German average.

This special situation in Brandenburg and Berlin, which to some extent already had been visible during the Volkskammer elections, may to some extent be due to the role of the former Protestant church official Manfred Stolpe who, as Brandenburg's premier, attracted a large number of Protestant voters originally committed to the CDU.

Considering the overall results of the 1994 Bundestag election, the realignment of social groups looks quite moderate, especially with regard to the expectations implied in the above scenario. The direction of change meets the expectations, however: the CDU slightly lost support among workers in East Germany, while it gained support from the self-employed. Thus, it came closer to the profile of its West German constituency. The SPD became more of an employees' party in the East by winning strong support from the new middle classes of employees and civil servants, while stagnating among workers and the self- employed. However, considering the speed and the impact of the economic transformation, the intensity of the conflicts connected to this and the completed establishment of new procedures of conflict resolution, the small size of these changes becomes even more obvious. Despite the disappearance of its constituent confrontation resulting from the fall of the GDR, the almost constant importance of the religious factor for voting behavior emphasizes the small degree of the change.

The results for the PDS can offer only a partial explanation for this situation. The party succeeded in mobilizing the protest potential of a broader constituency, exceeding its milieu core of supporters and beneficiaries of the old system. However, the party's disproportionately low resonance among workers and its success among higher employees and civil servants as well as among the self-employed shows that its attractiveness is limited to the subjective losers of unification (those who feel disadvantaged and keep holding on to certain elements of the socialist creed) and among the objective winners of the unification, who were

Figure 3.4. SPD Vote 1994 by Region, Occupation, and Religious Affiliation

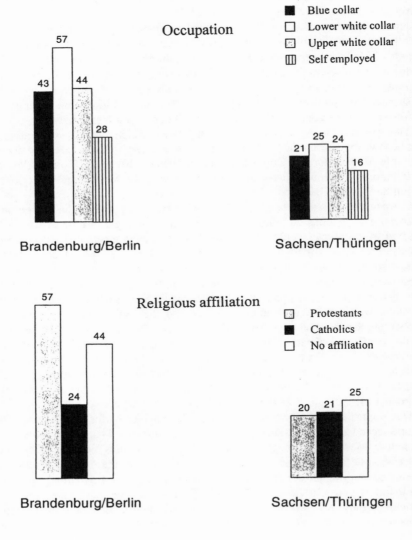

probably at the same time privileged supporters of the old system (Falter and Klein 1994: 26ff.; Neugebauer and Stöss 1996: 303ff.; Moreau and Neu 1994: 75ff.).

INTEREST MEDIATION AND GROUP-ORIENTED VOTING

The explanation for the relatively constant alignments of social groups with the CDU and the SPD suggests the need to examine the structures and mechanisms of interest mediation that have developed between the members of the individual groups and the parties. While organizations of free interest mediation did not exist in the GDR (with the exception of the churches), the creation of a widespread system of federations and organizations modeled after the West German pattern has rapidly been taking place since 1990.

For the new system of interest mediation to gain importance for voting behavior, it is first of all essential that the members of the individual groups feel connected to, and represented by, the respective organization. This is the case in both East Germany and West Germany (Table 3.2).

More than four-fifths of the respondents in the East and the West consider themselves represented by one interest organization (out of five choices). Questioned about the most important organization, trade unions rank first in the East as opposed to the West, irrespective of the respondents' occupational position. Although the two churches on average were named relatively infrequently, church members in the East–Protestants as well as Catholics–regarded them as their representatives of interests to a much larger degree than church members in the West.

Once such ties to interest organizations and social institutions exist, they can affect voting behavior if coalitions between these organizations and certain parties are actually perceived by the people who feel represented by the respective group. In 1990, when associations were still in their early phase of being (re)organized, East Germans had not been able to gain much experience with them and were therefore much more insecure about their party alignments (Weßels 1994). However, by 1994, almost as many East Germans perceived coalitions between interest groups and parties (Table 3.3).

Although the patterns of alliance are by and large perceived similarly, there are some notable East-West differences. In the West, three-quarters of the respondents consider the unions to be linked with the SPD. In the East, however, only 55 percent see them in a coalition with the SPD, 3 percent see them close to the PDS, and 15 percent do not see them linked to any party at all. Compared to the West, business groups are to a smaller degree linked to the FDP in the East. The clearest difference appears in the perception of the Protestant church: only a quarter of the respondents in the West consider it linked to the CDU, compared to about half in the East.

To answer the question of how the individual attachments to the organizations and their perceived proximity to the parties is translated into voting behavior, the two most important dimensions of conflict–the role of the trade unions for the SPD on one hand and the role of the churches for the CDU on the other–have to be

Table 3.2. Interest Group Best Representing Respondent (column percentages)

		All	Blue collar/ Lower white collar	Upper white collar/ self-employed	Protestants	Catholics
Unions	West	25	31	19	25	20
	East	44	46	44	27	31
Business	West	10	7	16	9	10
groups	East	11	9	17	11	5
Protestant	West	5	3	8	11	0
church	East	6	8	4	25	0
Catholic	West	8	8	7	1	19
groups	East	2	2	2	0	38
Environ.	West	35	32	37	37	32
groups	East	22	21	22	21	20
Don't	West	17	19	13	17	18
know/	East	14	15	12	15	5
none						

Source: 1990: Konrad Adenauer Foundation survey, ZA No. 2133, August/September 1990, 5,106 respondents (West: 3,033, East: 2,073); 1994: German Science Foundation "Transformation of the Political Culture in the New Federal States" survey, September/November 1994, 4,114 respondents (West: 2,033, East: 2,081). For reasons of comparison, both data sets were weighed according to the actual election results.

considered. Therefore, the impact of union ties on support for the SPD was examined separately for two occupational groups: employees in blue-collar and lower white-collar occupations on one hand, and those in upper white-collar positions (including the self-employed) on the other (Figure 3.5).

A comparison between East and West demonstrates that West Germans who feel represented by unions and consider them to be linked with the SPD vote for the party considerably more frequently than the average voter (+15 percent). In the East, however, the combined effect of subjective representation and perception of a coalition is much smaller (with +5 percent in the lower and +10 percent in the higher strata of occupational positions). Comparing these findings with data available for 1990 (Weßels 1994), it is evident that the moderate importance of the unions for a vote in favor of the SPD has not changed since then.

Table 3.3. Perceived Coalitions 1994: Groups and Parties (row percentages)

		CDU	SPD	FDP	B'90/ Greens	PDS	None	Don't know
Unions	West	7	74	1	1	0	4	13
	East	6	55	1	1	3	15	20
Business groups	West	59	4	18	0	0	3	13
	East	60	4	11	0	0	5	17
Protestant church	West	25	16	3	1	0	26	27
	East	49	6	1	1	0	19	23
Catholic church	West	61	1	0	0	0	17	19
	East	61	1	1	0	0	15	22
Environ. groups	West	1	3	1	83	0	3	8
	East	2	2	1	79	0	3	12

Source: 1990: Konrad Adenauer Foundation survey, ZA No. 2133, August/September 1990, 5,106 respondents (West: 3,033, East: 2,073); 1994: German Science Foundation "Transformation of the Political Culture in the New Federal States" survey, September/November 1994, 4,114 respondents (West: 2,033, East: 2,081). For reasons of comparison, both data sets were weighed according to the actual election results.

Examining the influence of church attachment in favor of the CDU, Protestants and Catholics have to be analyzed separately (Figure 3.6). Protestants who consider themselves to be represented by the church and perceive it as having close ties to the CDU vote for the party more frequently than the average voter (with 31 percent in the West and 16 percent in the East); Catholics who consider themselves to be represented by their church and see it as close to the CDU support it more frequently than the average voter (with 21 percent in the West and 24 percent in the East). The fact that Protestants as well as Catholics in the East see themselves as represented by their church more frequently and at the same time consider it to be close to the CDU more often increases this effect for the party. However, it has to be taken into account that members of both churches represent only a minority within the East German electorate.

Thus, these findings suggest important differences in the relevance of church attachment and trade union attachment in favor of the CDU or the SPD. The strong effect of church ties demonstrates the longevity of social milieus once they are established, even if the conflicts that created them belong to the past. In contrast, it is obvious that a subjective representation by the unions, even in combination with a perception of their proximity to the SPD, do not necessarily translate into SPD support. The economic and social adjustment to the West German model does

Figure 3.5. SPD Vote by Occupational Class, Attachment to a Union, and Perceived Coalition (in percent; number of cases in parentheses)

WEST

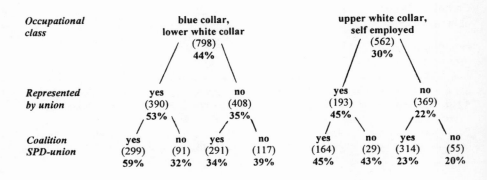

	blue collar, lower white collar				upper white collar, self employed			
Occupational class	(798) 44%				(562) 30%			
Represented by union	yes (390) 53%		no (408) 35%		yes (193) 45%		no (369) 22%	
Coalition SPD-union	yes (299) 59%	no (91) 32%	yes (291) 34%	no (117) 39%	yes (164) 45%	no (29) 43%	yes (314) 23%	no (55) 20%

EAST

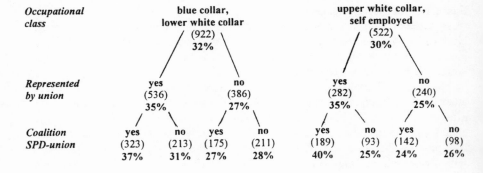

	blue collar, lower white collar				upper white collar, self employed			
Occupational class	(922) 32%				(522) 30%			
Represented by union	yes (536) 35%		no (386) 27%		yes (282) 35%		no (240) 25%	
Coalition SPD-union	yes (323) 37%	no (213) 31%	yes (175) 27%	no (211) 28%	yes (189) 40%	no (93) 25%	yes (142) 24%	no (98) 26%

not automatically entail benefits for one particular party, as is demonstrated by the extremely diverse party constellations in the eastern Länder. In the recent history of German federalism this is not the first time that a variety of different options is available in different Länder (see most prominently the Bavarian example)—options that allow parties of various backgrounds to prove their competence as agents of modernization.

TWO ELECTORATES: INTRA- AND EXTRAPARTY TENSIONS

Although the electorate and the party system still offer an inconsistent picture by 1996, an all-German party system with uniform national organizations has emerged: western CDU and FDP fused with the reformed bloc parties in the East, as did the SPD and the Greens with their respective counterparts that had been newly founded in the GDR. The traditional cleavages appeared again, and the party images of the voters were nearly identical in East and West at the end of 1990.

However, it would be wrong to conclude that a homogeneous all-German party landscape exists. Diverging party constellations in East and West contradict this. To be sure, the extreme scenario—the division into two regional party systems, made up of the CDU, SPD, and the Greens in the West and of the CDU, SPD, and PDS in the East—has not become reality for the time being, due to the consolidation of the FDP in some West German states. However, the strong presence of the PDS as the main proponent of an East German regional political culture influenced by the experience of the GDR as well as by the consequences of the unification determines party competition in the East in an entirely different manner than in the West. The role of the PDS within the East German party system reflects a new conflict between center and periphery as a result of the integration of the GDR territory into the Federal Republic. This conflict combines two traditional conflict dimensions. The PDS, which did not succeed in gaining a foothold in the West German states, took over the role of a regional party. It cultivates the resistance of East German society against the dominant culture, and it successfully presents itself as the representative of East German interests (Schultze 1994: 489; von Winter 1996: 315; see also chapter 11 on the PDS in this volume, which points at the importance of regional identifications for the electoral support for this party).

The East-West contrast, however, is not limited to the level of party constellations, but also affects the internal conditions of the two *Volksparteien* (people's parties) CDU and SPD. Because no major realignment of the various groups has taken place since 1990, the profile of the East German electorate of both parties differs considerably from the one in the West (Figure 3.7). Thus, blue-collar workers in the West represent only a quarter of the voters of the CDU, compared to about one half in the East. The SPD has to deal with the reverse constellation.

With regard to the religious cleavages, the structure of the conflict and of the alliances is quite similar in East and West. Yet, differences between East and West come in a different guise here: the composition of the East German population differs dramatically from that of the West, where a quantitative balance between the

Figure 3.6. CDU Vote by Religious Affiliation, Church Attachment, and Perceived Coalition

WEST

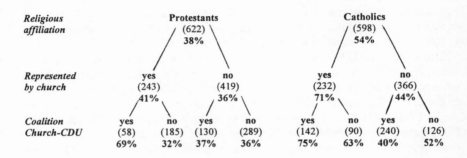

EAST

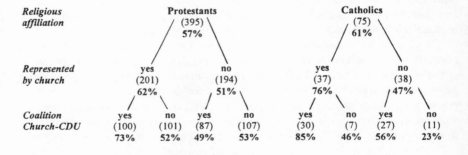

Figure 3.7. Composition of the CDU Electorate, 1994

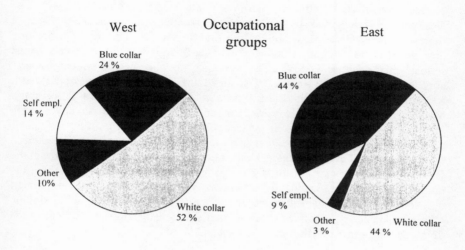

Occupational groups

West

Blue collar
24 %

Self empl.
14 %

Other
10%

White collar
52 %

East

Blue collar
44 %

Self empl.
9 %

Other
3 %

White collar
44 %

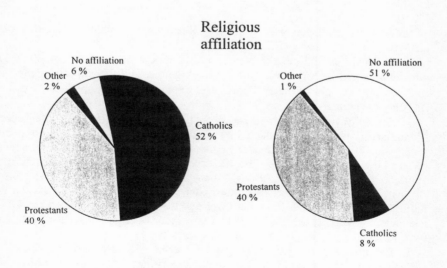

Religious affiliation

No affiliation
6 %

Other
2 %

Catholics
52 %

Protestants
40 %

Other
1 %

No affiliation
51 %

Protestants
40 %

Catholics
8 %

denominations exists. In the East–historically the heartland of German Protestantism–Catholics represent less than 10 percent of the population, while Protestant church members decreased to a minority of about one-third of the population during the four decades of the GDR era. Therefore, the Catholics represent the majority of CDU supporters in the West, while in the East it is the nonreligious voters who are most numerous.

It is obvious that the marked differences in the composition of the electorates produce considerable intraparty tensions (Dalton and Bürklin 1995: 94). The tensions are intensified by the minority position in which East German representatives within the two big parties find themselves. This minority position is rendered even more important by the weak party organizations in the East (most seriously in the case of the SPD). The tensions materialize in continuing intraparty conflicts (most recently in the CDU about the discussion paper of Eckhardt Rehberg, leader of the parliamentary group in Mecklenburg-Western Pomerania). Most typically, Brandenburg's Prime Minister Manfred Stolpe and Saxony's Prime Minister Kurt Biedenkopf both pursue policies that are in conflict with their national parties and try to court their specific electorate–a strategy which has been successful so far. On the federal level, the orientation of the eastern members of the Bundestag toward their constituencies makes it more difficult to guarantee the minimum of discipline within the parliamentary groups essential to the process of decision-making in parliamentary systems. Therefore, the strains on the functioning of a parliamentary system in a federal state are considerably intensified by the divergent electorates of the parties in East and West.

NOTES

1. Group sizes: 6.1 percent Catholics, 34.2 percent Protestants, 55.8 percent no affiliation.

2. Group sizes: 42.7 percent blue collar, 22.6 percent lower white collar, 4.0 percent upper white collar, 12.7 percent intelligentsia, 4.2 percent self-employed.

3. Yearly averages of the Politbarometer. Note that PDS support continued to rise over the course of the year.

4. The following analysis is based on two data sets: for 1990, the survey (Zentralarchiv No. 2133) conducted by GETAS in August/September 1990 under supervision of the Konrad-Adenauer-Foundation with a total of 5,106 respondents (West: 3,033, East: 2,073); for 1994 the survey conducted by Basis Research from September to November 1994 (German Science Foundation [DFG]-project "Transformation der politischen Kultur in den Neuen Bundesländern," Jürgen W. Falter, Oskar W. Gabriel, Hans Rattinger und Karl Schmitt) with a total of 4,114 respondents (West: 2,033, East: 2,081). For reasons of comparison, both data sets were weighed according to the actual election results.

5. Group sizes in Brandenburg and Berlin (Saxony and Thuringia in parentheses): 37.5 percent (37.7) blue collar, 26.9 percent (24.4) upper white collar, 5.8 percent (8.5) self-employed, 20.3 percent (31.0) Protestants, 2.8 percent (5.4) Catholics, 76.3 percent (63.0) no affiliation.

4

A Third Face of Dealignment?
An Update on Party Identification
in Germany, 1971-94

Carsten Zelle

As in a number of other countries, dealignment is en vogue in German electoral research. The term denotes a weakening of traditional alignments between segments of the electorate and political parties. By now it is generally accepted that the alignments identified by Lipset and Rokkan (1967) are less relevant for electoral behavior than they used to be–the frozen cleavages of the old days are thawing. Yet, a dealignment can come about in different ways. In principle, the following three processes could take place independently of each other, but they all come under the heading of dealignment:

- Dealignment as change in the composition of the electorate. This process takes place when social groups that are linked to a political party by a cleavage shrink in size, while groups that are not part of a cleavage expand simultaneously. Thus, in Germany as elsewhere, the working class, which the economic cleavage links to the Social Democrats, decreased in size during the past decades, while the new middle class, which did not enter an alliance with any party, expanded. Simultaneously, the electoral core groups of the Christian Democrats shrank. As a result, the portion of the electorate that is part of a cleavage decreases. Evidence for this first type of dealignment is presented in the introduction and in chapter 2 by Peter Gluchowski and Ulrich von Wilamowitz-Moellendorff in this volume.
- Dealignment as weakening of intragroup cohesion. Regardless of its size, a social group may be loyal to its party to varying degrees. Dealignment occurs when this intragroup cohesion decreases over time. For example, decreasing shares of the workers' party in the working class could be considered a dealignment in the shape weakening intragroup cohesion. In Germany, electoral research for a long time had not found any evidence of weakening intragroup cohesion (see Klingemann and Steinwede 1993). However, the chapter by Gluchowski and Wilamowitz-Moellendorff provides evidence for this second type of

dealignment. The electoral core groups identified by the cleavage approach stand less unanimously behind the parties they are associated with than they used to.

- Dealignment as a weakening of individual attachments to a party. In analyzing alliances between social groups and parties, the cleavage approach addresses the aggregate level. Consequently, the two faces of dealignment sketched out above talk about social groups, not about individual voters. Yet dealignment theory frequently is employed to draw inferences about individuals from the aggregate. Thus it is commonly regarded as an implication of a strong alignment that the individual voters within its core group have a strong sense of allegiance to the respective political party. Party identification is hypothesized to be strong, and vote stability is said to be high within the core groups identified by the cleavage approach. Consequently, when one or both types of aggregate dealignment occur, the percentage of strong partisans and standpatters is said to decrease. In this view of a dealignment, these party loyals are replaced by a new type of voter who is less party bound, more reactive to politics of the day, and more likely to switch parties. This third face of dealignment is the subject matter of this chapter.

Note that the empirical status of the three faces of dealignment differs. Thus, there is no doubt that the first type of dealignment did indeed take place. Evidence is more ambiguous regarding the second type, but the chapter by Gluchowski and Wilamowitz-Moellendorff provides strong support. With regard to the third face of dealignment, the evidence is simply contradictory.

It is the goal of this chapter to first lay out the major hypotheses that have been proposed regarding individual- level dealignment. Then I will sketch some recent evidence relating to these hypotheses. A conclusive examination of the diverging propositions is beyond the boundaries of this volume. The discussion largely will be restricted to party identification as an indicator of partisan loyalty (see Zelle 1998 for an up to date analysis of vote switching). Elaborated in the American context (see Campbell et al. 1960; see chapter 5 by Angelika Vetter and Oscar W. Gabriel for a discussion of this model), this concept has developed into a standard tool for the analysis of long term attachments to political parties in other countries as well–though the question of whether the concept can travel to the German context, and how it is to be measured, aroused some debate in the 1970s (see Gluchowski 1978, among many others). From this debate, a specific operationalization, which will be used here as well, emerged as the standard adaptation to the German context.[1]

WHY SHOULD INDIVIDUAL DEALIGNMENT OCCUR: SOCIAL AND POLITICAL VIEWS

Theoretically, different processes are conceivable as potentially causing a weakening of party identification. Electoral research on Germany predominantly focuses on social change as the relevant variable. In the U.S. context, political variables are more frequently considered as well. In this section, I will briefly present some possible predictor variables for a dealignment as well as their predictions for the German case.

Social Dealignment

This model takes firm ties between parties and voters, which are said to have been in place in the past, as a baseline. Over time, demographic changes led to a weakening or erosion of these partisan ties. Different variants of this approach exist, although there is some overlap. Thus, durable party preferences of the past were seen as being stabilized either (1) through shared political interests stemming from a similar position in the social structure (which may be enhanced by membership in a mediating organization), or (2) through interaction between individuals in a politically homogenous social milieu (see Pappi 1977). Party identification, once in place, was passed on through the processes of socialization.

From the baseline of this interpretation of the past, electoral change is said to have resulted from demographic changes. Again, different variants were put forward: (1) The new middle class lacks a clear position in the conflict structure between working class and old middle class, as it does with regard to the conflicts over religiosity and denomination. Its constant growth increases the percentage of the population lacking clear voting clues that stem from shared (class) interests (Klingemann 1985, Rose and McAllister 1986). (2) Traditional social milieus eroded in a process of "individualization," thus reducing social cues for political preferences (Gluchowski 1987; Veen 1991; Zapf et al. 1987). (3) Rising educational attainment has increased the "cognitive competence" of the public, thus enabling voters to do without "functional partisan ties" and judge political actors according to available information (Dalton 1984; Shively 1979; Dalton and Rohrschneider 1990). The differences in detail notwithstanding, these three variants of the social dealignment thesis concur in the diagnosis of rising partisan independence as a consequence of social modernization. The "modern floating voter" represents the altered demands the electorate puts on the political elites.

All these variants of the social dealignment thesis are highly plausible. Yet in all cases plausible rival hypotheses exist, making the social dealignment perspective somewhat less than a sure bet. Thus, the obscurity of socioeconomic interests need not necessarily imply their absence, even though they are harder to assess empirically (Oberndörfer and Mielke 1990). By the same token, the erosion of the traditional milieus may well have led to evolution of numerous smaller ones which may be equally effective in stabilizing partisan attachments (for examples see Vester et al. 1993; Müller-Schneider 1994). With regard to the effects of education, it is at least debatable whether better educated citizens are indeed capable of evaluating political phenomena without making use of attachments of some kind. In particular, given the increasing complexity of politics, it is by no means a sure thing that higher education makes it possible to base party choice merely on policy evaluations.

One final doubt relates to all of these variants. The close psychological attachments to the parties that the dealignment theory assumes to have existed in the past has not usually been ascertained empirically (for findings that raise doubts see H.A.Winkler 1993; J.Winkler 1995). After all, the perception of extreme stability in the past is based on a certain reading of the classics of the cleavage structure approach. It is important to note that these were not based on survey data (Lipset and Rokkan 1967; see also Lepsius 1973). Particularly in the case of Germany, where highly volatile electoral results made the decline of the Weimar Republic possible, it is uncertain how closely a model of stable ties between certain social segments and certain parties fits reality. If the past was not as stable as these theories assume, the idea of a dealignment, which claims an erosion of this stability, loses ground. Given these plausible rival hypotheses, empirical tests of the social dealignment approach are necessary.

Political Frustration

In earlier research, I have contrasted these social dealignment hypotheses with another group of explanatory factors that can be categorized as political approaches. For the present chapter, I limit the discussion to political frustration as a potential explanation for variations in party identification. The hypothesis is very straightforward: When citizens' satisfaction with the political system declines, so will the attachments to political parties as major agents in the political realm. Note that the ultimate cause of these variations may be located in the functioning of the political system itself, in its presentation through the media, or in changing expectations on the part of the public. The first two are cases of supply-side explanations, while the latter focuses on the demand side. Thus, pinning down the ultimate cause of a development of this kind may require additional research.

While political satisfaction plays little role in studies of party identification in the German case (but see Dalton and Rohrschneider 1990), it is considered more frequently in the United States. Thus, the public's evaluation of politics is a key variable for the explanation that Nie, Verba, and Petrocik (1976) offer for the sudden decline in party identification in the United States in the 1960s and early 1970s. Converse adhered to a similar logic when he employed what he called a "hapless, post hoc procedure" to point at a number of specific political events that he held responsible for this decline in partisanship (Converse 1976: 104). More recently, MacKuen, Erikson, and Stimson (1989) demonstrated that the aggregated party identification, termed macropartisanship, indeed depends on stimuli at the macrolevel of politics and the economy.

From this perspective, the degree of the public's satisfaction with politics becomes the key potential explanation for the development of party identification. Therefore, Figure 4.1 plots the development of satisfaction and dissatisfaction with the German political system for the period from 1973 to 1994 in western Germany. It makes clear that there has been a notable decline in satisfaction after 1990. The

Figure 4.1. Satisfaction with the Political System in Western Germany, 1973-94

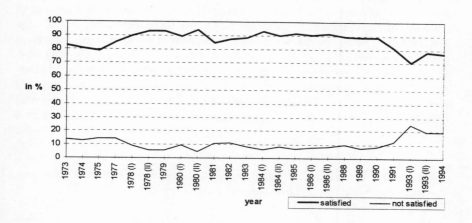

Source: Konrad Adenauer Foundation, Department of Political Research.

portion of the dissatisfied had never exceeded 14 percent for the entire time span before 1990. In fact, dissatisfaction was below 10 percent for most of the 1980s. Yet, dissatisfaction then rose from 9 to 12 percent between 1990 and 1991, peaked at 25 percent in early 1993 and remained at 20 percent until the federal election of 1994. This is by far the highest level of dissatisfaction in the entire period under consideration—reflecting that the heavily employed term *Politikverdrossenheit* (political disenchantment) indeed has some empirical basis (for other indicators see also Rattinger 1993; and Gabriel 1993). Unfortunately, however, it is impossible here to identify the exact cause of this sudden drop. Yet, given its very suddenness, it is more likely to result from short-term factors—such as macrophenomena—than from societal developments, which take place over a longer period of time. This notion is corroborated by the fact that the decline took place across social strata (see Zelle 1995b). One would have to apply Converse's "hapless" procedure in order to pin down the ultimate stimulus. Since the present focus is on party identification, this subject is left aside here. What is important here is that according to the political frustration perspective, the development described here should have an effect on the level of partisanship in the western German population.

THE DEVELOPMENT OF PARTY IDENTIFICATION IN
WESTERN GERMANY, 1971-94

The two approaches sketched out in the preceding section make claims about the development of party identification over time. Therefore, a longitudinal analysis of party identification appears to be a good way to test these approaches empirically. Unfortunately, however, the predictions derived from the social and frustration perspectives overlap to a substantial degree: viewed over the long term, both specify a decline in party identification. Yet, since dissatisfaction rose notably only after 1990, while social modernization has been taking place for a longer period of time, the respective time frames differ substantially. In particular, any decline that is visible before 1990 fits the social view only. Declining party identification after 1990 is consistent with both approaches. Applying this yardstick leads to the following hypotheses:

Social view: Continuous decline in party identification over the entire period.
Frustration view: Drop in party identification after 1990.

The trends of party identification in western Germany are presented in Figure 4.2. It contains the total portion of party identifiers as well as the portion of strong identifiers as measured by the surveys conducted by the Konrad Adenauer Foundation (KAS) between 1972 and 1994. Strikingly, the findings regarding the total percentage of party identification are in contrast to the expectations of both explanatory frameworks presented here. By the time of the federal election of 1994, party identification was no less frequent than it had been in 1972. In fact, it was slightly up from 65 percent in November of 1972 to 70 percent in 1994. The general picture, however, is one of trendless fluctuation rather than of either decline or increase. True, the last legislative period under consideration here saw some low levels in party identification, but earlier periods did so as well. This impression is confirmed by an aggregate correlation (Pearson's r) that is essentially nonexistent (.02, p=.91) for the forty-eight measurements from 1971 to 1994. Taking only the time span from 1990 to 1994–the time span on which the frustration approach focuses–yields a much higher correlation (-.53), but no statistical significance (p=.28, N=6). Hence, from these data, neither one of the two approaches fits the empirical evidence. Party identification did not become less frequent in western Germany in the course of the past decades.

It is important to point out that data from different sources produce different results in this respect. In particular, on the basis of the monthly Politbarometer conducted by IPOS in Mannheim, Falter and Rattinger (1997: 497-500) do find a statistically significant decline in the portion of party identifications between 1977 and 1994 in western Germany. Unfortunately, the procedure Falter and Rattinger chose makes it impossible to apply their evidence neatly to the approaches examined here. Their results do make clear, however, that this decline was much stronger in the 1990s (between 1991 and 1994) than it was when the entire period is considered. Falter and Rattinger do not investigate if there is a significant decline

Figure 4.2. Party Identification in Western Germany, 1971-94

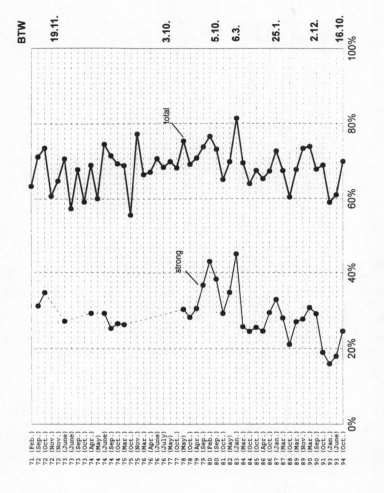

Source: Konrad Adenauer Foundation, Department of Political Research.

Figure 4.3. Percentage of Party Identifiers in the Data of the Politbarometer, 1977-94

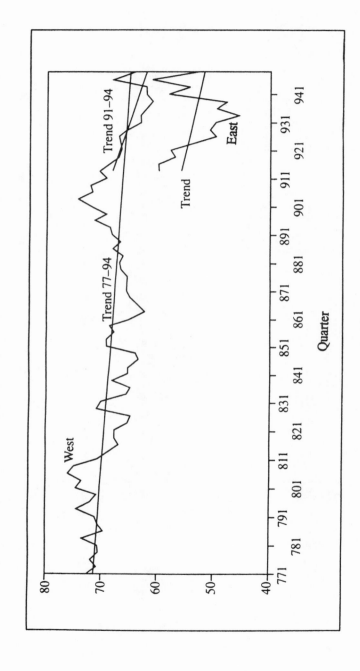

Source: From Falter and Rattinger (1997: 500). The trend lines arefrom the regression analyses conducted by Falter and Rattinger.

prior to 1990, however. Yet their graph suggests that there had been no steady decline before 1990, with that year marking one of the highest levels of party identification over the entire period (see Figure 4.3). Thus, these findings may be indicating fluctuations until 1990 and decline since, which taken together fits the frustration approach better than the social dealignment approach.

When we examine the strength of party identification, the picture is complicated further. In the KAS-data analyzed here, this indicator indeed testifies to a decline. The portion of strong identifiers reached its lowest level ever during the electoral period between 1990 and 1994. Never before had this portion gone below 20 percent, where it remained from the time from 1991 to 1993. Moreover, the 25 percent measured in 1994 marks the lowest value ever at the time of an election. This is reflected in a statistically significant aggregate correlation between the percentage of strong identifiers and the year of measurement of -.40 (p=.02).

When it comes to attributing this development to the social or political approach, however, once again the matter cannot be settled beyond any doubt. In fact, the data can be interpreted to favor either view. Viewed from the social dealignment perspective, it is important that the decline in strong party identification is not restricted to the time span between 1990 and 1994, but can be traced back to the early 1980s. Limiting the attention to election times, strong party identifications were most frequent in 1983 and declined gradually over the elections of 1987, 1990, and 1994. This gradual development cannot be accounted for by the short-term perspective of the frustration approach. On the other hand, this gradual decline is visible only during the second half of the time span covered here. During the earlier years, strong party identifications increased rather than declined. Thus, while strong party identifications were much less frequent in 1990 when compared to 1983 (by about 15 points), they were only slightly less frequent than they had been at the beginning of this period (5 points). For this reason, I had been reluctant to take the trend until 1990 as evidencing a decline at all in earlier research. This hesitancy is supported by the statistical insignificance of the aggregate correlation between the portion of strong identifications and the year of measurement between 1971 and 1990 (r=-.13, see Table 4.1).

Table 4.1. Aggregate Party Identification Over Time: Pearson Correlations

	Total PID			Strong PID		
	r	sig.	N	r	sig.	N
1971-94	.02	.91	48	-.40	.02	33
1971-90	.17	.27	44	-.13	.52	29
1990-94	-.53	.28	6	-.62	.19	6

Source: Surveys conducted by the Konrad Adenauer Foundation, Department of Political Research. Calculations based on the proportion of total and of strong identifiers in a survey, by year.

On the other hand, the evidence is too weak to attribute the decline to the period after 1990 only. To be sure, the aggregate correlation with time is much higher (-.62) but below statistical significance. In sum, then, the way the data are in 1994, it is impossible to decide between these approaches on the basis of this evidence. Thus, while it is accurate to talk about a decline in party identification in recent years, assigning a specific cause to this development is an endeavor that is much more speculative in character.

In a first attempt to solve this puzzle I reviewed the evidence collected by other data sources. Yet the numerous findings complicate the riddle instead of solving it. Most sources concur that some type of partisanship declined between 1990 and 1994–though not a dramatically so (see Falter and Rattinger 1997; Gehring and Winkler 1997). The crucial question for discriminating between the approaches relates to the period before 1990, however. For that period, the data fail to support any conclusion with a sufficient degree of certainty (see the discussion in Zelle 1995a: 147-157). Thus, given the contradictions in the longitudinal findings regarding party identification, it is very well possible that social dealignment is indeed taking place (as many electoral researchers, including some authors in this volume, assume), but it appears inaccurate to take this as a thesis that has passed all the tests necessary in empirical analysis.

In order to step beyond this point of uncertainty resulting from the longitudinal findings in the aggregate, the following section examines the implications of the two approaches regarding partisanship within certain groups.

WHO IDENTIFIES WITH A POLITICAL PARTY?

The social dealignment approach and the political frustration approach both make claims not only about the development of party identification (PID) over time, but also about its distribution among different groups. In their pure forms, both approaches imply compositional arguments. That is, both claim that the frequency of party identifications changes as the composition of the population with regard to certain groups changes. In particular, the social dealignment approach expects decreasing party attachments as a consequence of rising proportions of the better educated and of third-sector employment. In contrast, the frustration perspective claims declining proportions of party identifiers as the politically satisfied become less frequent. The baselines of these arguments are relationships at the individual level; namely, the claim that partisanship is weaker among the better educated and the individuals in the new middle class in the case of the social approach, and the claim that party identification is weaker among those who are dissatisfied with the political system. Both claims are open to empirical scrutiny.

Table 4.2 contains the relevant findings relating to the social view. The entries are means on a three point "intensity of party identification" scale, which scores '3' for a strong identification. In the first column, data sets from the election years from 1972 to 1994 (except 1976, when party identification intensity was not asked), have been pooled to yield a total of 17,576 respondents.[2] Given this remarkable sample size, the findings are indeed stunning: The relationship between party identification and either education or occupation are so weak that they remain well below the threshold of statistical significance (t-test). Hence, there is no reason whatever to assume a difference in party identification between these groups. It is clear from this point that in its pure form as a compositional argument relating to education and occupation, the social dealignment approach cannot possibly explain changes in party identification over time.

Yet there is an alternative to this focus on the composition of the electorate. When social characteristics are not decisive in accounting for the strength of party identification at any given time, they might affect changes in party identification over time nonetheless. Thus, though certain strata are not particularly prone not to identify with a party, they might be particularly vulnerable to changes in the environment that trigger a weakening of partisan ties. When this is the case, social factors (and social change) still are important factors for a theory of party identification change. This is the approach Dalton and Rohrschneider (1990) take in their analysis of German party identification in 1972 and 1987. Dalton and Rohrschneider argue that respondents who are high on cognitive mobilization are more likely to react to the changes of the media environment, making a decrease in

Table 4.2. Party Identification Among Occupational and Educational Groups, Election Years 1972-94, Western Germany

	Mean '72-'94	'72	'80	'83	'87	'90	'94	Change '72-'94	eta '72-'94
Total	2.1	2.0	2.1	2.3	2.1	2.0	1.9	-.07	.05**
Occupation:									
Worker	2.1	2.0	2.2	2.3	2.0	1.9	1.9	-.08	.05*
Salariat	2.1	2.1	2.1	2.3	2.1	2.0	2.0	-.13	.08**
Self-employed & farmer	2.1	2.0	2.2	2.3	2.0	2.1	1.9	-.04	.03
eta	.01	.07**	.03	.03	.06	.05	.03		
Education:									
Lower	2.1	2.0	2.1	2.3	2.0	2.0	1.9	-.04	.03
Middle	2.1	2.1	2.1	2.3	1.9	2.0	1.9	-.23	.16**
Higher	2.1	2.1	2.1	2.2	2.2	2.0	2.0	-.10	.06
eta	.02	.09**	.01	.02	.13**	.02	.06*		
r		.08**	.00	-.01	.07*	.01	.04*		
N	17,576	2,976	5,945	2,082	1,053	3,033	2,487		

Notes: Means, 1 = no identification, 3 = strong identification. * p < .05, ** p < .01.
Source: Surveys conducted by the Konrad Adenauer Foundation, Department of Political Research.

party identification more likely in this group (for the theoretical argument see Dalton 1984). In this argument, the mechanism behind changes in party identification is an interaction between membership in a certain group and changing stimuli on the macro level. The effect on party identification can take place without a change in the level of cognitive mobilization—that is, a compositional effect, though it might be enhanced by it.

To investigate whether the development of party identification took different courses among the different educational and occupational groups, Table 4.2 also lists the mean strength of party identification for each of the election years from 1972 to 1994 (except 1976). It turns out that all groups were affected by the mild decline in the intensity of party identification between 1972 and 1994, though there are utterly slight variations as well. Thus, the decline appears to have been a bit more pronounced among the new middle class (eta .08) than among the workers (.05) and the old middle class (.03, n.s.). Weak as it is, this finding at least identifies the very group the social dealignment approach focuses on as the one that appears to be most prone to be affected by a dealigning trend. Yet, at the same time, it is this very group that started out with the strongest identifications to begin with: In 1972, when the occupational groups differed significantly, the new middle class topped the other groups (though very weak in its level of party identification [eta .07]). Never again is there is a significant relationship between occupation and party identification: the new middle class is no less partisan than the other groups. These results are definitely too weak to be interpreted as supporting the social dealignment approach.

In the case of educational attainment, this general result is similar. Interestingly, the decline in party identification is most visible among those with an intermediate level of formal schooling (*Mittlere Reife*), evidenced by a statistically significant eta coefficient of .16 for the contrast between 1972 and 1994. For both the lowest and the highest educational groups, this comparison does not yield significant results. When considering the individual years, it turns out that education is positively related to party identification strength in a number of years, including 1994, while the reverse is never the case. Thus, if anything, education proliferates party identification rather than leads to its steady decline. Neither of these findings is impressive in magnitude, but both run counter to the expectation of the social dealignment perspective in substance. While the longitudinal data in the aggregate had left leeway for an interpretation in the spirit of the social dealignment approach (though certainly not favoring it over the frustration approach), this approach does poorly with this analysis of different social groups.

Table 4.3 contains the relevant evidence for the frustration approach. Unlike the case in the analysis of social groups presented above, this analysis cannot cover the entire time span, because the various indicators are not contained in the same data sets. Therefore, the analysis is limited to data from 1989 and from 1994. This procedure is sufficient for the present purpose since the decline in political satisfaction took place during this time span.

The results confirm that party identification intensity is related to political satisfaction, though the link is not very strong (Pearson's r .16 in 1989 and .14 in

Table 4.3. Party Identification and Political Satisfaction, 1989 and 1994, Western Germany

	1989	1994	Change 1989-94	Eta 1989-94
Total	2.0	1.9	-.06	.04**
Satisfaction with political system:				
Very satisfied	2.3	2.2	-.05	.03
Somewhat satisfied	2.0	1.9	-.03	.02
Not satisfied	1.9	1.8	-.05	.03
eta	.17**	.15**		
r	.16**	.14**		
N	4,981	2,485		

Notes: Means, 1= no identification, 3 = strong identification. * p < .05, ** p < .01.
Source: Surveys conducted by the Konrad Adenauer Foundation, Department of Political Research.

1994). Hence, the decline in party identification after 1990 has to be seen in conjunction with the increased level of political dissatisfaction. Though causal connections cannot be inferred from the evidence, the interpretation of the political frustration approach—which holds that the changing composition of the public with respect to political dissatisfaction is the explanation for partisanship decline—is compatible with these data. It is reflected in the fact that the decline is slightly weaker when political satisfaction is controlled (see the distances and the etas in Table 4.3). This is further supported by the fact that in the regression analysis, the significant, though utterly small, effect of the year on the intensity of party identification drops below statistical significance once political satisfaction is entered (from .04 to .01, data not shown). Weak as these findings are, they do support the political frustration perspective on changes in party identification.

PARTY IDENTIFICATION IN EASTERN GERMANY: THE DESCRIPTIVE EVIDENCE

One of the explanatory frameworks discussed in this update, namely the social dealignment approach, is heavily attuned to societies undergoing continuous processes of modernization rather rapid transformation as the result of a shock. Therefore, the discussion had to be limited to western Germany. For descriptive purposes, Figure 4.4 charts the development of party identification in eastern Germany. The surveys indicate that party identifications are present in eastern Germany as well, even though the issue of measurement may be particularly vexing here. The literature has examined different sources for these party identifications, namely prewar traditions, Western TV, the event of unification, and, in the special case of the former system party Party of Democratic Socialism, attachments developed during the socialist regime (see chapter 3 by Karl Schmitt in this volume; Bluck and Kreikenbom 1991; Gluchowski and Zelle 1992; Kaase and Klingemann 1994b; Neu 1994; Rattinger 1994a).

Figure 4.4 shows that party identification is less frequent and less intense in the East when compared to the West. Moreover, and maybe more interestingly, identifications declined in the East as well. Possibly, this is connected to the decline in satisfaction with the political system, which declined simultaneously (see chapter 11 on the PDS in this volume) and with which it is correlated at .10 (1994). From the perspective of the united Germany, then, unification sped up the decline in party identification intensity that was observed in the western data. In this case, East and West do indeed converge–although the reasons for this have yet to be ascertained in both parts of the country.

CONCLUSION

Complementing an earlier analysis of vote switching (see Zelle 1995b), this chapter contrasted social dealignment and political frustration as explanations for the development of party identification in western Germany. Theories of a social dealignment claim a gradual decline of party identifications during the process of modernization. The political frustration approach focuses on the degree of the public's (dis)satisfaction with politics. Since the cause of political frustration could also rest in social change, these two approaches are not necessarily incompatible. Yet, in the present case, they arrive at distinct predictions about the long-run dynamics of partisanship.

After establishing that political satisfaction hit a low in the early 1990s, the political frustration approach led to the expectation of a sudden decline in party identification after 1990. This should be discernible from the continuous decline expected from the social dealignment approach. However, the trend of party identification is such that it is not entirely compatible with either approach and partially compatible with both. Thus, party identification declined in strength (though the same cannot be ascertained beyond doubt for its frequency), but this development is neither as long-term as the social approach would have predicted nor as short-term as the political frustration approach led one to expect. Both views can be defended with these data. In this situation, researchers should be cautioned against too much intransigence on either side of the theoretical dispute. Also, they should be cautioned against employing truncated trends: given the fluctuations in party identification, the impression of decline or stability may be reached by accident, or it may be manufactured by starting the observation at a time when party identification is unusually high (to reach the conclusion of decline) or unusually low (to conclude stability or increase).

The analysis of aggregated party identification thus provided evidence for a dealignment of the third type, but it did not succeed in identifying the cause(s) for

Figure 4.4. Party Identification in Germany 1990-94

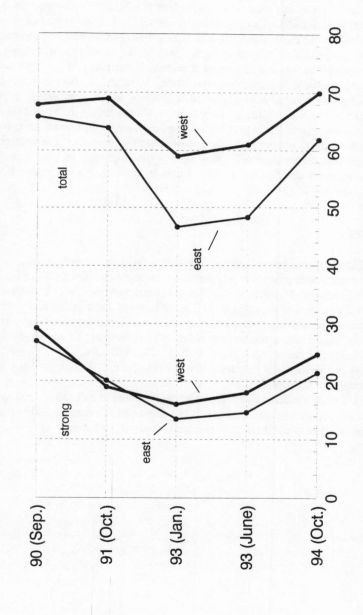

Source: Konrad Adenauer Foundation, Department of Political Research.

this development. Analyzing party identification among different groups also falls short of providing an answer to this question in a more or less definitive way. Yet it hints at the frustration approach, which fared somewhat better than the social dealignment view. In essence, the strength of party identification turned out to be unrelated to an individual's occupation or educational attainment. The same holds for the decline in party identification, which was not primarily a phenomenon of specific groups. The few weak findings that did emerge ran counter to the expectation of the social dealignment approach. In particular, if anything, education promotes party identification rather than degrades it. In contrast, political satisfaction is linked with party identification, thus constituting a potential explanation for the decline in partisanship after 1990 in light of the political frustration approach. Though these findings tip the overall balance in favor of the political frustration approach, they cannot totally outweigh the indeterminacy resulting from the longitudinal examination in the aggregate. In sum, therefore, the present research can offer an empirical update to an academic dispute, but it falls short of settling it.

NOTES

1. The questions read: "Denken Sie jetzt einmal an die politischen Parteien in Deutschland. Wenn Sie es insgesamt betrachten: Neigen Sie da einer Partei mehr zu als den anderen Parteien oder ist das bei Ihnen nicht der Fall? Welche Partei ist das?" "Think about the political parties in Germany for a moment. On the whole, do you tend more toward one party than others, or is this not the case for you?"; (if yes): "Wie stark oder schwach neigen Sie–alles zusammengenommen–dieser Partei zu: Würden Sie sagen: Eher stark, mäßig, oder eher schwach?" "In general, how strongly or weakly do you tend toward this party? Would you say strongly, moderately, or weakly?"

2. I am deeply indebted to Peter Gluchowski (Konrad Adenauer Foundation) for letting me use this pooled data set. It is a subset of the data he and Wilamowitz-Moellendorff employed for their research reported in chapter 2.

5

Candidate Evaluations and Party Choice in Germany, 1972-94: Do Candidates Matter?

Angelika Vetter and Oscar W. Gabriel

INTRODUCTION

Elections in Western democracies increasingly have been criticized for having degenerated into beauty contests between candidates who lack any notable differences regarding their policy positions. This trend toward a diminishing relevance of political issues in favor of candidates as determinants of voting behavior is said to have two different sources: First, the emergence of so-called catch-all parties in most Western democracies has been interpreted as going along with a decline of ideologies and a convergence of clearly differentiated party platforms (see Kirchheimer 1965; Lipset 1981). Second, the growing role of electronic media as an intermediary institution in the exchange between the governors and the governed is said to have fundamentally altered the processes of political communication: It is difficult to communicate differentiated policy positions of candidates and parties via TV or radio, and the trend toward reducing politics to a competition between prominent leadership figures seems to be strengthened by the nature of media-set politics (see, among others, Sarcinelli 1987; Kepplinger and Brosius 1990; Schrott 1990b).

This rather pessimistic interpretation of the electoral process and the candidates running for office is counterbalanced by a competing approach that stresses a new map which structures voters' decisions. Following the arguments made by Nie, Verba, and Petrocik (1976), the changing voter is by no means a victim of the public relations agencies and campaign managers who seek to manipulate him or her. As modernization and rationalization of social and political life in Western societies have progressed, voters appear to have become increasingly sophisticated. Instead of casting their ballots according to their long-standing party loyalties, they make deliberate choices between the party programs and leaders offered to them in the electoral campaign. They even take into account parties' and party leaders' performance during the electoral period preceding the current campaign. The modern voter is thus perceived by some observers as coming close to the ideal described by rational choice theories.[1]

In this chapter, we investigate the perception and evaluation of candidates as determinants of party choice in Germany, thereby focusing on the candidates for the office of the chancellor (see chapter 13 by Thomas D. Lancaster in this volume for an examination of candidate effects on the district level). We ask whether attitudes toward candidates affect electoral decision-making in Germany, and whether these effects have changed over the years. In other words, have elections in Germany really degenerated to beauty contests between the chancellor candidates? In the first part of the chapter, we discuss the role of candidate evaluation in a more encompassing model of explaining electoral behavior (Campbell et al. 1954; 1960). Also, we raise the issue of how the concept of candidate evaluation may be applied in the particular institutional setting of Germany. The empirical analyses provide information on the development of candidate evaluations in Germany since 1961. In the final part of the chapter, we investigate the relevance of attitudes toward candidates in the context of the so-called Michigan model. Again, the strategy of analysis is longitudinal. We present data from German Bundestag elections in 1972, 1983, and 1990 for an overview over the development within the last three decades and conclude with a comparative analysis of the determinants of electoral behavior in West and East Germany in the most recent election held in the fall of 1994.[2]

THE AMERICAN VOTER RECONSIDERED: THE GENERAL STRUCTURE OF THE MICHIGAN MODEL

One of the most important concepts for explaining electoral behavior was developed by Angus Campbell and his associates (Campbell et al. 1954, 1960). The so-called Michigan model was applied for the first time in an analysis of the American presidential campaign in 1952. It successively has been refined and partially revised (Nie, Verba, and Petrocik 1976; for further details see Dalton and Wattenberg 1993; Miller 1995). According to the logic of the Michigan model, the individual voting decision is considered the dependent variable to be explained by an interplay of the three independent or intervening variables: party identification, issue orientation, and the evaluation of candidates.

Campbell et al. characterized the relevance of these factors in the explanation of vote choice as follows: "If we are to understand what leads the voter to his decision at the polls we must know how he sees the things to which the decision relates. In casting a vote, the individual acts toward a world of politics in which he perceives the *personalities*, *issues*, and *parties*. ... As a result, measuring perceptions and evaluations of the elements of politics is a first charge on our energies in the explanation of the voting act" (Campbell et al. 1960, 42). Campbell et al. thought of these variables as being embedded in a more encompassing psychological field that contains political as well as nonpolitical factors. Moreover, they take different positions on the time axis. Party identification is assumed to have a long-term impact on the voters' decisions, and, therefore, to remain stable over a long period

Figure 5.1. The Michigan Model's Funnel of Causality

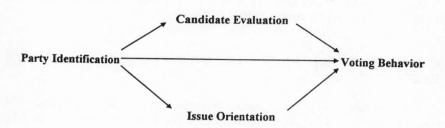

of time. In contrast, issue and candidate orientations are thought to be bound to particular situational circumstances. They may be responsible for short-term fluctuations in electoral behavior and probably change from one electoral contest to another.

Among others, stability and instability over time are important factors accounting for the position a particular variable takes in a complex explanatory model (see Asher 1976: 11). Accordingly, the variables incorporated by Campbell et al. (1960: 24) in the social-psychological concept of electoral behavior were regarded as making up a "funnel of causality." While party identification was attributed the status of an independent variable that was located at the beginning of the funnel, voting behavior was placed at its end. Issue orientations as well as candidate evaluations were placed in an intermediary position (see also Bürklin 1988: 55; Falter, Schumann, and Winkler 1990: 8; Miller 1995: 252; and Figure 5.1).

The concept of the funnel of causality makes two assumptions concerning the role and nature of party identification. First, party identification has been interpreted as a central, enduring, deeply ingrained, and stable affective-evaluative orientation toward a particular party, and as being less dependent on situational influences than other elements of an individual's attitudinal system (see Campbell et al. 1960: 121). Second, if the relationship between party identification and voting intention is embedded in the larger context of the Michigan model, three paths link the former to the latter. On one hand, party identification shapes party choices directly. On the other hand, two indirect relationships exist between party identification and voting intention, mediated by voters' candidate and issue orientations. These indirect paths represent the impact of party identification on the short-term determinants of voters' choices.

In most cases, party identification, candidate, and issue orientation will be in an equilibrium where these variables tend to reinforce each other. Party identification works as a main force in the complex interplay of determinants of electoral behavior. Whenever an equilibrium of this type prevails, consistent and stable voting in accordance with the long-term party identification is the most probable result. Only if inconsistencies between party identification and short-term influences appear, voters' defections from their established party identification become likely, leading to vote switching, split voting, or abstention from the vote (see Campbell 1960, 121, 123, 136; Eltermann 1980, 28).

CANDIDATE EVALUATIONS AS A DETERMINANT OF ELECTORAL CHOICE

Although party identification is considered the most important determinant of electoral choices, the Michigan model assumes that additional factors need to be taken into account in the explanation of voting behavior, foremost issue and candidate orientations. These two variables may perform a different function as determinants of the voters' choices. First, not every voter has developed a long-term attachment to a particular party. For a considerable number of independents–and probably weak party identifiers as well–factors other than party identification will be decisive for their party choice. Second, in the case of strong inconsistencies between party identification and issue and candidate orientations, people may defect from their long-term party identification and cast their ballots in accordance with their candidate or issue orientation. Since the strength of party identification as a long-term determinant of electoral behavior appears to have declined in a number of Western democracies during the last few decades (see, for the United States Nie, Verba, and Petrocik 1976: 47; Wattenberg 1984; for Western Europe Gabriel 1994a; see also chapters 2 and 4 in this volume), candidate evaluations and issue orientations may have become more important determinants of voting behavior (see Dalton and Wattenberg 1993: 206).

Before assessing the impact of the candidate evaluation on electoral choices in Germany, some remarks on the properties of the respective variable in general, and in the particular German context, are in order. The evaluation of candidates is interpreted as a short-term determinant of electoral behavior. As far as candidates for the positions of the American president or the German federal chancellor are concerned, this view is highly plausible. In almost all American presidential elections since World War II, candidates running for office changed from one election to the next. In Germany, the situation is slightly different. With regard to the candidates for chancellorship presented by political parties–particularly opposition parties–since 1949, change and discontinuity prevail. Consequently, voters have to make up their minds on candidates anew from one federal election to the next.

Candidate evaluation as well as issue orientation are multidimensional concepts composed of cognitive as well as affective-evaluative components (see Eltermann 1980: 13; Lass 1995). Therefore, candidates and some of their attributes need to be perceived by the electorate in order to become relevant as determinants of electoral choice. While candidates running for president of the United States or chancellor of Germany are probably well known to the electorate, this does not necessarily apply to candidates for other political positions. Focusing on the candidates for the chancellorship, the perception of candidates does not seem to be a problem. Playing a prominent role in the political game, either of them might be sufficiently known to the electorate in order to become a factor in the voter's decision making process (see Eltermann 1980: 17; Lass 1995).

Another source of variation refers to the evaluative standards shaping the candidates' images. Candidates are normally evaluated on the basis of criteria rather different in nature (see Eltermann 1980: 64; Lass 1995). The most important attributes regarding the evaluation of candidates for leadership positions may be classified into two broad categories, a personality-related dimension and a performance-related one. Each of them consists of a variable number of elements. These criteria may have a different meaning for the voters' decision-making process. At the same time, they may be linked to the candidates in different ways. Sometimes, general or specific policy performance may be the most important criterion. In other instances, performance does not count very much, but personal qualities like integrity, honesty, fairness, or responsiveness become preeminent image factors. Moreover, the available information on the properties of different candidates may vary strongly according to the position they hold, how long they have been known to the electorate, and other situational influences. Finally, party identification may work as a screen in the perception and evaluation of candidates (see Campbell et al. 1960: 54; Dalton and Wattenberg 1993: 208; Norpoth 1977: 561).

Either way, information about the electorate's knowledge of general and specific properties of candidates has to be gathered by way of empirical research. Candidate evaluation can be expected to play a role in the process of electoral decision-making only if at least one of the candidates is known to the respective voter, and if instrumental, affective, or evaluative orientations toward the candidates have been formed. Unfortunately, detailed empirical data on candidate perception in Germany is rather poor. Most empirical analyses of candidates as determinants of electoral behavior have used very different measures of candidate evaluation. Despite these shortcomings, Lass (1995: 95) showed a clear increase in the complexity of candidate perceptions in an analysis of data from 1969, 1976, and 1987. Therefore, at least one precondition supporting the hypothesis of increased candidate effects on voting behavior in Germany appears to be fulfilled.

THE CONCEPT OF CANDIDATE ORIENTATION IN THE GERMAN CONTEXT

Since the Michigan model was originally developed to explain electoral behavior in the United States, its value as a theoretical concept in other institutional contexts is by no means self-evident. Political dispositions influencing the selection of political leaders in the United States do not have to play the same role in a different system. Therefore, we need to ask whether candidate orientations can have a similar effect on electoral choices in Germany, given the particular German institutional setting.

One of the major problems facing cross-national survey research is the operationalization of concepts. Thus, the operationalization of candidate orientations appropriate for the United States may not be appropriate in the German context (see Niedermayer 1992: 75; Budge, Crewe, and Fairlie 1976; Falter 1977: 283; Gluchowski 1978; Küchler 1986: 201). Another serious problem is posed by the differing institutional frameworks of electoral contests in Germany and the United States. The competencies attributed to particular institutions—as well as their interrelationships, the electoral laws, and the structure of the party systems in the respective nations—are completely different.

In the United States, the president and the members of Congress are elected by direct vote. In Germany, the Bundestag (federal parliament) is the only political institution legitimized directly by popular vote. The German government as well as the chancellor owe their offices to parliamentary processes of leadership recruitment. Moreover, the powers of the American president and Congress are clearly separated from each other. As a consequence, voters may employ a separate voting calculus for presidential and congressional elections. The situation is different in Germany. As in every parliamentary system, government and parliamentary majority are closely interrelated. A situation of divided government cannot occur. Unlike the United States, the fate of the chancellor and his government rests on a majority in parliament. The loss of parliamentary majority inevitably leads to a change in government. Hence, government and parliamentary majority are considered as one by the electorate.

Further differences in the process of leadership recruitment result from the provisions of electoral laws. In the United States, leaders are selected by simple majority vote, whereas members of the Bundestag are elected by a system of proportional representation. As a result of electoral laws and the types of political parties controlling the process of leadership recruitment, the candidates' personalities may have a greater impact on the electoral choice in the United States than in Germany. From a formal-institutional point of view, American voters cast their ballots in favor of particular candidates, while party labels are of minor importance. In Germany, the opposite is true. Casting one's vote primarily means a party choice.

Another problem concerning the possibility of transferring the concept of candidate orientation to Germany has been raised by Eltermann (1980: 9). He argues that a strong governmental orientation as a part of the German political culture might lead to the formation of a so-called *Kanzlerbonus* (chancellor bonus)—that is, an advantage attributed to the incumbent head of the government irrespective of the personality and performance of the particular officeholder. If an influence of this type could be established empirically, candidate effects would be a constant rather than a variable, and thus become largely irrelevant in an explanatory model of voting behavior.

Finally, the types of parties involved in the struggle for power in the United

States and Germany should be taken into account when discussing the possibility of transferring the Michigan model to Germany. American political parties come very close to the ideal form of a rational-efficient party. In contrast, German parties may be regarded as a mixed type that combines elements of the rational-efficient and the party-democracy ideal type (see Wright 1971). One of the most important differences between the rational-efficient and the party-democracy model is that ideologies and clear-cut party platforms play a far stronger role in the former than in the latter. If this assumption could be validated empirically, candidate effects would be more important in the United States than in Germany because German political parties provide their voters with more effective ideological clues than their American counterparts.

Overall, the relevance of candidate orientation as a determinant of electoral choice in Germany might thus be doubted for several reasons. However, any such conclusion in the absence of empirical tests seems inappropriate. Because of the close interrelation between choosing a parliamentary majority on one hand and the federal chancellor on the other, candidate orientation in Germany has to be equated with the perception and evaluation of the candidates vying for the chancellorship. Although the German federal chancellor is not subjected to direct popular vote, virtually all voters know that casting a ballot in favor of a particular party implies a clear decision on the future leader of the German government.

This assumption is not invalidated by the fact that governments almost always are a result of negotiations between at least two parties. In each election since 1972, the small parties (FDP and Greens) have stated their coalition preferences prior to the election. Thus, voters always could decide between two clear-cut alternatives of potential political coalitions and their respective chancellor candidates. From a more empirical instead of a formal-institutional point of view, parliamentary elections are plebiscites on the preferred federal chancellor (see Norpoth 1977: 551). Candidate orientation can therefore be a meaningful concept in the German institutional context, too, when interpreted as evaluation of candidates for the position of federal chancellor.

To sum up the foregoing discussion: the model of electoral behavior developed by Campbell and his associates may in principle be used in studies conducted outside the United States. However, various components of the model may have a different meaning and weight when applied in political analyses conducted elsewhere. Moreover, such analyses have to take variations in institutional arrangements into account. Therefore, when applying the Michigan model to the German electoral context, candidate orientation will be equated with perception and evaluation of the candidates for chancellorship. Moreover, even then candidate orientation might be linked more closely to party identification in Germany than in the United States. Nevertheless, we can state the hypothesis that—as a consequence of the decline of party identification and the more complex candidate perception—candidate orientations may have gained in importance as determinants of electoral behavior over time (see Dalton and Wattenberg 1993).

REVIEW OF THE LITERATURE

During the past thirty years, the Michigan model was transferred to most Western democracies, although there has been considerable debate over how this was done (the German case is described by Kaase and Klingemann 1994a). In Germany, the explanatory concept was applied for the first time in the German Election Study of 1961 when the Scheuch-Wildenmann group established a tradition of systematic, theory-oriented, methodologically sophisticated, and continuous electoral research: "Thus, the Michigan 'funnel of causality' approach ... and the core explanatory factors of party identification, issue orientation and candidate orientation are factors which on an operational level can be found in every national election study conducted in Germany since the early sixties" (Kaase and Klingemann 1994a: 346). Since then, a considerable number of electoral studies have used the Michigan model as their theoretical foundation (see, e.g., Klingemann and Taylor 1977; Berger et al. 1983, 1986, 1990; Jagodzinski and Kühnel 1990; Forschungsgruppe Wahlen 1994b; Rattinger 1994a; Zelle 1994). Others have examined particular components of the model, primarily the role of party identification (Zohlnhoefer 1965; Kaase 1970; Falter 1977; Gluchowski 1978, 1983; Norpoth 1978; Küchler 1986).

In contrast to the rich body of the literature mentioned above, empirical research on the role of candidate orientation is rather poor, not to mention the theoretical foundation these analyses are based on. There are only a handful of empirical studies on the effects of candidate orientation on electoral behavior in the German case. Norpoth (1977) as well as Klingemann and Taylor (1977) were the first scholars to focus on the role political candidates play in the electoral decision-making processes of German voters. Following the trends of candidate preferences in the National Election Studies from 1961 to 1976, Norpoth discovered an increasing gap between the competitors in the period under observation. However, when trying to separate the effects of party identification and candidate orientation, he did not find an increase in candidate effects on voting decisions. Similar results were reported by Klingemann and Taylor. Party identification was clearly the more important variable. Candidates had a strong direct influence on voting decisions only in 1969, when party effects had probably been lessened by the proximity of the share of the vote gained by CDU/CSU and the SPD, leading to a coalition government in the following parliamentary term.

Using trend data on candidate preferences for 1972 to 1976 from the Konrad Adenauer Foundation, Eltermann (1978, 1980) observed a phenomenon he called *Kanzlerbonus* (chancellor bonus): Incumbents always had an advantage over their various challengers. By analyzing actual candidate features in comparison to an ideal chancellor in 1972 and 1976, Eltermann found an influence of voters' images of the SPD candidates Willy Brandt and Helmut Schmidt on vote choice. Thus, in contrast to Norpoth and Klingemann and Taylor, he presumed an increasing importance of candidate images in the middle of the 1970s, especially among opinion leaders and politically isolated voters.

Introducing the normal vote analysis in Germany, Falter and Rattinger (1983,

1986) also tried to investigate the particular effects of party identification and issue and candidate orientation on vote intention. In an analysis of the 1980 and 1983 Bundestag elections, they found genuine candidate effects that changed with the different personalities of the competitors. In 1980 the incumbent Chancellor Helmut Schmidt convinced more voters to cast their ballot in favor of the SPD than Franz Josef Strauß did in favor of the CDU/CSU. The situation was different in 1983, when Helmut Kohl, the candidate of the CDU/CSU, had a stronger influence on vote choice than Hans Jochen Vogel, the candidate of the SPD. Comparing the 1980 and 1983 elections, Falter and Rattinger showed that the impact of the chancellor candidates on the voting decisions were stronger in the 1980 election when the preference gap between the two candidates was more obvious than in 1983. However, in both years, candidate effects were weaker factors influencing voters' decisions than party identification.

In contrast to the results obtained in the analysis of the 1980 and 1983 elections, Rattinger (1994a) found extremely high candidate effects on party sympathy in the beginning of the 1990s. He also found that candidate orientations were the most important variable besides party identification, left-right self-placement, and issue orientation in determining the sympathy for the CDU, and the second important variable in determining the sympathy for the SPD. These results held for both East and West Germany. They could indeed be supportive of our hypothesis of an increased personalization in German elections, even though multicollinearity problems among the independent variables were not taken into account. Rattinger's results for 1990 and 1991 are in line with the candidate effects Zelle (1995c: 55, see also Anderson and Zelle 1995) reported for Helmut Kohl and the CDU in the 1994 election. However, unlike Rattinger, Zelle found that party identification was still the most important determinant of vote intention.

Two of the most recent contributions on candidate orientation–Kepplinger, Brosius, and Dahlem (1994b) as well as Lass (1995)–focused primarily on different dimensions of candidate perceptions and their impact on candidate or party preference. Using data from a survey conducted in Mainz in 1990, Kepplinger et al. found that the issue competence of the candidates played only a negligible role in determining candidate and party choice. The attribution of personal characteristics, however, proved to have a strong impact on the voting decisions. These effects remained even after controlling for past voting behavior. Lass' results support the notion that the integrity dimension is the most important variable for the evaluation of political candidates. Moreover, Lass showed that candidate perceptions are far more differentiated in the voters' minds at the end of the 1980s than they were in 1969. Despite these results, an increased direct impact of candidates on party choice did not emerge (see Lass 1995: 187). However, given the fact that the group of voters without or with weak party affiliation is growing, stronger indirect effect of candidates in more recent elections might be observed.

Summing up the results on candidate effects on voting behavior so far, three points can be made. First, there are indications that candidates have indeed gained in importance as influences on voters' decisions over the past twenty years (for the 1970s see Eltermann 1978, 1980; for the 1990s see Rattinger 1994a; Zelle 1995c;

Anderson and Zelle 1995), even though authors like Lass (1995) cast doubt on increased direct candidate effects. Second, an investigation of changing patterns of candidate evaluation and candidate effects requires the analysis of long-term trends. Trend data analyses of candidate evaluations do not exist for the 1980s and 1990s. Whenever candidate orientations in the 1980s and 1990s were included in a more complex research design, they were not analyzed for more than two parliamentary terms. The third conclusion we draw is that some of these studies show methodological deficiencies, in particular a neglect of multicollinearity among the explanatory variables.

DATA AND RESEARCH DESIGN

We start with a description of long-term ratings of the different candidates from the beginning of the 1960s on. The trend analysis also will compare East and West Germany in the 1990s, when a more detailed item battery on the perception and evaluation of chancellor candidates in the 1994 Bundestag election can be used. Group comparisons and multiple regression analyses will be used to answer the question whether or not chancellor candidates affect the decisions of German voters, and whether these effects have changed over the years.

A few methodological remarks are in order. As mentioned above, party identification and issue and candidate orientations are likely to be highly correlated. Hence, interpreting the size of effect coefficients included in multivariate analyses does not seem an appropriate strategy for assessing the impact of candidate orientation on party choice. Therefore, we will investigate two different regression models. The first model includes only party identification and issue orientation as explanatory variables. To assess the explanatory power of candidate orientations in the more encompassing Michigan model, they will be included additionally in a second regression model. We then interpret the increase in size of the coefficient of determination as the explanatory power of the variable under observation. In a last step, we seek to answer the question whether and to what degree candidate orientation affects party choice among party identifiers and nonidentifiers. Compared to the effects among party identifiers, candidate effects might be far stronger in explaining voting behavior of nonidentifiers, given that their decisions are dependent exclusively on issue and candidate orientations.

For the purposes of this analysis, we focus primarily on the long-term trends. Data on the perceptions and evaluations of candidates has been gathered in Germany since 1961 in the form of the German National Election Studies (Bundeswahlstudien), conducted during every Bundestag election year. Starting in 1977, when the Politbarometer-Studies were introduced, annual data sets for more continuous trend analyses are available. For the East/West comparison in 1994, we use additional data that were gathered in the context of a DFG (German Science Foundation) project on political attitudes and political behavior in the unified Germany (for more details on the data used here, see the Appendix at the end of this chapter).

LONG-TERM TRENDS IN CANDIDATE EVALUATION IN GERMANY, 1961-94

We can get a first view of the role candidates have played in the electoral contests by analyzing data on candidate preferences, the only available indicator for time series starting in the beginning of the 1960s. However, one serious problem arises when we try to conduct long-term analyses using the candidate preferences. The question format of the indicator changes somewhat over the years. From 1961 to 1969, respondents were asked about a number of different political personalities, not just the candidates for the chancellorship. At the beginning of the 1970s, the question format was changed for the first time. The number of candidates was reduced to the two competitors for chancellorship and a third "neither of them" category was added. This category was dropped at the end of the 1980s. The last available question format was used for the first time in 1987. As a result of the changes in the question wording, the marginals on candidate preferences cannot easily be compared over time.

Despite these problems, several interesting observations can be made on the basis of these data (see Table 5.1). The first refers to the development of candidate orientations over time. They turn out to be rather unstable. In other words, there is no linear trend in candidate evaluations. However, this could partly be the result of changes in the question format. Although the trend appears rather erratic at first glance, two points can be made concerning the patterns of attitudes. The first one has to do with the relationship of winning parties and preferred candidates, whereas the second one refers to the gap existing between the competing candidates.

Regarding the relationship between winning parties and preferred candidates up to 1983, the candidate for chancellorship preferred by the majority of the electorate always became chancellor during the following parliamentary term. From 1987 on, this was no longer the case. There are several possible reasons for this. Maybe strong and charismatic political leaders like Willy Brandt and Helmut Schmidt had a strong impact on party choice, thus leading to an electoral victory of their party. Moreover, a *Kanzlerbonus* may have been at work as well. However, given the strong position of political parties in German politics, an alternative interpretation seems plausible. The candidates of the victorious parties could have been rated higher than their opponents simply because of the strong position of their parties, thus indicating a carryover effect from party to candidate. Either way, the correspondence of preferred candidates and the winning parties vanished in 1987 when the incumbent Helmut Kohl was rated lower than his opponent. The exception of 1990 is probably due to the special situation in the first Bundestag election after the reunification, when Helmut Kohl got strong support for his position in the reunification process. The second observation parallels these findings. With the exception of 1961, one of the competitors generally had a clear advantage until 1980, regardless of the changing question format (see also Norpoth 1977). This preference gap disappeared as well. From 1983 on, the ratings of the candidates may have become more similar because of their personalities were less charismatic.

Table 5.1. Preferred Candidates for Chancellor, 1961-94 (in percentages of respondents)

	1961	1965	1969	1972	1976	1980	1983	1987	1990	1994
CDU										
Adenauer	28.2 (35.3)									
Erhard		50.2								
Kiesinger			41.5							
Barzel				27.4						
Kohl					36.0		46.0	47.7	53.2 (60.0)	47.7 (43.0)
Strauß						24.4				
SPD										
Brandt	25.6	24.8	29.8	59.5						
Schmidt					51.5	64.4				
Vogel							36.6			
Rau								52.3		
Lafontaine									46.8 (40.0)	
Scharping										52.3 (57.0)
others	10.9	25.0	28.7	13.1	12.4	11.2	17.4			
none of them										

GAP	2.6	25.4	11.7	32.1	15.5	40.0	9.4	4.6	6.4 (20.0)	4.6 (14.0)
N (app.)	1,400	1,200	700	1,900	2,000	6,300	1,000	2,000	7,000 (2,000)	9,000 (10,000)

Data and question wording:
Bundeswahlstudien 1961(S0057), 1965(S0556) and 1969(S0427): "Whom would you prefer to be Federal Chancellor?"
Possible Answers: **1961:** 1. Adenauer, 2. Brandt, 3. Erhard, 4. Mende, 5. Schmid, 6. Strauß, 7. Schröder, 8. Gerstenmaier, 9. Ollenhauer, 10. others, 99. n.a./d.k.; **1965:** 1. Erhard, 2. Schröder, 3. Brandt, 4. Erler, 5. Mende, 6. Adenauer, 7. Gerstenmaier, 8. Strauß, 9. to 12. others, 99. n.a./d.k; **1969:** 1. Brandt, 2. Schiller, 3. Schmidt, 4. Scheel, 5. Kiesinger, 6. Schröder, 7. Strauß, 8. others, 99. n.a./d.k.
Bundeswahlstudien 1972(S0635), 1976(S0823), 1980(S1053), 1983(S1275), 1987(S1537), Politbarometer 1990, 1994: "Whom would you prefer to be Federal Chancellor: ... or .....?"
Possible Answers: **1972:** 1. Willy Brandt, 2. none of them, 3. Rainer Barzel, 8. n.a., 9. d.k.; **1976:** 1. Helmut Kohl, 2. Helmut Schmidt, 3. none of them, 9. n.a.; **1980:** 1. Helmut Schmidt, 2. Franz-Josef Strauß, 3. none of them, 9. n.a., 0; **1983** : 1. Helmut Kohl, 2. Hans-Jochen Vogel, 3. none of them, 9. n.a., 0; (February only); **1987:** 1. Helmut Kohl, 2. Johannes Rau, 9. n.a., 0; **1990:** 1. Helmut Kohl, 2. Oskar Lafontaine, 9. n.a.; **1994:** 1. Helmut Kohl, 2. Rudolf Scharping, 9. n.a.

Note: The numbers in parentheses refer to East Germany; the grey areas indicate the governing parties during the following parliamentary term and their Chancellors; the GAP indicates the difference between the two candidates; the value in parentheses for 1961 was added, to show the strong position of Erhard at the time, even though he was not nominated by his party. All percentages were calculated without n.a., d.k.; own calculations.

A first and rather tentative result derived from these data at the macro level is that candidates did not play a central role in influencing election outcomes (at least from 1983 on). Relatively low ratings of Kohl did not prevent his party from winning the elections. However, since this conclusion refers exclusively to trends at the aggregate level, we will not proceed too far with our interpretation.

Because of the measurement problems mentioned, we decided to analyze the annual sympathy scalometers of the candidates as well starting in 1977. Thereby, we can present a more continuous even though shorter time series on the evaluation of candidates (see Table 5.2). Given the many changes of the candidates presented

Table 5.2. Sympathy Ratings for the Chancellor Candidates, 1976-94 in West Germany (means)

| | Year | | | | | | | | | | | |
	76	**77**	**78**	**79**	**80**	**81**	**82**	**83**	**84**	**85**	**86**	**87**
		Kohl		Strauss					Kohl			
CDU candidate	**7.7**	7.1	6.8	6.1	**5.8**	7.2	6.9	**7.4**	6.8	6.2	6.2	6.5
			Schmidt						Vogel		Rau	
SPD candidate	8.5	8.0	8.4	8.8	8.8	8.2	8.2	**6.9**	6.6	6.3	7.0	**7.1**
GAP	**0.8**	0.9	1.6	2.7	**3.0**	1.0	1.3	**0.5**	0.2	0.1	0.8	**0.6**
N (in 1,000)	2	10	10	11	12	12	10	10	11	11	11	11

| | Year | | | | | | | | |
	88	**89**	**90**	**91**	**92**	**93**	**94**	**Mean**	**Std Dev.**
	Kohl								
CDU candidate	6.0	6.0	7.3	6.6	6.2	5.6	**6.5**	6.6 (Kohl)	0.55 (Kohl)
		Lafontaine			Engholm	Scharping			
SPD candidate	7.0	7.3	**7.5**	8.0	7.8	7.3	**6.9**	8.4 (Schmidt)	0.28 (Schmidt)
GAP	1.0	1.3	**0.2**	1.4	1.6	1.7	**0.4**		
N (in 1,000)	11	11	11	11	10	11	11		

Question wording: "What do you think of....?"
Possible Answers: 1. "don't like at all" to 11. "like .... very much."

Note: Bold numbers indicate Bundestag election years. Italicized numbers indicate the governing party during the following parliamentary term.
Sources: 1976: Bundeswahlstudie; 1977-1994: Politbarometer; own calculations.

by the Social Democrats between 1983 and 1994, we will focus on the two most prominent figures, Helmut Schmidt (SPD) and Helmut Kohl (CDU), for whom we can observe a relatively long time series. Two points deserve our interest. First, there is a clear difference in the overall levels of the candidates' sympathy ratings. As candidate and chancellor, Schmidt was rated highest in sympathy during the whole period examined (8.0 to 8.8 on an 11 point scale). Kohl's average level of sympathy is clearly lower (mean 6.6). Even during election years, Helmut Kohl did not manage to beat his challengers in the race for sympathy (a result that has to be revised partly later on). Despite this, Kohl and the CDU have been in power since 1982.

Second, although there are obvious differences in sympathy levels, an interesting similarity remains between Schmidt and Kohl. This similarity seems to be closely connected to the role of the incumbent chancellor. Both Kohl and Schmidt were rated relatively highly during election years. They tended to lose public support during the rest of the parliamentary term, only to rise again in sympathy with an upcoming election. These popularity cycles are less obvious in the case of Schmidt (variance 0.28) and much more evident for Kohl (variance 0.55). Obviously the concept of popularity cycles does not only apply to particular officeholders, but to political institutions like the German Bundestag or the government as well (see Gabriel 1993: 5). Given these trends, the declines in sympathy for Kohl and Schmidt at the midterm can be interpreted as general performance ratings depending on the perception of the actual state of political affairs. These trends may differ in degree, but they exist irrespective of the personalities and parties in power.

When we look at the candidates' quarterly sympathy figures in East and West Germany in the 1990 to 1994 period (see Table 5.3), note that the SPD candidates changed twice while Kohl remained the CDU candidate for chancellor throughout the entire period under investigation. Bjoern Engholm was nominated after the defeat of Oskar Lafontaine in the 1990 election, but had to resign as party leader in 1993 because of his ambiguous role in the so-called Barschel scandal. He was succeeded as party chair and challenger to Kohl by Rudolf Scharping.[3] We find that the ratings attained by the incumbent chancellor and his challengers turn out to have roughly the same pattern in East and West Germany. Kohl received worse average ratings than all of his opponents (Kohl East: 6.2; SPD candidates East: 7.4). Moreover, popularity cycles are obviously not limited to West Germany. Finally, despite of his loss of support in the midterm, Kohl managed to catch up to the sympathy level of this challenger Scharping within a few weeks of the 1994 Bundestag election. And even though Kohl and his party finally won the election, he did not succeed in attaining a significantly higher sympathy rating than his challenger (1994/4 East: Kohl 6.5 vs. Scharping 6.6; 1994/4 West: Kohl 6.9 vs. Scharping 6.8).

So far, this chapter has focused on sympathy scalometers as indicators of candidate evaluations. However, candidate orientations are multidimensional and include various components attributed to the candidates (see Eltermann 1980; Lass 1995). The Politbarometer 1994, which contains a battery of items referring to particular attributes of the candidates, allows a closer investigation of the perception

Table 5.3. Quarterly Sympathy Ratings for the Chancellor Candidates, 1989-94, in East and West Germany (means)

		East Germany		West Germany		N (in 1,000)	
		CDU	SPD	SPD	CDU	East	West
Year/quarter							
1989	1			7.1	5.8		3
	2			7.3	5.8		3
	3			7.4	6.3		2
	4			7.3	6.3		3
1990	1			7.9	6.8	2	3
	2	6.7	7.6	7.9	7.0	2	3
	3	7.0	6.5	7.3	7.4	2	2
	4	**8.1**	**6.7**	**7.0**	**8.0**	3	3
1991	1	6.8	7.9	8.0	6.8	3	3
	2	6.3	8.3	8.2	6.4	3	3
	3	6.6	8.4	8.1	6.5	2	2
	4	6.8	8.0	7.9	6.7	3	3
1992	1	6.9	8.1	8.1	6.7	3	3
	2	6.0	8.0	7.8	5.9	3	3
	3	5.4	7.6	7.5	5.7	2	2
	4	5.9	7.8	7.8	6.1	3	3
1993	1	5.4	7.6	7.4	5.5	3	3
	2	5.4	6.7	7.4	5.8	3	3
	3	5.3	7.2	7.2	5.7	2	2
	4	5.4	7.0	7.2	5.5	3	3
1994	1	5.2	7.2	7.1	5.7	3	3
	2	5.9	6.9	6.9	6.4	3	3
	3	6.6	6.8	6.9	6.9	3	3
	4	**6.5**	**6.6**	**6.8**	**6.9**	3	3
Mean		6.2	7.4	7.5	6.3		
Std. Dev.		0.75	0.59	0.41	0.63		

Question wording: "What do you think of ...?" Possible Answers: 1. "Don't like ... at all." to 11. "Like ... very much."

Note: The bold numbers indicate the quarters of the Bundestag elections. CDU candidate: Kohl, entire period. SPD candidate: Lafontaine (89/1-90/4); Engholm (91/1-93/2); Scharping (93/3-94/4).
Source: Politbarometer 1989-94.

of Kohl and Scharping. Some of the items ask about personal attributes of the candidates. Others refer to their presumed performance.[4] We decided to present the results in a simple ordering of the items (see Figure 5.2). The ordering starts on the left side with the typical leadership or performance-related attributes and ends on the right side with the personality-related ones.

While the sympathy scalometers presented in the preceding part of our analysis showed rather low ratings for Kohl compared to his opponents, the two charts in Figure 5.2 offer a somewhat different result. Unlike the more diffuse candidate ratings reflected in sympathy scalometers, the candidates have very differentiated profiles when we examine particular attributes. While Scharping is rated more highly on social- and personality-related items (more public-minded, more honest, more credible), Kohl achieves higher scores on all items indicating leadership qualities. Thus, we have to partially revise the conclusions drawn from the analyses of the sympathy scalometers. Sympathy scalometers apparently do not give an encompassing and sufficient impression of voters' orientations toward candidates in that they seem to be related more strongly to personal attributes of the respective candidates. While the data presented in Tables 5.2 and 5.3 showed a rather weak rating of Kohl, quite a different conclusion concerning candidate effects on voting decisions can be drawn now: Kohl was perceived much more favorably by the voters than his challenger Scharping with regard to the performance-related dimension of candidate evaluation. This result might explain the success of his party in the 1994 election and, therefore, support the hypothesis of strong candidate effects. Whether this interpretation can be supported by the multivariate analyses will be investigated in the following part of this chapter.

We can summarize several findings of our descriptive analyses on candidate perception and evaluation so far. There are popularity cycles of the incumbent chancellor during every parliamentary term in both West and East Germany. Whether the fluctuations reflect performance ratings of the government that carry over to incumbents or rather reflect fluctuations in affective orientations toward political institutions and leaders cannot be answered here. What is apparent, however, is that cross-sectional analyses of candidate evaluation may yield unreliable results, given that evaluations change systematically during the parliamentary term. We also found that the observed congruence between winning party and preferred chancellor candidate that existed in Germany in the 1960s and 1970s disappeared in the middle of the 1980s. Since 1987, the challenger was rated more highly than the incumbent chancellor most of the time. Only within the last weeks of the elections was Kohl able to catch up to the sympathy level of his challenger (with the exception of the reunification election in 1990). Yet the opposition party did not succeed in winning the elections. This may imply only small candidate effects on voting behavior. At the same time, the more detailed analyses of candidate orientation showed rather differentiated evaluations. Such results could be supportive of the beauty-contest hypothesis. Up to now, however, we have presented results only from aggregate data. The next section presents multivariate analyses at the level of individuals.

Figure 5.2. Qualities Attributed to Kohl and Scharping, 1994 (in % of respondents)

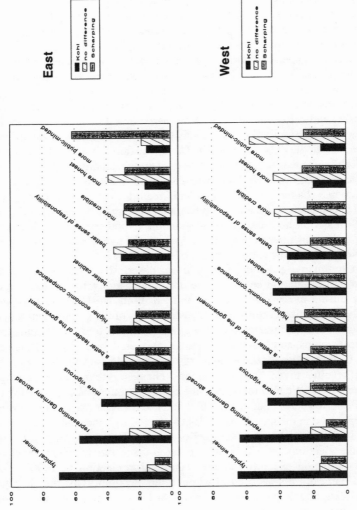

Possible Answers: 1. Helmut Kohl, 2. Rudolf Scharping, 3. No difference, 4. None of them.

Notes: The category "none of them" is not shown in the charts, as the number of respondents for this category is very small.

Source: Politbarometer 1994 East and West Germany; own calculations.

DO CANDIDATES MATTER AND HOW?

According to Campbell et al., party identification is the most important factor explaining party choice. And, in fact, in each German election held during the last twenty years, there was a considerable degree of consistency between party identification on one hand and voting intention on the other. However, despite the strong predictive power of party identification, the impact of short-term factors like candidate orientation may have gained importance during the last decades because the group of weak or nonidentifiers has increased and the perception of candidates has become more complex and differentiated. This section investigates the candidates' impact on the individual voting decisions beginning in the 1970s in order to find out whether this impact has changed over time. In addition, we examine whether there are differences in candidate effects in East and West Germany for the 1994 Bundestag election.

As the data in Table 5.4 show, about 70 percent of voting intention in favor of the CDU/CSU can be attributed to party identification and issue orientation (1972 to 1994, West Germany). In the case of the SPD, the proportion of the variance explained by the respective variables turns out to be slightly lower. When we include candidate orientation in the model, the increase in the amount of variance additionally explained ranges between 2 (SPD, 1994 West) and 15 percentage points (CDU, 1994 East). Thus, we conclude that candidate preferences do matter for voters' choices.

Please note the following caveat regarding the role of party identification in East Germany. Given the fact that the western parties are new institutions in eastern Germany, one may doubt the value of the idea of stable long-term attachments to political parties in this part of the country (see Gabriel 1997; see also chapters 3 by Karl Schmitt and chapter 4 by Carsten Zelle in this volume). Therefore, some doubts can be raised regarding the relevance of the Michigan model in its entirety for explaining voting behavior in the so-called *New Länder* (new states) of the Federal Republic. If the core variable of the model, party identification, cannot be considered a meaningful concept in this particular context, the status of the other explanatory variables becomes problematic as well. Since there is no way out of the dilemma, a tentative and cautious interpretation of the comparative results appears reasonable.

Because East German voters do not possess a long experience in an institutional context of a competitive party system, voting behavior in the new part of the Federal Republic may be expected to rest partly on chance or nonstructural factors. Moreover, measurement error may distort the explanatory power of the model. The first of these two expectations, however, is not confirmed by the data. Although party identification and issue orientation contribute less to the explanation of voting intentions in East than they do in West Germany, these two variables explain a considerable share of the variance in vote choice (58 percent SPD, 66 percent CDU). In contrast, candidate effects appear to be stronger in the East, but not dramatically so. This seconds a finding reported by Hans Rattinger and Jürgen Krämer in the following chapter; they also find only gradual differences between eastern and western Germans with regard to the short-term influences of economic considerations. Furthermore, candidate orientation has a higher impact on CDU/CSU vote than on SPD vote. This conclusion is particularly valid in East Germany. The strongest candidate effects appear in 1994 for Chancellor Kohl.

When we investigate the amount of variance attributable to candidate orientations since 1972, however, the hypothesis of an increased candidate effect has to be rejected. In 1972, 1983, and 1990, candidate orientations add similar amounts of explained variance in voting intention. Only in 1994 the preference of Helmut Kohl as chancellor seemed to have had a considerable impact on CDU/CSU voters (candidate effect West: .10; East: .15). This may be the result of the rather personalized campaign strategy of the CDU/CSU in this election (see also Anderson and Zelle 1995; Zelle 1995c, 1998).

Table 5.4. Candidate Effects on CDU or SPD Vote Intention, 1972-94 (simultaneous regression)

Vote Intention		**Model 1** Party ID Issue Comp. (R_1^2)	**Model 2** Party ID Issue Comp. Cand. Pref. (R_2^2)	**Candidate Effect** Difference $(R_2^2 - R_1^2)$	N
1972	CDU	.70	.74	.04	
	SPD	.66	.72	.06	1,233
1983	CDU	.72	.80	.08	
	SPD	.73	.78	.05	1,005
1990	CDU	.73	.78	.05	
	SPD	.71	.75	.04	1,219
1994 West	CDU	.69	.79	.10	
	SPD	.66	.68	.02	1,141
1994 East	CDU	.62	.77	.15	
	SPD	.58	.63	.05	1,091

Notes: Vote Intention (CDU resp. SPD): 1=Vote Intention CDU resp. SPD; 0=no Vote Intention CDU resp. SPD; Party Identification (Party ID): -2=strong SPD PI, 0=no PI, +2=strong CDU PI; Attribution of Issue Competence (Issue Comp.): Index from Competence in Economic Stability, Environmental Protection, Law and Order, -2=strong attribution to SPD, 0=no diff. or attrib. to no party, +2=strong attribution to CDU; Candidate Preference (Cand. Pref.): 1= preference for CDU resp. SPD candidate; 0=no preference for CDU resp. SPD candidate; Model 1 = Two-Variable-Model including PI and Competence as independent variables; Model 2 = Three-Variable-Model including PI, Competence and Candidate Preference as independent variables.
Sources: Bundeswahlstudien 1972, 1983, 1990, DFG Study "Politische Einstellungen und politisches Verhalten im vereinigten Deutschland 1994"; almost the same results were obtained recoding all independent variables as dummy variables; own calculations.

Table 5.5. Candidate Effects on the Probability of Voting for CDU or SPD Among CDU/CSU and SPD Party Identifiers, 1972-94

		1972	1983	1990	1994 West	1994 East
Probability of Voting for CDU/CSU						
when controlling for Party ID CDU/CSU	N	.96 (389)	.94 (385)	.96 (428)	.95 (461)	.95 (375)
when controlling for Party ID CDU/CSU and Attrib. of Issue Competence to CDU/CSU	N	.98 (325)	.95 (345)	.97 (357)	.97 (344)	.97 (289)
when controlling for Party ID CDU/CSU and Attrib. of Issue Competence to CDU/CSU and CDU/CSU Candidate Preference	N	.98 (260)	.96 (339)	.97 (349)	.98 (328)	.97 (279)
Probability of Voting for SPD						
when controlling for Party ID SPD	N	.93 (630)	.95 (421)	.95 (540)	.92 (459)	.91 (329)
when controlling for Party ID SPD and Attrib. of Issue Competence to SPD	N	.95 (452)	.99 (271)	.96 (406)	.95 (331)	.94 (249)
when controlling for Party ID SPD and Attrib. of Issue Competence to SPD and SPD Candidate Preference	N	.95 (446)	.99 (266)	.96 (387)	.95 (275)	.95 (217)

Notes: Probability of Voting for... : CDU/CSU: 1=vote intention CDU/CSU, 0= no vote intention CDU/CSU; SPD: 1=vote intention SPD, 0=no vote intention SPD; Attribution of Issue Competence: Index from Competence in Economic Stability, Environmental Protection, Law and Order, ranging from -1=SPD competent, 0= no diff. or no party competent, 1=CDU/CSU competent. The Competence index for 1994 was built from the variables 1st and 2nd most impoartant problem combined with the problem solving party. Candidates in 1972: Barzel and Brandt, in 1983: Kohl and Vogel, in 1990: Kohl and Lafontaine, in 1994: Kohl and Scharping.
Sources: Bundeswahlstudien 1972 (S0635), 1983 (S1276), 1990 (S1919, 2nd panel wave), DFG Study "Politische Einstellungen und politisches Verhalten im vereinigten Deutschland"; own calculations.

Table 5.6. Candidate Effects on the Probability of Voting for CDU or SPD Among Nonidentifiers, 1972-94

		1972	1983	1990	1994 West	1994 East
Attribution of Competence to no Party						
Probability of Voting for CDU/CSU						
- when only controlling for Attrib. of Issue Competence to no Party	N	.30 (63)	.20 (51)	.21 (61)	.25 (97)	.28 (197)
- when controlling for Attrib. of Issue Competence to no Party and CDU/CSU Candidate Preference	N	*	.45 (20)	.40 (25)	.70 (30)	.75 (64)
Additional Candidate Effects		*	+.25	+.19	+.45	+.47
Probability of Voting for SPD						
- when only controlling for Attrib. of Issue Competence to no Party	N	.44 (63)	.39 (51)	.38 (61)	.24 (97)	.36 (197)
- when controlling for Attrib. of Issue Competence to no Party and SPD Candidate Preference	N	.63 (38)	.58 (31)	.53 (36)	.43 (28)	.62 (74)
Additional Candidate Effects		+.19	+.19	+.15	+.19	+.26

		1972	1983	1990	1994 West	1994 East
Attribution of Competence to CDU/CSU						
Probability of Voting for CDU/CSU						
- when only controlling for Attrib. of Issue Competence to CDU/CSU		.67	.77	.70	.74	.86
	N	(82)	(92)	(81)	(58)	(99)
- when controlling for Attrib. of Issue Competence to CDU/CSU and CDU/CSU Candidate Preference		.89	.90	.79	.87	.96
	N	(38)	(70)	(67)	(47)	(85)
Additional Candidate Effects		+.22	+.13	+.09	+.13	+.10
Attribution of Competence to SPD						
Probability of Voting for SPD						
- when only controlling for Attrib. of Issue Competence to SPD		.84	.77	.77	.74	.83
	N	(80)	(61)	(109)	(68)	(99)
- when controlling for Attrib. of Issue Competence to SPD and SPD Candidate Preference		.89	.78	.81	.78	.86
	N	(71)	(58)	(99)	(45)	(64)
Additional Candidate Effects		+.05	+.01	+.04	+.04	+.03

Notes: * indicates that the number of cases is < 20. For the Probability of Voting for … vote intention was built from: Competence in Economic Stability, Environmental Protection, Law and Order, ranging from -1=SPD competent, 0=no party competent, to 1=CDU/CSU competent. The Competence index for 1994 was built from the variables 1st and 2nd most important problem combined with the problem solving party. Candidates were in 1972: Barzel and Brandt, in 1983: Kohl and Vogel, in 1990: Kohl and Lafontaine, in 1994: Kohl and Scharping.
Source: Bundeswahlstudien 1972 (S0635), 1983 (S1276), 1990 (S1919, 2nd panel wave), DFG Study "Politische Einstellungen und politisches Verhalten im vereinigten Deutschland;" own calculations.

Our last question addresses the differences between candidate effects on CDU/CSU or SPD party identifiers and on nonidentifiers. We first examine party identifiers who attribute a problem-solving competence to the party they identify with (see Table 5.5). Despite some slight variations over the years, a positive evaluation of the respective party's candidate does not greatly alter things. Since almost all party identifiers hold issue orientations that are in line with their general disposition toward the respective party, they tend to cast their votes in accordance with the attitudes mentioned before. There is hardly any room for candidate effects. The additional changes in probability of voting for CDU/CSU or SPD are almost zero.

Because stable long-term party loyalties are absent, the situation among nonidentifiers turns out to be more promising for assessing short-term effects like candidate orientations on the vote (see Table 5.6). First, we examine the vote choice of respondents who lack party identification and who have a positive evaluation of the problem-solving capacity of the CDU/CSU or SPD. We ask whether and to what degree candidate orientation induces an additional push toward voting in favor of the party assessed by voters to be more able to resolve the most urgent problems. The second group of interest encompasses people who do not identify with a party and who do not attribute problem solving capacity to any party.[5]

When we examine the effects of candidate orientations among nonidentifiers not attributing competence to any particular party on the vote, we find clear candidate effects in 1983, 1990, and 1994, which raised the probability of voting for the CDU/CSU.[6] In 1983, the effect of a preference for Helmut Kohl as federal chancellor was rather high (+0.25), and in 1994 it was striking in East as well as in West Germany (+0.47 and +0.45, respectively). The figure obtained by Rudolf Scharping in 1994 in East Germany also was above average (+0.26), whereas the candidate of the SPD in 1990, Oskar Lafontaine, performed somewhat worse (+0.15).

Similarly, the question of whether candidate evaluations influence voting intention among nonidentifiers who attribute competence to one of the parties can be answered positively. Again, the situation differs over the years. We find particularly strong effects in the case of the CDU/CSU vote in 1972 (+0.22), and a smaller, but nevertheless significant, effect in other years, ranging between 9 and 13 percentage points. In contrast, candidates nominated by the Social Democrats normally do not matter if the party is regarded as the more competent alternative. In these cases, voting intention increases only by about 5 percentage points at best.

CONCLUSION

This chapter focused on the perception and evaluation of candidates for chancellorship as determinants of party choice in German elections. We asked whether national elections in Germany have degenerated into mere beauty contests between the candidates. When embedded in the more encompassing Michigan model developed by Angus Campbell et al. (1954), candidate orientations were expected to have a short-term impact on voters' choices in addition to party identification and the attribution of issue competence to a certain party.

We first discussed whether the Michigan model, originally developed within the American political context, can be used to explain voting behavior in Germany. Taking the typical institutional settings of the German political system into account, party identification was expected to play a stronger, and candidate orientation a weaker, role in Germany compared to the United States. Because the literature on the role of candidates in Germany is rather poor, we first described trends in candidate preferences from 1961 to 1994. Despite considerable problems concerning the changes in the format of questions on candidate preference, we found that, first, the candidate of the governing party had always been ranked more highly in sympathy ratings than his opponent until the middle of the 1980s. From 1987 on, however, Kohl's average sympathy ratings were usually lower than those of his challengers. A closer look on the basis of annual data showed that there are popularity cycles for the incumbent chancellor, which exist in both West and East Germany. Only within a few weeks before the Bundestag elections, Kohl managed to catch up to the sympathy level of his SPD opponent, to decline again in sympathy ratings after the elections. Second, we found that sympathy ratings of the candidates became increasingly similar during the 1980s.

However, we also found that there is more to the evaluation of candidates than a simple like-dislike decision on the part of voters. Using a detailed item battery on candidate evaluation in 1994, we also showed that candidate orientations are multidimensional. In contrast to results derived on the basis of sympathy scalometers, we found that Kohl had a clear advantage with regard to his leadership and performance qualities, while his opponent Scharping was evaluated more highly only on social-and personality-related items.

To assess whether candidate images affect voting behavior in Germany, whether these effects have changed over the years, and what kind of effects candidates have among different groups of voters like party identifiers and nonidentifiers, we performed multivariate regression analyses based on individual-level survey data. The multivariate analyses presented in the final part of this chapter show that candidate orientations play a role as short-term determinants of voting behavior in Germany. Applying a conservative strategy of analysis, we found variable candidate effects from 1972 to 1994. The effects were particularly strong in the case of Kohl during the 1994 election. However, on the basis of empirical data available for the last two decades, the contention that electoral contests have increasingly become beauty contests between particular candidates is not supported by the analysis.

Although candidate effects did not change much during the period investigated here, they differed considerably among various segments of the electorate. And while candidates do not seem to play an important role among party identifiers, they have a strong impact on the vote behavior of nonidentifiers. Although it appears that party identification has remained the most important determinant of vote intention, we have to keep in mind that the number of nonidentifiers has increased considerably over the years (for a discussion of this claim see chapters 2 and 4 in this volume). In the aggregate, this may produce stronger effects of short-term forces like candidate orientations on election outcomes. Thus parties, in order to be successful at the polls, should definitely pay attention to their candidates for the highest office in the land.

NOTES

1. Although this interpretation applies primarily to issue voting, the formation of attitudes toward candidates is also an element of the process of electoral choice to be interpreted in a rational choice perspective (for a short introduction, see Dalton and Wattenberg [1993]).

2. All data used in this chapter are available from the Zentralarchiv für empirische Sozialforschung (ZA), University of Cologne. The data were collected by the staff and institutions named in the Appendix. Preparation and documentation for the empirical analysis were supervised by the ZA. Neither the Project Teams nor the Zentralarchiv are responsible for the analyses and interpretation of the data in this chapter. Most of the Federal Election Studies also are available from the Inter-University Consortium for Political Research, Ann Arbor, Michigan. Special thanks to Christiane Kolb for her help in translating this chapter.

3. The Barschel scandal involved the hiring of a private investigator to probe into the life of the then incumbent premier in the state of Schleswig-Holstein, Uwe Barschel (CDU), against whom Engholm ran as the SPD's nominee. Barschel subsequently committed suicide. After we finished this chapter, the SPD party leader had changed again, with Oskar Lafontaine becoming the successor to Rudolf Scharping.

4. The differentiation between a personality- and a performance-related dimension was also supported by factor analysis, which we do not present here separately.

5. Due to the small number of cases, analyses for an interesting third group of people subjected to dissonant short-term influences cannot be presented.

6. In 1972 an assessment of the role of candidate orientation as a determinant of CDU/CSU voting intention fell short due to the small number of cases.

APPENDIX: DATA

Bundeswahlstudien

1961: Kölner Wahlstudie 1961: Postelection study November/December 1961 (S0057); Head of Project: Gerhard Baumert, Erwin K. Scheuch, Rudolf Wildenmann (DIVO-Institut, Frankfurt, Forschungsinstitut für Soziologie, Institut für Politische Wissenschaft, University of Köln.).

1965: Bundestagswahl 1965: Preelection study September 1965 (S0556); Head of Project: Max Kaase and Rudolf Wildenmann (Lehrstuhl für politische

Wissenschaft, University of Mannheim).

1969: Bundestagswahl 1969: Postelection panel study October/November 1969 (S0427); Head of Project: Hans-Dieter Klingemann (ZUMA, Mannheim) and Franz Urban Pappi (University of Kiel).

1972: Wahlstudie 1972: Preelection panel study September/October 1972 (S0635); Head of Project: Manfred Berger, Wolfgang Gibowski, Max Kaase, Dieter Roth, Uwe Schleth, Rudolf Wildenmann (University of Mannheim).

1976: Wahlstudie 1976: Preelection panel study May/June 1976 (S0823); Head of Project: Manfred Berger, Wolfgang Gibowski, Edelgard Gruber, Dieter Roth, Wolfgang Schulte (Forschungsgruppe Wahlen e.V. Mannheim), together with Max Kaase, Hans-Dieter Klingemann (ZUMA Mannheim) and Uwe Schleth (University of Heidelberg).

1980: Wahlstudie 1980: Pooled data from ten single surveys January to November 1980 (S1053); Head of Project: Forschungsgruppe Wahlen e.V., Mannheim, in cooperation with Dieter Fuchs (ZUMA, Mannheim), Max Kaase (University of Mannheim), Hans-Dieter Klingemann (FU Berlin), Uwe Schleth (University of Heidelberg).

1983: Wahlstudie 1983: Pre- and postelection trend study (S1275); Head of Project: Manfred Berger, Wolfgang Gibowski, Dieter Roth, Wolfgang Schulte, Forschungsgruppe Wahlen e.V., Mannheim.

1987: Wahlstudie 1987: Pre- and postelection panel study September 1986 to February 1987 (S1537); Head of Project: Manfred Berger, Wolfgang Gibowski, Dieter Roth, Wolfgang Schulte, Forschungsgruppe Wahlen e.V., Mannheim, together with Max Kaase (University of Mannheim), Hans-Dieter Klingemann (FU Berlin), Manfred Küchler (Florida State University, Tallahassee), Franz Urban Pappi (University of Kiel).

1990: Wahlstudie 1990 West (S1919), only the second panel wave was used.

Politbarometer

1977: Kumulierter Politbarometer 1977 (ZA S2160)
1978: Kumulierter Politbarometer 1978 (ZA S2171)
1979: Kumulierter Politbarometer 1979 (ZA S2182)
1980: Kumulierter Politbarometer 1980 (ZA S1053)
1981: Kumulierter Politbarometer 1981 (ZA S2194)
1982: Kumulierter Politbarometer 1982 (ZA S2201)
1983: Kumulierter Politbarometer 1983 (ZA S2209)

1984: Kumulierter Politbarometer 1984 (ZA S2220)
1985: Kumulierter Politbarometer 1985 (ZA S1901)
1986: Kumulierter Politbarometer 1986 (ZA S1536)
1987: Kumulierter Politbarometer 1987 (ZA S1899)
1988: Kumulierter Politbarometer 1988 (ZA S1762)
1989: Kumulierter Politbarometer 1989 (ZA S1551)
1990: Kumulierter Politbarometer 1990 West (ZA S1920)
1990: Kumulierter Politbarometer 1990 Ost (ZA S1987)
1991: Kumulierter Politbarometer 1991 West (ZA S2102)
1991: Kumulierter Politbarometer 1991 Ost (ZA-Nr. 2114)
1992: Kumulierter Politbarometer 1992 West (ZA-Nr. 2275)
1992: Kumulierter Politbarometer 1992 Ost (ZA-Nr. 2287)
1993: Kumulierter Politbarometer West 1993 (ZA-Nr. 2378)
1993: Kumulierter Politbarometer Ost 1993 (ZA-Nr. 2390)
1994: Kumulierter Politbarometer West 1994 (ZA-Nr. 2546)
1994: Kumulierter Politbarometer Ost 1994 (ZA-Nr. 2559)

DFG Study "Political Attitudes and Political Behavior in Unified Germany," 1994

Head of Project: Jürgen W. Falter (University of Mainz), Oscar W. Gabriel (University of Stuttgart), Hans Rattinger (University of Bamberg), and Karl Schmitt (University of Jena).

Economic Conditions and Voting Preferences in East and West Germany, 1989-94

Hans Rattinger and Jürgen Krämer

INTRODUCTION

One of the most important problems resulting from German unification in 1990 was the economic integration of the two parts of the new Germany. The solution that was adopted was to expose the ex-GDR to an economic shock therapy (see, e.g., Singer 1992). According to some theorists, radical transition from a socialist economy to a free social market economy promises a faster, but also a much rougher, way to economic prosperity than moderate reorganization (see, e.g., Przeworski 1991). In the special case of Germany (which is not comparable with the transition processes in other East-Central European countries), the successful West German political and economic system should provide the model and resources to enable East Germany to quickly catch up with the West. Politicians and commentators presented a vision of a second "economic miracle," comparable to the postwar experience of the Federal Republic (see, e.g., Glastetter, Hägemann, and Marquardt 1991). Five years after unification, however, the high expectations created during the campaign prior to the first all-German Bundestag election in December 1990 have given way to more realistic assessments. Indeed, it is now obvious that the process of economic and social integration of Germany is much more difficult than was anticipated immediately after the Wall came down (see Wenzel 1993).

If economic performance since 1990 has failed to meet expectations, the hypothesis that this could have affected citizens' political preferences is obvious. Much prior evidence exists to support this hypothesis. Earlier research on the impact of economic conditions on voting behavior in West Germany has supplied broad empirical support for such relationships, both at the macro and the microlevels (see, e.g., Kirchgässner 1986, 1991; Rattinger 1980, 1985, 1986, 1991; Rattinger and Puschner 1981; for systematic reviews of the relevant literature, see Jung 1982 and 1985; for results within a cross-national perspective, see, e.g.,

Lewis-Beck 1988). Moreover, the current discussion about electoral dynamics in Germany—especially rising levels of nonvoters, successes of so-called protest parties, and declining trust in the established political parties (CDU/CSU, Christian Democrats; SPD, Social Democrats; and FDP, Free Democrats)—often refers to growing dissatisfaction with economic outputs (see, e.g., Hoffmann-Jaberg and Roth 1994; Rattinger 1993; Roth 1994). Such impacts of economic conditions on voting and political attitudes should be stronger for East than for West Germany, of course, given the more frequent personal exposure to economic hardship in the new Länder. Also, since long-term influences on electoral choice can be expected to be less powerful in the East, short-term factors—such as the state of the economy—might be of greater importance (see in particular chapter 3 by Karl Schmitt in this volume on the relevance of long-term influences in East Germany).

Research on the relationship between economic conditions and voting comes in many versions, often making it difficult to compare different studies over time and across nations. First, many analyses focus on the aggregate level, relating objective indicators of the economic situation (e.g., the unemployment rate, the inflation rate, or the growth of GNP) to support for the government. Cross-national comparisons of this sort often remain inconclusive because of the assumption of an equal political context over different nations (see Powell and Whitten 1993). At the individual level more consistent cross-national results usually are reported (see, e.g., Lewis-Beck 1988). But since other relevant factors of the individual voting decision are usually controlled for in such studies (e.g., party identification), the evidence for voting that is economically driven generally is much weaker. Moreover, objective economic indicators almost always have to be replaced by subjective perceptions of personal or national economic conditions at the microlevel. Thus, the change in the level of analysis is mostly correlated with a change of indicators.

Second, there is an important theoretical and empirical distinction between personal and collective economic conditions (for an example of the different political effects of both types of economic variables see Markus 1988, 139). On one hand there is the "pocketbook-voter" hypothesis, which suggests that individual economic experiences will be politicized. The importance of personal economic conditions for vote choices should be higher in nations with a strong welfare state tradition (as in East *and* West Germany) than in countries with a traditional ethics of "coping and self-reliance" (like in the United States; see, e.g., Feldman 1982, 1983; Sniderman and Brody 1977). One of the major weaknesses of this hypothesis is that not *every* individual economic experience can be reasonably attributed to politics (e.g., losses of income due to illness or death; see Rattinger and Juhász 1990, 283).

In contrast, national economic conditions are seen as more relevant by the rival hypothesis of "sociotropic voting" (see, e.g., Kinder and Kiewiet 1981). Because of the permanent claims by political competitors to be more competent in terms of economic policies, responsibility for national economic performance can be almost automatically attributed to the political system. While personal economic conditions are seen as idiosyncratic, general conditions that are regularly publicized as standardized figures lend themselves as an easy benchmark for how well the government is doing its job. If performance is lacking, loss of diffuse system support, lower turnout, and voting for protest parties can result (see Lewis-Beck and Lockerbie 1989; Lockerbie 1993; Rattinger and Juhász 1990).

Third, voters can assess (personal or general) economic conditions within different reference systems. The primary judgment, of course, is about the current economic situation. But it can also be set against some point of reference, be it in the past or in the future. Retrospective voters evaluate past economic development in order to make their choice (see, e.g., Fiorina 1981). Prospective voters focus on expectations about future economic performance (of the current or an alternative government), which makes higher cognitive demands regarding knowledge and evaluation of relevant economic data and of future policies of competing political parties.

Fourth, research on the impact of economic conditions on voting can follow two different theoretical conjectures (for a comprehensive discussion, see, e.g., Kiewiet 1983). The classical hypothesis proposed by Downs (1957), the incumbency-oriented hypothesis, assumes that the individual probability to vote for incumbents depends upon economic evaluations. However, this hypothesis ignores the relationships between the economic interests of different social groups or classes and their long-term attachment to the policy goals of political parties. The alternative policy-oriented hypothesis takes such traditional economic policy preferences of political parties into account. In this view, bad times will not necessarily hurt parties in power because the political consequences of economic crisis will depend upon the type of economic problem and upon which political party is in power. High rates of unemployment should lead to increased electoral support for left/labor parties, while conservative parties should benefit if the economy suffers from inflation. As for the United States and some West European countries, empirical evidence for this latter hypothesis is reported for West Germany, too (see, e.g., Hibbs 1982; Rattinger 1983, 1986). One major problem with both hypotheses is that they will not always contradict each other, so that it can be difficult to decide which is superior. Moreover, in their basic version both hypotheses assume that voters react by switching (or staying put) between the established political parties. If we also allow nonvoting or support for protest parties as forms of political response, the need to further refine these hypotheses becomes obvious.

In sum, if we combine these four distinctions of economic judgments (personal or national), by levels of analysis (micro or macrolevel), by theoretical framework (incumbency-oriented vs. policy-oriented), and by operationalization of economic conditions (objective vs. subjective economic data), it becomes obvious why it is so difficult to find universally consistent relationships between the economy and electoral outcomes over time and in cross-national perspective (not to speak of different data analysis techniques; see, e.g., Leithner [1993]; Weatherford [1986]).

In this chapter we set out to make use of several of these distinctions in order to shed some light on the interactions between economic conditions and electoral dynamics in unified Germany. We proceed as follows: First we discuss the database for our analyses. Then we first take a look at trends in the development of economic perceptions and examine the longitudinal aggregate-level evidence for the impact of economic conditions on voting intentions. We then turn to cross-sectional individual-level analyses. In a final step, two panel studies will be analyzed in order to ascertain whether over time associations between voting preferences and economic perceptions run parallel in macro and micro data.

DATA

For both the longitudinal analysis at the aggregate level and the cross-sectional analysis at the individual level we use the monthly Politbarometer surveys collected by Forschungsgruppe Wahlen (FGW) in Mannheim. For the period of 1990 to 1994, more than 50,000 interviews are available both for East and West Germany (about 1,000 individuals are interviewed each month). Because evaluations of economic conditions were not gauged every month, missing values in time series had to be interpolated (see the Appendix at the end of this chapter). For the same reason, the available number of complete surveys for cross-sectional analyses is reduced to 20 in West Germany and 41 in East Germany.

For the longitudinal analysis at the individual level we use two three-wave panel surveys that were collected by the first author in the context of research projects funded by the German Science Foundation (Deutsche Forschungsgemeinschaft, DFG). The first panel was in the field in May 1990 (only West Germany) with 2,007 respondents. After unification, the panel was extended to East Germany, so that 932 individuals in West and 606 in East Germany were interviewed in May 1991. In the last wave (May 1992) 716 and 325 individuals participated for a third/second time. The second panel initially started with 1046 individuals in West and 1,043 in East Germany in May and June 1992. In March and April 1993, 703 respondents from the old and 740 from the new Länder were reinterviewed. This study concluded in October and November 1993 with 514 and 597 interviews, respectively.

For all analyses we use individual voting intentions as the dependent variable and measure perceptions of economic conditions by *evaluations* and *expectations* of *general* and *personal* economic conditions. In addition, we could use data on *retrospective* economic evaluations only for the panel surveys. In the Politbarometer surveys retrospective evaluations were only very rarely collected.

TRENDS IN ECONOMIC PERCEPTIONS

West German public opinion about general economic conditions declined between August 1990 and November 1994 (see Figure 6.1). Up to the middle of 1991 the ratings were relatively stable between .6 and .7 on a scale from -1 to +1. Thereafter, average evaluations decreased rapidly and reached the neutral point of the scale by the end of 1992. This trend continued into the first half of 1993, and stagnated in the second half at a mean score of -.3. Finally, in 1994 ratings

Figure 6.1. Perceptions of General and Personal Economic Conditions in West Germany, 1990-94

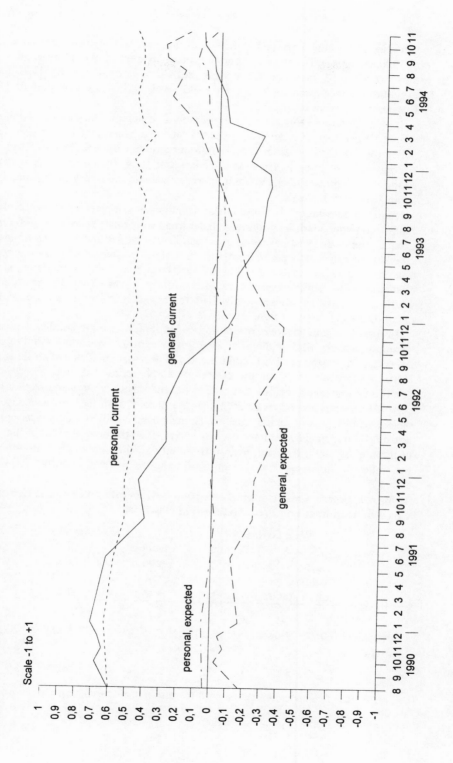

increased again somewhat, and at the end of that year became positive. At the end of 1990 expectations of general economic conditions started to deteriorate, too. By the end of 1992, they had fallen to a mean score of -.4. During 1993 these expectations recovered back to their 1990 level, and in the first half of 1994 increased to a mean score of .3.

In comparison, evaluations and expectations of personal economic conditions changed much less. Evaluations of personal economic conditions in late 1990 were about the same as of general economic conditions (.6), and fell slightly but continuously up to early 1994, to a mean score of .4. Expectations of personal economic conditions over the whole period fluctuate only very little around the neutral point of our scale.

Table 6.1 clarifies to what extent these developments of perceptions of actual and future economic conditions follow a linear trend over time. With the exception of expectations of the personal economic situation, we find significant linear trends for all other indicators. The negative coefficient for evaluations of individual economic conditions is highly significant, but not very large in absolute terms. In contrast, evaluations of general economic conditions follow a very strong downward trend while the highly significant coefficient for expectations of general economic conditions has a positive sign.

In *East* Germany, average evaluations of general economic conditions exhibit strong variations during the first year for which we have data (Figure 6.2). Afterward, from summer 1991 until the end of 1993, they oscillate only little around a mean score of -.6. Over the course of 1994, ratings of general economic conditions improved steadily to between -.2 and -.3. In contrast, expectations of general economic conditions deteriorated substantially from 1990 to 1993. Up until the end of 1991, their average clearly remained positive–with some stronger ups and downs. Thereafter they declined rapidly and reached the neutral point of the scale at the end of 1992; they stayed in this vicinity all through 1993. But similar to general evaluations, they clearly improved to between .2 and .3 during 1994.

Table 6.1. Linear Trends in the Perception of General and Personal Economic Conditions in East and West Germany, 1990-1994

| | West Germany | | | | East Germany | | | |
| | General economic conditions | | Personal economic conditions | | General economic conditions | | Personal economic conditions | |
	Evalua-tion	Expec-tation	Evalua-tion	Expec-tation	Evalua-tion	Expec-tation	Evalua-tion	Expec-tation
R^2	.75	.34	.68	.02	.59	.34	.66	.29
Coefficient	-.019[c]	.008[c]	-.003[c]	.001	.006[c]	-.006[c]	.004[c]	-.003[c]
Constant	.82-	.37	.61	-.01	-.74	.38	.07	.23
N	52	52	52	52	53	53	48	56

Notes: All coefficients are unstandardized regression coefficients; a: p<.05; b: p<.01; c: p<.001.

Figure 6.2. Perceptions of General and Personal Economic Conditions in East Germany, 1990-94

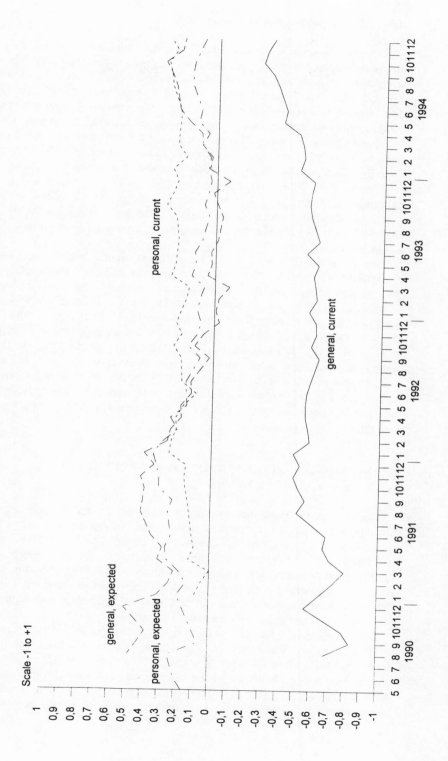

Regarding evaluations of individual economic conditions, we can observe an almost monotonous increase over time if we disregard some minor dips. The series starts close to the neutral point in 1991, and reaches up to between .2 and .3 for all of 1993 and 1994. Expectations of personal economic conditions seem to have developed in two phases. First, there was growing optimism up until the end of 1991, followed by a decline, so that (after a short period of brighter views in summer of 1994) by the end of our time period the average expectation was that personal economic conditions would remain about unchanged.

In East Germany, we can report highly significant linear trends for *all* economic perceptions (see Table 6.1). For both evaluations of the general and personal economic situation weak and positive coefficients are obtained, while both expectations of future economic developments exhibit negative trends. Moreover, the coefficients for general economic perceptions are higher in magnitude than for individual ones.

In sum, between 1990 and 1993 we discern trends toward more negative evaluations of general *and* individual economic conditions in West Germany; in the East we find a similar decline of both expectations, but simultaneous improvement of evaluations of the general and individual economic situation. In 1994 we find somewhat improved ratings for all indicators, which also might have something to do with the upcoming national elections in October. Evaluations of economic conditions in the old Länder are at a higher level than in the East. Those of the general situation, however, declined almost to the level of the East, while those of the personal situation in the East increased toward the western level. Conversely, up to the end of 1993 expectations about the future were considerably higher in the new Länder than in the West, and there is convergence in 1994—toward the notion that things will stay as they are.

ECONOMIC CONDITIONS AND VOTING PREFERENCES AT THE AGGREGATE LEVEL

We now turn to the question whether these economic variables have affected the electoral fortunes of the competing political parties during the first four years after unification. To investigate this question at the aggregate data level, we have regressed the shares of voting intentions for each party, the combined percentage of the coalition parties, and the share of nonvoters on average monthly scores of economic judgments and on shares of party identification in a stepwise fashion, so that party identification was entered first, and economic perceptions in the second step—provided their effect was statistically significant.

For *West* Germany, we observe (with one exception for the SPD) positive effects of evaluations of the economic situation on voting intentions for the three established parties (see Table 6.2). For the CDU/CSU, the major government party, electoral success is positively related to expected personal economic conditions, while for the FDP a significant impact of current personal economic conditions on voting intentions can be observed. Combining the two parties into the government

Table 6.2. Impact of Perceived Economic Conditions on Voting Preferences at the Aggregate Level in West Germany, 1990-1994

	CDU/ CSU	SPD	FDP	GRU[e]	REP[f]	Govern- ment[g]	Non- voting
			% Voting Preference For				
General economic conditions							
Evaluation	-	.77[c]	.33[a]	-.54[c]	-.46[c]	-	-.42[c]
Expectation	-	.68[b]	-	-	-.58[c]	-	-.73[c]
Personal economic conditions							
Evaluation	-	-	.37[a]	-	-	.21[a]	-
Expectation	.24[b]	-.51[a]	-	-	-	.22[c]	-
% Party Identification	.71[c]	.95[c]	.25[a]	.41[c]	.38[c]	.66[c]	.37[b]
R^2 (only PID)	63.5	41.1	54.8	63.3	40.1	77.9	29.7
R^2 (finalmodel)[d]	68.7	64.9	76.0	78.1	74.9	83.8	82.1
Change of R^2	5.2	23.8	21.2	14.8	34.8	5.9	52.4
N	52	52	52	52	52	52	52

Notes: - Not significant. [a], [b], [c]: Significance as in Table 6.1[d]. : After significant general and personal economic perceptions have been entered. [e]: Green Party.[f]: Republikaner. [g]: CDU/CSU+FDP. All R^2s have been multiplied by 100; coefficients are standardized.

vote share, both the perceived and the expected individual situation are significant.

The impact of general economic conditions on SPD share is positive while the effect of expected personal conditions is negative. The strongest effect is due to perceived general economic conditions. The coefficient of the same variable is negative for the Green Party. The right-wing Republikaner Party benefits considerably from negative evaluations of the general economic situation. Another possibility for voters to show their dissatisfaction with the economic policies of the government is not to vote for the opposition but to abstain. And indeed, both negative evaluations and expectations of the general economic situation over time are associated with higher proportions of nonvoters.

In *East* Germany, the electoral fortunes of the parties depend on economic expectations to a somewhat greater extent than in the old Länder (see Table 6.3). The success of the CDU/CSU is weakly related to evaluations of the general economic situation, while the effect of perceived general economic conditions is strongly negative for the FDP. Additionally, projections of future individual economic conditions are positively associated with the proportion of voting preferences for the FDP. When we combine CDU/CSU and FDP into the government vote share, we find a positive impact of expectations of general economic conditions on electoral success. For the SPD positive expectations about the general economic situation are here linked with higher levels of voting intentions, and vice versa. This is exactly opposite in the case of the Green Party, and a second significant negative effect exists for evaluations of personal economic conditions. Economic conditions have no significant impact on the vote share of the PDS (the successor party of the East German Communist party, SED). For the right-wing Republikaner, the negative effects of personal economic expectations underscore their role as a protest party; they benefit if times are seen to become worse. Similar to West Germany, finally, there is a negative relationship between abstention rates and evaluations of general economic conditions at the aggregate level. Additionally, positive individual expectations are associated with higher proportions of nonvoters in East Germany as well.

Table 6.3. Impact of Perceived Economic Conditions on Voting Preferences at the Aggregate Level in East Germany, 1991-1994

	CDU/ CSU	SPD	FDP	GRU[e]	PDS[f]	REP[g]	Govern-ment[h]	Non-voting
	\% Voting Preference For							
General economic conditions								
Evaluation	$.18^b$	-	$-.39^c$	-	-	-	-	$-.60^c$
Expectation	-	$.24^b$	-	$-.35^b$	-	$-.22^a$	$.23^b$	-
Personal economic conditions								
Evaluation	-	-	-	$-.22^a$	-	-	-	-
Expectation	-	-	$.49^c$	-	-	-	-	$.31^b$
\%Party Identification	$.81^c$	$.80^c$	$.33^c$	$.61^c$	$.96^c$	$.74^c$	$.74^c$	$.75^c$
R^2(only PID)	85.7	62.8	83.7	61.0	93.0	75.9	86.7	34.8
R^2(finalmodel)[d]	87.8	68.8	92.2	70.4	93.0	79.2	88.7	80.1
Change of R^2	2.1	6.0	8.5	9.6	0.0	3.3	2.0	45.3
N	45	45	45	45	45	45	45	45

Notes:
- Not significant.
[a], [b], [c]: Significance as in Table 6.1.
[d]: After significant general and personal economic perceptions have been entered.
[e]: Green Party.
[f]: The successor party of the communist SED.
[g]: Republikaner.
[h]: CDU/CSU+FDP.
All R^2s have been multiplied by 100; coefficients are standardized.

In sum, for both the old and new Länder we find strong effects of economic evaluations and expectations on the electoral prospects of the parties measured by monthly vote intentions. In both parts of Germany such economic judgments are largely related to vote shares according to the predictions of the anti-incumbent hypothesis: when times are seen as bad or getting worse, government parties suffer, and vice versa. There are four major East-West differences, however. First, the effect of personal pocketbook concerns is slightly weaker in the East than in the West. Second, while current conditions have a stronger impact in the West, in the East it is prospective orientations that matter. Third, the split of who benefits and who does not is not clearly along the classical government-opposition divide either in East or in West Germany. But because of the stronger effects of economic conditions on vote shares for the SPD in the old Länder, the distinction between competing parties along a new line of established versus nonestablished parties (with the SPD on the side of the establishment) seems to be more important for the West German electorate than in the East. Finally, a surprising result of this aggregate analysis is that the relationship between pessimistic economic judgments and nonvoting is quite strongly negative in the old Länder, but partially positive in the new ones.

ECONOMIC CONDITIONS AND VOTING PREFERENCES AT THE INDIVIDUAL LEVEL

For our cross-sectional analyses at the individual level we could only use those surveys from the Politbarometer series with a complete set of variables (i.e., voting intention, four economic perceptions, and party identification). In East Germany, party identification was first measured in April 1991 (for a discussion of the applicability of this concept in the new Länder, see Rattinger 1994c). In the West many studies do not contain all four economic variables. The number of available cross-sections thus is 20 for West and 41 for East Germany. To make the results from this multitude of cross-sections manageable, we present only the average coefficients of economic variables from stepwise regression analyses, in which party identification is controlled for in a procedure that is analogous to that described in the previous section.

Table 6.4 shows that the variance in vote intentions in the *West* German cross-sections explained only by the strength of party identification is considerably higher for the two major parties than for all others. This conforms to earlier results reported in the literature (see, e.g., Jagodzinski and Kühnel 1990). Second, compared to the findings at the aggregate level, we find a much lower impact of economic judgments on voting. The average minimum variance explained by those variables ranges from .4 percent for the SPD, FDP, and the Green Party to 2.1 percent for nonvoting.

The strongest partisan effect of economic conditions can be observed for the CDU/CSU. The most frequently significant variable here is general economic expectations, followed by general evaluations. For both variables, all estimated

Table 6.4. Average Impact of Perceived General and Personal Economic Conditions on Voting Preferences at the Individual Level in West Germany, 1990-1994

% Voting Preference For

	CDU/ CSU	SPD	FDP	GRU[e]	REP[f]	Govern-ment[g]	Non-voting
General economic conditions							
Mean beta of evaluations	.048	.003	.001	.012	-.018	.050	-.062
% of significant coefficients	30.0	15.0	0.0	0.0	10.0	55.0	55.0
% of coefficients with sign different from average	0.0	45.0	45.0	30.0	20.0	0.0	10.0
Mean beta of expectations	.056	-.013	.010	-.018	-.014	.057	-.055
% of significant coefficients	60.0	15.0	5.0	10.0	5.0	55.0	55.0
% of coefficients with sign different from average	0.0	30.0	20.0	25.0	20.0	0.0	5.0
Personal economic conditions							
Mean beta of evaluations	.033	-.012	.024	-.005	-.014	.044	-.056
% of significant coefficients	25.0	15.0	5.0	5.0	20.0	50.0	45.0
% of coefficients with sign different from average	5.0	40.0	20.0	35.0	40.0	0.0	10.0
Mean beta of expectations	.005	.001	.016	.013	-.010	.011	-.004
% of significant coefficients	10.0	5.0	5.0	10.0	20.0	15.0	15.0
% of coefficients with sign different from average	30.0	60.0	20.0	25.0	40.0	30.0	55.0
Mean beta of strength of PID	.619	.638	.529	.570	.369	.627	.161
Mean R^2 (only strength of PID)	44.2	41.1	28.9	32.7	15.2	42.1	3.3
Mean R^2 (final model)[d]	45.3	41.5	29.2	33.1	15.7	43.4	5.4
Change of mean R^2	1.1	0.4	0.4	0.4	0.6	1.4	2.1

Notes: Average N over all 20 surveys is 1,072. Reported coefficients are standardized regression coefficients. [d]: After all general and personal economic perceptions have been entered. All other notes as in Table 6.2.

(significant or insignificant) coefficients have an anti-incumbent (i.e., positive) sign. In comparison, individual economic judgments have only minor effects. This is also the case for the second government party, the FDP, where economic perceptions seldom have a significant effect on the vote. However, when we combine CDU/CSU and FDP into government voters, the pattern found for the former prevails, with general economic evaluations and expectations having positive and significant effects more than half of the time.

From the increases in the R^2 for the SPD, the Green Party, and the Republikaner, we can deduce only rather low effects of these economic variables on voting preferences. The estimated coefficients seldom are significantly different from zero, and their signs are often "wrong" and change frequently between subsequent months. The strongest overall impact of economic judgments on vote intention is obtained for abstention. The increase in R^2 is more than two percentage points, and all average coefficients have the expected negative sign. For three out of the four economic variables, "wrong" signs are seldom estimated, and the effect of general economic evaluations is significant in more than half of the surveys.

The impact of party identification on voting preferences in *East* Germany is lower than in the West (see Table 6.5). Since the effects of economic perceptions are of a similar magnitude (the average increase of R^2 varies from .4 to 2.9 percentage points), the fit of the models in total is below that in the old Länder. For the CDU/CSU we identify strong associations with general economic perceptions and personal evaluations. The coefficients of these three variables are frequently significant and seldom have a "wrong" sign. Most average coefficients are stronger than in West Germany. For the FDP the West German nonresult is replicated. The same holds for the government parties, where the equation deviates only marginally from that for the CDU/CSU: Two-thirds of the coefficients of the first three economic indicators are significant, and never is a "wrong" sign obtained.

For the SPD, the Green Party, and the Republikaner the additional variance explained by economic judgments is as low in the East as in the old Länder. Significance is rare, and "wrong" signs are frequent. However, the results for the East German protest party, the PDS, deserve the following qualification. All its average coefficients are negative, as expected, indicating that the probability of a vote for this party increases as economic judgments get worse. General economic assessments and personal expectations seem to be most important. Similar to the West, the strongest increase in average explained variance (2.9 percentage points) is found for abstention. All average coefficients are negative; for general economic expectations and individual evaluations they are quite strong, often significant, and most of the time consistent in direction. In both parts of the country skeptical economic judgments thus contribute to increase the probability of nonvoting.

So far we have only analyzed average effects of economic perceptions on voting intentions for the period 1990 to 1994 in order to reduce the complexity of the data effectively. However, we also have lost information about whether the importance of economic conditions for voting preferences has changed during this period. To recover some of that information we estimated bivariate regressions of the monthly values of increases in R^2 and of the coefficients of the economic variables on a time

Table 6.5. Average Impact of Perceived General and Personal Economic Conditions on Voting Preferences at the Individual Level in East Germany, 1991-1994

% Voting Preference For

	CDU/CSU	SPD	FDP	GRU[e]	PDS[f]	REP[g]	Government[h]	Non-voting
General economic conditions								
Mean beta of evaluations	.069	-.015	.005	-.024	-.031	-.003	.068	-.017
% of significant coefficients	68.3	7.3	2.4	12.2	22.0	7.3	73.2	14.6
% of coefficients with sign different from average	0.0	22.0	43.9	14.6	9.8	41.5	0.0	31.7
Mean beta of expectations	.053	.023	.008	-.005	-.028	-.020	.057	-.075
% of significant coefficients	46.3	12.2	9.8	7.7	22.0	19.5	58.5	56.1
% of coefficients with sign different from average	2.4	24.4	34.1	48.8	9.8	39.0	0.0	2.4
Personal economic conditions								
Mean beta of evaluations	.052	.006	.014	.022	-.001	-.008	.059	-.110
% of significant coefficients	53.7	17.1	4.9	12.2	9.8	14.6	68.3	94.1
% of coefficients with sign different from average	2.4	41.5	46.3	22.0	53.7	46.3	0.0	0.0
Mean beta of expectations	.017	-.001	.002	-.009	-.019	.011	.018	-.005
% of significant coefficients	17.1	2.4	6.7	4.9	22.0	14.6	12.2	9.8
% of coefficients with sign different from average	31.7	46.3	43.3	31.7	22.0	34.1	26.8	46.3
Mean beta of strength of PID	.586	.523	.539	.503	.695	.443	.563	.209
Mean R^2 (only strength of PID)	38.3	27.6	30.0	25.9	49.9	22.7	35.7	5.0
Mean R^2 (final model)[d]	40.1	28.0	30.4	26.3	50.5	23.2	37.7	7.8
Change of mean R^2	1.8	0.4	0.4	0.4	0.5	0.5	2.0	2.9

Notes: Average N over all 41 surveys is 1,094. Reported coefficients are standardized regression coefficients. [d]: After all general and personal economic perceptions have been entered. All other notes as in Table 6.3.

variable. A significant coefficient would indicate that economic voting and/or a particular variable has become more or less important over time, depending on the sign.

Unfortunately, there are very few significant results obtained by this procedure–probably due to the comparatively low number of cases. These can be summarized briefly. For the *old* Länder, significant trends can be reported only for SPD vote intention and for nonvoting. For the former, the (positive) impact of evaluations of general economic conditions has decreased over time, while in the case of abstention the (negative) impact of general economic expectations has grown.

In the *new* Länder there are three trends that deserve attention. For the CDU/CSU, the PDS, and the government parties combined, the explanatory power of economic conditions for voting intentions has significantly increased between 1991 and 1994. We find a growing (positive) impact of personal economic evaluations in the case of the CDU/CSU, stronger positive associations between general economic perceptions and voting preferences for the government parties, and a higher negative effect of general and individual economic evaluations on support for the PDS.

Our cross-sectional analyses can be summarized as follows: The impact of economic judgments on voting in both parts of Germany emerges as rather limited, but somewhat higher in the new Länder. The strongest effects of these variables can be found for the CDU/CSU, the government as a whole, and for abstention. For these dependent variables, the directions of estimated associations are consistent with the anti-incumbent logic and significantly different from zero. For the second government party, the FDP, our findings are as weak and volatile as for the SPD and the Green Party. In the case of the two protest parties (PDS and Republikaner), economic judgments usually are negatively related to their electoral prospects, but this impact is lower than one might expect, given the frequently voiced dissatisfaction with the performance of the established parties. However, over the period analyzed here there are notable trends of economic perceptions growing in importance as far as voting for the government parties, protest parties, or abstention are concerned. Finally, we can say that in East and West Germany the effects of national economic conditions generally are stronger than those of personal conditions. The only (but important) exception is evaluations of the current personal economic situation in the new Länder, which have a rather strong impact overall.

ECONOMIC CONDITIONS AND VOTING PREFERENCES AT THE INDIVIDUAL LEVEL OVER TIME

We now turn to the final part of our analysis–that is, panel data from 1990 to 1993. We begin with a brief look at the comparability of the cross-sectional and the panel data. Table 6.6 reports the aggregate changes in general and personal economic judgments between subsequent panel waves and corresponding Politbarometer data (in parentheses). In most cases the direction of change is the same in both sets of data, and the two corresponding values do not deviate much. When they do, the changes in the Politbarometer data are stronger in magnitude. There are two explanations: First, later responses by panel participants are constrained by their earlier responses. Second, there are different scales. The Politbarometer uses 3-point scales, in our panels we used 5-point scales (see the Appendix), which allow more graded judgments. Nevertheless, we can conclude that both sets of data are highly comparable as far as the development of economic perceptions is concerned.[1]

Our procedure here is completely analogous to the previous section; the only deviation involves the substitution of first differences between subsequent panel waves for the original variables, and the inclusion of retrospective evaluations in the analysis. For *West* Germany we see rather few significant effects of changing economic perceptions on changes in voting (see Table 6.7). The most consistent such effect can be observed for the CDU/CSU, the government vote, and for abstention. For all other dependent variables insignificance prevails. This is parallel to our cross-sectional analysis. For all dependent variables the R^2 of the final models decreases over time, indicating declining predictive power of changes in partisanship for voting behavior. Another common pattern is that the most relevant economic perception rarely stays the same over time. Nevertheless, in terms of direction all significant coefficients are consistent with the cross-sectional results in that improving economic judgments, if at all, strengthen the CDU/CSU, the FDP, the government in total, and the SPD, while the opposite is the case for the Greens, the Republikaner, and the "party of the nonvoters."

Table 6. 6. Comparison of Changes of Economic Perceptions Between Panel Waves with Simultaneous Cross-Sections

	Change of				
	General		Personal		
	Economic Conditions				
Year of fieldwork	Evaluation	Expectation	Evaluation	Expectation	N
West Germany					
1990/1991	-.02 (.05)	-.12 (.05)	.02 (-.01)	-.09 (-.02)	932
1991/1992a	-.21 (-.35)	-.12 (-.15)	-.05 (-.11)	-.05 (-.03)	587
1992b/1993a	-.29 (-.39)	-.13 (.02)	-.02 (.00)	-.07 (.02)	703
1993a/1993b	-.02 (-.19)	.05 (.19)	-.01 (-.02)	-.03 (-.02)	489
East Germany					
1991/1992a	.25 (.12)	.07 (-.09)	.18 (.07)	.09 (-.12)	325
1992b/1993a	-.06 (-.03)	-.17 (-.18)	.01 (.02)	-.09 (-.08)	740
1993a/1993b	.07 (.04)	.02 (.06)	.06 (.12)	.00 (-.02)	556

Notes: First panel: 1990, 1991, 1992a (May of each year). Second panel: 1992b: June/July, 1993a: March/April, 1993b: October/November. Without parentheses: Panel results. Within parentheses: Politbarometer results (interpolated when not available for the same month).

Table 6.7. Impact of Changes in Economic Perceptions on Changes in Voting Preferences at the Individual Level in West Germany, 1990-93

Change in voting preference for

	CDU/CSU	SPD	FDP	GRU[e]	REP[f]	Govern-ment[g]	Non-voting
1990/1991							
General economic conditions							
Δ in evaluation	-	-	-	-	-	-	-.086[b]
Δ in expectation	-	-	-	-	-	-	-
Δ in retrospection	-	-	-	-	-	-	-
Personal economic conditions							
Δ in evaluation	-	-	-	-	-	-	-
Δ in expectation	.071[a]	-	-	-	-	.078[b]	-
Δ in retrospection	-	-	-	-	-	-	-
R² (only change of strength of PID)	52.9	31.3	33.8	23.8	0.0	24.2	5.8
R² (final model)[d]	53.4	31.3	33.8	23.8	0.0	24.8	6.5
Δ in R²	0.5	0.0	0.0	0.0	0.0	0.6	0.7
1991/1992a							
General economic conditions							
Δ in evaluation	-	-	-	-	-.080[a]	-	-
Δ in expectation	.102[b]	-	-	-	-	.091[a]	-
Δ in retrospection	-	.074[a]	-	-	-	-	-.105[b]
Personal economic conditions							
Δ in evaluation	-	-	-	-	-	-	-
Δ in expectation	-	.081[a]	-	-.107[b]	-	-	-
Δ in retrospection	-	-	-	-	-	-	-.096[a]
R² (only change of strength of PID)	21.1	21.2	13.3	22.9	16.2	15.2	1.7
R² (final model)[d]	22.2	22.6	13.3	24.0	16.8	16.0	3.8
Δ in R²	0.9	1.4	0.0	1.1	0.6	0.8	2.1

(continued)

Table 6.7. continued

	Change in voting preference for						
	CDU/ CSU	SPD	FDP	GRU[e]	REP[f]	Govern- ment[g]	Non- voting
1992b/1993a							
General economic conditions							
Δ in evaluation	-	-	-	-	-	-	-
Δ in expectation	-	-	-	-	-	.093[b]	-
Δ in retrospection	-	-	-	-	-	-	-
Personal economic conditions							
Δ in evaluation	-	-	-	-	-	-	-
Δ in expectation	-	-	-	-	-	-	-
Δ in retrospection	.082[a]	-	-	-	-	-	-.102[b]
R^2 (only change							
of strength of PID)	16.8	18.3	19.6	20.3	12.0	16.6	0.0
R^2 (final model)[d]	17.4	18.3	19.6	20.3	12.0	17.5	1.0
Δ in R^2	0.6	0.0	0.0	0.0	0.0	0.9	1.0
1993a/1993b							
General economic conditions							
Δ in evaluation	-	-	-	-	-	-	-
Δ in expectation	.092[a]	-	.089[a]	-	-	-	-
Δ in retrospection	-	-	-	-	-	-	-
Personal economic conditions							
Δ in evaluation	-	-	-	-	-	.102[a]	-.104[a]
Δ in expectation	-	-	-	-	-	.093[a]	-
Δ in retrospection	-	-	-	-	-	-	-
R^2 (only change							
of strength of PID)	10.8	12.5	21.0	8.7	9.2	10.9	0.0
R^2 (final model)[d]	11.6	12.5	21.8	8.7	9.2	13.2	1.1
Δ in R^2	0.8	0.0	0.8	0.0	0.0	2.3	1.1

Notes: All R^2s have been multiplied by 100; coefficients are unstandardized. - Not significant. [a], [b], [c]: Significance as in Table 6.1. [d]: After significant economic perceptions have been entered. All other notes as in Table 6.2.

Table 6.8. Impact of Changes in Economic Perceptions on Changes in Voting Preferences at the Individual Level in East Germany, 1991-93

	CDU/CSU	SPD	FDP	GRU[e]	PDS[f]	REP[g]	Government[h]	Non-voting
1991/1992a								
General economic conditions								
Δ in evaluation	-	-	-	-	-	-.096[a]	-	-
Δ in expectation	-	-	-	-	-	-	-	-
Δ in retrospection	-	-	-	-	-	-	-	-
Personal economic conditions								
Δ in evaluation	-	-	-	-	-	-	-	-
Δ in expectation	-	-	-	-	-	-	-	-
Δ in retrospection	-	-	-	-	-	-	-	-
R^2 (only change in strength of PID)	13.8	6.3	20.3	8.2	15.3	30.2	17.6	3.1
R^2 (final model)[d]	13.8	6.3	20.3	8.2	15.3	31.1	17.6	3.1
Δ in R^2	0.0	0.0	0.0	0.0	0.0	0.9	0.0	0.0
1992b/1993a								
General economic conditions								
Δ in evaluation	-	-	-	-	-	-	-	-
Δ in expectation	-	-	-	-	-	-	-.071[a]	-
Δ in retrospection	-	-	-	-	-	-	-	-
Personal economic conditions								
Δ in evaluation	.097[b]	-	-	-	-	-	.094[b]	-.153[c]
Δ in expectation	-	-	-	-	-	-	-	-
Δ in retrospection	-	-	-	-	-	-	-	-
R^2 (only change in strength of PID)	20.0	12.7	9.2	8.1	2.6	4.1	16.6	3.1
R^2 (final model)[d]	21.0	12.7	9.2	8.1	2.6	4.1	18.2	5.5
Δ in R^2	1.0	0.0	0.0	0.0	0.0	0.0	1.6	1.4
1993a/1993b								
General economic conditions								
Δ in evaluation	-	-	-	-	-	-	-	-
Δ in expectation	-	-	-	-	-	-	-	-
Δ in retrospection	-	-	-	-	-	-	-	-
Personal economic conditions								
Δ in evaluation	.093[a]	-	-	-	-	-	-	-.089[a]
Δ in expectation	-	-	-	-	-	-	-.096[a]	-
Δ in retrospection	-	-	-	-	-	-	-	-
R^2 (only change in strength of PID)	9.6	5.8	6.5	16.2	4.0	14.3	9.8	1.5
R^2 (final model)[d]	10.4	5.8	6.5	16.2	4.0	14.3	10.8	2.2
Δ in R^2	0.8	0.0	0.0	0.0	0.0	0.0	1.0	0.7

Notes: All notes as in Table 6.3.

In *East* Germany changing perceptions of economic conditions affect changes in voting preferences even less often than in the West (see Table 6.8). Significant effects can be found only for the CDU/CSU, the government as a whole, the Republikaner, and for nonvoters. Most of what has been said about the West holds here as well. Rarely is one particular economic variable associated with voting changes in a stable fashion over time. To the extent that results are significant, they again conform to the anti-incumbent logic, if one accepts abstention as one form of antigovernment behavior within that logic. Surprisingly, and contrary to the findings in the previous section, the PDS is not found to benefit from deteriorating economic perceptions. Finally, most of the associations with changes in the vote occur for changes of perceptions of personal economic circumstances, not general ones, while in the West both were equally likely to have an effect.

In sum, the impact of changing economic perceptions on changes in voting intentions at the individual level is found to be rather limited both in East and West Germany. Those effects that can be discerned predominantly support the anti-incumbent hypothesis. Abstention again emerges as an especially plausible reaction to deteriorating economic perceptions in both parts of the country. In the East, finally, this analysis of panel data shows citizens to politically respond to economic pocketbook concerns almost exclusively, and much less to collective ones.[2]

CONCLUSION

The German economy has been called a "colossus at the crossroads" (Smyser 1993). It might well be that the future role of the German economy within the European Union and the world will depend upon how quickly the economic problems resulting from unification can be overcome by a successful economic policy. But our analysis of individual attitudes toward economic conditions and of their effects on voting preferences does not give very strong support to the widely held notion that social and political integration of the citizens in both parts of Germany requires another economic miracle. This conclusion can be based upon the rather limited effects of economic evaluations on voting decisions that have been described here at the cross-sectional and longitudinal individual level. Although they are sometimes somewhat stronger in the new Länder, our results show once more (as has been demonstrated for many other social and political attitudes in both parts of Germany) that the differences between East and West are gradual rather than categorical. It is interesting to note that Angelika Vetter and Oscar W. Gabriel report a similar conclusion regarding the other short-term factor considered in chapter 5 of this volume, namely candidate orientations. In our analysis, one of these important gradual differences is that individuals in East Germany pay more attention to their personal economic situation when deciding about their vote.

Our analyses also revealed three problems that deserve further research. First, it seems as if the traditional contrast between government versus opposition has shifted for economic voting in Germany. Negative economic judgments not only hurt the government parties, but also the SPD. Thus, a distinction between established and nonestablished parties appears to have become more important for voters' reactions. Second, nonvoting and support for nonestablished parties seem to be functional equivalents when negative economic perceptions create the desire to punish the "ins." Under what circumstances one or the other is chosen requires clarification—especially because recent research has shown that the effect of economic perceptions on turnout in Germany is only marginal when other important variables like the perceived social norm to participate in elections are controlled for (Rattinger and Krämer 1995).

Finally, there is a considerable discrepancy between the results derived from aggregate data over time and those obtained from analyses of individual-level data. The most obvious differences are, first, that the impact of economic conditions on voting emerged as more visible in the aggregate and stronger in the West, while at the individual level our results support the opposite conclusion. Second, the results at the micro and macrolevels are not consistent enough to provide much of a firm answer to the questions whether evaluations or expectations, individual or collective economic assessments have a stronger effect on voting preferences. Third, the aggregate findings suggest that there is an impact of economic conditions for almost every party. But at the individual level in cross-sectional and longitudinal perspective we find that effects of economic variables are mainly limited to the shares of the major government party (the CDU/CSU), the government in total, and the proportion of voters not intending to vote. This is not the first time such discrepancies are reported, and it will not be the last. Even though the view has been expressed that aggregate results should be accepted when in doubt (Kramer 1983), we find this far too simple a recommendation in the present context. We prefer to conclude that this chapter cannot be the final word either on the political effects of economic developments in Germany since unification or on the theoretical and methodological issues raised by any attempt to reconcile micro and macrolevel research on this important subject.

NOTES

1. This conclusion is not valid, of course, regarding retrospective evaluations, which were collected only very rarely in the Politbarometer.

2. These main results of panel analysis remain largely the same if we restrict it to only those individuals who have changed their voting intention between two subsequent panel waves. Due to the lower number of cases there are even less significant coefficients, and the finding that West German voters respond more to general and East Germans more to personal economic concerns becomes more pronounced.

APPENDIX: CODING OF VARIABLES

Politbarometer Data

Evaluation of general and personal economic conditions: 3-point scales from -1 ("bad") to +1 ("good").

Expectation of general and personal economic conditions: 3-point scales from -1 ("worse") to +1 ("better").

Voting preference: Percentage of voting preference for each party and every month (for the aggregate level); dummy-variables (for the individual level), coded as 1 (will vote for this party) and 0 (all other responses). The abstention variable consists of the percentage of individuals for each month who explicitly indicate they would not vote (for the aggregate level); dummy-variable (for the individual level), coded as 1 (will not vote) and 0 (all other responses).

Party identification: Percentage of party identification for each party and every month (for the aggregate level); strength of party identification (for the individual level), coded as 1 ("very weak") to 5 ("very strong"), and 0 (all other responses). For abstention the variable consists of the percentage of individuals for each month without party identification (for the aggregate level); dummy-variable (for the individual level), coded as 1 (no party identification) and 0 (all other responses).

For every analysis at the aggregate level (except the trend analysis of the data in Tables 6.4 and 6.5) missing monthly values in time series are substituted by linear interpolation. For every analysis at the individual level missing values are removed by mean substitution for each month.

Panel Data

Evaluation of general and personal economic conditions: Differences between subsequent panel waves, based on 5-point scales from -1 ("very bad") to +1 ("very good").

Retrospective evaluation and expectation of general and personal economic conditions: Differences between subsequent panel-waves, based on 5-point scales from -1 ("much worse") to +1 ("much better").

Voting preference: Coded as -1 (will no longer vote for this party), +1 (will now vote for this party), and 0 (all other responses). For abstention this variable is coded as -1 (will now vote), +1 (will no longer vote), and 0 (all other responses).

Party identification: Differences between subsequent panel-waves of the strength of party identification. For abstention this variable is coded as -1 (now identifies with a party), +1 (no longer identifies with a party), and 0 (all other responses).

For all analyses missing values are removed by mean substitution.

7

The Stability of the Meaning of Left and Right in Germany, 1976-90

Wolfgang Jagodzinski and Steffen M. Kühnel

INTRODUCTION

There is a long-standing debate about the fate of ideology in advanced societies. While scholars such as Seymour M. Lipset (1972) predicted a decline of ideological politics, empirical evidence presented by Hans-Dieter Klingemann (1979; Inglehart and Klingemann 1976) demonstrated that there had been no decline in ideological thinking by the late 1970s. Given the fact that the proportion of ideologues was larger among the better-educated in these analyses, one might even go so far as expecting an increase in ideological thinking as a result of rising cognitive mobilization. The same might be expected to result from value change.

Although the question remains controversial to date, it has important implications for electoral change. After all, due to its presumed stability at the individual level, ideological thinking might influence electoral choice beyond the short-term politics of the day. Hence, the proposition that the weight of the candidates increases for voting behavior as personalization of politics proceeds may be considered the flip side of Lipset's position of a decline in ideology. Yet, Angelika Vetter and Oscar W. Gabriel have demonstrated in chapter 5 of this volume that, unlike in the United States, candidates have not become substantially more important in Germany (for further references to the American case, see Lass 1995; Wattenberg 1994; Zelle 1995a). While the impact of this short-term component seems not to have increased over time, the impact of other long-term causes of voting behavior is often assumed to decline: For example, according to Peter Gluchowski and Ulrich von Wilamowitz-Moellendorff (chapter 2 in this volume) the long-term forces of the social cleavages are weakening (but see Jagodzinski and Quandt 1997), and a decline in party identification continues to be a popular thesis with electoral researchers as well (see Carsten Zelle's critical discussion in chapter 4 of this volume). Possibly, then, ideological orientations are among the very few stable long-term causes of electoral choice which have survived in a time of rapid change.

While it is beyond the scope of this present chapter to investigate the implications of this proposition in an encompassing way, we will investigate whether there are changes in the meaning of the ideological labels of "left" and "right" that might hint at a potential decline of their relevance over time.

To do that, ambiguities surrounding the very concept of ideology as much as its specific shape in the form of the left-right dimension have to be overcome. European intellectuals usually hold a negative attitude toward ideologies. In their view, ideologies are based on a distorted and simplified picture of reality. To many, these concepts have at best a vague meaning and are used merely as catchwords in political debates. The labels "left" and "right" allow political opponents to stigmatize one another. If a rightist politician classifies an opponent's position as being on the left, this position is declared wrong and unacceptable for his or her followers; a substantive discussion is no longer needed. Clearly, a leftist politician can use the term "right" for the same purpose.

Political scientists may add that the notions of left and right become more problematic the higher the complexity of political reasoning. They believe that politically sophisticated persons often hold a mixture of left and right positions on different issues, and that such individuals therefore cannot be classified as being left or right. Essentially the same argument can be reformulated in more technical terms: Left and right, it is argued, can be applied only if the political space of a person can be reduced to a single dimension without any significant loss of information. Since this does not seem to be the case for most people, there is a limited range of applicability for these concepts.

This criticism largely ignores the positive function of the left-right scheme. First of all, critics often forget that the ranking of persons, parties, or other political objects on a left-right scheme requires much more political knowledge than the average citizen can be expected to have. Converse (1964) has shown that the majority of American voters either does not have an understanding of the liberal-democratic continuum[1] at all or defines the continuum in terms of societal groups. At this level of conceptualization, a party is classified as being left if it acts in the interest of the poor or blue-collar workers, and it is classified right if it acts in the interests of the rich or the employers.

Only a small fraction of the electorate–the so-called ideologues or near-ideologues–reaches a higher level of understanding where the relationship between the left-right continuum and general issues or underlying values is recognized. An even smaller fraction is able to conceptualize politics in these terms. Ideologues have the ability to use the left-right dimension as an overarching principle to guide their political belief system, thereby integrating political attitudes and positions toward a multitude of issues into one coherent structure. Although Converse tends to treat group thinking and ideological thinking as two exclusive alternatives, we are inclined to see them as complementary concepts. Left and right partly can be defined on the basis of groups (group component of the left-right continuum) and on the basis of issues and values (ideological component).

This chapter addresses the question of whether the relative weights of these two components have varied among the German electorate both over time and between groups. Moreover, it seeks to understand the content of the ideological component. One may argue that–at least in most West European countries–the left-right dimension received its dominant meaning during the Industrial Revolution, and that this situation has not changed to this day. While left-wing has always been associated with an egalitarian, socialist, or communist ideology, right-wing has been equated with a position that emphasizes the freedom of the individual in general, and that of the entrepreneur in particular.

The right side of the continuum presumably never has been fixed in some absolute sense. Right could mean the defense of national interest, of law and order, of fascism, or–more generally–the defense of the established order. The meaning of left also may have undergone minor changes. For instance, while in past years socialist ideologies frequently had supported the expansion of governmental activities and state control because the state was regarded as a safeguard of the underprivileged in the power struggle with the economic elite, today even the moderate leftist ideologues turn against an omnipotent state because it is perceived as a menace to freedom and autonomy (see Inglehart 1990).

Despite such changes, the core meaning of the left-right dimension may have remained more or less stable. We call this assumption the *stable meaning hypothesis*. On the other extreme, one may argue that left and right are nothing but catchwords that are defined by each group in its own way. If there is a common element at all, it comes from the distinction of progressive and conservative orientations. Advocates of change are classified as being left and advocates of the existing order as being right (see van Deth and Geurts 1989). Given that the direction of change is not, or at best rudimentarily, specified, we should see a variety of left-wing and right-wing positions at any given point in time. We call this the *variable meaning hypothesis*.

Both the *stable* and the *variable meaning hypotheses* are poles on a continuum that runs from maximum to minimum stability. How variable is the meaning of left and right? It is the major purpose of this chapter to develop an analytic design for answering such questions. In the theoretical part, we first explicate our concept of meaning more precisely. We then turn to the meaning components of left and right, distinguishing between a group component and an issue component. In a third step we identify strategic groups for empirical analysis.

THE EMPIRICAL SOCIAL MEANING OF A CONCEPT

Social science methodology usually distinguishes between analytical and descriptive statements. Definitions and meaning postulates belong to the former, empirical hypotheses to the latter. For the purposes of this chapter, we are not interested in analytical statements about left and right. Rather, we will try to find out how members of particular groups or societies understand these terms. Because our descriptions can be false or true, they belong to the class of empirical statements. Thus, we are interested in the average meaning or the average understanding of the concept in a group.

Several strategies can be applied in order to identify this average meaning. First of all, we can simply ask the group members what they understand by left and right. This procedure measures the active understanding of the concept (Klingemann 1979, 1982). According to Klingemann's results, roughly half of the respondents relate left and right to value orientations and political movements, roughly a third use the concepts as labels for political parties, and roughly a sixth do not associate any meaning at all or a false meaning with these concepts.[2] Second, we can show respondents a list of alternative definitions or characterizations of left and right and ask them to identify the one(s) which come(s) closest to their own understanding. Clearly, this method focuses on the passive recognition of a concept.

We will apply a third strategy that aims at the measurement of the implicit meaning. Central to our conceptualization is the assumption that an individual's own position on the left-right scale, as well as the position which he or she ascribes to other actors are ultimately determined by values, issue positions, and group affiliations regardless of whether the individual is aware of these relationships. If an individual places him/herself on a left-right scale, his or her own values and beliefs will be used as implicit criteria. If other political actors are located on the continuum, the perceived[3] values and properties of these actors becomes decisive.

An example may help fix ideas: Assume a single individual and two variables–say the left-right ranking of at least three parties and the perceived position of the parties on the issue of privatization.[4] The latter scale may be coded in such a way that the category "opposition to privatization" appears on the left and the category "support for privatization" on the right. Supposing that respondent A places the socialist party to the very left end and the most conservative party to the very right end on both scales, and all other parties somewhere in between, we can then define the meaning of the left-right party ranking in the following way: The more it depends on the issue of privatization, the more we can improve our prediction of a given party's left-right position by knowing its perceived position on the issue of privatization. If we further assume both scales to be continuous, the bivariate product moment correlation coefficient reflects the degree to which the meaning of the left-right scale is determined by the issue of privatization. The stronger the correlation the more strongly the meaning of one scale is determined by the other.

Two features of our concept of an empirical meaning are important. First, the meaning obviously does not require any kind of awareness: In our example, although the individual may not be aware of the relationship between the left-right placement and the issue of privatization, the meaning of the former scale nevertheless may be completely determined by the other. Second, empirical meaning in the way used here must not be confused with causality. Even if the meaning of a first concept is completely determined by a second, it does not need to be causally dependent on it. "X determines the meaning of Y" is not a causal relationship. While causality is asymmetric,[5] we consider the empirical meaning relationship symmetric. To the extent that X determines the meaning of Y, the latter also determines the meaning of X.

So far we have focused on correlations within individuals–that is, we have treated individuals separately. As a consequence, the meanings that are implicitly or explicitly attributed by two individuals A and B may not only differ from one another, but also may be based on highly idiosyncratic cognitions and evaluations. Supposing that the individual A erroneously classifies a right-wing extremist party as being left and in opposition to privatization, and a socialist party as being right and in favor of privatization, then his implicit understanding of the left-right continuum may be determined by the issue of privatization to the same degree as the implicit understanding of B who rank-orders the parties correctly on both scales. In other words, wrong perceptions do not necessarily need to weaken a meaning-relationship that is unique for each individual. Correlations within individuals do not tell us whether A uses the terms left and right in the same way as other individuals.

If the correlation coefficient is also supposed to reflect the degree of social consensus, the calculations have to be based on the party rankings *of all group members*. We have opted for this alternative. The resulting correlation coefficient reflects the average meaning in the group or—as we prefer to call it—the *social* meaning. Because its calculation is based on the party rankings of all group members, the sample size usually is sufficiently large for estimation. If the correlation is high, there is not only a close correspondence between the two scales on the individual level but also a high group consensus. Vice versa, a low correlation is either due to a lack of a relationship between the scales or to a lack of a consensus among the group members or both.

Our measure of the empirical *social* meaning requires that all variables have sufficiently large variances, or at least variances above zero. Because the self-placement of a single individual has no variation, we started with the left-right ranking of a larger number of parties. If we move from the individual to the group, the variation will not necessarily increase. For example, if all group members perceive the left-right position of a party correctly, we still will have no variation of that position. And if all group members place themselves on the same position of the left-right continuum, we still have no variation in the self-placement scales. Thus, the requirement of sufficiently large variances restricts our group selections in the empirical analyses.

Three specific recommendations can be made: (1) It is useful to focus on groups whose members can be expected to have variable positions on the left-right continuum when analyzing the meaning of self-placement scales. For example, it makes little sense to analyze the empirical *social* meaning of left-right self-placement scales among socialists because their left-right positions will not differ very much. The same holds true for other political groups like the Greens or right-wing extremists. (2) Aside from a few exceptions, it makes little sense to analyze the placement of a single party on the left-right scale. The placement of the same party at different locations frequently is due to misperceptions or measurement error. Clearly, if we want to investigate whether members of a particular group systematically place a given party too far to the left or too far to the right, the placement of this party may be of interest. However, it generally is more adequate to analyze the ranks of all parties along the left-right continuum as it has been described in our initial example.

The essence of the two previous rules can be summarized in a third: (3a) If all group members can be expected to hold similar positions on the left-right continuum and/or the relevant values and issues, the implicit meaning of left and right should not be derived from self-placement scales but from the rankings of a larger number of political actors on the left-right continuum. These actors should differ in the left-right position and in the values and issue positions as well. (3b) However, if the variation within a group is sufficiently large, the implicit meaning can also be derived from self-placement scales.

So far we have examined a situation where the implicit meaning of left and right is determined by a second variable. In general, a much broader spectrum of variables will influence the meaning of a concept. Throughout this chapter we assume that the relationships among all these variables are linear and additive. If we regress the left-right ranking of the parties (or the left-right self-placement scale) on all other variables under consideration, the *coefficient of determination R^2* reflects the degree to which the meaning of the dependent variable is determined by these other variables. If R^2 is equal to 1 the meaning is completely determined by the other variables. If R^2 is equal to 0, the meaning is completely independent of these other variables. Numerical values between 0 and 1 reflect varying degrees of determination. R^2 measures the overall influence on the meaning of the dependent variable Y. In many situations, however, we are not so much interested in the overall influence as in the degree to which the meaning of Y is determined by a particular variable X when all other variables in the system are held constant. We plan to use the *partial correlation coefficient* $r_{XY.UV...Z}$ for this purpose. The larger the partial correlation, the more the meaning of Y for given levels of the variables U, V,..., Z is determined by X, and vice versa.[6]

THEORETICAL CONSIDERATIONS ON THE EMPIRICAL SOCIAL MEANING OF LEFT AND RIGHT

Having precisely defined the concept of an empirical *social* meaning, we can turn to the more substantive questions. What determines the meaning of left and right? On the basis of the analyses conducted by Converse (1964, 1970) one may draw the conclusion that people either use groups (*group component*) or issues and abstract value orientations (*ideological component*) to define the content of the left-right continuum. Moreover, the cleavage theory of Lipset and Rokkan (1967) allows the identification of some of the relevant groups and/or values and issues, while authors like Inglehart (1990) may help us identify new values and issues that may gain an influence on the meaning of left and right in contemporary Western societies.

The Group Component: Groups, Organizations, and Social Movements

During the socialization process a child may learn to divide the existing political parties into three—left, middle, right—or more categories. The child has no deeper understanding of left and right but only an extensional definition: left are the communists and socialists, middle are the liberals, and right are the conservatives, etc. Nevertheless, later in life the child will be able to determine her/his own position on the left-right continuum on the basis of party attachment or party choice. The child will place her/himself in the left-right category of the party that is most preferred. This may be the easiest way to determine the meaning of left and right. We can call this the *party-defined meaning of left and right*. It requires nothing more than the knowledge of the names of the parties and their assignment to the left-right categories.

Only slightly more sophistication is required if the meaning of left and right is determined on the basis of *group interests*. We have already mentioned the distinction between the poor and the rich. Parties that protect the former are called left-wing and parties that serve the interests of the latter are called right-wing. Rightist and leftist groups may also be defined on the basis of a country's cleavage system. Since most of the West European countries including Germany have been shaped by the industrial conflict, the citizens will be able to translate the conflict between workers and employees, on the one hand, and employers or entrepreneurs, on the other hand, into the left-right terminology. Accordingly, a left-wing party or leader should act in the interest of the workers and employees, a right-wing party in the interest of the entrepreneurs and employers.

Principally, the left-right distinction could also be applied to other cleavages. Countries that are divided along religious lines, and where the Catholic church formerly was an ally of the conservative elites, politics in the interest of the Catholics could be called right-wing.[7] However, if we generalize from answers on open-ended questions,[8] the left-right distinction rarely seems to be applied to the religious cleavage.

This should be even more true with respect to the other historical cleavages that make it difficult to define the conflict parties in social-structural terms. Who is the opponent of the peasants in the urban-rural conflict, and who is the opponent of an ethnic, linguistic, or culturally defined minority in the center periphery conflict? Furthermore, should we call these minorities left-wing because they usually intend to change the existing order, or should we call them right-wing because they mostly defend traditional customs and values? Regarding these complications, we do not expect cleavage groups other than employers and employees to play an important role in determining the meaning of left and right.

When we turn to the so-called new cleavages, the social structural basis of the conflict regarding emancipation is most easily identified. Politics in the interest of women may be called left-wing by at least some groups. The parties of the other value conflicts are less visible. If there is a division between older and younger generations regarding environmental issues, lifestyle issues, postmaterialism, and individualism, the question remains whether old and young form homogeneous interest groups. Nevertheless, if some groups consider environmental protection, a liberalization of the family law as a policy in the interest of the young generations, the meaning of left and right may be marginally influenced by this social division.

We will not discuss whether the so-called new value conflicts in fact constitute new cleavages or not (see Knutsen and Scarbrough 1995; on the electoral relevance of these dimensions see also Markus Klein in chapter 8 of this volume). They may be loosely related to social divisions, which, in turn, may marginally influence the empirical social meaning of left and right. In Table 7.1 we have listed historical cleavages and persistent general issues in modern societies that have contributed or may contribute to the emergence of social divisions (first column), social organizations and social movements (second column), specific issues (third column), general issues and value conflicts (last column). As mentioned above, we have little doubt that the meaning of left and right mainly has been shaped by the Industrial Revolution. Therefore we have declared workers/employees as left-wing and employers as right-wing interest groups. In all other instances we have used question marks (L?, R?), since it is at least doubtful whether these social groups are perceived as being left- or right-wing.

Organizations and social movements often are more visible than social groups. Therefore, some citizens may find it easier to define left and right in terms of the former. In the case of the industrial cleavage (second row in Table 7.1), support of the unions indicates a leftist political measure and the support of the employers' associations a rightist one. Several cleavages are asymmetric in the sense that only one side is represented by societal organizations with clearly defined interests. For instance, where the religious cleavage divides between religious and secular groups, the latter usually are not represented by strong organizations. Where a cleavage has emerged from the conflict between the ruling elite or the dominant cultural elite and a disadvantaged social group, usually only the latter is represented by special interest organizations. In Table 7.1 we have denoted a question mark where a social group is not represented by a strong interest organization. Apart from these peculiarities, our former considerations also apply to organizations and social movements. The meaning of left and right is presumably most strongly influenced by the organizations of the industrial cleavage and less strongly by other organizations and movements.

The Ideological Component: Issues and Values

Contrary to Converse we assume that *all* voters–at least implicitly–make use of specific issues and/or of abstract principles and value orientations in order to define their positions on the left-right continuum. The relative weight of the ideological and the value components may vary with the centrality of politics, but they should have an impact in all subpopulations. The distinction between abstract values and specific issues is often less relevant in practice than in theory because many empirical studies derive abstract value orientations from a respondent's position toward specific issues. Accordingly, these two factors are not measured independently from each other.

In the last two columns of Table 7.1 we show a few examples of specific and general issues or values for each cleavage or new conflict dimensions. The list is by no means complete. Typical economic issues are working conditions, social security expenditures, income taxes, worker participation, strike regulations, and so on. On a more abstract level, most of these conflicts center around the trade-off between freedom and equality. While a right-wing position stresses the importance of freedom, a left-wing position gives a higher priority to equality. As far as the relationship between the state and the economy is concerned, a right-wing position emphasizes private initiative, favors privatization and a lean state, whereas a left-wing position emphasizes public control and favors a welfare state with comprehensive responsibilities in the field of social security. Even though socialist and social democratic parties have changed their position after the breakdown of communism, the basic distinction between left and right seems still to be valid.

In contrast to commonly held beliefs, the religious cleavage is still alive in Germany and most other West European countries. It manifests itself not only in conflicts over crucifixes or prayer in schools, but also in issues on sexual morality, family life, and the like. On a more abstract level, these issues affect the moral standards in Christian religion, the relationship between religion and politics, and the limits of religious freedom and religious pluralism. In the long run, other topics such as the privileges enjoyed by the dominant Christian churches may come under attack.

Because other historical cleavages do not play any role in the subsequent analysis, we do not need to comment on the respective rows in Table 7.1. The so-called new value conflicts are more interesting because they are believed to change the meaning of left and right. Emancipation, postmaterialism, individualism, or postmodernism could contribute to a new understanding of left and right. However, apart from postmaterialism, there do not exist any established operationalizations, and the distinction between specific and general issues has not been carefully elaborated. Although we provide some examples in Table 7.1, our data set does not include suitable measurement instruments. We only introduce a surrogate measure for postmaterialism. Thus, a systematic treatment of the so-called new values conflicts in this framework has to be postponed (but see Markus Klein in chapter 8 for a different treatment of postmaterialism).

Selecting the Relevant Groups

To subject the stable meaning hypothesis to a stringent test, it is important to select groups that can be expected to assign different meanings to left and right. While *workers* and *employers in the productive sector* may define left and right by means of economic interest groups and issues, *highly integrated church members* may use religious issues for the same purpose. In the *younger generations*, particularly in the highly educated segments, left and right may be less determined by attitudes toward economic security and equality but by attitudes toward environmental issues, emancipation, and lifestyle issues. *Employees in the tertiary sector*, and in particular public servants, may be more similar to younger generations than to the workers. Thus, it is easy to find a large number of groups

Table 7.1. Possible Interpretations of Left and Right

Domains	Social Groups	Organizations, Movements	Specific Issues	General Issues/Values
Political Parties		Left: Communists, Socialists Right: Conservatives, Nationalists		
		Historical Cleavages		
Industrial Conflict	Left: Workers, Employees versus Right: Employers, Managers	Left: Unions versus Right: Employer organizations	Working conditions, Wages, Privatization, Strikes and lockouts, Income taxes, Welfare expenditures	Welfare state versus liberal market economy, Equality versus freedom, Capitalism versus communism
Religious Conflict	L?: Secular Groups versus R?: Religious Groups	L?: Freemasons and other secular organizations versus R?: Churches	Sexual morality, Abortion, Divorce, Religious education	Religious versus humanistic-scientific meaning system, State and religion, Religious freedom
Center Periphery Conflict	L?: Minority Groups versus R?: Dominant Groups	L?: Minority organizations versus R? ?	Education, Linguistic and ethnic issues, Political representation	Meaning of Equality, Range of the subsidiarity principle, Cultural pluralism, (national) unity versus autonomy
Urban Rural Conflicts	L?: Urban Elites versus R?: Peasants	L?: ? versus R?: Peasant orgs.	Land ownership, Taxes, State subsidies	Equality, Exploitation of the peasants, Role of agriculture in modern societies

Other Enduring Conflicts

Nationalism, Ethnocentrism

L?:	High Education versus	Peace movement versus	Asylum, Immigration, Political participation	Parochialism versus universalism, Human rights and legitimate national interests
R?:	Low Education	Right-wing orgs.		

Order and Freedom

L?:	Young, highly educated generations	? versus	National defense, Prevention of crime, Economic and internal security	Security versus freedom, Materialism vs. postmaterialism(?), Order and freedom
R?:	vs. Older gens.	Old hierarchical organizations		

Environmental Protection

L?:	Young, highly educated generations	Environ. orgs. versus	Speed limit, Air pollution, Nuclear energy, Environmental laws	Economic growth versus environmental concerns, Nature versus technical progress, Limits of freedom
R?:	vs. Older gens.	Old hierarchical organizations		

Emancipation

L?:	Women versus	Women's orgs. versus	Female work participation, Political participation, Family laws	Relationship between genders, Interpretation of equality, Self-determination
R?:	Men	?		

Other cultural Conflicts

L?:	Young, highly educ. generations versus	Cultural avant-garde vs.	Homosexual couples, Other lifestyle issues	Individualism, Autonomy, Self-determination
R?:	Older generations	Cultural establishment		

that can be expected to differ in their implicit and explicit understanding of left and right.

As long as we try to infer the meaning of left and right from the positions of the parties on the left-right continuum, each of these groups can be analyzed separately. However, if we can only make use of the left-right self-placement scale, we have to take the problem of homogeneity into account: We are likely to find little variation in some groups with regard to the left-right position of the group members. In order to increase the variance, we create new groups. For instance, the combination of *highly integrated church members and unaffiliated persons* has a sufficiently large variance both on the dependent left-right self-placement scale and the religious issues. Similarly, we create a contrast group of *young and highly educated individuals and older generations*. One shortcoming of this strategy could be that we produce artificial relationships. We will return to this topic later.

ANALYSIS

We have outlined two broad research questions. Above all, we seek to decompose the contribution of the various ideological subcomponents to the meaning of left and right. The meaning can be determined by the issues and values of the industrial and/or religious conflict and/or by other permanent conflicts as well. In the first section, we focus on the *left-right self-placement scale* and begin with the bivariate relationship between this scale and various issues and values. Subsequently, we calculate partial correlation coefficients in order to estimate the contribution of each issue or value when all other ideological sub-components are held constant. In a third step, we also control for the party-defined group component that can be expected to reduce the influence of ideology on left and right considerably (see Jagodzinski and Kühnel 1994). Given that we are interested in group comparisons, we repeat the analysis for the social groups mentioned before. Finally, we estimate the relative weights of the ideological and the party-defined group components.

As mentioned above, self-placement scales severely restrict the possibilities of group comparisons because the members of the groups that are theoretically most interesting tend to be rather homogeneous in their left-right and issue positions. This is the major reason why we extend and improve the original design of Jagodzinski and Kühnel (1994) in the second part and use the *perceived party positions on the left-right continuum* as dependent variables. This requires a transformation of the original data set. The steps of the analysis are essentially the same as in part 1. In a first step we first investigate the influence of issues and values regarding the meaning of left and right. Then we include a group component. This time around, however, we do not use the party-defined meaning of left and right but the left-right assignment on the basis of interest groups.[9]

THE IMPLICIT SOCIAL MEANING OF LEFT-RIGHT
SELF-PLACEMENT SCALES: 1976

Even though the election study 1976 still is the best German database for analyzing the various components of left and right, the list of issues covers only a small part of the topics mentioned in Table 7.1. The study includes two general issues of the industrial cleavage. Both are measured by 11-point scales. The first addresses the conflict between entrepreneurial freedom (coded 1) and *governmental control* (coded 11), the second one the conflict between private initiative (coded 1) and the *welfare state* (coded 11). The study includes another 11-point scale on one of the persistent issues of the religious cleavage. It concerns the *influence of the churches* in politics; respondents could choose between the alternatives "the churches should have a say in politics" (coded 1) and "the churches should completely keep out of politics" (coded 11).

Since other historical cleavages do not play a major role in the German party system (Pappi 1977, 1985), the lack of additional cleavage issues does not create any serious problem for our analysis. Other deficits are more disturbing. We have a position issue on the conflict between order (coded 1) and freedom (coded 11) that is related to materialism/postmaterialism (MPM). However, it is not an established measure of this general orientation. As a surrogate for the latter, we will use an index (MPM-surrogate in Table 7.2) that was constructed from three valence issues "stable prices," "maintaining order," and "more say in governmental decisions" (see Jagodzinski and Kühnel 1994 for details). Thus, we will call it an MPM-surrogate but it can be better described as a measure for the conflict between materialism and political participation. Given that we could not balance the materialistic and postmaterialist priorities, the correlation of about 0.5 with the original MPM 4-point scale[10] is remarkably good. While we have a second-best solution in the case of postmaterialism, we do not have any indicator for environmentalism, emancipation, and–above all–nationalism and ethnocentrism in the 1976 data set. Thus, the meaning of left and right can only be partly determined.

The five indicators of the ideological component that have been measured are shown in Table 7.2. In each row we report the simple correlation (r_1) and the partial correlations (r_2, r_3) of an 11-point left-right self-placement scale with these variables. The results in Table 7.2 are almost identical with those reported in Jagodzinski and Kühnel (1994). We have marginally improved some of the operationalizations,[11] and we have consistently replaced of R^2s and R^2-changes by correlation coefficients.

When we look at the bivariate correlations for the total sample (first row)–one variable of the industrial conflict (*governmental control*), *church influence,* and the surrogate variable for *postmaterialism*–we find that these variables have a considerable impact on the meaning of left and right. The correlations between -0.28 and -0.36 are all in the expected direction: people who have a relative preference for governmental control, who reject the influence of the church in politics, and who have postmaterialist priorities tend to place themselves to the left side of the scale. The impact of order/freedom is somewhat weaker but still close

Table 7.2. The Ideological Components of Left and Right: Self-Placement Scale (West German Election Study 1976)

	Economic Cleavage		Religious Cleavage	Other Conflicts	
	Governmental Control	Welfare State	Church Influence	Order vs. Freedom	MPM-Surrogate
Total Sample					
r_1 (n = 1,745)	- 0.360*	- 0.080*	- 0.330*	- 0.188*	- 0.287*
r_2 (n = 1,745)	- 0.260*	0.075*	- 0.228*	- 0.074*	- 0.197*
r_3 (n = 1,718)	- 0.138*	0.060*	- 0.108*	- 0.099*	- 0.139*
High Political Interest					
r_1 (n = 141)	- 0.633*	- 0.370*	- 0.355*	- 0.356*	- 0.454*
r_2 (n = 141)	- 0.445*	- 0.026	- 0.125	- 0.050	- 0.250*
r_3 (n = 135)	- 0.261*	- 0.071	- 0.023	- 0.005	- 0.184*
Low Political Interest					
r_1 (n = 243)	- 0.303*	0.095	- 0.403*	- 0.189*	- 0.098
r_2 (n = 243)	- 0.293*	0.231*	- 0.344*	- 0.121	0.019
r_3 (n = 238)	- 0.130*	0.180*	- 0.214*	- 0.157*	- 0.003
Industrial Sector					
r_1 (n = 615)	- 0.322*	- 0.065	- 0.327*	- 0.051	- 0.163*
r_2 (n = 615)	- 0.225*	0.023	- 0.232*	0.038	- 0.102*
r_3 (n = 605)	- 0.126*	0.015	- 0.086*	- 0.026	- 0.071
Service Sector					
r_1 (n = 841)	- 0.329*	- 0.042	- 0.274*	- 0.227*	- 0.306*
r_2 (n = 841)	- 0.271*	0.131*	- 0.194*	- 0.120*	- 0.220*
r_3 (n = 837)	- 0.129*	0.099*	- 0.088*	0.132*	- 0.145*
Religious vs. Nonreligious					
r_1 (n = 760)	- 0.403*	- 0.124*	- 0.424*	- 0.233*	- 0.362*
r_2 (n = 760)	- 0.253*	0.053	- 0.304*	- 0.082*	- 0.241*
r_3 (n = 743)	- 0.154*	0.039	- 0.174*	- 0.150*	- 0.168*
Young Educated vs. Old					
r_1 (n = 511)	- 0.532*	- 0.241*	- 0.490*	- 0.305*	- 0.433*
r_2 (n = 511)	- 0.356*	- 0.017	- 0.344*	- 0.092*	- 0.222*
r_3 (n = 498)	- 0.214*	- 0.032	- 0.252*	- 0.089*	- 0.168*

Notes: r_1 Simple correlations; r_2 Partial correlations controlled for other issues; r_3 Partial correlations controlled for other issues and party components. *$p < 0.05$

to -0.2: a left-wing position indicates a preference of freedom before order. The welfare state has the smallest effect on the left-right self-placement, presumably because it has been highly accepted among voters. Protagonists of the welfare state are only slightly more left-wing than the rest of the population.

The bivariate correlations in the first row do not control for the influence of the other variables. When these influences are controlled, the correlation coefficients shrink considerably. However, the rank order remains stable: *governmental control* still is highest in magnitude, followed by *church influence* and *postmaterialism*. The partial correlation coefficient of *order versus freedom* has shrunk to -0.075. *Welfare state* now changes its sign and becomes positive–that is, when we look at the influence of welfare state mentality independently of all other ideological orientations, we find that it is associated with a rightist position. Because the German welfare state was rooted in the authoritarian empire, this relationship is not surprising at all. On balance, even in the total sample the implicit social meaning of left and right is by no means determined by the issues of the industrial conflict alone. The religious issue as well as the conflict between materialism and political participation and between freedom and order shape the implicit meaning of the left-right continuum.

Do we observe the same pattern in all social groups? To answer the question, we divided the total population into several subgroups. First, we distinguished between individuals with a very high interest in politics (second row of Table 7.2) and individuals with a very low interest in politics (third row). Apart from *church influence*, the ideological items have a much greater influence on the meaning of left and right in the high than in the low interest group. And while the meaning among the high interest group is mostly determined by the ideology of the industrial cleavage and of *postmaterialism*, it appears to be predominantly influenced by the religious issue in the low interest group.

The pattern becomes even more pronounced when we control for the influence of the other ideological items. Now, only the coefficients for *governmental control* (-0.45) and *postmaterialism* remain significant in the high interest group (-0.25); all other coefficients fall below the 5 percent confidence interval. In contrast, attitudes toward the welfare state gain in strength among the low interest group (+0.23), and correlations of the economic and the religious issue become more similar.

According to these results, the pattern in the high interest group comes closest to the assumption that the implicit meaning of the left-right continuum is almost exclusively shaped by the value conceptions of the industrial conflict. However, it is less the question of the welfare state but that of governmental control of the economy that divides left and right. Even among individuals with high levels of political interest, the conflict between materialism and participation contributes to the implicit understanding of the ideological dimension. In contrast, religious orientations are even more important than economic issues in the low interest group. Thus the empirical evidence is hardly compatible with our stable meaning hypothesis. Moreover, the content of the left-right continuum is not predominantly determined by economic issues or left-right materialism, nor is the implicit social meaning the same among groups with high or low political interest.

It has been argued in the tradition of Max Weber that values as well as rationality differ between the industrial and the service sectors. Although the service sector–that is, workers and employers-is strongly affected by the economic development, an economic-rational orientation predominates. Cultural values and fundamentalist orientations should be more widespread in the service sector, particularly in the public sector in Germany where job security is high. To test these assumptions, we distinguish between two groups. Employers, self-employed persons, skilled and unskilled workers were assigned to the industrial sector; self-employed, white-collar workers, and public servants to the service sectors.

The results shown in the fourth and fifth rows of Table 7.2 partly confirm our expectations. On one hand, we do not observe particularly high correlations between economic issues and the left-right self-placement scale in the industrial sector. The meaning is determined to more or less the same extent by religious and industrial issues and values. On the other hand, the cultural variables *order versus freedom* and the *MPM-surrogate* influence the meaning of left and right only in the service sector.

The remaining two subgroups may appear unusual because both were constructed from two very heterogeneous subgroups. In the first instance, we combined religiously unaffiliated individuals and nuclear church members;[12] in the second one, we combined individuals above age 65 and highly educated persons below age 31. In each case we have tried to produce a group with sufficiently large variance on the self-placement scale and on one of the ideological variables–that is, on the religious issue in the first instance and on the MPM-surrogate in the second.

One may object that the procedure is biased against industrial conflict because we did not try to increase the variance of the economic orientations at the same time. However, when we look at the results in the last two rows of Table 7.2, we find that *governmental control* is always among the best determinants. It is particularly strong in the last contrast group where the bivariate correlation is below -.50 and the partial correlation is below -.35. Aside from this, the patterns in the last two rows are very similar: The meaning of left and right mainly is determined by the issues of the economic and religious conflicts, and to a lesser degree by the conflict between *materialism and participation (MPM-surrogate)* and *freedom versus order.*

So far we have not examined the third entry of each row of Table 7.2–that is, the second partial correlation coefficient that eliminates the effect of the partisan component. If we do not account for this component, we may heavily overestimate the impact of ideology. Taken to an extreme, people may be able to define their own position on the left-right scale without any reference to issues and values. To control for the partisan component, Huber (1989) has suggested to regress the left-right self-placement scale not only on the relevant issues but also on a set of as many dummy variables as there are parties. The numerical value 1 is assigned to the dummy variable for party X if the respondent identifies her/himself with party X, and the numerical value 0 otherwise. As Jagodzinski and Kühnel (1994) have shown, this procedure only leads to optimal results if all identifiers of party X locate this party at the same point on the left-right continuum. The more they deviate in their views, the less effect the party dummy variable has. To correct for this effect, we suggested that the dummy variable be multiplied by the perceived position of party X on the left-right scale. The party component for West Germany is then computed in this equation:

$$\text{Party Component} = \beta_1(P^{GREENS} \bullet LR^{GREENS} + P^{SPD} \bullet LR^{SPD} + P^{FDP} \bullet LR^{FDP} + P^{CDU} \bullet LR^{CDU} + P^{CSU} \bullet LR^{CSU}) + \beta_2 P^{NON}$$

P^X is a dummy variable for the identification with party X, LR^X is the position on the left-right scale the respondent assigns to party X, and P^{NON} is the dummy variable for respondents without party identification. The weights β_i are estimated. The influence of the partisan component on the left-right scale is considerably strengthened as a consequence of these modifications (see Jagodzinski and Kühnel 1994: 344). For the purposes of this chapter, we operationalized the partisan component in the same way with one exception: a respondent is also considered an identifier if he or she intends to vote for the same party in the present election as in the last election.

Our operationalization of the partisan component explains more than 50% of the variation in the left-right self-placement scale. Therefore, it is not surprising that the partial correlation coefficient between the left-right self-placement scale and an issue or value position declines considerably if we control not only for other issues but also for the partisan component. Aside from the decreased magnitude, however, the structure of the partial correlations remains very stable. In the total sample, *governmental control, church influence,* and the *MPM-surrogate* were the main determinants of the left-right meaning. Only these three partial correlations (in the last row) are above 0.1 in magnitude.

In row 2 (high political interest) only the correlations of *governmental control* and the *MPM-surrogate* remain significant. We can say that the determinants with the strongest bivariate correlations thus usually remain significant even after we control for the partisan component. The *welfare state* issue is exceptional in two respects. First, in some cases the partial correlations become significant while the bivariate correlations are not (service sector and low political interest). Furthermore, in several cases the partial correlations have positive signs while the bivariate correlations have negative ones. In 1976, the welfare state was not only widely accepted in general–it was even slightly more accepted in the conservative groups. However, this becomes obvious only once we control for the influences of all other components.

We may gain the impression from the partial correlations r_3 in Table 7.2 that ideology plays only a minor role in determining the meaning of left and right. However, we would like to point out that the ideological component so far was divided in many subcomponents. In order to estimate the entire influence of the ideology, we computed a linear combination of all ideological variables–that is, the variables in the header of Table 7.2 (the *ideological component*).[13] The *partisan component* is defined in the equation. In the left part of each column in Table 7.3,

Table 7.3. The Ideological and Partisan Components of Left and Right: Self-placement Scale (West German Election Study 1976 and 1990)

	Ideological Component		Partisan Component		Multiple Correlation Coefficient	
Year	1976	1990	1976	1990	1976	1990
Total Sample						
r	0.478	0.490	0.722	0.748	0.750	0.764
$r_{part.}$	0.291	0.230	0.671	0.676		
High Political Interest						
r	0.679	0.749	0.794	0.757	0.835	0.814
$r_{part.}$	0.428	0.305	0.710	0.553		
Low Political Interest						
r	0.511	0.438	0.730	0.675	0.767	0.748
$r_{part.}$	0.342	0.442	0.675	0.692		
Industrial Sector						
r	0.407	0.454	0.730	0.747	0.744	0.760
$r_{part.}$	0.211	0.181	0.687	0.688		
Service Sector						
r	0.474	0.494	0.732	0.771	0.758	0.784
$r_{part.}$	0.291	0.228	0.681	0.713		
Religious vs. Non-religious						
r	0.559		0.736		0.784	
$r_{part.}$	0.403		0.640			
Young Educated vs. Old						
r	0.661	0.551	0.786	0.754	0.838	0.777
$r_{part.}$	0.469	0.269	0.708	0.662		

Note: All coefficients are significant at the 5% level.

we report the magnitude of the simple (first entry) and the partial correlations of the two components with the left-right self-placement scale in 1976.[14]

We should not be surprised that the partisan component always performs better. In causal terms, we would argue that issues and values almost certainly have also an indirect impact via the partisan component. The bivariate correlation between the left-right self-placement scale and the partisan component is always is above 0.7. The bivariate correlations of the ideological component come close to 0.7 only in the high political interest group and in the last contrast group. Even though the influence of the ideological component of the meaning of left and right is weaker, it is still remarkable. In the first column of Table 7.3, the partial correlation coefficients vary between 0.21 in the industrial sector and roughly 0.47 in the contrast group of *young and educated versus old*. The coefficient for persons with high political interest is almost 0.43.

Although the influence of the ideological component varies between groups, it contributes to the meaning within each groups. As the earlier decomposition has shown, the issues of the industrial cleavage, and surprisingly also the ones of the religious cleavage, determine the implicit social meaning of left and right. The conflict between materialism and participation (MPM-surrogate) has an influence on some groups but not on all. Given that it is particularly strong in the last contrast group, this might be a result of our variance maximizing strategy. We examine this possibility below.

THE IMPLICIT SOCIAL MEANING OF LEFT-RIGHT SELF-PLACEMENT SCALES: 1990

Do the relationships we found in 1976 still exist in the 1990s? Unfortunately, we cannot provide a complete answer to this question because the 1976 election study was never replicated. The only German election study that includes left-right scales for parties and respondents and a large number of position issues was conducted by Kaltefleiter for the 1990 election. Although the study did not make any direct attempt to measure the issues and values of the industrial conflict, a number of items can be related to a socialist or liberal ideology.

The 7-point scale concerning the reform of income taxes we use here is a crude measure because it does not really indicate the conflicting positions on the industrial cleavage. "Tax reductions for all" and "higher taxes for the high incomes and lower taxes for the low incomes" were the poles of the continuum. The two other 4-point-scales are from the German portion of the General Social Survey (ALLBUS) and can be related to the ideology of a liberal market economy. A first statement, with which the respondent could either agree or disagree,[15] stresses the positive function of profits. The respondents were also asked to agree or disagree with a second statement concerning the fairest distribution of profits in the Federal Republic. Since the liberalization of abortion[16] is only partly related to the religious conflict, we use church attendance as an indirect indicator of religiosity. One advantage of the election study 1990 is its inclusion of indicators of national pride,[17] free asylum,[18] and national strength,[19] which allows an estimation of the impact of nationalism and ethnocentrism.[20] Finally, materialistic orientations may partly be measured by the issue of disarmament,[21] and attitudes toward environmental affairs by the issue of nuclear energy.[22] The study included two other items on materialism and environmental issues that have no significant influence on the left-right meaning. Since we do not have any indicator for emancipation and postmaterialism, we were not even able to construct a surrogate measure.

As far as the groups are concerned, the election study 1990 measures political interest differently than the 1976 study. To obtain a roughly comparable distribution with the earlier survey, we combined *education* with this alternative measure. Furthermore, the distinction between the industrial sector and the service sector could not be perfectly replicated. Thus, the social groups in 1976 and 1990 are also somewhat dissimilar. Given these caveats, it is more than astonishing that the patterns of the correlation coefficients correspond closely. The ideological and the partisan component for the right part of each column in Table 7.3–that is, for the year 1990–were calculated in the same way as before. As the third column shows, both components determine the meaning of left and right to a very large extent (the multiple correlations are always above 0.7).

On average, ideology seems to have had a slightly stronger impact in 1976 than in 1990, even though the latter survey includes more issues and value indicators. The bivariate correlations between the ideological component and the left-right self-placement scale are of similar magnitude but the control for the party component reduces these coefficients in 1990 to a greater extent than was the case in the earlier study.[23]

The ideological component is further decomposed in Table 7.4. This time we do not report correlations for each indicator,[24] but for all indicators of a given cleavage or value conflict.[25] In general, the issues of the two historical cleavages seem to have less influence in 1990 because the correlations are smaller. This is not indicative of a decline in ideological thinking. It is presumably because some central and general issues were used in 1976, while the issues are more strongly related to the actual political debate in the country in the 1990 study. We partly compensated for these deficiencies by using more indicators per cleavage/conflict.

When we look at the partial coefficients,[26] the issues of the industrial cleavage in most cases maintain their predominant position. After controlling for the other ideological components, the correlation with the left-right self-placement scale is among the highest not only in the total sample, but also in the service sector and in the contrast group *young and highly educated versus old*. These results are similar to those shown in Table 7.2. It is remarkable that the new issue, measured by the issue of nuclear energy, has a similarly strong influence in the latter group and in the service sector.

The high political interest group is the one that deviates the most from the former pattern. Here, national issues become the major determinant of left-right meaning (-0.40) in 1990. It is even stronger than the economic issues (-0.35). Because we do not have a comparable economic item for 1990, and no comparable nationalism items for 1976, we unfortunately cannot determine whether this was unique for the unification period. In all other groups the influence of nationalism is much weaker. As far as the so-called new conflicts are concerned, they have only a moderate impact in the high political interest group if we consider *military strength and disarmament* as a new issue.

Finally turning to the partial correlation r_3, Table 7.4 does not offer much of a surprise. In general, the inclusion of the partisan component lowers the correlation coefficients. However, the economic issues have a significant influence on the meaning of left-right in almost all groups. Though the effects of the religious cleavage are less consistent than in Table 7.2, we would not like to draw far-reaching conclusions from these results. It may simply be a problem of sufficiently reliable indicators. As expected, environmental issues have an influence on the meaning of left-right in the contrast group *young and highly educated versus old* and in the service sector.

Table 7.4. The Ideological Components of Left and Right: Self-Placement Scale (West German Election Study 1990)

	Economic Cleavage	Religious Cleavage	Other Conflicts		
			Nationalism	Materialism	Environment
Total Sample					
r_1 (n = 1,307)	- 0.326*	- 0.278*	- 0.339*	- 0.336*	- 0.300*
r_2 (n = 1,307)	- 0.189*	- 0.154*	- 0.122*	- 0.190*	- 0.110*
r_3 (n = 1,293)	- 0.098*	- 0.079*	- 0.035*	- 0.086*	- 0.059*
High Political Interest					
r_1 (n = 82)	- 0.597*	- 0.071	- 0.630*	- 0.611*	- 0.533*
r_2 (n = 82)	- 0.348*	- 0.066	- 0.404	- 0.205	- 0.010
r_3 (n = 80)	- 0.256*	- 0.171*	- 0.329*	- 0.141	- 0.089
Low Political Interest					
r_1 (n = 98)	- 0.206*	0.309*	- 0.264*	- 0.227*	- 0.158
r_2 (n = 98)	- 0.199*	0.255*	- 0.161	- 0.131	- 0.041
r_3 (n = 97)	- 0.242*	0.147	- 0.204	- 0.237*	0.074
Industrial Sector					
r_1 (n = 484)	- 0.287*	- 0.276*	- 0.257*	- 0.266*	- 0.227*
r_2 (n = 484)	- 0.192*	0.208*	- 0.157*	0.165*	- 0.075
r_3 (n = 478)	- 0.105*	0.106*	- 0.071	- 0.047	- 0.007
Service Sector					
r_1 (n = 622)	- 0.343*	- 0.255*	- 0.358*	- 0.341*	- 0.322*
r_2 (n = 622)	- 0.192*	0.093*	- 0.152*	- 0.172*	- 0.129*
r_3 (n = 616)	- 0.115*	0.034*	- 0.047	0.073	- 0.098*
Young Educated vs. Old					
r_1 (n = 482)	- 0.363*	- 0.348*	- 0.186*	- 0.349*	- 0.411*
r_2 (n = 482)	- 0.216*	- 0.182*	- 0.065	- 0.141*	- 0.219*
r_3 (n = 478)	- 0.113*	- 0.104*	- 0.098*	- 0.057	- 0.103*

Notes: r_1 Simple correlations; r_2 Partial correlations controlled for other issues; r_3 Partial correlations controlled for other issues and party components. *$p < 0.05$

DERIVING THE IMPLICIT SOCIAL MEANING FROM THE PERCEIVED POSITIONS OF PARTIES ON THE LEFT-RIGHT SCALES

The surveys under consideration not only include self-placement scales but also left-right scales for each party. Respondents were asked to indicate the position of the major parties on this scale as well as their position on various issues. This offers an alternative way of analyzing the meaning of left and right. We simply examine to what extent the positions of the parties on the left-right scale are determined by their positions on the other scales. By doing so, individual differences in the assignment of positions can be eliminated much more easily than in the former analyses. This design has a second advantage: we do not need to worry about the variances in subgroups and are able to investigate the meaning components in whatever subgroup we like.

We first define a new unit of analysis. It is no longer the respondent but the party per respondent. The more parties that were located on the left-right scale by the respondent, the more cases per respondents or the more units of analysis we can analyze. In the election study 1976, respondents were asked to locate only the SPD (Social Democratic Party), FDP (Free Democratic Party), CDU (Christian Democratic Union), and CSU (Christian Social Union) on the scales; in the 1990 election study the Greens were included as well.[27] Thus we can use four cases per respondent in 1976 and five per case in 1990.

For our analysis, we follow a strategy that allows us not only to correct for differences in scale means but also for differences in the variances. Some individuals may use the whole range of the 11-point scale to locate parties while placing all parties close to the middle category. These idiosyncrasies can be eliminated by standardizing the scale positions of the party separately for each individual. We calculate partial correlation coefficients for n x 4 and n x 5 units of analysis, respectively. Since we did not correct for the reduced number of the degrees of freedom so far, we do not report significance levels. However, regarding the large number of cases, almost all of our correlation coefficients are significant.

THE 1976 ELECTION STUDY

When analyzing the positions of parties we cannot control for a partisan component. However, the 1976 election study permits us to control for a group component. Respondents were asked which party does most for the workers, the pensioners, the self-employed, the Catholics, the Protestants, and so on. From these items we constructed several variables that assign parties to cleavage groups. The variables *workers versus employers*, *underprivileged groups*, and *privileged groups* all belong to the economic cleavage.[28] Assuming that the transformation of a formerly denominational cleavage into a religious cleavage still has not come to an end in Germany, we constructed two variables for the religious cleavage. The first one, *Protestants versus Catholics,* considers Protestants and Catholics as opposing groups.[29] By contrast, the indicator for the *religious cleavage* group is based on the assumption that the members of both churches gradually come into opposition to an increasingly large secular group.[30] Finally, we distinguished between parties that support the interests of rural residents (*rural*=1) and others (*rural*=0). The combination of these variables is used as group component in the subsequent analysis.

In Table 7.5 we report the correlation coefficients for this analysis. Compared to Table 7.2, two features of the new table have changed. First, we cannot order parties on one of the so-called new conflict dimensions given that neither the *MPM-surrogate* nor any other suitable indicator is available. We only can use the conflict *order versus freedom*. Second, we can drop the contrast groups and analyze *older citizens, young and highly educated citizens, highly integrated church members*, and *unaffiliated persons* separately. When we inspect the bivariate correlation coefficients, it turns out that they usually are much higher than in Table 7.2.

When we move from the bivariate over the first partial to the second partial correlation, a simple structure emerges. In almost all groups, the meaning of left and right is shaped by only two out of four issues: *governmental control* and *church influence in politics*. Sometimes the issue of the economic cleavage has a somewhat stronger influence (*high political interest, church unaffiliated*) but usually both coefficients are of similar magnitude. The results also show that nuclear church members and the unaffiliated are in fact very different from each other. While the former at least implicitly make use of the religious conflict dimension in order to locate parties on the left-right continuum, the religious conflict is of much less relevance to the second group. The two subgroups of the other contrast are more similar to each other.

In Table 7.6 we decomposed the interest group component in the same way as the ideological component in Table 7.5. While it is not necessary to go into many details, two results are worth mentioning. According to the bivariate correlations, four pairs of conflicting groups are particularly relevant: *workers and employers* (first column), *underprivileged and privileged groups* (second and third columns), *Protestants and Catholics* (fourth column), and *secular and religious groups* (fifth column). When the effects of the other group variables and of the ideological component are controlled for, only the two indicators for the religious/denominational cleavage display substantial correlations. We draw two tentative conclusions from this. First, it provides further evidence for the continuation of the religious cleavage. It not only exists in issues and value conflicts, but also can be found on the level of group thinking. Second, even the older denominational cleavage still seems to retain a moderate impact on the ideological thinking of individuals.

THE 1990 ELECTION STUDY

Because the election study 1990 does not allow us to isolate a group component, comparisons between the elections 1976 and 1990 are even more difficult than in

Table 7.5. The Ideological Components of Left and Right: Perceived Party Positions (West German Election Study 1976)

| | Economic Cleavage | | Religious Cleavage | Other Conflicts |
	Governmental Control	Welfare State	Church Influence	Order vs. Freedom
Total Sample				
r_1 (n = 7,164)	- 0.673	- 0.345	- 0.705	- 0.341
r_2 (n = 7,164)	- 0.379	0.025	- 0.451	- 0.082
r_3 (n = 7,164)	- 0.282	0.011	- 0.262	- 0.063
High Political Interest				
r_1 (n = 577)	- 0.780	- 0.569	- 0.776	- 0.422
r_2 (n = 577)	- 0.468	- 0.172	- 0.472	- 0.101
r_3 (n = 577)	- 0.342	- 0.140	- 0.283	- 0.088
Low Political Interest				
r_1 (n = 956)	- 0.573	- 0.078	- 0.667	- 0.227
r_2 (n = 956)	- 0.272	0.090	- 0.472	- 0.012
r_3 (n = 956)	- 0.192	0.075	- 0.234	- 0.006
Industrial Sector				
r_1 (n = 2,552)	- 0.632	- 0.277	- 0.664	- 0.267
r_2 (n = 2,552)	- 0.354	- 0.008	- 0.429	- 0.028
r_3 (n = 2,552)	- 0.262	0.005	- 0.247	- 0.009
Service Sector				
r_1 (n = 3,431)	- 0.679	- 0.384	- 0.726	- 0.364
r_2 (n = 3,431)	- 0.374	- 0.019	- 0.476	- 0.110
r_3 (n = 3,431)	- 0.261	0.012	- 0.267	- 0.096
Young Highly Educated				
r_1 (n = 892)	- 0.713	- 0.509	- 0.743	- 0.527
r_2 (n = 892)	- 0.406	- 0.044	- 0.425	- 0.198
r_3 (n = 892)	- 0.291	- 0.017	- 0.243	- 0.133
Age Above 65				
r_1 (n = 1,225)	- 0.704	- 0.352	- 0.720	- 0.340
r_2 (n = 1,225)	- 0.412	- 0.089	- 0.461	- 0.092
r_3 (n = 1,225)	- 0.325	- 0.061	- 0.230	- 0.083
High Church Integration				
r_1 (n = 1,478)	- 0.670	- 0.129	- 0.735	- 0.228
r_2 (n = 1,478)	- 0.415	0.004	- 0.549	- 0.038
r_3 (n = 1,478)	- 0.303	0.001	- 0.370	- 0.006
Church Unaffiliated				
r_1 (n = 1,638)	- 0.676	- 0.467	- 0.703	- 0.449
r_2 (n = 1,638)	- 0.350	- 0.042	- 0.391	- 0.114
r_3 (n = 1,638)	- 0.268	0.001	- 0.194	- 0.074

Notes: r_1 Simple correlations; r_2 Partial correlations controlled for other issues; r_3 Partial correlations controlled for other issues and party components.

Table 7.6. The Group Components of Left and Right: Perceived Party Positions (West German Election Study 1976)

	Industrial Cleavage			Religious Cleavage		Urban/ Rural Cleavage
	Workers vs. Employers	Under-privileged Groups (Workers and Pensioners)	Privileged Groups (Civil Servants and Entrepreneurs)	Protestants vs. Catholics	Interest of One or Both Churches)	Interests of Peasants
Total Sample (n=7,164)						
r_1	0.624	- 0.290	0.520	0.528	0.495	0.348
r_2	0.079	- 0.040	0.060	0.182	0.206	0.098
High Political Interest (n=577)						
r_1	0.730	- 0.334	0.554	0.638	0.538	0.271
r_2	0.105	- 0.044	0.163	0.199	0.260	0.072
Low Political Interest (n=956)						
r_1	0.598	- 0.200	0.566	0.470	0.492	0.334
r_2	0.114	- 0.020	0.080	0.180	0.194	0.136
Industrial Sector (n=2,552)						
r_1	0.596	- 0.255	0.505	0.509	0.468	0.302
r_2	0.099	- 0.011	0.047	0.190	0.211	0.038
Service Sector (n=3,431)						
r_1	0.664	- 0.332	0.544	0.549	0.514	0.371
r_2	0.081	- 0.094	0.077	0.183	0.209	0.121
Young Highly Educated (n=892)						
r_1	0.677	- 0.390	0.545	0.613	0.534	0.286
r_2	0.047	- 0.069	0.063	0.229	0.227	0.115
Age Above 65 (n=1,225)						
r_1	0.630	- 0.270	0.510	0.529	0.537	0.418
r_2	0.092	- 0.035	0.017	0.234	0.275	0.140
High Church Integration (n=1,478)						
r_1	0.512	- 0.037	0.588	0.475	0.567	0.449
r_2	0.075	- 0.020	0.045	0.201	0.220	0.110
Church Unaffiliated (n=1,638)						
r_1	0.665	- 0.423	0.486	0.589	0.497	0.293
r_2	0.052	- 0.063	0.040	0.222	0.224	0.195

Notes: r_1 Simple correlations; r_2 Partial correlations controlled for five other group components and four ideological components.

Table 7.7. The Ideological Components of Left and Right: Perceived Party Positions (West German Election Study 1990)

	Economic Cleavage	Religious Cleavage	Other Conflicts		Nationalism		Materialism		Environment
	Progressive Taxation	Liberalization of Abortion	Against Unification		Free Asylum	National Strength	Disarmament	Antiterrorist Laws Sufficient	No Nuclear Energy
Total Sample (n=6,717)									
r_1	- 0.357	- 0.653	- 0.633		- 0.515	0.392	- 0.638	- 0.514	- 0.734
r_2	- 0.079	- 0.210	- 0.229		- 0.083	0.039	- 0.151	- 0.066	- 0.303
High Political Interest (n=430)									
r_1	- 0.727	- 0.836	- 0.721		- 0.664	0.633	- 0.826	- 0.616	- 0.851
r_2	- 0.256	- 0.272	- 0.110		- 0.177	0.040	- 0.189	0.074	- 0.259
Low Political Interest (n=511)									
r_1	- 0.288	- 0.519	- 0.571		- 0.446	0.331	- 0.524	- 0.407	- 0.647
r_2	- 0.152	- 0.129	- 0.246		- 0.215	0.039	- 0.120	0.001	- 0.307
Industrial Sector (n=2,499)									
r_1	- 0.321	- 0.623	- 0.646		- 0.431	0.318	- 0.640	- 0.534	- 0.698
r_2	- 0.077	- 0.203	- 0.272		- 0.017	0.037	- 0.185	- 0.108	- 0.243

Service Sector (n=3,184)								
r_1	- 0.393	- 0.682	- 0.627	- 0.534	0.439	- 0.644	- 0.481	- 0.758
r_2	- 0.086	- 0.228	- 0.202	- 0.097	0.028	- 0.154	- 0.019	- 0.344
Young Highly Educated (n=1,004)								
r_1	- 0.317	- 0.669	- 0.584	- 0.635	0.523	- 0.694	- 0.523	- 0.775
r_2	- 0.039	- 0.146	- 0.108	- 0.161	0.132	- 0.114	- 0.076	- 0.340
Age Above 65 (n=1,517)								
r_1	- 0.308	- 0.648	- 0.651	- 0.520	0.386	- 0.663	- 0.541	- 0.760
r_2	- 0.074	- 0.154	- 0.262	- 0.097	0.008	- 0.189	- 0.0668	- 0.368
High Church Integration (n=1,828)								
r_1	- 0.357	- 0.661	- 0.633	- 0.497	0.319	- 0.598	- 0.564	- 0.756
r_2	- 0.079	- 0.225	- 0.242	- 0.078	0.019	- 0.130	- 0.105	- 0.356
Church Unaffiliated (n=1,423)								
r_1	- 0.365	- 0.681	- 0.672	- 0.587	- 0.384	- 0.669	- 0.519	- 0.732
r_2	- 0.078	- 0.232	- 0.238	- 0.131	0.007	- 0.160	- 0.063	- 0.241

Notes: r_1 Simple correlations; r_2 Partial correlations controlled for five other group components and four ideological components.

the case of self-placement scales. Even comparisons between the two analyses for 1990 would create problems because the positions of the parties depend on issues other than the left-right self-placement scale. The most important findings in Table 7.7 are as follows. Despite the fact that the economic indicator has low face validity, it correlates moderately with the perceived party positions among almost all groups. However, the influence of the religious indicator is much more significant. It has a substantial impact in all groups even when we control for the other ideological components.

SUMMARY AND CONCLUSION

In this chapter we tried to determine the sources of the implicit meaning of left and right with the help of survey data collected in the Federal Republic of Germany. Following Converse (1964, 1970) we distinguished between a group element and an ideological element in the left-right terminology. The former was further divided into a partisan component and an interest group component.[31] In our analyses of two German election studies conducted in 1976 and 1990, we showed that the partisan component consistently explains more than 50 percent of the variance in the left-right self-placement scales. This amounts to a multiple correlation of above 0.7. While the influence of issues and values–that is, the ideological component–is weaker, it is by no means irrelevant. Even if we control for the partisan component, ideology determines the meaning of left and right to a substantial degree.

There are differences between groups, and many of them are expected theoretically. If political interest is high, and if individuals are young and highly educated, the ideological component seems to be more influential than in other groups. The left-right meaning of young and highly educated persons or of individuals with an occupation in the service sector is affected by environmental issues, issues on political participation, or other so-called new value conflicts. However, these differences partially disappear when the partisan component is taken into account. While the influence of these new value conflicts appears variable from group to group, the influence of the two historical cleavages remains remarkably stable. This finding was not unexpected in the case of the economic cleavage. We did not anticipate, however, the constant impact of the religious cleavage. Although it is rarely associated with left and right in open-ended questions, religion obviously survives not only in issues on sexual morality and family life but also on the level of group thinking. Clearly, these are findings that apply to the German case and that may not be valid in other countries.

Overall, we find more stability than change in our analyses of the meaning of left and right in Germany. The two historical cleavages still have a strong and consistent impact on the meaning of left and right. The so-called new values did not alter the meaning of this dimension across the board. The question whether these values exhibit their relevance by establishing a new dimension of conflict that is unrelated to the ideological dimension of the traditional cleavages is investigated by Markus Klein in the next chapter.

Our analysis of the self-placement scales improved on existing designs. Moreover, our investigation of the perceived positions of parties tried to suggest a less well-known approach. Hopefully, the advantages of this procedure are transparent. In the end the question remains how these two strategies of analysis fit together. Do we really analyze the same meaning with both techniques? From a technical point of view the answer is a clear-cut "no." Given that the left-right variables are not the same, the meaning also cannot be the same. Or, to say it in less technical terms: If all citizens hold the same attitude toward the welfare state, this variable cannot explain the differences on the left-right self-placement scale. However, if the same citizens perceive large differences between the parties on the welfare state issue, we may be able to explain party differences on the left-right continuum. The determinants of the empirical meaning in the second case do not need to have an influence in the first. However, as long as the party positions largely reflect the issue distribution in the population, discrepancies like these will not occur. In our study both strategies of analysis in fact led to very similar conclusions.

NOTES

1. The American equivalent of a left-right scale.

2. The percentages vary across surveys (see Fuchs and Klingemann 1990). A more recent analysis by Wilamowitz-Moellendorff (1993) comes to the conclusion that the understanding of left and right has markedly increased between 1971 and 1991 in Germany.

3. By perceived values or perceived positions we understand properties which an observer attributes to another person or object. Clearly, the perceptions can be wrong–that is, perceived properties need not to coincide with the real properties of an object.

4. He could also place himself and other political actors on these scales.

5. Simultaneous causality is sometimes seen as an exception.

6. Please note that the partial correlation is a symmetric coefficient, that is, $r_{XY.UV...Z} = r_{YX.UV...Z}$. By contrast, the coefficient of determination does not need to be the same for pairs of variables in the system.

7. The religious cleavage has manyfold faces. In countries like France it has always been a conflict between Catholic and secular groups. In Germany, the conflict gradually transforms from a denominational conflict between Catholics and Protestants into a religious cleavage between religious and secular groups (see Pappi 1985; Schmitt 1985).

8. The German election study 1976 included an open question on the meaning of left and right. Clericalism and the Catholic church have almost never been associated with the label "right."

9. We use the German election study 1976 (ZA-No. 0823) by the Forschungsgruppe Wahlen and the German election study 1990 (ZA-No. 1959) which was carried out by W. Kaltefleiter. In the latter case we have restricted our

analysis to the West German sample.

10. In the election study 1983 of the Forschungsgruppe Wahlen the correlation is 0.48. This is slightly higher than the test-retest correlation of the postmaterialism index between the first and the third panel wave. The length between the waves was approximately six months.

11. In particular, we have improved the operationalization of party identification.

12. That is, individuals going to church almost every Sunday or more.

13. Each variable has been weighted by the unstandardized regression coefficient of a model where the left-right self-placement scale is regressed on all ideological variables and on the partisan component in the equation.

14. The partial correlation is that between the left-right self-placement scale and one of the components by controlling for the other component. The signs of the correlation coefficients have been omitted.

15. 1= strongly agree, 4= strongly disagree.

16. Abortion: 1=only if the health of the mother or the child is at risk, ..., 7=without restriction during the first three months.

17. I am proud to be a German in the unified Germany (1=strongly agree, ..., 7=strongly disagree).

18. The right of asylum should be 1= further restricted, ..., 7= left as it is.

19. German politics should 1=exercise restraint in international relations, ..., 7=act self-confidently.

20. We have to be conscious of the fact that the year 1990 was the first year after German unification, and that the influence of nationalism thus might have been inflated by a period effect.

21. 1=Peace by military strength, ..., 7=peace by one-sided prior concessions.

22. 1= Cautious use of nuclear energy, ..., 7=Immediate stop of nuclear energy production.

23. Since we used different indicators with reliabilities that are likely to differ, we should abstain from speculations about these differences.

24. The correlations for each indicator are reported in Appendix Table 7.A1.

25. Again each single variable is weighted by the unstandardized regression coefficient of a model in which the left-right self-placement scale is regressed on all ideological subcomponents (r_2) or on all ideological subcomponents and on the partisan component (r_3).

26. We have slightly simplified the calculation and have controlled for the linear combinations where several indicators for the same cleavage/value conflict have been used. However, if we had controlled for the indicators instead of the linear combination we would have obtained almost the same results.

27. We have dropped the PDS, which at that time had no clear profile for many West Germans.

28. The numerical value -1 is assigned to party X on the variable *workers versus employers* if the party is believed to support the workers, the numerical value 1 if X is believed to support the entrepreneurs, and 0 is assigned otherwise. Coding of *underprivileged groups:* 1=support of workers or pensioners, 2=support of both, 0=support none of these. *Privileged groups:* 1= support of public servants, self-

employed, or entrepreneurs, 2=support of two out of three, 3=support all three, 0=support none of these.

29. Coding: -1= support of Protestants, 1= support of Catholics, 0=neither.

30. Coding: 1=support for Protestants or for Catholics, 2= support for both, 0=no support.

31. When analyzing self-placement scales, the partisan component always should be taken into account. Otherwise, we are likely to heavily overestimate the influence of ideology.

8

A Postmaterialist Realignment? Value Change and Electoral Behavior in Unified Germany

Markus Klein

INTRODUCTION

The process of changing value orientations among mass publics appears to be one of the most important developments in modern societies. It produces changes in many facets of human behavior. Because of its importance, there has been and continues to be a lot of research concerning the causes and consequences of value change. One of the major realms of modern life in which changing values should have considerable consequences is the field of electoral behavior. In fact, it has been argued that the process of value change has produced a new cleavage that cuts across the old left-right cleavage (Dalton 1988; Kitschelt 1994, 1995). This new value cleavage deals primarily with postmaterialist issues concerning quality of life, environmental protection, and more rights for citizens to participate in politics. Following this perspective, the emergence of a new type of parties, the so-called Green alternative parties, seems to be one of the most important results of value change.

This chapter examines the relationship between social value orientations and voting behavior in unified Germany. Before going into the empirical analysis, I give a short definition of the concept of values. I then present the basic ideas of the most important theory of value change–the so-called theory of the silent revolution formulated by Ronald Inglehart. This discussion will show that the process of value change is theoretically conceptualized as a long-term force that gradually shifts the bases of politics in modern societies. This is why Inglehart speaks of it as a kind of silent revolution. Furthermore, it points to the necessity of analyzing long time series in order to describe this process adequately. In the theoretical part of the chapter, I also discuss some methodological problems associated with the most popular survey instrument for the measurement of values, the so-called Inglehart (or materialism/postmaterialism) index.

In the empirical part of this chapter, I first examine whether the postulated relationship between value orientations and voting behavior exists and, if so, whether it is stable over time. I also will examine if this relationship differs between West and East Germany. Subsequently, I ask whether social values really are changing. If there is a relationship between value orientations and voting behavior while social values are not undergoing change, the relationship between value orientations and voting behavior is not of great practical relevance. But if there is a process of value change and the relationship between values and party choice is stable over time, we will be able to make predictions about the future direction of the German party system.

THE CONCEPT OF VALUES

Values are defined as conceptions of the desirable (Kluckhohn 1951: 395). They can serve as selection standards when decisions have to be made. *Private values* are conceptions of the desirable order of private life, while *social values* are conceptions of the desirable type of society (Parsons 1980: 185). As abstract conceptions, values are not part of the belief systems of individuals. They are cultural objects that exist independently from their supporters (Gabriel 1986: 42). But individuals can internalize such values, so that they become individual *value orientations* (Friedrichs 1968: 48, 74). Viewed from this theoretical perspective, a value orientation is a value a person has accepted as a guideline for her/his personal life. In contrast to attitudes, value orientations are conceptualized as being more central and deeply rooted in the belief systems of individuals (Rokeach 1973: 18). Thus, value orientations determine attitudes and are more resistant to change. This relative stability of value orientations is one of their most central and defining elements.

The term *value space* describes the sum of all values existing in a culture that are different with regard to their content (cf. Maag 1991). The term *dimensionality of value space* is devoted to the way people structure their orientations toward the different values. In this context, *value dimensions* are subjective ordering patterns along which individuals organize their value orientations into belief systems. Value dimensions bundle value orientations which are seen by the individual as belonging together.

VALUE CHANGE AS VIEWED BY THE "THEORY OF THE SILENT REVOLUTION"

The most important theory of value change was developed by Ronald Inglehart (Inglehart 1971, 1977, 1987, 1989). This theory is based on two hypotheses: the *scarcity hypothesis* and the *socialization hypothesis*. The first states that "an individual's priorities reflect one's socioeconomic environment," while the second postulates that "to a large extent, one's basic values reflect the conditions that prevailed during one's preadult years" (Inglehart 1985: 103). To put Inglehart's theory in a nutshell: he argues that the need structure of human beings develops as Abraham Maslow predicts in his theory of the need hierarchy (Maslow 1954). There are lower order needs like hunger, thirst, and the need for housing and security. Inglehart calls these needs material. Furthermore there are higher order needs, like the desire for social integration, esteem, and self-realization. Inglehart calls these needs postmaterialist. In the logic of the need hierarchy, individuals only develop higher order needs once lower needs have been satisfied. Inglehart further assumes that the fundamental need structure of a person is cognitively transformed into social value orientations during one's preadult years and remains relative stable during one's adult years. The next step in his argument is that the great majority of the population grew up under conditions of security and material prosperity after World War II. Because their material needs were satisfied, they developed higher order needs, which were then transformed into postmaterialist value orientations. Even if Inglehart allows for period effects–that is, short-term value fluctuations in response to altered environmental circumstances–he sees the major force of value change in generational replacement. The postwar generations thus are the demographic basis of postmaterialism; as older generations become smaller in size because of the deaths of their members, the society as a whole develops toward attaching greater importance to postmaterialist values. Inglehart calls this process the silent revolution because generational replacement works very slowly.

One peculiarity of Inglehart's theory has to be mentioned: it deals with value *priorities*. Inglehart is not interested in the absolute importance people give to different values but in their relative importance. He is especially interested in the question of whether a person gives greater priority to materialist or postmaterialist concerns. This focus on value priorities has several causes. First, it follows directly from the Maslowian need hierarchy, which is the theoretical basis of Inglehart's argument and deals with relative priorities. Furthermore, Inglehart argues that in the field of politics, priorities are crucial. Most people will find *materialist and* postmaterialist concerns important: they want to have economic growth *and* a clean environment, wealth *and* greater possibilities to participate in politics. But because politics is about choices and it is not possible to have everything–so Inglehart's argument goes–people have to decide between different desirable political goals (Inglehart 1994; Inglehart and Klingemann 1996). In this situation, value priorities serve as selection standards. In a representative democracy people do not have to choose between concrete policy options but between different parties offering them different policy bundles. So it can be expected that value priorities have a significant impact on voting behavior.

The fact that Inglehart's theory deals with value priorities implies that the value space in his concept is necessarily a unidimensional continuum with the poles of materialism and postmaterialism. People are either materialists or postmaterialists, but they cannot have strong orientations toward both materialist *and* postmaterialist values.

THE MEASUREMENT OF VALUES IN SURVEYS:
SOME METHODOLOGICAL CONSIDERATIONS

The most important and widespread survey instrument for the measurement of social value orientations is the so-called Inglehart (or materialism/postmaterialism) index. It was constructed by Ronald Inglehart in order to measure value priorities in which he is primarily interested. For that reason the Inglehart index forces the respondents to rank-order four political goals, each of which by itself would be rated as very important by the respondents. The underlying assumption is that the respondents rank-order these goals according to their basic value priorities.

Because this instrument has been included in the biannual Eurobarometer surveys of the European Commission since the beginning of the 1970s, there exists a long time series enabling us to analyze the causes and consequences of value change adequately.[1] In the Eurobarometer surveys the Inglehart index is implemented in the following form:

> There is a lot of talk these days about what Germany's goals should be for the next ten or fifteen years. On this card are listed some of the goals that different people say should be given top priority. Would you please say which one of them you yourself consider to be most important in the long run?
> * Maintaining order in the country (MAT)
> * Giving people more say in important government decisions (POSTMAT)
> * Fighting rising prices (MAT)
> * Protecting freedom of speech (POSTMAT)
> And what would be your second choice?

In the empirical analysis, respondents who give top priority to the two materialist goals (MAT), are classified as materialists, while those who give top priority to the two postmaterialist goals (POSTMAT) are coded as postmaterialists. Finally, respondents who name a materialist and a postmaterialist goal at the top of their priority list or vice versa are classified as mixed types.

The big advantage of the Inglehart index is its simplicity and its ability to predict a number of attitudes and patterns of behavior. One problem with the Inglehart index, however, is that its validity cannot be taken for granted. The instrument is very sensitive to changes in the rate of inflation: when inflation rates are high, the percentage of materialists in a country is high as well; when inflation rates are low, the issue of "fighting rising prices" loses importance and the percentage of postmaterialists is high (Gabriel 1986). However, given that value orientations are conceptualized as relatively stable constructs, it is possible that the Inglehart index does not measure value priorities but measures issue priorities instead. Even if we assume that these issue priorities are a function of underlying value orientations, we have to take into account a certain degree of measurement error resulting from the fact that we try to measure values via issues. The strong relationship between changing rates of inflation and the percentage of the different value types may thus not necessarily be an argument against the validity of the Inglehart index, but constitutes an argument against its reliability.

SOCIAL VALUE ORIENTATIONS AND VOTING BEHAVIOR IN WEST AND EAST GERMANY

Is there a relationship between social value priorities and voting behavior? If so, is this relationship stable or does it change over time? How do these relationships compare across East and West Germany? To answer these questions, I take several analytic steps. First I look at the development of social value orientations in Germany between 1970 and 1994. Subsequently, I examine the development of voting behavior in Germany over the same time span. By doing so, it is possible to get a first impression if there is a relationship between the two variables. Such a relationship should exist if substantial variations in the distribution of value orientations among the mass public lead to substantial variations in the distribution of voting intentions. In the following, I will examine the voting behavior among the two pure value types distinguished by Inglehart -materialists and postmaterialists–in greater detail. Finally, I will examine the thesis that a new value cleavage has been added to the old left-right cleavage.

Figure 8.1 shows the development of value orientations among West and East Germans. According to the strategy of analysis preferred by Inglehart (see, for example, Inglehart 1989: 113), Figure 8.1 shows the percentage of postmaterialists minus the percentage of materialists at each point in time (in the following, this is called the PMM index). The calculation of such a percentage difference is

Figure 8.1. Value Change in Germany Between 1970 and 1994

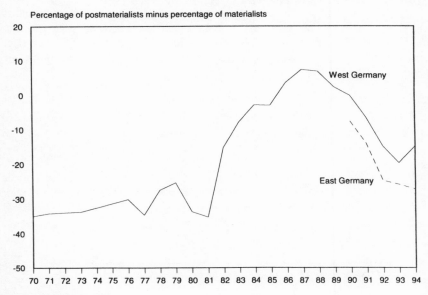

Source: Eurobarometer.

appropriate when the process of value change is unidimensional as assumed by Inglehart. In this case the trend goes from materialism to postmaterialism and the mixed type is not more than a transitional station. A quick look at Figure 8.1 reveals that there is no unidirectional linear trend in West Germany toward postmaterialism as Inglehart's theory predicts. Beginning in the 1980s, there was a sharp increase in postmaterialism; this increase levels off in 1987, and afterward there is a kind of rollback to materialism. Given this somewhat uneven development, the question of whether there are any long-term trends that could be labeled "value change" will be examined in a later section. In East Germany, there is a constant decline in postmaterialism. This might be explained by the fact that the goal "giving the people more say in important government decisions" was extraordinarily highly valued in 1990 because of the experience with the peaceful revolution in fall 1989.

If the values under consideration here were related to partisan choice, a likely consequence would be a parallel development for at least part of the time. Yet, when we compare the development of voting intentions in both parts of Germany (Figures 8.2 and 8.3) with the respective developments of value orientations, there are no striking correlations at first glance. Only the emergence of the Green alternative party ("the Greens" or Grüne) in West Germany coincides with the beginning of the short-time trend toward postmaterialism at the beginning of the 1980s. This fact matches our theoretical expectations. However, the decline of postmaterialism at the end of the 1980s is not accompanied by a simultaneous decline of electoral support for the Greens.

Figure 8.2. Vote Intention in West Germany Between 1970 and 1994

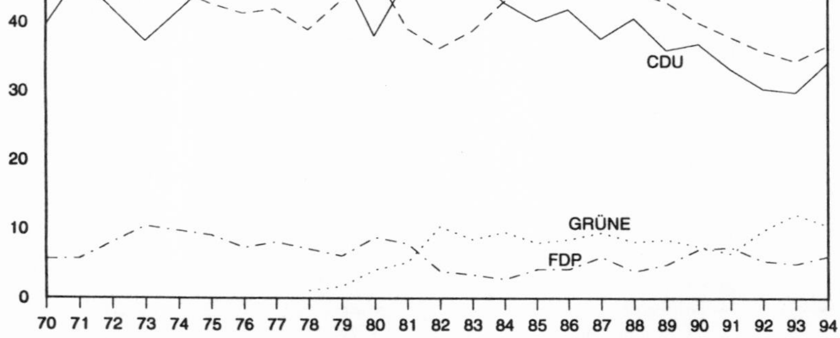

Source: Eurobarometer.

In East Germany there has been a sharp decline of electoral support for the Christian Democrats (CDU) after 1990, resulting from the exaggerated promises Chancellor Kohl made to the East German population before unification. This decline cannot reasonably be explained by the rise of materialism. The second trend in East Germany is the rise of electoral support for the Party of Democratic Socialism (PDS). This trend also cannot be explained by a rise of materialism but as a result of the frictions during the process of unification and as a relict of political socialization under the communist GDR regime (see chapter 11 by Carsten Zelle on support for the PDS in this volume).

Thus, with the exception of the emergence of the Greens, there seems to be little evidence for a great impact of value priorities on electoral behavior in the aggregate. However, when we take the analysis a bit further, we can see some differences. Figures 8.4 and 8.5 examine the group of materialists exclusively. Among this group the voting share of the Christian Democrats is about 10 percent higher than among the population as a whole. The results of the Social Democrats are slightly lower than among all voters. Support for the Greens is most striking. They obtain only about 2 or 3 percent among the materialists, even though their vote share rises at the beginning of the 1990s to almost 8 percent of the population as a whole. This might explain why the electoral success of the Greens remains stable even after the decline of postmaterialism at the end of the 1980s. In East Germany, however, the voting behavior of the materialists differs only marginally from the electorate as a whole. Only the share of the Greens is slightly lower, but nevertheless reaches 10 percent at almost every point in time.

Figure 8.3. Vote Intention in East Germany Between 1990 and 1994

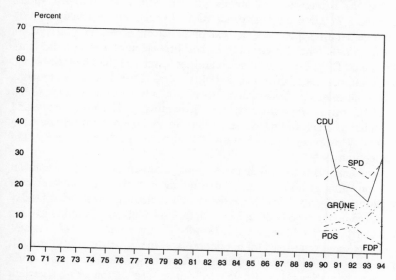

Source: Eurobarometer.

Figure 8.4. Vote Intention Among Materialists in West Germany Between 1970 and 1994

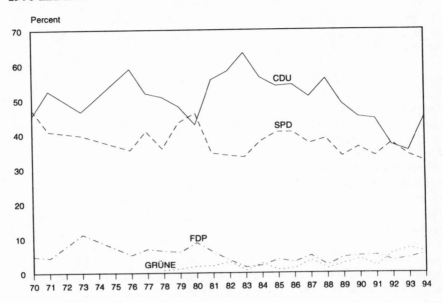

Source: Eurobarometer.

When we look at the postmaterialists, we find that in West Germany the Social Democrats are the strongest party among persons with postmaterialist values (Figures 8.6 and 8.7). Until the emergence of the Greens they reached up to 68 percent of postmaterialist support with a mean of 60 percent across the years. At the beginning of the 1980s, when the Greens had their first electoral success, the share of the SPD (Social Democrats) became somewhat lower and the Greens reached between 20 and 30 percent of the postmaterialist voters. The Christian Democrats are relatively weak among postmaterialists and obtain only about 20 percent of the votes. In East Germany, the structure is a bit confusing. The Greens reached between 20 and 30 percent, while the share of the Social Democrats dropped from 25 to 15 percent. However, the share of the PDS rose from 10 percent in 1990 to nearly 40 percent in 1994.

The empirical analysis presented up to this point is somewhat limited because it focuses only on value priorities even though the most important determinant of party competition in Germany is still the old left-right cleavage, which until today is primarily based on the class conflict (see chapter 7 by Wolfgang Jagodzinski and Steffen M. Kühnel in this volume; see also Jagodzinski and Kühnel 1994). The new value cleavage is supposed to add to, but not replace, the left-right controversy. It thus seems to be appropriate to analyze these two cleavages simultaneously (for a similar approach, though based on different techniques, see Dalton 1988; Kitschelt 1994, 1995). This is represented in Figures 8.8 and 8.9. Given the findings reported

Figure 8.5. Vote Intentions Among Materialists in East Germany Between 1990 and 1994

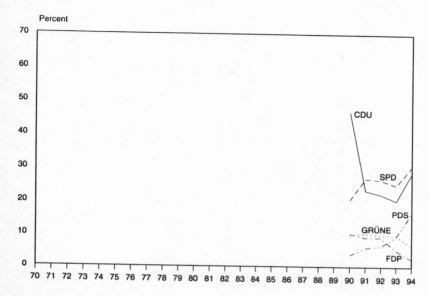

Source: Eurobarometer.

by Jagodzinski and Kühnel, it is appropriate to employ the respondents' self placement on the left-right scale as a summary measure of their old cleavage positions. Thus, the percentage difference between those on the right and those on the left supporting the different parties is shown on the horizontal axis.[2] The vertical axis represents the percentage difference between postmaterialists and materialists. To analyze the dynamics of the German party system, I calculate these differences for each year of our time series. This permits an analysis of how the electorates of the different parties develop over time.

Figure 8.8 shows the two-dimensional space of party competition in West Germany, divided into four quadrants: The old materialist right, the new postmaterialist right, the old materialist left, and the new postmaterialist left. The Christian Democrats are a typical party of the old right. Their supporters locating themselves on the right outnumber those on the left by about 50 percentage points. Moreover, at each point in time, there are more materialists than postmaterialists. The Free Democrats (FDP) take a middle position on both the left versus right axis and the materialist versus postmaterialist value cleavage. The Social Democrats seem to develop from a party of the old left to a leftist party in-between old and new politics. While there usually are 50 percent more leftists among SPD voters than rightists at most points in time, the balance between materialists and postmaterialists changes over time. In the 1970s there are more materialists than postmaterialists, while in the 1980s the postmaterialists dominate slightly within the electorate of the

Figure 8.6. Vote Intentions Among Postmaterialists in West Germany Between 1970 and 1994

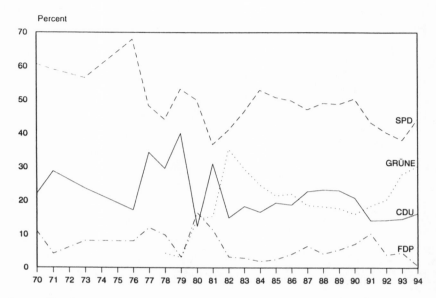

Source: Eurobarometer.

Social Democrats. In contrast, the Greens clearly are a party of the new left. Among their electorate, postmaterialists outnumber materialists at each point in time; the same is true for supporters with left inclinations compared to those placing themselves on the right. Thus, for the case of West Germany there really seems to be a new value cleavage along which the Greens found their market niche.

The East German situation (Figure 8.9) differs from the West German case: here, the political polarization is exclusively organized along the left-right axis. Except for the PDS in 1990 and the Greens in 1990 and 1991, the electorates of all parties are dominated by materialists at each point in time. Even the electorate of the Greens is composed almost equally of materialists and postmaterialists. With regard to the left-right dimension, the relative position of the different parties is equal to West Germany: the CDU is on the right, the Free Democrats take a middle-of-the-road position, and the SPD and the Greens are leftist parties. The PDS is a party of the extreme left; its voters are almost all pronounced left wingers. Along the value cleavage, the PDS takes a middle position with a trend toward materialism over time.

The finding that there is a new kind of cleavage based on social value orientations in West Germany would not be very interesting, unless one can demonstrate that this cleavage is gaining importance through the process of value change. When there is no process of value change, there also is no reason to believe that the German party system reorganizes itself along this new value

Figure 8.7. Vote Intentions Among Postmaterialists in East Germany Between 1990 and 1994

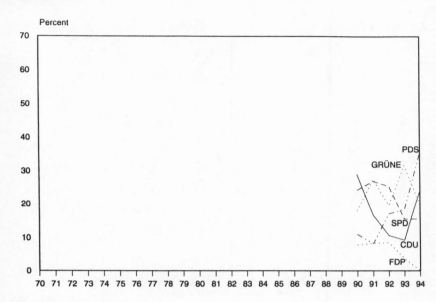

Source: Eurobarometer.

cleavage. Thus, this chapter poses the question whether social values really are changing or whether the often-discussed process of value change is possibly a chimera. To answer this question, I take several analytical steps. First, I compare the development of the distribution of social value orientations among the electorate with the development of two macroeconomic indicators: the rate of inflation and the rate of unemployment. Then I take a closer look at value orientations, examining the development of the percentages of materialists, mixed types, and postmaterialists over time without further relying on the PMM index constructed by Inglehart. Finally, I analyze if there really is a trend toward more postmaterialism as predicted by Inglehart. This analysis is restricted to the case of West Germany because the available time series for East Germany is too short to draw valid conclusions.

ARE SOCIAL VALUES REALLY CHANGING? A CRITICAL REANALYSIS OF THE EUROBAROMETER TIME SERIES

Figure 8.10 shows the development of the rate of inflation and the postmaterialist/materialist gap. There is a strong negative correlation between the two time series. This indicates that high rates of inflation lead to a high percentage of materialists compared to the percentage of postmaterialists. The trend toward

Figure 8.8. The Two-Dimensional Space of Party Competition in West Germany Between 1973 and 1994

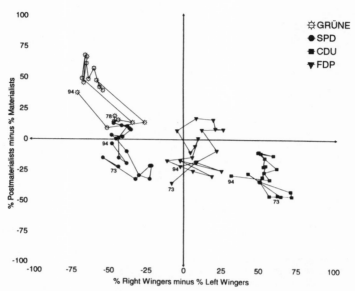

Source: Eurobarometer.

postmaterialism, which started at the beginning of the 1980s, coincides with a sharp decline in inflation, which was induced by the strict monetarist macroeconomic policy of the conservative federal government and the German central bank. When the rate of inflation went up again at the end of the 1980s because of the economic problems related to German reunification, the trend toward postmaterialism reversed. At least in the German case, the supposed process of value change is probably not more than the result of declining rates of inflation. Or in other words: the so-called silent revolution was a result of the monetarist counterrevolution against Keynesian macroeconomic policies.

Should we expect an influence of unemployment on the distribution of value orientations among the public? Clarke and Dutt developed the following argument in order to explain such a relationship:

In many Western countries high rates of inflation were followed in the early 1980s by a deep recession accompanied by decreases in inflation and sharp increases in joblessness. ... many persons formerly concerned with inflation abandoned the 'fight rising prices' statement in the four-item battery and sought an alternative that reflected their current preoccupation with unemployment. Since there is no such item, which one did they choose as their top priority? We hypothesize that many selected "give people more say in government" to express their preference for policies to alleviate the problem at hand (Clarke and Dutt 1991: 910).

Figure 8.11 shows the development of the rate of unemployment and the

Figure 8.9. The Two-Dimensional Space of Party Competition in East Germany Between 1990 and 1994

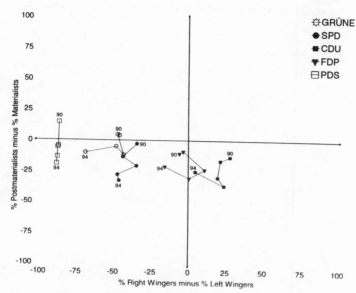

Source: Eurobarometer.

development of the percentage difference between postmaterialists and materialists. It shows that there is a strong positive relationship between the two time series. Joblessness, ironically, coincides with higher levels of postmaterialism.

To sum up: on the basis of the empirical results presented above, it cannot be taken for granted that the Inglehart index is a good instrument for the measurement of values. It is possible that the Inglehart index does not measure value priorities but issue priorities. This would mean that the index is an invalid instrument. The second possibility is that the Inglehart index does measure fundamental value orientation but with great measurement errors because it measures these value orientations via issues. If this is the case, the Inglehart index may not be a reliable instrument. Either way, it is difficult to establish if social values are really changing because we are not able to measure them adequately (see also the debate by Clarke, Dutt, and Rapkin and Abramson, Inglehart, and Ellis [1997]).

However, even if we assume that the Inglehart index is a reliable and valid instrument, other problems remain. The Inglehart index was designed to measure a construct that was unidimensional; thus, a ranking format was chosen. However, is this assumption of unidimensionality realistic? In my view, the arguments provided by Inglehart are not very convincing (Bean and Papadakis 1994a, b; Bürklin, Klein, and Ruß 1994, 1996; Klein 1995). First of all, the transfer of the Maslowian need hierarchy onto the analysis of social value orientations can be

Figure 8.10. Value Change and the Development of Inflation in West Germany Between 1970 and 1994

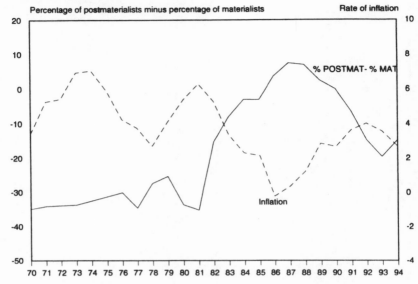

Source: Eurobarometer.

Figure 8.11. Value Change and the Development of Unemployment in West Germany Between 1970 and 1994

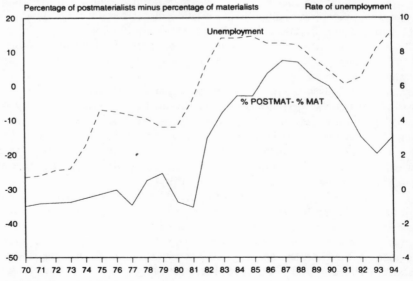

Source: Eurobarometer.

criticized for several reasons. There is no striking argument why the escalation of political wants should follow the same logic as the escalation of private needs. And there is no reason why need structures should directly be transformed into value orientations (Flanagan 1982a; Marsh 1975). Moreover, there is no reason why politics should always be about choices. It is unclear, for example, why there is an inherent conflict between a low rate of inflation and the right of freedom of speech. Why should more rights to participate in politics necessarily conflict with the goal of maintaining order in the country? Why should people not have strong orientations toward materialist *and* postmaterialist values? But Inglehart denies the possibility of such a synthesis between old and new values (Inglehart 1994, Inglehart and Klingemann 1996).

We are not able to correct the fundamental construction principles of the Inglehart index–that is, the ranking format–in order to be able to draw a more realistic picture of value change. However, by using the data collected with the Inglehart index we are at least able to present the findings in a way not as burdened by theoretical assumptions as the percentage-point difference between postmaterialists and materialists. The calculation of this index is appropriate only if one makes the assumption that value change necessarily shifts from materialism to postmaterialism. But it can also be assumed that value change develops toward a new synthesis of materialist and postmaterialist values (Klages 1985, 1992). According to the logic of the Inglehart index this group would fall into the mixed category (Klein 1995). However, the mixed category is not included in the PMM-index used by Inglehart, so the possibility of value synthesis is not taken into account.

To avoid this focus on the two pure types, Figures 8.12 and 8.13 show the development of all three value types separately. They show that the mixed category is the only one that follows a clear linear trend over time. In 1970, 43 percent of the West Germans were mixed value types, while in 1994, 55 percent fall in this category. The varying shares of pure postmaterialists and pure materialists show great nonlinear variations over time due to varying rates of unemployment and inflation. However, there is a straightforward way to control for the influence of inflation by comparing different time points during which inflation rates were similar (1970 and 1993; see Figure 8.10). We find that the percentage of materialists drops from 45 (1970) to 30 (1993), while the percentage of postmaterialists is nearly identical in these two years (about 10). Meanwhile the mixed type gains almost 15 percentage points. It may thus be possible that the process of value change does not lead to the emergence of a majority of pure postmaterialists, but to a majority of persons with a synthesis of materialist and postmaterialist values.

Up to this point, the empirical evidence for our value synthesis argument has been somewhat preliminary. To test the notion of a value synthesis in a statistically more stringent fashion, I reproduce an analysis presented by Inglehart and Abramson (1994). They computed a simple OLS regression model for the time series of their PMM index that includes the rate of inflation, the rate of unemployment, and the years passed since the baseline study in 1970 as

Figure 8.12. The Development of Social Value Orientations in West Germany Between 1970 and 1994

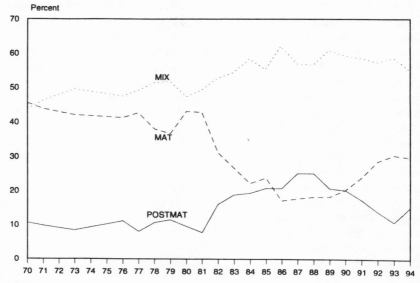

Source: Eurobarometer.

Figure 8.13. The Development of Social Value Orientations in East Germany Between 1990 and 1994

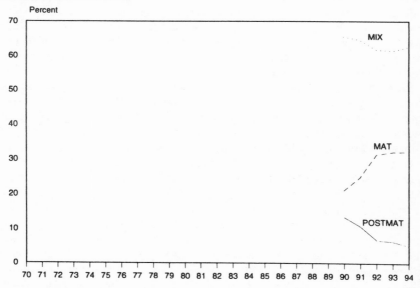

Source: Eurobarometer.

independent variables. They do this in order to test if there is a significant trend toward postmaterialism when the influence of the macroeconomic development is controlled for. My analysis includes the years from 1970 to 1994; I compute this model for the PMM index as well as for the share of the three value types separately. The results can be summed up as follows (see Table 8.1): There is no statistically significant trend toward pure postmaterialism, using neither the PMM index nor the absolute percentage of postmaterialists as the dependent variable. There also is no significant trend away from pure materialism. However, there is a significant trend toward a greater share for the mixed type and thus a greater relevance of value synthesis. Given that the three value types must always sum up to 100 percent, the trend toward the mixed type has to be accompanied by a significant downward trend of at least one of the two other value types. The materialist category shows such a trend, although it fails to achieve conventional levels of statistical significance. Although these results should be interpreted with caution and need further validation because of possible problems with autocorrelation, they provide empirical evidence that stands in contrast to Inglehart's theory of a silent revolution.

Table 8.1. Predicting Social Value Orientations in West Germany, 1970-94

	b	SE b	beta	t-value	sig.	R^2	Durbin-Watson
% Postmaterialists							
- % Materialists							
Years since baseline	.378	.422	.174	.896	.382	.793	.808
Inflation	-3.947	1.234	-.452	-3.199	.005		
Unemployment	2.147	1.240	.386	1.731	.101		
% Postmaterialists							
Years since baseline	-.036	.178	-.047	-.207	.839	.722	.933
Inflation	-1.600	.520	-.503	-3.077	.007		
Unemployment	.950	.523	.470	1.818	.086		
% Mixed Value Types							
Years since baseline	.452	.139	.620	3.245	.004	.800	1.920
Inflation	-.741	.407	-.253	-1.819	.086		
Unemployment	.255	.409	.137	.624	.540		
% Materialists							
Years since baseline	-.415	.259	-.293	-1.602	.127	.816	.910
Inflation	2.347	.757	.413	3.100	.006		
Unemployment	-1.197	.761	-.331	-1.573	.133		

Notes: SE: Standard Error; sig.: significance level.
Source: Eurobarometer and Federal Statistical Office of Germany.

CONCLUSION: THE QUESTION REMAINS OPEN

It is not easy to draw unequivocal conclusions from the empirical analysis presented in this chapter. Because of the nonexistence of other time series, I was forced to utilize data collected with the help of the Inglehart index, even though I believe that it may not be a reliable instrument and possibly not even a valid one. However, I tried to deal with the data in a manner that would enable me to test some of the assumptions underlying Inglehart's theory of value change. In my view, Inglehart's theory failed this test. It thus cannot be taken for granted that social values really are changing. Moreover, if they are changing, the trend in all likelihood does not go in the direction of pure postmaterialists but toward a value synthesis.

Figure 8.14 shows the placement of the German electorate within the two-dimensional space of party competition over time. The most striking development in Figure 8.14 is the rapid movement of the East German electorate toward the left. Along the new value cleavage, only the West German electorate shows a slight tendency toward the postmaterialist pole. However, this movement can be explained to a large extent by short-term macroeconomic trends, while the East Germans

Figure 8.14. The Position of the West and East German Electorates in the Two-Dimensional Ideological Space Between 1973 and 1994

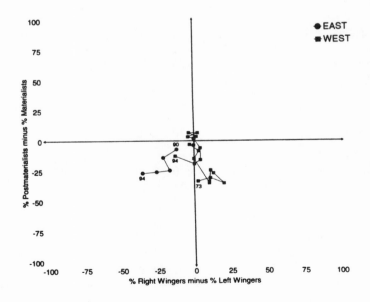

Source: Eurobarometer.

became more materialist since reunification. Overall, West German voters have shown a great amount of stability in their attitudes since the early 1970s.

The mixed category is not included in the analysis as the vertical axis shows only the percentage difference between postmaterialists and materialists. However, the majority of Germans belong to the mixed type, which has gained significantly over time (see Figure 8.12). In other words, the politics of value change seem to be in the mixed category. It is thus necessary to take a closer look at this group. As Figures 8.15 and 8.16 reveal, the voting behavior of the mixed value type differs only slightly from the electorate as a whole. So if there is a process of value change and if this process trends toward a greater relevance of the mixed value type, it may not have sizable effects on electoral choice.

In the end, the question of whether anything is changing remains open. The existence of value change cannot be taken for granted because of the deficiency of the available time series. And if such a process of value change indeed exists, there is considerable evidence, which indicates that it leads to a synthesis of materialist and postmaterialist values and not to an exchange of both. If this is the case, there is no need to expect significant consequences with regard to how voters make their choices.

Figure 8.15. Vote Intentions Among Mixed Value Types in West Germany Between 1970 and 1994

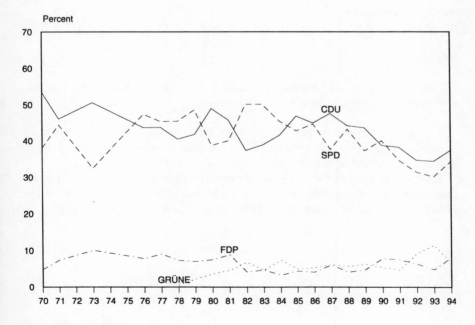

Source: Eurobarometer.

Figure 8.16. Vote Intentions Among Mixed Value Types in East Germany Between 1990 and 1994

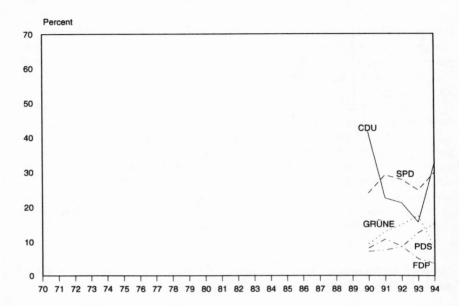

Source: Eurobarometer.

NOTES

I would like to thank Timothi Maywood and Friederika Priemer for valuable comments on an earlier version of this chapter.

1. The Eurobarometer surveys 1 to 42 and 44 constitute the database for the empirical analysis in this chapter. For each year in which two surveys were available, the mean of their results is presented.

2. I coded respondents as being on the right if they place themselves in one of the four right-most categories of the 10 point left-right scale included in the Eurobarometer surveys since 1973. Those on the left were coded analogously.

A New Type of Nonvoter? Turnout Decline in German Elections, 1980-94

Thomas Kleinhenz

Until the Bundestag elections of 1990 and 1994, nonvoting or abstention was virtually unknown in the study of German elections. In both elections, more than 20 percent of the German electorate did not go to the polls. Although these record low turnouts surprised many at the time, the origins of turnout decline in German elections can be traced back to the early 1980s, when turnout in elections at the federal, state, and local levels started to decrease at a steady rate.

Declining turnout rates can be observed in most West European countries. However, Germany is a special and particularly interesting case of rising abstention rates. For many years, West German voters were among the most active participants in elections held in the Western world. In fact, turnout had increased to 90 percent in national elections until the 1970s (up from 78.5 percent in the first federal election of 1949), and to about 80 percent in state elections. Then, within two elections' time (1983-1990), turnout dropped by 10 percentage points. Subsequently, turnout in the first national elections of the united Germany—two months after reunification in 1990—reached just 77.8 percent in the nation as a whole and 78.6 percent in the former West Germany. Four years later, turnout increased only slightly to 79.0 percent.

These developments raise a number of questions. Most fundamentally, they include the following: Who are the nonvoters? Why did turnout decline? This chapter constitutes an attempt to answer these and related questions.

NONVOTING AND TURNOUT

Because turnout was high over much of the Federal Republic's existence, nonvoting only recently became an issue for researchers interested in German elections. In 1971 Kaack referred to the nonvoters as the "terra incognita of voting behavior research." More than twenty years later, the conclusion would have been

Figure 9.1. Turnout in Federal (Bundestag) and State (Landtag) Elections, 1949-94

Percent who did not vote

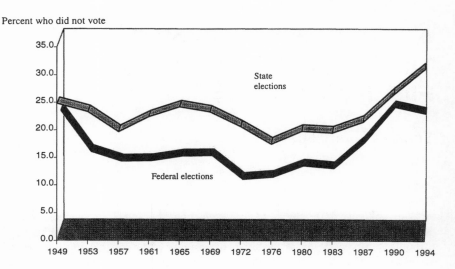

Source: Federal Department of Statistics.

equally appropriate. Nonvoters were not the focus of election studies for obvious reasons: High turnout combined with overreporting in surveys left very few cases of reported abstention for systematic examination (Steiner 1969; Eilfort 1994; Kleinhenz 1995). In addition, high turnout rates did not exactly ignite an interest in nonvoting research.

In contrast to the small number of studies on turnout in the German case, there are numerous studies in the literature on U.S. elections that deal with the phenomenon of low turnout and the question of turnout decline (Lazarsfeld et al. 1944; Campbell et al. 1960; Lipset 1960; Verba, Nie, and Kim 1978; Wolfinger and Rosenstone 1980, Abramson and Aldrich 1982, Kleppner 1982; Teixeira 1987, 1992; Leighley and Nagler 1992). However, because voting depends on legal as well as cultural settings, findings regarding the nature of nonvoting may not travel very easily across cultures. For instance, race and particularly registration laws have consistently been shown to influence turnout in the United States (Wolfinger and Rosenstone 1980: 90; Crewe 1981:, 240; Leighley and Nagler 1992: 718). These variables are irrelevant to the German case. In most European countries, citizens do not have to make any efforts to vote, except for traveling to the polling station. What is more, the absence of legal hurdles affects the relationship of other variables–particularly social demographic ones–with turnout (Verba, Kim, and Nie 1978).[1]

In the German case, Faul (1965) and Gunzert (1965) were the first scholars to deal with the issue of nonvoting. Somewhat more extensive research on nonvoting started to appear in the late 1960s with Steiner's (1969) work on the Swiss national election of 1963 and the federal election in Germany 1965, and Radtke's (1972) study of the 1965 Bundestag election. Lavies (1973) was the first to examine electoral participation over time, dealing with data from the Federal Department of Statistics and selected statistical material of local elections. Later Golzem and Liepelt (1976), Wernicke (1976), Marciniak (1978), and Schoof (1980) examined turnout in light of social and demographic factors on the basis of aggregate data. Only Steiner (1969), Radtke (1972), and Golzem and Liepelt (1976) used survey data for their research. However, the study by Golzem and Liepelt (1976) was limited to the analysis of one state, North Rhine-Westphalia.

This brief overview includes virtually all scholarly work on turnout in the German context prior to 1990. The topic disappeared from the research agenda in the late 1970s because of Germany's high turnout rates of around 90 percent. Studies of nonvoting in Bundestag elections in 1980, 1983, and 1987 do not exist. After taking note of the turnout decline in 1990, however, the electoral research community as well as the mass media developed a new interest in the subject. Aside from this author, Eilfort (1994) as well as Falter and Schumann (1993, 1994) were among the first to examine nonvoting on the basis of large-scale quantitative analyses. While Eilfort's study is limited to the city of Stuttgart, Falter and Schumann's (1994) analysis concentrated on the parliamentary election of 1990, neither incorporating other types of elections nor more recent trends. Since then, a number of articles and studies dealing with various aspects of nonvoting were published in recent years (see e.g. Roth 1992; Armingeon 1994; Feist 1994; Hofmann-Jaberg and Roth 1994; Klingemann et al. 1998; Rattinger and Krämer 1995).

RESEARCH DESIGN AND RESEARCH QUESTIONS

The theoretical framework employed here attempts to integrate two approaches: voting behavior theory and participation research. While these are related, they also have distinct theoretical traditions. Both these theoretical perspectives underline the strong relationship of turnout with socioeconomic status, age, social connectedness and particularly other forms of political involvement (Lazarsfeld et al. 1944; Campbell et al. 1960; Verba, Nie, and Kim 1978; Wolfinger and Rosenstone 1980). Most nonvoting studies in Germany exclusively employ variables related to the social and demographic background of the individual, searching for differences in turnout between social groups. The results resemble those derived in other countries with a few exceptions that appear specific to the German case.

Scholars have found that individuals with low socioeconomic status, single persons, women and young people as well as the very old tend to vote less (Steiner 1969; Radtke 1972; Lavies 1973, Mayer 1991). These findings support the common view that turnout is lowest among those at the bottom of the social ladder (Radtke

1972, 69; Lavies 1973, 162; for the U.S., see Key 1952; Reiter 1979; Burnham 1987, Bennett 1991). In addition, religion was found to be a relevant factor for explaining turnout differences in West Germany (Faul 1965, 13; Lavies 1973, 121).

Unfortunately, most analyses of the decline in German turnout were limited by the widely-used cross-sectional design of German election studies, thus leaving trends largely unexamined. In this chapter, I address this problem by employing a longitudinal design based on survey data. The basic question is this: Among which groups of the population has voting participation decreased most, and what are the reasons for the decline? This approach leads us to the next question: Can we apply explanations based on social and demographic factors to longitudinal research? In the last twenty years the social structure of German society has changed fundamentally. As a result, a number of socio-demographic trends do not fit well with declining turnout rates. Particularly, increasing levels of cognitive mobilization should have promoted higher levels of participation. I will try to explain this apparent paradox.[2]

An examination of the question of turnout decline requires two different kinds of information: data at the level of both the individual and the aggregate. While individual-level research looks for differences in turnout decline between social groups, aggregate-level data identify changes in the composition of the electorate and their potential effects on turnout. A final answer to the question of why turnout has declined can be given only with the help of a combination of individual-level and aggregate-level effects. An example may serve to illustrate this point. Individual data show that the probability of voting is lower among persons with low levels of education. At the same time, the proportion of individuals with low education has decreased in the population as a whole. In a situation like this, the total impact of the indicator education on declining turnout can be measured only by the combined effect of decline within the group and shrinking size of the group.[3, 4]

The research reported here covers the parliamentary elections from 1980 through 1994, the period during which most of the turnout decline took place. The analyses rely on three longitudinal data sources. The three data bases are: Election surveys of the Federal Department of Statistics from 1983 to 1990; ALLBUS-surveys (General Population Survey) from 1980 to 1994; and election studies of the Konrad Adenauer Foundation from 1983 to 1990.[5] In addition, a survey of the national election in 1990 is included.

Except for the official statistics, which measure actual behavior, overreporting of participation has to be taken into account. It is well known that a sizable portion of actual nonvoters claims to have voted when asked in a survey. Moreover, indications are that the overreporting phenomenon became even more pronounced as turnout rates dropped (Kleinhenz 1995: 88). Similar to other contributions in this volume, this study is devoted to both the examination of an electoral phenomenon over time and the comparison between East and West. Unfortunately, the analysis of demographic variables has to be limited to western Germany because the social structure of eastern Germany continues to be in transformation. Moreover, the interest in long-term trends inhibits detailed scrutiny of the East. Therefore, this study will proceed by first examining nonvoting and its rise in the West.

Subsequently, it investigates to what extent the results regarding political attitudes can usefully be applied to nonvoting in eastern Germany.

Against the background of previous findings in Germany as well as in other countries, I reexamine standard conclusions about nonvoting. Are nonvoters less connected socially? Are they generally of low status, in particular measured by low levels of education? Does religion, a key element of the cleavage structure in West European societies, play a role? Do these factors help understand the findings regarding age and gender? How do political attitudes such as interest in politics and political satisfaction fit in? These aspects are first investigated with the help of cross-sectional data. I will then move to the longitudinal perspective, asking what role these factors play in the decline of electoral participation.

SOCIAL STRUCTURE AND TURNOUT DECLINE

Religion

Despite the important role religion has played in German electoral behavior for decades, and despite the earlier findings testifying to an effect of religion on electoral participation, there is no significant relationship between religion and turnout in any of the surveys examined here. The most impressive finding in this regard is that persons who do not belong to any religious group vote somewhat less frequently, but this difference never exceeds 4 percentage points. Adherents of religions other than the Protestant or Catholic churches vote rarely, but they constitute only a very small group of only between 2 and 3 percent of the German electorate (see also Falter and Schumann 1994, 179). Thus, compared to earlier analyses (Steiner 1969; Lavies 1973; Falter and Schumann 1994), religion has lost much of its relevance for explaining turnout in German elections.

While denomination does a poor job in explaining turnout, church attendance does a lot better. Persons who never go to church also vote less frequently (see Table 9.1). Likewise, the decline of turnout in this group was notably above average. From 1982 through 1992, nonvoting rose by 15 percentage points among persons who never went to church. This stands in contrast to an increase in nonvoting of 4.8 percentage points among those who went to church regularly. Yet, even when we control for frequency of church attendance, there are no significant differences between Catholics and Protestants. Hence, we can speculate that church attachment is more of an indicator of social connectedness rather than of religious differences.

Social Connectedness

Past studies suggest that people who are well connected into social life are more likely to vote (Falter and Schumann 1994: 178). Here, social connectedness is measured by the indicators marital status, household size, and club membership.

Table 9.1 Nonvoting by Religion and Church Attendance, 1980-92 (percent who did not vote)

	1980	1982	1984	1986	1988	1990	1991	1992
% not voting (total)	3.2	5.7	9.3	9.8	10.9	11.8	12.9	14.9
Religion								
Catholic	3.2	5.5	8.3	8.9	10.6	9.6	11.9	13.0
Protestant	2.5	4.4	8.3	9.8	9.9	11.4	14.5	15.2
Others	13.0	16.7	19.0	13.2	23.3	17.1	10.5	27.1
No religion	2.8	7.4	13.0	13.7	13.5	21.7	10.9	18.1
Church Attendance								
Regularly	3.4	4.4	6.1	6.4	10.1	8.4	5.1	9.2
Sometimes	2.2	4.1	7.8	6.9	8.4	8.0	11.9	9.8
Rarely	3.9	5.6	8.3	10.7	11.4	12.2	11.4	15.7
Never	-	9.0	15.2	16.7	14.8	18.2	22.0	24.1

Source: ALLBUS.

Table 9.2 Nonvoting by Marital Status, Size of Household and Club Membership, 1980-92 (percent who did not vote)

	1980	1982	1984	1986	1988	1990	1991	1992
% not voting (total)	3.2	5.7	9.3	9.8	10.9	11.8	12.9	14.9
Marital Status								
Married	2.0	3.7	6.8	8.4	8.3	7.1	9.4	10.9
Separated, widowed, divorced	5.2	9.5	12.7	10.8	14.6	15.0	16.8	20.6
Single	5.1	7.8	13.3	13.1	14.1	19.3	18.8	20.4
Size of Household								
One person	4.5	9.4	11.7	11.6	13.3	17.9	19.1	20.3
Two persons	1.9	5.0	10.1	8.9	8.9	10.0	10.5	12.0
Three persons	3.4	4.7	8.0	10.7	10.5	9.9	13.3	14.7
Four+ persons	3.5	3.9	6.9	8.7	11.2	8.8	10.4	13.3
Club Membership								
Yes	2.7	4.1	6.1	6.6	8.9	8.4	9.3	10.1
No	3.6	6.9	10.5	12.7	12.1	15.3	15.8	18.8

Source: ALLBUS.

As Table 9.2 indicates, marital status in particular is a good predictor of electoral participation.

How does social connectedness fit into an explanation of turnout decline? During the period from 1980 to 1992, the share of nonvoters increased by 15 percentage points among single, divorced, and widowed persons compared to 8.9 percentage points among married people. Similar results can be observed when we consider household size. Among people who do not live alone, the decline in turnout was smaller than it was in single households. Once we go beyond the single household, the exact number of inhabitants does not matter. Yet lower electoral participation of those who are single or widowed and live in single households also has to be viewed in light of another variable: age. The very young as well as the very old tend to live alone and tend to be single.

The findings regarding the various measures of social connectedness support the well-known proposition that social isolation promotes abstention, while people who are well integrated in societal life vote more often (Anderson 1996). Thus it comes as a surprise that longitudinal analyses showed a drop in turnout by 8 to 10 percentage points even among socially integrated persons—a figure that is very similar to the average decrease of participation in West Germany. Hence, social connectedness does not prevent people from abstention and indifference. However, among the isolated persons the process of turning away from electoral participation is developing even more rapidly.

Socioeconomic Status

When we examine indicators of socioeconomic status, the analyses support well-established findings regarding its relationship with turnout in the cross-section. Less educated people and people with smaller incomes vote less frequently. Government employees have a very high probability to vote compared to other occupational groups. Yet socioeconomic status cannot explain the trend toward an increasing number of nonvoters in the population as a whole.[6]

Education

In contrast to Wolfinger and Rosenstone, who found education to be of prime importance for the explanation of electoral participation (Wolfinger and Rosenstone 1980: 34), there are no large differences in turnout between the various educational groups in the German case.[7] Particularly in light of the overreporting phenomenon, small differences in the range between 2 and 4 percentage points should not be considered significant, given that better educated individuals are most likely to misreport participation (Steiner 1969; Silver, Anderson, and Abramson 1986; Granberg and Holmberg 1991).

Over the years, nonvoting increased slightly less among the better educated. Yet the rate of decline in turnout was nearly equal among grammar school graduates and secondary school graduates. The participation rate fell disproportionately only among persons who did not finish school at all. However, due to its small size of the population as a whole (between 1.8 and 2.3 percent), this group does not play an important role for explaining turnout decline (see Table 9.3).

Table 9.3. Nonvoting by Level of Education, 1980-92
(percent who did not vote)

	1980	1982	1984	1986	1988	1990	1991	1992
Without Degree	6.8	11.8	20.7	21.6	33.9	29.4	20.8	37.2
Grammar School (9 Years)	3.3	5.8	9.5	11.0	12.2	13.2	15.6	16.5
Secondary School (10-11 years)	3.4	5.3	8.9	8.0	10.1	11.1	11.4	14.7
High School/ College (12+ years)	1.8	3.3	8.3	7.4	5.7	10.0	12.0	10.0
Total	3.2	5.7	9.3	9.8	10.9	11.8	12.9	14.9

Source: ALLBUS.

Two facts become apparent when we examine the decline in electoral participation among the better educated. On one hand, the effect of education on turnout has grown somewhat over time. That is, the difference between the lowest and highest educational categories in the percentage of nonvoters rose from 5 to 27 points. On the other hand, the close relationship between high education and voting has eroded over time. In 1980 almost every person with a high school diploma or college degree went to the polls (2 percent nonvoters). In contrast, in 1992 the percentage of nonvoters among this group increased to 10 percent. Thus the erosion in participation affects individuals of all levels of education.

Occupation

Occupation does not help much to flesh out the picture of the German nonvoter. The one notable finding is that government employees are more likely to vote, and that the drop in turnout was smaller in this group relative to the others. We may speculate that government jobs lead to a close attachment to the state. In contrast to the findings reported by Eilfort (1994: 214) as well as by Falter and Schumann (1994: 176), there is no difference in turnout between white-collar workers and blue-collar workers, either in the cross-section or over time (see Table 9.4).

Closer scrutiny reveals that differences in turnout rates between the occupational groups have lost their significance in comparison to those reported in earlier studies (Radtke 1972: 69; Lavies 1973: 91). Because of the small number of cases in certain occupational groups, I pooled two consecutive surveys for this analysis. The only exception to the generally weak effects of occupation is that unemployed persons are less likely to vote. Apparently, a low-status interpretation of abstention continues to make sense in the case of unemployment, though social connectedness may play a role here as well. When considering occupation over time, turnout decline does not correlate with occupational status (with some exceptions). Electoral participation seems to decrease uniformly among skilled, semiskilled, and

Table 9.4. Nonvoting by Occupation and Union Membership, 1980-92 (percent who did not vote)

	1980	1982	1984	1986	1988	1990	1991	1992
Percent who did not vote (total)	3.2	5.7	9.3	9.8	10.9	11.8	12.9	14.9
Occupation								
Self-employed	1.8	4.7	7.1	7.9	4.0	10.1	6.3	13.8
Government Employees	0.7	3.6	7.3	7.2	4.7	3.7	6.7	5.0
White-collar	3.3	4.0	7.6	9.3	9.4	13.1	12.6	14.2
Blue-collar	4.1	4.7	12.7	10.9	13.2	17.0	17.2	17.4
Not in labor force	3.3	7.0	9.5	10.3	12.1	11.1	13.4	15.7
Union Membership								
Yes	4.0	4.9	6.3	6.2	6.4	10.9	14.4	11.1
No	3.0	5.8	9.8	10.5	11.5	11.9	12.6	15.6

Source: ALLBUS.

unskilled blue-collar workers. Even among the unemployed turnout dropped by 11 percentage points—roughly at the same rate as among blue-collar workers and white-collar workers (see Table 9.5).

In sum, aside from government employees and professionals, participation rates declined largely uniformly in various occupational groups. The relatively marked decline in turnout among skilled blue-collar workers as well as among lower and upper white-collar workers demonstrates that the new middle class contributed its share to the decline in turnout.

Gender and Age

According to the large samples of the Federal Department of Statistics, the traditional difference in turnout between men and women diminished over the years, dropping to 1.5 percentage points in the 1980s and 1990s. In the United States, Wolfinger and Rosenstone (1980: 43) found that most of the gender gap is due to low electoral participation of women over age 70 whose political socialization took place in the 1930s and 1940s. They had accepted that political life is dominated by men. Hence they were less engaged to demonstrate their own involvement.

The right side of Table 9.6 reports the analysis of the election samples. The left side shows the analysis of the ALLBUS surveys. The lower rates of abstention measured with the help of the ALLBUS surveys are due to overreporting. A comparison to the quite accurate data of the Department of Statistics reveals that there was more overreporting among men and especially among young people.

Table 9.5. Nonvoting by Occupational Status, 1982/84-1991/92
(percent who did not vote)

	1982/84	1988	1991/92	Difference 1991/92 - 1982/84
Unskilled/semiskilled workers	12.9	25.3	18.3	+ 5.4
Skilled blue-collar workers	5.5	8.3	16.4	+ 10.9
Lower white-collar	7.1	15.6	17.8	+ 10.1
Upper white-collar	4.7	7.6	14.4	+ 9.7
Professionals	6.0	2.8	10.5	+ 4.5
Lower government employees	9.0	7.4	5.7	- 3.3
Upper government employees	2.5	2.7	6.8	+ 4.3
Unemployed	15.2	23.6	26.2	+ 11.0
Housewives	8.4	-	18.0	+ 9.6
Total	7.5	10.9	14.1	+ 6.6

Source: ALLBUS.

Table 9.6. Nonvoting by Sex and Age: ALLBUS Surveys and Elections Samples of the Federal Department of Statistics, 1982/84-1991/92 (percent who did not vote)

	ALLBUS				Federal Department of Statistics			
	1982/84	1986/88	1991/92	Change '82-'92	1983	1987	1990[1]	Change '83'-90
Sex								
Male	5.9	8.9	11.0	+ 5.1	9.9	14.3	20.4	+ 10.5
Female	8.8	12.6	16.9	+ 8.1	10.9	16.0	21.7	+ 10.8
Age								
18-24	11.0	16.6	23.1	+12.1	16.0	23.6	32.8	+ 16.8
25-34	9.1	12.5	18.3	+ 9.2	13.2	20.1	27.9	+ 14.7
35-44	6.1	7.7	10.8	+ 4.7	8.9	14.0	20.7	+ 11.8
45-59	5.3	8.3	11.4	+ 6.1	6.9	10.3	14.9	+ 8.0
60-69	7.0	8.6	10.1	+ 3.1	6.9	9.2	12.3	+ 5.4
70+	8.4	8.9	13.0	+ 4.6	12.6	16.7	21.7	+ 9.1
Total	7.4	10.3	14.1	+ 6.3	10.4	15.2	21.1	+ 10.7

Notes: [1] West Germany without Berlin.
Source: ALLBUS; Federal Department of Statistics.

The data show that turnout decline was most pronounced among very young and very old citizens. It is well established in cross-sectional analyses that these groups participate less. Although life-cycle interpretations may work well in the cross-section, they do not help to explain turnout from a longitudinal perspective. Among the 18 to 24 year olds, the proportion of nonvoters climbed by 16.8 points from 16 percent in 1983 up to 32.8 percent in 1990. We find similar results for the second youngest group, the 25 to 35 year olds, among whom turnout fell by 14.6 percentage points during the same period.

The decline of turnout within the younger electorate could be the result of two distinct developments. On one hand, changing participation behavior may reflect a change in attitudes relating to voting participation in the younger postwar generations, particularly the generations born in the 1960s and 1970s during times of affluence. Socialized in times of a stable democracy, these generations feel little need to support the idea of democracy by going to the polls (generational view). On the other hand, changes in more general political attitudes among the young could have caused the decrease in turnout. Interest in politics, party attachment, and political satisfaction perhaps weakened among the younger generations (modified life-cycle interpretation).

Life-Cycle and Generational Effects

Miller (1992) argued that the decline in turnout in the United States can be attributed to the changing generational composition of the electorate. This explanation supposes that voting behavior among younger generations differs fundamentally from that of older generations. Since the analyses presented so far have demonstrated a weakening or disappearance of the traditional differences in turnout between social groups, one might suspect that the younger generations show different patterns of turnout than the older generations. To evaluate this possibility, we rely on differences in levels of education. This is justified because a major aspect of social change is the growth in educational attainment. To increase the number of cases, two subsequent samples were pooled once again.

We find that the proportion belonging to the lowest educational category fell from 39.1 percent (1982/84) to 25.9 among the younger generations. During the same period the share of persons who finished high school rose to 40 percent. Table 9.7 evaluates the different cohorts.

When we examine the effects of education on turnout over time, we find that there are no significant differences in turnout within cohorts between grammar school graduates and secondary school graduates. However, we also find that nonvoting did not increase among the better educated born before 1956. This result favors the generational hypothesis. Within the older generations, particularly among the prewar generations as well as the war generation, turnout decline among persons with high levels of education was significantly lower than among those of other educational levels. Therefore, the effect of education is much stronger among these generations than in the sample as a whole.

Turnout is remarkably low among the better educated in the young cohort. Moreover, differences between various educational groups increased in the youngest cohort even though turnout declined. In 1991/92, 15 percent of high

Table 9.7. Nonvoting by Education Within Different Generations, 1982/84-1991/92 (percent who did not vote)

	Percent not voting 1982/84			Percent not voting 1991/92			Difference 1991/92 -1982/84		
	Gram- mar school	Secon- dary school	High school	Gram- mar school	Secon- dary school	High school	Gram- mar school	Secon- dary school	High school
Year of birth									
1903-11	10.2	9.7	3.6	[2]	[2]	[2]	-	-	-
1912-20	6.6	3.2	4.8	15.8	3.9	14.3[2]	+ 9.2	+ 0.7	+ 9.5[2]
1921-29	5.0	8.2	5.5	13.0	2.7	5.6	+ 8.0	- 5.5	+ 0.1
1930-38	5.0	7.6	3.0	11.1	15.9	5.6	+ 6.1	+ 8.6	+ 2.6
1939-47	6.6	4.9	7.2	12.1	8.2	6.9	+ 5.5	+ 7.2	- 0.3
1948-56	8.6	4.4	9.1	13.4	10.5	5.9	+ 4.8	+ 6.1	- 3.2
1957-65	15.2	10.8	8.4	25.8	15.6	9.3	+ 10.4	+ 4.8	+ 1.1
1966-74	-	-	-	32.3	23.9	15.0	-	-	-

Notes: [1] Persons without graduation not included. [2] Number of cases less than 30.
Source: ALLBUS 1982/84 and 1991/92.

Table 9.8. Proportion of Nonvoters by Level of Education Within Different Generations, 1982/84-1991/92 (percentage share of nonvoters)

	Education level of nonvoters 1982/84[1]			Education level of nonvoters 1991/92[1]		
	Grammar School	Secondary School	High School	Grammar School	Secondary School	High School
Year of birth						
1903-11	82.6	15.2	2.2	[2]	[2]	[2]
1912-20	85.4	7.3	7.3	84.9	6.1	9.0[2]
1921-29	66.0	23.4	10.6	87.5	4.2	8.3
1930-38	66.7	26.2	7.1	67.9	26.4	5.7
1939-47	62.3	19.7	18.0	64.7	21.6	13.7
1948-56	57.3	14.7	28.0	64.2	22.4	13.4
1957-65	47.9	31.9	20.2	52.3	30.0	17.7
1966-74	-	-	-	36.2	36.2	27.6

Notes: [1] Persons without degree not included . [2] Number of cases less than 30.
Source: ALLBUS 1982/84 and 1991/92.

school graduates report not going to the polls compared to 8.4 percent in 1982/84. When we look at the aggregate level, we notice that the educational composition of nonvoters had changed dramatically given that 35 to 40 percent of the younger generations had graduated from high school and 27.6 percent of the nonvoters born between 1966 and 1974 hold a high school degree. In 1991/92 only 36.2 percent of the nonvoters fell into the lowest educational category as opposed to 47.9 percent among the youngest cohort in 1982/84. Hence, among the young nonvoting is not primarily a phenomenon of the less educated (see Table 9.8).

Overall, we find that the rise in educational attainment of the younger generations did not lead to a boost in turnout. Instead, shifts in education levels at the aggregate level go hand in hand with changing behavioral patterns at the individual level. An increasing number of young Germans do not vote regularly. Thus, the education level of the youngest generation of nonvoters differs tremendously from that observed among the older prewar generations of nonvoters. However, because generational replacement does not explain most of the decline, we detect two parallel developments in voting participation. The majority of voters within the older generation who had a low or average education contributed largely to the decline in turnout. Within the younger generations, the nature of the effect is ambiguous. Although the differences in participation rates between various educational groups remained constant or became even larger, the portion of nonvoters with high education also rose to a great extent.

Furthermore, we should not underestimate the drop of turnout among the middle and older cohorts. The decline reached between 5 and 8 percentage points. Likewise, in the oldest cohorts we observe even higher rates of decline. This result does not support the generational hypothesis and leads to the conclusion that the institution of voting is weakened in a general sense. Apparently, the generational effects accelerate a process that is taking place in most parts of German society. Aside from civil servants and aside from persons who regularly attend church, there are hardly any differences between social groups examined here with respect to the rate of turnout decline. With a few notable exceptions, turnout decline is thus a phenomenon that can be detected in the entire German electorate.

THE MIDDLE-CLASS NONVOTER

The findings at the individual level revealed only slight variations in electoral participation across social groups. As we will demonstrate on the following pages, compositional changes of the population led to a shift of the social characteristics of nonvoters. It should be noted first, however, that these distributional changes of the German population did not enlarge the proportion of the groups known for relatively low participation rates. When considering the period since the 1980s, persons without even a grammar school diploma, unemployed people, and members of religious communities other than Catholic or Protestant represent only a small and largely unchanging minority in German society.

There is only one compositional effect that is in line with the correlations observed at the individual level. German society became somewhat younger. At the same time, however, the education level of the electorate has grown considerably. Thus, turnout would have had to *rise* as a result (see Teixeira 1992 for similar observations in the United States). As shown in the preceding section, differential effects are at work at both the aggregate and the individual levels when it comes to education. This section analyzes the compositional effects, first by comparing the distribution of German nonvoters with regard to social characteristics at the beginning of the 1980s and ten years later; and second by building an index of disproportionality that reports how the social characteristics of the nonvoters deviate from the social structure for the entire electorate.

This index was constructed by dividing the percentage of a certain social group among nonvoters by the share of this social group within the entire population over age 18. For measuring the variables age and household size, averages instead of percentages are used. An index value of 1 indicates that there is no deviation between the proportion of nonvoters and the proportion of the entire electorate, while lower and higher values testify to a disproportionality of some sort.

The findings, shown in Table 9.9, are not surprising. Most of the variables confirm the claim that voters and nonvoters have become more similar in their social composition over time. We come to the opposite observation only in the cases of age and education. Regarding education, the index of disproportion increased largely because of the high abstention rates among individuals who left school without a diploma. Nonetheless, the share of nonvoters with an educational level higher than average (top two categories) increased to 39.1 percent in 1991/92, up from 35.5 in 1982/84. Similarly, the portion of nonvoters holding a grammar school degree dropped from 62.2 percent to 56.9 percent at the beginning of the 1990s. Hence the net impact of education on declining turnout is rather negligible because the growth in education can be observed in both groups. With respect to age, however, we find that the age composition of voters and nonvoters was very similar at the beginning of the 1980s, whereas German nonvoters became younger by 1991/92. Specifically, almost half of the nonvoters were younger than 35 years (48.9 percent) in 1991/92 compared to 41 percent in 1982/84.

In sum, nonvoters have become more middle class in outlook. Moreover, given that only 20 percent of German nonvoters indicate that they never participate in any election, the majority of German nonvoters only occasionally stays away from the polls. This leads to the conclusion that about 30 to 40 percent of the German electorate can be considered "occasional nonvoters." These findings make it difficult, if not impossible, to uphold the claim that German nonvoting is confined to the fringes of German society. In fact, German nonvoters are in most cases part of the mainstream of middle-class society.

We can confirm this claim on the basis of so-called self-report measures. Consider the variable "self-reported status in society," as shown in Table 9.10. Respondents had to judge their own position in society on a scale ranging from 1 (lowest) to 10 (highest). When we collapse the indicator to a 5-point scale, the data show that German nonvoters have started to think of themselves more frequently as "middle class" than they used to. Only 27.4 percent of the German nonvoters in 1991/92 judged their own status as being "lower class" or "lower middle class" compared to 38.9 percent in 1980/82.

Table 9.9. Proportion of Nonvoters by Sociostructural Indicators, 1982/84, 1986/88, and 1991/92 (percentage of nonvoters)

	'82/84	'86/88	'91/92		'82/84	'86/88	'91/92
Occupation				**Religion**			
Civil servant	4.4	3.2	2.3	Catholic	37.0	43.5	37.4
Self-employed	4.7	3.2	3.8	Protestant	40.8	40.3	46.2
White-collar	15.4	19.9	25.4	Others	11.7	6.0	3.8
Blue-collar	15.6	15.8	16.5	No religion	10.5	10.2	12.6
Not in labor force	59.9	57.9	52.1				
Disproportion index	*0.76*	*0.90*	*0.96*	*Disproportion index*	*1.39*	*1.31*	*1.10*
Education				**Church attendance**			
No degree	2.3	5.5	4.0	Regularly	20.3	19.0	14.3
Grammar sch.	62.2	61.3	56.9	Sometimes	17.7	17.9	16.6
Secondary sch.	0.8	20.1	23.6	Rarely	25.9	32.3	33.8
High school/ college	14.7	13.1	15.5	Never	35.1	30.8	35.3
Disproportion index	*1.02*	*1.10*	*1.09*	*Disproportion index*	*0.91*	*0.91*	*0.90*
Club membership				**Age**			
No	76.9	67.0	68.6	18-25 years	16.2	21.9	17.1
Yes	23.1	33.0	31.4	26-35 years	24.9	26.6	31.8
Disproportion index	*1.07*	*1.10*	*1.09*	36-45 years	15.7	12.6	14.3
				46-65 years	23.7	23.9	22.6
				65+ years	19.5	14.9	14.3
Union membership				*Disproportion index*	*1.00*	*1.08*	*1.08*
Yes	11.0	8.5	13.5				
No	89.0	91.5	86.5				
Disproportion index	*1.02*	*1.03*	*1.01*	**Size of household**			
				One person	34.3	28.0	33.1
				Two persons	31.0	27.0	27.3
Marital status				Three persons	16.6	20.7	20.3
Married	42.7	47.8	42.9	Four +	18.1	24.3	19.3
Widowed, divorced	29.8	21.7	25.0	*Disproportion index*	*1.10*	*1.02*	*1.05*
Single	27.5	30.5	32.1				
Disproportion index	*1.44*	*1.32*	*1.40*				

Source: ALLBUS.

Although lower-class self-identifications continue to be overrepresented among nonvoters, almost every second German nonvoter considered him- or herself middle class at the beginning of the 1990s. Similarly, upper-middle-class identifications rose from 15.7 percent to 23.2 percent. When we consider the ideological orientations of the population–assuming that middle-class orientations tend to be moderate–self-placements on the left-right continuum provide additional support for the notion of the middle-class nonvoter (see Table 9.11).

Apparently, political radicalism does not promote electoral abstention. To the contrary: those who placed themselves in the middle of the ideological space were overrepresented among nonvoters. 55.3 percent of German nonvoters placed themselves in one of the two middle categories on the left-right-continuum compared to 42.9 percent of the voters. This result reinforces the key claim that most German nonvoters come from the political center.

Table 9.10. Self-Reported Class Status: Voters and Nonvoters, 1980/82-1991/92

| | 1980/82 | | 1991/92 | | Change | |
	Nonvoters	Voters	Nonvoters	Voters	Nonvoters	Voters
Lower	9.6	2.4	5.4	2.2	- 4.2	- 0.2
Lower middle	29.3	16.2	22.0	14.6	- 7.3	- 1.6
Middle	42.2	51.0	48.4	51.6	+ 6.2	+ 0.6
Upper middle	15.7	27.5	23.2	29.8	+ 7.5	+ 2.2
Upper	3.2	2.9	1.0	1.9	- 2.2	- 1.0
Total	100	100	100	100		

Source: ALLBUS 1980/82 and 1991/92.

Table 9.11. Proportion of Voters and Nonvoters Along the Left/Right-Continuum, 1991/92

	Extreme Left	Left	Middle	Right	Extreme Right	Total
Nonvoter	3.7	20.4	55.3	16.3	4.3	100
Voter	4.9	24.7	42.9	21.1	6.4	100
Disproportion -index[1]	0.74	0.85	1.24	0.80	0.71	

Notes: [1] The disproportion index was constructed as in Table 9.9.
Source: ALLBUS 1980/82 and 1991/92.

POLITICAL INTEREST AND TURNOUT DECLINE

Given that social and demographic indicators are only marginally helpful for explaining turnout decline in German elections, this section explores the attitudinal underpinnings of turnout. Both voting behavior research and participation research have identified political interest as the main predictor of turnout (Lazarsfeld et al. 1968; Campbell et al. 1960; Verba, Nie, and Kim 1972; Radtke 1972; Golzem and Liepelt 1976). Our data show that political interest has gained in importance for predicting electoral participation over the 1980 to 1992 period. Although the probability that a person who is very interested in politics would vote in federal elections has remained high, nonvoting increased tremendously among persons who were not interested in politics (see Table 9.12).

In 1992 the share of nonvoters among persons without any political interest reached 47.6 percent. This constitutes an increase of more than 35 percentage points over the course of the period examined here. The findings are similar when we look at individuals who are only slightly interested in politics. From 1980 to 1992, nonvoting rose by 21.4 percentage points. However, despite the strong bivariate relationship between political interest and electoral participation, political interest cannot explain the dramatic decline of turnout in the last ten years. In a trend that may be related to the rise in educational levels, the percentage of individuals who showed much or very much interest in politics increased from 26 percent in 1980 to 33.2 percent in 1992 (see Figure 9.2). This growing political interest of the German electorate as a whole runs counter to the decrease in turnout.

Note that interest in politics dropped slightly in 1991 and in 1992. However, this appears to signify a process of normalization after reunification in 1990 when political interest was unusually high. The average level of political interest still remained at a high rate equivalent to that of the late 1980s. As Figure 9.2 shows, in 1992 the percentage of persons not interested in politics was about half the level observed in 1980. Although in 1992 only 5.7 percent of the German electorate was not interested in politics, about 20 percent of the electorate did not vote.

Table 9.12. Nonvoting by Level of Political Interest, 1980-92 (percent who did not vote)

	1980	1982	1984	1986	1988	1990	1991	1992
Political Interest								
Very much	2.2	5.2	6.3	3.3	3.4	5.5	6.3	8.8
Much	1.2	3.4	5.1	6.2	5.4	6.7	6.5	9.4
Somewhat	1.5	4.3	6.1	7.7	9.5	10.3	10.0	11.3
Little	3.6	7.2	12.5	14.1	15.3	16.4	22.1	25.0
Not at all	12.7	16.1	24.5	29.6	35.6	43.0	39.6	47.6
Total	3 2	5.7	9.3	9.8	10.9	11.9	12.9	14.9

Source: ALLBUS.

Figure 9.2. Trends in Political Interest in West Germany, 1980-92 (means)

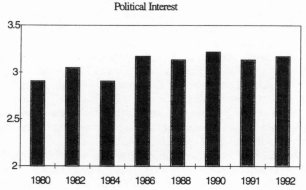

Source: ALLBUS.

However, the most sizable group (40 percent) is composed of those who are somewhat interested in politics. Because these respondents place themselves in the middle of the scale, the meaning of the response and thus the behavioral implications are more difficult to interpret. As Table 9.12 indicates, given that the share of nonvoters increased by 9.8 percentage points in this group, they contributed significantly to the overall decline.

If we were to account for overreporting, the findings would be even more marked. Overreporting is most frequent among the respondents who claim to be interested in politics (Eilfort 1994, 141). Hence, we can assume that abstention among the highly interested is even more frequent than the results indicate. But even if we ignore overreporting, the changing composition of the nonvoters with regard to political interest is apparent.[8]

The share of people who were very or somewhat interested in politics is on the rise among German nonvoters. As the more recent data indicate, the majority of nonvoters cannot be characterized as uninterested. While 68.1 percent of the nonvoters had little or no interest in politics in 1980s, just 45.6 percent reported similarly low levels of political interest in 1992 (see Figure 9.3).

This does not mean that individuals who are not at all or only weakly interested in politics are a minority among German nonvoters. However, those of little or no interest are not responsible for most of the turnout decline. The expansion of education as well as the growing interest in politics should have led to a higher cognitive mobilization and therefore to more participation. Yet, by the 1990s, nonvoters are not that different from voters. The analysis of political interest provides additional evidence to support this conclusion.

How can we explain the fact that educational levels are much higher among younger generations while young people also vote less often than before? Perhaps this riddle can be solved when we combine political interest with education and age. Table 9.13 presents the interest-related turnout by level of education.

Figure 9.3. Proportions of Nonvoters by Level of Political Interest, 1980, 1984, 1988, and 1992 (percentage share of nonvoters)

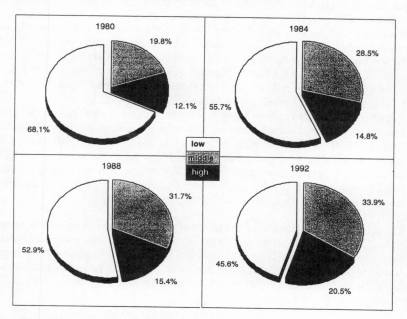

Source: ALLBUS 1980, 1984, 1988, 1992.

Table 9.13. Nonvoting by Levels of Education and Political Interest, 1982/84-1991/92 (percent who did not vote)

Education[1]	Political Interest 1982/84			Political Interest 1991/92			Difference 1991/92-1982/84		
	High	Middle	Low	High	Middle	Low	High	Middle	Low
Grammar school	3.0	4.5	13.9	12.5	10.8	28.6	+9.5	+6.3	+14.7
Secondary school	4.8	6.5	11.7	4.5	12.2	31.5	-0.3	+5.7	+19.8
High school	6.8	6.2	11.0	6.3	9.0	27.0	-0.5	+2.8	+16.0
Total	4.7	5.2	13.4	8.2	10.8	29.0	+3.5	+5.6	+15.6

Notes: [1] Persons without degree not included.
Source: ALLBUS 1982/84 and 1991/92.

The findings presented above support the view that the better educated are more likely to vote. Since the well-educated are more frequently interested in politics, there should be an indirect effect of education on turnout as well. As it turns out, once the level of interest is held constant, education does not affect the likelihood of nonvoting. Hence, the effect of education can be considered an indirect effect via political interest. People with high education behave in the same manner as other groups with different education levels within different categories of political interest. This is exactly what Lazarsfeld et al. (1968) demonstrated in their seminal study of voting behavior in 1944. Quite obviously, it is not education, but political interest that is the direct predictor of turnout.[9]

Because the young were least likely to vote, this may indicate that the decline in turnout is due to a political demobilization of the German youth (Falter and Schumann 1993: 49). However, the empirical evidence runs counter to this assertion. Most important, contrary to Falter and Schumann's assumption, political interest did not decline among the young. While it is true that the increase in political interest was strongest among those born 1947 or earlier, levels of political interest still rose slightly or remained constant among the younger cohorts (see Table 9.14).

Thus, the youngest portion of the German electorate did not show less interest than had been the case about ten years ago. In fact, average scores of interest increased to 3.01 in 1991/92, up from 2.94 in 1982/84. At the same time, nonvoting increased in nearly every cohort, as the results in Table 9.15 indicate. Hence, there is no indication that the decline in participation is due to the rise of a young and less involved part of the electorate.

Table 9.14. Changes in Levels of Political Interest Within Different Generations, 1982/84-1991/92 (means[1])

	Political interest 1982/84	Political interest 1991/92	Difference 1991/92 -1982/84
Year of birth			
1903-11	2.65	2.85	+0.20
1912-20	2.86	3.13	+0.27
1921-29	2.99	3.29	+0.30
1930-38	3.00	3.17	+0.17
1939-47	3.12	3.35	+0.23
1948-56	3.16	3.17	+0.01
1957-65	2.94	3.05	+0.09
1966-74	-	3.01	-

Notes: [1] Scale of political interest: 1=not at all interested to 5=very interested. A positive difference value means that political interest has increased.
Source: ALLBUS 1982/84 and 1991/92.

Table 9.15. Nonvoting by Levels of Political Interest Within Different Generations, 1982/84-1991/92 (percent who did not vote)

	Political Interest 1982/84			Political Interest 1991/92			Difference 1991/92-1982/84		
	High	Middle	Low	High	Middle	Low	High	Middle	Low
Year of birth									
1903-11	4.2	4.7	16.4	0.0	6.7	31.0	-4.2	+2.0	+14.6
1912-20	2.9	4.9	9.9	6.5	10.3	26.4	+3.6	+5.4	+16.5
1921-29	4.2	2.5	11.2	7.5	5.9	25.0	+3.3	+3.4	+13.8
1930-38	3.5	3.6	10.2	8.3	9.6	20.8	+4.3	+6.0	+10.6
1939-47	4.6	5.6	9.8	8.5	6.5	23.6	+3.9	+1.1	+14.8
1948-56	4.7	5.6	16.4	6.7	9.1	22.4	+2.0	+3.5	+6.6
1957-65	7.5	9.0	19.8	9.8	13.3	33.5	+2.3	+4.3	+14.7
1966-74	-	-	-	9.5	19.4	40.8	-	-	-

Source: ALLBUS 1982/84 and 1991/92.

The results do confirm the argument made by Falter and Schumann (1993) in one respect. At the beginning of the 1990s, the probability that young people with low or no interest in politics stayed away from the polls was very high. The proportion of nonvoters in this group was 40.8 percent. However, over the years the decline in turnout among those less interested in politics was largely independent of generational factors. The right side of Table 9.15 indicates that nonvoting seems quite uniform across cohorts. The effects of generation differences are weaker when interest in politics is used as an indicator instead of education.

What are the reasons for this surprising observation? It is likely that better educated people still feel a stronger obligation to vote, independent of their level of interest. Within the younger generations, nonvoting was relatively high among persons who had a medium level of interest. This result leads to the conclusion that interest in politics was not a sufficient motivation to go to the polls for younger generation.

NONVOTING IN EAST GERMANY

Do these findings apply to the eastern part of the new Germany? When we investigate social structure variables with the help of cross-sectional data, the results indicate that the better educated, white-collar workers, and the self-employed are more likely to vote. However, the differences between various social groups were not very large. In the following analysis, I examine age as a relevant demographic factor affecting turnout because it contains the least ambiguity.

With respect to the age composition of the two electorates, nonvoters in East Germany are quite similar to their counterparts in West Germany. In East and West, young citizens were least likely to vote. Almost half of all nonvoters were less than 35 years old. According to the election samples of the Federal Department of

Table 9.16. Nonvoting by Age in East Germany (percent who did not vote)[1]

	Percent who did not vote	Composition of all nonvoters
Age		
18-24	44.7	20.7
25-34	35.6	27.6
35-44	24.1	15.5
45-59	17.4	17.6
60+	19.5	18.6
Total	26.0	100.0

Notes: [1] Excluding those who voted by mail.
Source: Federal Department of Statistics.

Statistics, turnout among young Easterners was even lower than among their West German counterparts (see Table 9.16). However, as we move up the age brackets, participation rates between East Germans and West Germans converge. What are the reasons for these differences among German youth? Generations born into the socialist regime experienced different socialization patterns, perhaps leading to a more distant attitude toward participation in a democracy. Below, we consider attitude differences between the (younger) generations of East and West Germany.

When we compare interest in politics among different generations, the findings correspond to those reported in the West German case. The proportion of East Germans who are uninterested in politics is just a bit larger than that of West Germans (24.8 vs. 23.0 percent) (Table 9.17). Similarly, given a certain level of political interest, turnout rates differ only slightly between East and West. As the middle section of Table 9.17 indicates, 40.2 percent of the East Germans not interested in politics stayed away from the polls (West: 44.2).

Overall, political interest is the strongest correlate of turnout in the cross-section. Yet, Easterners who are interested in politics voted slightly less frequently than the respective group of Westerners (by 5 points). Regarding the composition of nonvoters, more than half of the East German nonvoters reported being politically interested. Considering the findings of the Konrad Adenauer Foundation studies, this proportion would amount to 64 percent (Klingemann et al. 1998: 175). Hence, any attempt to explain low turnout in East Germany by the degree of political involvement is likely to be misleading. Moreover, it is generally surprising how little variation there is between East and West in the results reported so far, despite the significant differences between their social and political settings.

Differences between East and West emerge when we consider the various indicators of political apathy. From 1990 to 1992, political alienation rose substantially. In 1992 and 1993, more than half of the East Germans report not being satisfied with the working of the political system (see Table 9.18).

Interestingly, however, the politically dissatisfied were not significantly more likely to abstain than the politically satisfied. 10.5 percent of the East Germans who claimed that the political system worked by and large did not vote compared to 22.5 percent of the alienated Easterners. While political dissatisfaction thus helps somewhat in explaining nonvoting in the East, it is far too widespread to interpret nonvoting as the behavioral outlet of political dissatisfaction (see Table 9.19).

Table 9.17. Turnout and Political Interest in East and West Germany, 1991/92

Political Interest	Composition within the population		Percent who did not vote		Composition of nonvoters	
	East	West	East	West	East	West
Very much	9.9	11.2	14.1	7.8	7.1	6.2
Much	17.7	21.9	12.1	8.3	11.1	12.8
Somewhat	43.1	44.0	16.2	10.8	35.9	33.8
Little	15.8	17.3	26.2	23.9	27.4	29.3
Not at all	9.0	5.7	40.2	44.2	18.5	17.9
Total	100.0	100.0	19.5	14.1	100.0	100.0

Source: ALLBUS 1991/92.

Table 9.18. Trends in Political Satisfaction in East Germany, 1991-94

Satisfied	Proportion satisfied in East Germany			
	1991	1992	1994	Difference 1994-91
Very	2.2	0.9	0.9	-1.3
Fairly	62.0	48.4	42.0	-20.0
Not very	32.5	44.3	47.2	+14.7
Not at all	3.3	6.4	9.9	+6.6
Total	100.0	100.0	100.0	
N	1,441	993	811	

Source: ALLBUS 1991, 1992, 1994.

Table 9.19. Turnout and Political Satisfaction in East Germany, 1991-94

Satisfied	Percent who did not vote			Proportion of nonvoters		
	1991	1992	1994[2]	1991	1992	1994
Very	6.5	[1]	[1]	0.7	0.5	1.0
Fairly	17.4	15.3	10.5	52.7	42.9	24.6
Not very	25.9	17.6	23.2	40.9	45.0	62.2
Not at all	35.4	31.4	22.5	5.7	11.6	12.2
Total	20.9	17.5	18.2	100.0	100.0	100.0

Notes: [1] Number of cases less than 30. [2] Data weighted.
Source: ALLBUS 1991, 1992, 1994.

In recent years, turnout rates in state elections have continued to decline. This was the case in state elections held in Saxony, Saxony-Anhalt, and Brandenburg in 1995. This trend, as well as the decline in turnout from 74.5 to 72.5 percent in the federal election of 1994, suggests that the trend toward abstention continues in East Germany. Though the current correlation of turnout and political dissatisfaction is not very strong, further research will have to establish whether there is a possible link between political alienation and turnout in East Germany.

CONCLUSION

The picture of German nonvoters has changed. Earlier characterizations of nonvoting as a phenomenon found among those of low social status no longer holds. At the beginning of the 1990s, German nonvoters do not differ tremendously from those who participate in elections with regard to their social composition as well as political attitudes. Thus, if we seek to explain the decline of turnout in German elections, persistent differences in electoral participation across different social groups are of limited help. The phenomenon of nonvoting has reached the German middle class.

Similarly, political attitudes commonly employed in the analysis of turnout are insufficient for explaining the trend in turnout. In addition to the attitudes presented in this chapter, even measures such as party attachment, satisfaction with the political system, as well as sense of citizen duty do not help explain most of the drop of electoral participation in West Germany (see Kleinhenz 1995). Because differences between voters and nonvoters are small, there are no easy explanations for turnout decline in the German case. In general, the German nonvoter has become more middle class in social background and has moved toward the political center. As a result, students of German elections have to solve the same puzzle as those engaged in research on American elections (Brody 1978). Part of the puzzle may be the increase in the repertoire of political acts in which individuals of high status now routinely engage (Barnes and Kaase 1979). This may make the act of voting one among several individuals consider when seeking to participate in political life.

With regard to turnout in East Germany, the findings obtained with the West German data were largely replicated. When we compare social demographics in East and West, largely similar structures emerge. And even the level of political dissatisfaction in eastern Germany adds only a small piece to the puzzle of nonvoting. As the results presented here show, theoretical approaches to nonvoting, incomplete as they are, will not have to be modified for studying turnout in East Germany.

NOTES

1. In their comparative research Verba, Nie, and Kim (1978) examined how institutional arrangements—for example, registration laws, and social factors—are intertwined and affect turnout in combination. Part of the achievement of Verba et al. is that they demonstrated that research on political participation has to take

differences across political systems into account.

2. As is the case in a large number of American studies, other sociopolitical characteristics such as party attachment and political efficacy also are included in the research program, and the reader is referred to my book, where the respective results are reported (Kleinhenz 1995).

3. In order to account for alternative explanations of declining turnout, the possibility of changes in political institutions must not be neglected. However, no such change comes to mind for the time until 1990. Then, German reunification in 1990 led to a redesign of institutional arrangements. As for West Germany, it is hard to imagine how these should have affected turnout. After all, except for its enlargement, no fundamental change of the political system had taken place in the West. In the East, however, German unification was accompanied by a decline of nearly 18 percentage points between the last election held in the GDR (March 1990, turnout 93.4 percent) and the first all-German federal election (December 1990, turnout 75.5 percent). However, explaining this development would require a theoretical framework much more attuned to the situation of system change. Therefore, the analysis here will only consider the decline between 1990 and 1994, when turnout dropped another few points in the East (to 73.4 percent). Once again, institutional changes are unlikely to play a large role in this trend. Hence, this set of explanations will not be considered in the analysis here.

4. Miller attributes turnout decline in the United States to "changes in the generational composition of the electorate." The younger generation "votes at a rate well below that of older generations" (Miller 1992: 1). In his analysis of German election data, Rattinger confirmed parts of Miller's findings (Rattinger 1994b: 83). Thus, in addition to social changes, this chapter investigates the impact of generational replacement. Unfortunately, due to data constraints, this part of the analysis will have to remain incomplete. The exact role the generational hypothesis plays in the explanation of the drop in turnout could not yet be ascertained. So far, the period of turnout decline in Germany is simply too short.

5. The largest and most reliable data source in Germany is provided by the Federal Department of Statistics (Amtliche Repräsentativstatistik des Statistischen Bundesamts). In each election until 1990, the electoral behavior of 3.7 percent of the German electorate was directly monitored. Due to legal constraints, however, this data source includes only party choice, turnout, sex, and age. Quite obviously, this information base is too small for most research purposes. Moreover, in 1994 no such data were collected. The General Population Surveys, referred to as ALLBUS, are usually released every second year and encompass about 3,000 respondents each time. In 1991 an additional survey was carried out–for the first time in both parts of Germany. The third data source is the election studies of the Konrad Adenauer Foundation that include between 2,000 and 3,500 respondents. These are conducted a few weeks before or after a parliamentary election. The following analyses employ the surveys of the elections in 1983, 1987, and 1990.

6. The results are similar for income. They are not shown here but are reported in Kleinhenz (1995).

7. The exception is low turnout among the small number of respondents who left school without any degree.

8. For purposes of presentation, the categories "very much" and "much" political interest were combined to form the category "high" political interest, the categories "not at all" and "little" to form the category "low political interest."

9. There is only one exception to this claim. Persons who attended grammar school participated at a much lower frequency in 1991/92 compared to 1982/84, even when they reported a high degree of interest in politics.

Part II

COLLISIONS BETWEEN EAST AND WEST? REGIONAL DIFFERENCES IN PARTY SYSTEMS

10

Voting Behavior in Subnational Elections: Local and State Elections in Three Länder, 1988-95

Ulrich Eith

In recent years, local politics in Germany has enjoyed increased scholarly attention. One reason for this lies in the growing dissatisfaction with political parties, which has led to a fundamental shift in the debate about how to involve citizens in democratic decision-making. Aside from changes in party structures, the principal demand has been for more opportunities to hold referendums at the local level. Proponents regard this as an effective way of giving citizens a greater say in various local matters that affect them directly. Local politicians also have started to call for a greater use of plebiscites in decision-making processes. They hope that majority support in fundamental questions of local politics will grant their decisions legitimacy and hence wider acceptance (Böhme 1994: 102-122).

An additional factor has put the spotlight on local politics. A core communitarian criticism of Western liberal democracy is that it neglects the principle of subsidiarity. Communitarians believe that strengthening the role of local communities, and hence their normative ability to promote integration, is a crucial step toward realizing civil society. Institutions such as the family, schools, and local networks can help to buttress society's moral foundations. But there is no escaping one indispensable prerequisite: politically active citizens (Etzioni 1993).

The extent to which normative expectations of citizens' political involvement reflect reality can be measured empirically. This chapter is intended as a small contribution to this question. It seeks to determine factors of voting behavior at the local level by examining voting behavior at different levels of government in Germany between 1988 and 1995.[1] While national elections in unified Germany have already been widely analyzed and documented (e.g., Klingemann and Kaase 1994; Dalton 1993b; Padgett 1993; Oberndörfer et al. 1994), voting behavior in local elections has received much less attention. Moreover, comparisons between the different levels of government are few and far between, and their findings generally are mixed. A particularly controversial point in the literature is the role of political parties in local elections (Kevenhörster 1983; Löffler and Rogg 1991).

Are voters in local elections primarily candidate- and issue-oriented? Does this mean that the longer-term party identifications and ideological positions that influence voters at Land and federal levels are less relevant in local elections? These questions cannot be answered in detail with survey data based on random national samples. The available aggregated data for municipalities, however, are an adequate source for a first analysis that we undertake below.

STRUCTURAL CONDITIONS

A comparison of voting behavior at different levels of government must take differences in structural conditions into account. Germany has a federal structure and a long tradition of strong local government. These two principles are part of the Basic Law. The functions of government are divided between the federal, Länder, and local authorities. The different levels of government, however, have noticeably less autonomy in exercising these powers and functions than in the United States, for example. Although the federal government's power to exert influence through statutory regulations has led to the sharing of functions and policies between the levels of government in many fields, foreign affairs remains the preserve of the federal government; and culture, education, and the police those of the Länder. Local authorities, in turn, are largely responsible for basic social welfare and public infrastructure (Conradt 1993).

Unlike the United States or France, the Federal Republic of Germany is a parliamentary democracy in which political parties play a crucial role. At the federal level and in the sixteen Länder each party puts up a slate of candidates. Voters choose among them in general, direct, free, equal, and secret elections. The members of state and national assemblies, in turn, elect the federal chancellor and the prime ministers of the Länder. The same system of proportional representation is used for all federal and Land elections. The number of seats each party holds in the Bundestag and the Länder parliaments is proportional to its total votes, not the number of directly elected candidates. Accordingly, voters can only choose indirectly who sits in parliament and the government.

In contrast, there is a variety of electoral systems at the level of local governments. In some Länder the mayor is elected by the local council, in others directly by voters. Different Länder use different systems. Baden-Württemberg, Bavaria, and Rhineland-Palatinate allow the electorate the greatest flexibility in casting their ballots. Voters have as many ballots as there are seats on the local council, and they are free to cast them for candidates from different tickets (ticket-splitting) or even, within limits, cast more than one vote for individual candidates (cumulation). In North Rhine-Westphalia, Hesse, and the Saarland, voters have just one vote, which they cast for the slate of a party or for a *Wählervereinigung* (WV–nonparty local citizen tickets). Lower Saxony and the new eastern Länder, with the exception of Thuringia, have adopted a middle position: each citizen has three votes that can be split in any combination among the different slates of candidates (Woyke 1994: 153-183).

Parliamentary elections at all three levels of government take place every four or five years. Given that legislative periods vary, Germany does not have a regular election cycle. Nonetheless, the results of regional elections always reflect to some degree attitudes toward federal politics (Anderson and Ward 1996). Thus, the ruling party in Bonn always does worse in midterm Länder elections than in those closer to federal elections (Dinkel 1989).

VOTING BEHAVIOR IN LOCAL ELECTIONS: A THEORETICAL OUTLINE

Voting behavior usually is analyzed in terms of either the sociological approach, the Michigan model, or the rational choice model. Regardless of the theoretical model, the determinants of voting behavior in local elections can, in principle, be divided into general, contextual, and local factors (Pappi 1976). The influence of general factors on voting behavior is much the same everywhere in the country and at all levels of government (federal, Land, and local). These include ascribed competence in dealing with problems, party images, and cleavages arising out of sociostructural conflicts. Contextual factors serve to explain differences between regions and local authorities. They too are independent of the level of government. Numerous studies have shown that in Germany regional traditions and peculiarities influence voting behavior and characteristics of the party system (cf. Oberndörfer and Schmitt 1991). Unfortunately, it is not always easy to distinguish between general and contextual determinants of voting behavior in local elections, because most studies deal with a single Land or individual cities.

The few studies that have been conducted so far emphasize for the most part the influence of contextual and general factors on voting behavior. Applying bivariate regression analysis to federal, Länder, and local election results in the Mannheim/Heidelberg metropolitan area in 1980, Dieter Hermann and Raymund Werle established that there is a high structural consistency in voting behavior that is independent of level of government. Qualifications apply, however, to party choice in local elections in smaller localities. The authors discovered that a significant segment of middle-class conservative voters voted for candidates rather than parties (Hermann and Werle 1983).

Thomas Czarnecki examined the influence of sociostructural variables on election results in Rhineland-Palatinate between 1979 and 1989. For the CDU and SPD in particular he found similar patterns at all three levels of government. Accordingly, the effects of social structures must be primarily contextual or general. At the same time, the correlation between social structure and election results is weaker in local elections across the board, especially in smaller localities, where local ties are stronger. This effect is more pronounced in flexible local election systems (Czarnecki 1992: 85-88). Local factors may influence results more strongly at this level.

By definition, local factors affect voting behavior exclusively at the local level, and may thus serve to explain differences between levels of government. The strength of these factors depends on local peculiarities, such as parties' structures, images, and competence, whether local politics tends to be issue- or candidate-oriented, or institutional peculiarities in the electoral system at the local level. Even if local voting behavior is largely independent of voting behavior at other levels of government, it is necessary to show that these local factors do have a significant and consistent effect on voting behavior.

One prominent difference between local party systems in southern Germany and those at the Land and federal levels is the success of Wählervereinigungen: non-party local citizen tickets organized expressly for the purpose of electing individuals to local offices. It would be wrong, however, to interpret the WV as expressions of politicized local conflict in terms of the cleavage model. Quite the contrary: the WV are part of a nonparty tradition in German local government that prefers to settle contentious local matters on the basis of the facts, rather than through political deals, political compromise, or majority vote (Wehling 1991). The share of the vote obtained by WV is thus a useful "indicator of consociational democratic structures" (Gabriel 1991: 376). In keeping with this view, Berthold Löffler and Walter Rogg do not employ peculiarities of local party structures or party images to explain singularities of voting behavior in Baden-Württemberg. According to them, local government prefers for the most part a nonpolitical, consensus- and issue-oriented approach rather than party-political conflicts (Löffler and Rogg 1991). One consequence—an effect strengthened by Baden-Württemberg's local government electoral system—is that voters tend to be candidate-oriented in local elections.

There is little doubt that the flexible electoral systems used in Baden-Württemberg, Bavaria, and Rhineland-Palatinate strengthen the effect of local factors. The smaller the city or town, the greater the degree of ticket splitting. The SPD and the Greens regularly poll the highest share of unsplit tickets (Löffler and Rogg 1991: 116). Apart from this, no systematic studies have been conducted of the conditions under which voters are likely to split their ballots. If, however, the electoral system encourages people to alter their voting behavior significantly in local elections, then—assuming other conditions are equal—there should be very little difference between the results of local elections on one hand and of Länder and federal elections on the other in Länder with inflexible voting systems at all levels. Yet the persistent success of the WV in Hesse stands in contrast to this expectation (Gabriel 1991: 377).

This leaves the question of the desire for harmonious regulation of conflict—problem-solving on the basis of consensus and facts. There is no reason why different attitudes toward politics at different levels of government should not encourage differences in voting behavior. For instance, voters may perceive local problems as a local concern. Similarly, if local party organizations are not taken seriously, this could strengthen the importance of individuals. Unfortunately, there is insufficient evidence to quantify the strength and effect of consensus-oriented attitudes among the electorate. Hence, it is necessary to resort to estimates based on various indicators.

The few representative surveys of voters' attitudes about local politics are limited to individual cities. Moreover, some of these have not been analyzed in sufficient detail to date. There is some evidence of an antiparty effect among voters in local elections in Baden-Württemberg. Surveys in different local authorities show that the feeling is fairly widespread that parties should stay out of the town hall (Löffler and Rogg 1991: 120). Oscar W. Gabriel investigated political competition in forty-nine municipalities in Rhineland-Palatinate. His variables included the percentage of votes cast for the WV, the fractionalization of the local partysystem, and indicators of the conflict behavior of the factions represented in the local council. For the period 1974-84, Gabriel found that the balance between consensus and conflict–"the combination of tradition and change"–was relatively constant (Gabriel 1991: 396).

Studies of attitudinal patterns among local representatives and candidates in North Rhine-Westphalia and Baden-Württemberg produced very similar findings (Gabriel et al. 1984; Köser 1991; Mielke and Eith 1994). Traditional, consociational attitudes are especially strong in rural areas. The larger the town, the higher the average level of education; or the younger the councilors, the more willing they are to accept conflict, particularly among left-wing and alternative parties. The influence of party structures in local politics gains the upper hand, though never to the complete exclusion of other forms of political conflict regulation. In short: on the basis of this evidence, we may cautiously conclude that some sections of the electorate perceive local politics as a distinct form of politics. This, in turn, must be regarded as a local determinant of voting behavior.

This discussion leads us to the following conclusions:

1. The analytical distinction between local and general or contextual factors of influence increases one's awareness of the complexity of voting behavior in local elections. This is by no means identical to voters' relative propensity for personalities rather than parties. The extent of this candidate-orientation is largely a function of the provisions of the respective electoral system. However, it also may reflect a specific local approach to politics.

2. We can identify the factors influencing local voting behavior only by comparative analysis. In ideal circumstances, this involves different levels of government and different regions. Difficulties of comparison often bedevil studies of local politics and voting behavior, and further regional case studies are needed to alleviate this shortcoming. If such studies are to deepen our understanding of voting behavior at the local government level, however, they will, at the very least, also have to examine the relevance of the independent variables at different levels of government.

3. Distinctions between the determinants of voting behavior in local elections are not tied to the use of any specific theoretical model of voting behavior. However, the choice of model affects the findings. From the sociological point of view, the factors obtained are primarily general or contextual. In the long run, the effects of sociostructurally determined group norms are felt at all levels. Should sociostructural variables explain local election results to a significantly lesser degree than they do Länder or federal election results, this is an indication that local factors are in play. Only in very rare cases, however, will this be a consequence of specifically local, permanently politicized, and sociostructurally entrenched

structures of conflict. Party images and issue- and candidate-orientations–which sociopsychological and rationalistic models treat as determinants of behavior–hold greater promise of pinpointing factors that influence local voting behavior. If results at the local level diverge significantly and consistently from those at the Land or federal level, it may be possible to develop a theoretical model to interpret these as effects of a specifically local approach to politics, and consequently as a reflection of local determinants of voting behavior.

DATA AND ANALYSIS

The following analysis is based on aggregated data for municipalities in Baden-Württemberg, North Rhine-Westphalia, and Brandenburg (data sources in Appendix A)–that is, three Länder with different electoral systems at the local level. As discussed above, the systems in Baden-Württemberg and North Rhine-Westphalia are fundamentally different. This analysis also takes into account differences in the party spectrums at the Land and federal levels. The inclusion of Brandenburg enables us to compare western and eastern Länder.

Table 10.1 shows the results of elections in the three Länder between 1988 and 1995. There are obvious differences between the party systems in eastern and western Germany. For several decades–until the rise of the Greens in the 1980s–West Germany had a stable three-party system consisting of CDU/CSU, SPD, and FDP. The FDP now safely exceeds the 5 percent threshold only in federal elections. The situation in the new eastern Länder is quite different. Apart from the CDU and SPD, the PDS–the former Communist party which has turned into an eastern German regional party–enjoys widespread support at all levels of government (Neu 1995a).

There are also differences between voting behavior at local and at other levels of government. Turnout is a good example (see also chapter 10 by Thomas Kleinhenz in this volume): the higher the level of government, the higher the turnout. The only exception is the 1994 local elections in North Rhine-Westphalia, which were held on the same day as the federal elections. Second, in Baden-Württemberg and Brandenburg more parties participate in local than in Land or federal elections. In particular, conservative WV, but also left-wing, environmental, and women's tickets, win considerable support. In both Länder, local electoral laws allow voters to split their ballots.

The differences between the results of federal, Land, and local elections in Table 10.1 require closer inspection. First, we look at the influence of sociostructural variables on voting decisions (for lack of data this analysis will exclude Brandenburg). Subsequently, we examine the relationship between local and other elections. The results of five local elections in the three Länder are the dependent variables, and the results of federal and Land elections the independent variables. In this case we are interested in determining whether, and to what extent, voting behavior in local elections can be explained by voting behavior in Land and federal elections.

Table 10.1. Results of Federal, Land, and Local Elections in Baden-Württemberg, North Rhine-Westphalia and Brandenburg, 1988-95 (party vote shares in %)

	WBT	CDU	SPD	FDP	GRU	PDS	REP	WV	oth.
Baden-Württemberg									
GRW 1989	61.6	34.3	24.4	4.4	5.2	-	1.9	26.5	3.3
GRW 1994	66.7	32.9	23.2	3.6	6.0	-	1.4	27.8	5.1
LTW 1988	71.8	49.0	32.0	5.9	7.9	-	1.0	-	4.1
LTW 1992	70.1	39.6	29.4	5.9	9.5	-	10.9	-	4.7
BTW 1990	77.5	46.5	29.1	12.3	5.7	0.3	3.2	-	2.9
BTW 1994	79.7	43.3	30.7	9.9	9.6	0.8	3.1	-	2.6
North Rhine-Westphalia									
GRW 1989	65.6	37.5	43.0	6.5	8.3	-	2.3	-	2.4
GRW 1994	81.7	40.3	42.3	3.8	10.2	-	0.6	-	2.8
LTW 1990	71.8	36.7	50.0	5.8	5.0	-	1.8	-	0.7
LTW 1995	64.1	37.7	46.0	4.0	10.0	-	0.8	-	1.5
BTW 1990	78.7	40.5	41.1	11.0	4.3	0.3	1.3	-	1.5
BTW 1994	81.9	38.0	43.1	7.6	7.4	1.0	1.3	-	1.6
Brandenburg									
GRW 1990	n.a.	26.6	28.2	6.0	3.4	16.4	-	8.9	10.5
GRW 1993	59.9	17.0	28.1	6.4	2.6	18.9	-	15.9	11.1
LTW 1990	67.1	29.4	38.2	6.6	9.2	13.4	1.2	-	1.9
LTW 1994	56.3	18.7	54.1	2.2	2.9	18.7	1.1	-	2.3
BTW 1990	73.8	36.3	32.9	9.7	6.6	11.0	1.7	-	1.8
BTW 1994	71.5	28.1	45.0	2.6	2.9	19.3	1.1	-	1.0

Notes: GRW = local elections (*Gemeinderatswahlen*): means of all municipalities, weighted by the number of persons entitled to vote; LTW = Land elections (*Landtagswahlen*); BTW = federal elections (*Bundestagswahlen*); WBT = turnout (*Wahlbeteiligung*); WV = *Wählervereinigungen*, GRU=Greens; REP=Republikaner.

Given the nature of this study, the findings are primarily descriptive. At best, the comparison between the Länder can provide systematic evidence of local factors in local election voting behavior as well as the conditions under which they have an effect. Empirical questions concerning the causes and shaping of attitudes to local politics or regional traditions are beyond the scope of this chapter. The following three groups of questions are central to the analysis.

The first concerns political fundamentals. What are the differences between the structures of the party systems in these three Länder? Since unification, the cleavage between western and eastern Länder is "the most conspicuous structural divide in the entire German electorate" (Oberndörfer et al. 1994). Because the national party system reflects political front lines, it also sets a framework for voting behavior at the local level. Accordingly, a detailed knowledge of possible structural differences is indispensable for this analysis.

The next question concerns the sociostructural bases of voting behavior. Are there significant differences between the levels of government? The relationship between social structure and voting behavior in Germany is generally accepted and need not be repeated here. If our analysis of elections at different levels reveals similar relationships, especially in the same direction, social structure may be taken as a general or contextual factor that works at all levels of elections. Should sociostructural variables be significantly less successful at explaining local election results, this may be interpreted as an indication of the influence of local determinants.

Finally, the relationship between the levels of government requires examination. To what extent can results at the local level be explained by the results at the Land and federal levels? Can we identify contexts that may provide further explanations of voting behavior at the local level? From the preceding remarks we can draw empirically verifiable conclusions, for instance, on the effect of the electoral system. If the electoral system influences voting behavior at the local level, then one would expect the model to be more successful at explaining the variation of the local election results in North Rhine-Westphalia than in Baden-Württemberg. Weak correlations in Brandenburg, in contrast, may reflect generally less rigid voting behavior. Furthermore, our investigations lead us to expect differences in voting behavior between the supporters of different parties. If the conservative wing of the electorate tends to place greater importance on issues and candidates, the model's elements for explanation–federal and Land election results–should perform better for left-wing and alternative parties.

STRUCTURES OF COMPETITION

The federal structure of the Federal Republic of Germany favors regional traditions. This is also reflected in voting behavior, such as the traditional strength of the FDP in Baden-Württemberg or the consistently high turnout in the Saarland. German unity has added another facet to the diversity of regional behavior. Analyses of federal and Land elections since 1990 point to independent elements in voting behavior among eastern Germans. They find expression in factors such as the strong position of the PDS or the unusually high support for the CDU among blue-collar workers.

We rely on factor analysis to provide a detailed insight into the structure of the party system, its dimensions, and cleavages. This analysis is based on results for all parties in the Bundestag in federal and Land elections between 1988 and 1995. The objective of this procedure is to distill the existing data into a few, easily interpretable basic structures. The factors obtained in the procedure are uncorrelated and may be regarded as dimensions of the political sphere. The interpretation of their meaning is based on their respective characterizing variables.

Interpretable models can be calculated for all three Länder (see Appendix B). The fact that variables with matching content converge with respect to the same factor without exception, underlines the pronounced and stable structure of the results for each party. The findings for Baden-Württemberg and North Rhine-Westphalia are similar: the political sphere in both Länder is defined by three factors. The first and most important factor reflects the competition for power between the two large political parties: support for the CDU and the SPD move inversely to each other. The correlation between the two parties is strongly negative. The strongholds of one party are generally the whipping posts of the other (see Figures 10.1 and 10.2).

Green and FDP voter support have much more independent structures. Thus the results of Alliance 90/Greens and to a lesser degree those of the PDS constitute a separate, second factor. The third factor is characterized by the results of the FDP. In essence, the findings for the two Länder correspond with the structural model for the western German electorate as a whole (Oberndörfer and Mielke 1990: 23-29).

The constellation in Brandenburg is very different. Calculations indicate four relevant factors—the crucial distinction compared to the western Länder lies in the battle lines between the parties. The first, and most important, factor is the political contest in the East. It consists of the cleavage between the CDU and the former Communists, PDS. Support for the two parties moves inversely. A second factor is the position of the SPD. In contrast to the West, the SPD's share of the vote is far less closely related to the distribution of CDU results. The two other factors are the showings of the FDP and the Alliance 90/Greens, respectively. In the 1994 federal and Land elections in Brandenburg, both parties failed to reach the 5 percent threshold. This structural pattern of voting behavior in Brandenburg is representative of political perceptions and party political contests throughout eastern Germany. In terms of election manifestos, the CDU and the PDS are at the opposite ends of the political spectrum (see Figure 10.3). Although this factor model was constructed specifically for Brandenburg, it is not unique to this Land. Political activity in Saxony-Anhalt, for instance, also fits this "eastern pattern" (Eith 1997).

The data on our two-dimensional presentation of the structures of political competition in our three Länder reveal crucial differences.[2] Baden-Württemberg has a structurally entrenched, dual system of party political competition. At each level of government there is a high correlation between the results of different elections, which is reflected by their close proximity in the diagram. Although there are no significant structural differences between the federal and Land levels, local elections have their own pattern of voting behavior.

In North Rhine-Westphalia, too, the pattern of party competition is one of strong structural consistency. Here, however, election results at all levels of government are in close proximity. The pattern of local election results is the same as those in federal and Land elections. The most obvious explanation for this pattern is the restrictive local electoral system in North Rhine-Westphalia, exacerbated by the fact that local elections take place on the same day as federal elections. Further surveys may show that the similarities in voting behavior in local and other elections reflect a particular attitude to local politics–that they are, in other words, a result of a specific cultural factors.

Figure 10.1. The Structure of Political Competition in Baden-Württemberg (factor analysis)

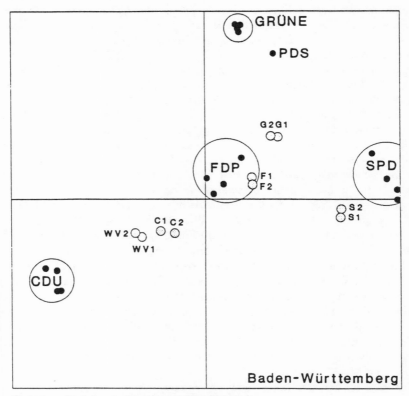

● federal- / land elections (1988-1994)
○ local elections (1: 1989, 2: 1994)

In Brandenburg, patterns of party competition reveal both consistency and change. There are strong structural similarities between PDS results in elections at all levels and in CDU results at the federal and Land levels. There is a noticeably larger spread in the federal and Land results of SPD, FDP, and Alliance 90/Greens. Local election results are relatively unstructured. With the exception of the PDS, the positioning of all parties at the local level shifted between 1990 and 1993. The difference between the results obtained by CDU and SPD at the local and federal/Land levels almost doubled during this period. Figure 10.3 supports the thesis that the Brandenburg electorate forms specific patterns of voting behavior for different levels of government as gains in voting experience.

Figure 10.2. The Structure of Political Competition in North Rhine-Westphalia (factor analysis)

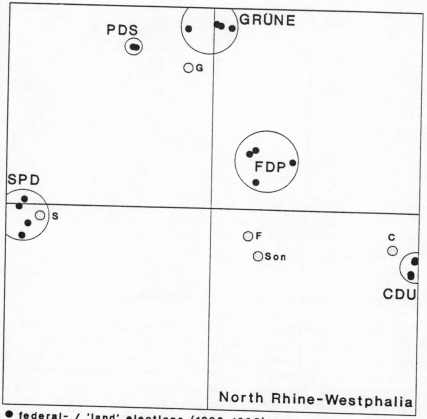

● federal- / 'land' elections (1990–1995)
◎ local election (1994)

Figure 10.3. The Structure of Political Competition in Brandenburg (factor analysis)

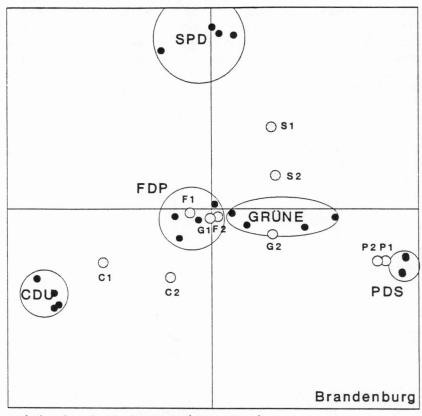

● federal- / land elections (1990-1994)
○ local elections (1: 1990, 2: 1993)

SOCIAL STRUCTURE AND VOTING BEHAVIOR

Throughout Western Europe, voting behavior is based on fundamental coalitions between social strata and the corresponding parties (Lipset and Rokkan 1967). Although real or media-created political figures and issues may cause significant fluctuations in the electorate's mood, these are short-term phenomena. However, the relationship between social structure and voting behavior also is not constant over time or the same at the federal and the Land levels. It is quite conceivable that existing regional or local peculiarities may produce changes in voting behavior at different levels of government. The coalition between electorate and party has to be confirmed and updated periodically at all levels of government. This is accomplished either through the ballotbox or through open expression of one's social interests. Thus, changes in the relationship between social structure and voting behavior are a result of both changes in social structure and in the specific policies that parties adopt to represent particular interests.

The next step is to examine the extent to which social structure can explain voting behavior at different levels of government. The available data on social structure also were examined with the help of a factor analysis (see Appendix C). Regression analysis was used to determine whether and how the factors obtained could explain the variation in the voting shares of the parties.[3] Turnout does not significantly affect the results. The table of regression coefficients has been omitted for reasons of space. For lack of data, the following calculations do not include Brandenburg.

In terms of content and factor analysis, five factors play a role for the relationship between social structure and election outcomes in Baden-Württemberg. The first is the cleavage between services/university cities and manufacturing centers. Factor two represents local authorities adjoining large centers. Factor three is the urban/rural cleavage. Factor four reflects the contrast between Protestant and Catholic areas. The proportions of in- and out-migration load highly on factor five.

The relationships between social structure and voting behavior are the same at the federal and Land levels. At the local level the findings for the conservative parties diverge slightly from the pattern. Thus, the CDU's share of the vote is always directly proportional to the percentage of Catholics. In addition, in federal and Land elections the CDU does well in small to medium-sized towns with a high proportion of manufacturing industry. At the federal and Land levels, voter support for the FDP has a positive correlation with the proportion of Protestants. In local elections the WV compete directly with both parties. The WV do well in towns with a high proportion of employment in manufacturing and skilled trades as well as in rural and Protestant areas. The support structures of the SPD and Alliance 90/Greens are similar across all levels of government. The SPD vote correlates positively with population density and proportion of Protestants. The strongholds of the Alliance 90/Greens lie in Baden-Württemberg's services / university centers.

A three-factor model adequately describes the social structure in North Rhine-Westphalia. Once again, factor one is the cleavage between the service and manufacturing sectors. Factor two distinguishes between urban areas and rural communities, and factor three represents the religious cleavage. The structural patterns of elections at all levels of government are similar in almost all respects. The CDU and the SPD compete directly with each other: the CDU benefits from a high proportion of Catholics and low population density, the SPD from a high proportion of Protestants and high population density. The Alliance 90/Greens' support rises with the share of services industries. The FDP finds its strength in the services-oriented towns and small cities.

There are only minor structural differences between the levels of government in both Länder. The factors studied have almost identical effects on voting behavior at the federal and Land levels as well as at the level of local government.

Accordingly, in both cases social structure is largely a general or contextual determinant of voting behavior in local elections.

This leaves the question of whether the sociostructural models in Baden-Württemberg and North Rhine-Westphalia can be used for quantitative predictions. The respective shares of explained variance are summarized in Table 10.2. Once again, the findings for federal and Land elections are the same in both Länder: the variation in election outcomes explained by the sociostructural variables is of much the same magnitude in elections for the Bundestag as for the state parliaments.

It is worth pointing out that in North Rhine-Westphalia, voting behavior in local elections also fits this pattern. The studies of this Land provide little evidence of specifically local determinants of voting behavior. The situation is different in Baden-Württemberg. Sociostructural factors have far less explanatory power in local elections than in federal and Land elections. An obvious cause are the flexible provisions inherent in Baden-Württemberg's local electoral law, which allows voters to split tickets and cast multiple votes for individual candidates. However, we should not disregard the possibility that this reflects other local factors as well.

Table 10.2. Multivariate Regression Analysis: The Dimensions of Social Strata as Predictors of Election Results in Baden-Württemberg and North Rhine-Westphalia (variation explained: R^2 x 100)

	WBT	CDU	SPD	FDP	GRU	PDS	WV
Baden-Württemberg (N = 1,110; 5 factors)							
GRW 1989	42.7	28.6	26.6	17.9	30.8	-	40.6
GRW 1994	39.9	27.5	23.9	13.7	36.3	-	41.8
LTW 1988	40.1	55.5	41.1	20.5	67.0	-	-
LTW 1992	35.4	61.3	27.0	25.9	59.3	-	-
BTW 1990	39.1	71.8	45.1	55.2	67.1	-	-
BTW 1994	20.9	65.1	32.9	37.7	73.0	68.6	-
North Rhine-Westphalia (N = 396; 3 factors)							
GRW 1994	57.4	54.0	46.6	17.4	44.3	-	-
LTW 1990	46.7	66.3	58.0	36.1	62.2	-	-
LTW 1995	41.5	66.8	55.0	31.5	65.0	-	-
BTW 1990	57.6	67.7	53.2	36.1	62.0	80.2	-
BTW 1994	55.6	66.0	51.5	40.0	64.1	84.8	-

Notes: significance level = .05; aggregated data for municipalities, weighted by the number of persons entitled to vote in 1994; GRW = local elections (*Gemeinderatswahlen*): means of all municipalities, weighted by the number of persons entitled to vote; LTW = Land elections (*Landtagswahlen*); BTW = federal elections (*Bundestagswahlen*); WBT = turnout (*Wahlbeteiligung*); WV = *Wählervereinigungen*, GRU=Greens.

THE RELATIONSHIP BETWEEN VOTING BEHAVIOR AT LOCAL, FEDERAL, AND LAND LEVELS

We now turn to the influence of federal and Land elections on voting behavior in local elections. To minimize the influence of a particular electoral cycle, we took the factors of the respective political level as the independent variables in our regression analysis.[4] In addition, we included the following characteristics to improve the explanation of variance: historical affiliation, primary administrative divisions of the Land, local authority size, number of factions active in local politics, stable majorities in the local council, and the share held in the local council by parties represented in the Bundestag.

Given that this study is intended primarily as a contribution to comparative research, the most important influences must be taken into account in an operational model that can be applied to all three Länder. The effect of historical and territorial affiliations on variance is minimal and may be neglected in this study. The different characteristics of party systems at the local level can be represented by the index of fractionalization, whose construction reflects different local political structures. The size of the local authority is a separate factor, even if its correlation with the index of fractionalization for Baden-Württemberg is slightly positive. Therefore, the model actually employed includes not only the factor scores of the three or four political factors–depending on the Land–but also the index of fractionalization[5] and the size of the local authority.[6] Including turnout does not substantially alter the amount of variance explained. Table 10.3 gives the share of variation explained by each predictor[7] as well as the sign of the corresponding regression coefficient. For reasons of space, we do not show a table with all regression coefficients.

The patterns of the 1989 and 1994 local elections in Baden-Württemberg are very similar. The three factors of political competition at the federal and Land levels explain only part of the results of these elections. Overall, left-alternative voters in these local contests paid more attention to the official party ticket than the conservative segment of the electorate. Political factors consistently failed to explain much variation in the results of CDU, FDP, and WV. This supports the thesis that their supporters are more issue- and candidate-oriented in local elections. Comparable findings are available for the 1980 local elections in Mannheim/Heidelberg (Hermann and Werle 1983: 397-398) as well as for the candidates for the 1989 local elections in Freiburg. In these cases, too, representatives of left-wing and alternative parties and groups were more likely to view local politics through the lens of party politics (Mielke and Eith 1994).

In contrast, the 1994 local elections in North Rhine-Westphalia could largely be explained by the three political factors. In addition, in the case of all four parties, the most influential factor was the strength of the respective party at the federal and Land levels. Thus, this approach provides few indications that local determinants are influential in North Rhine-Westphalia. Voting behavior at the local level correlates very strongly with the results at federal and Land levels.

Table 10.3. Multivariate Context Analysis: The Dimensions of Political Competition and Selected Context Variables as Predictors of Local Election Results in Baden-Württemberg, North Rhine-Westphalia, and Brandenburg (increase in variation explained: R^2 x 100, sign of the stand. regression coefficients)

Increase in Variation explained:		Pol. Comp.	Index Fract.	City Size	R^2 (total)
Baden-Württemberg (N = 1,098)					
CDU	1989	18.5	30.2 (+)	0.2 (-)	48.9
	1994	16.2	37.8 (+)	*	54.0
SPD	1989	46.3	17.8 (+)	*	64.1
	1994	46.8	18.5 (+)	*	65.3
FDP	1989	16.1	2.3 (+)	10.0 (+)	28.5
	1994	14.6	2.0 (+)	8.8 (+)	25.3
GRU	1989	25.4	1.0 (+)	7.5 (+)	33.9
	1994	23.3	0.5 (+)	10.8 (+)	34.6
WV	1989	17.4	47.1 (-)	2.4 (-)	66.8
	1994	18.7	50.5 (-)	2.4 (-)	71.5
North Rhine-Westphalia (N = 396)					
CDU	1994	81.3	5.4 (-)	*	86.7
SPD	1994	86.2	6.0 (-)	*	92.2
FDP	1994	57.9	0.7 (-)	1.2 (-)	59.9
GRU	1994	58.0	2.2 (+)	0.8 (+)	60.9
Brandenburg (N = 1,690)					
CDU	1990	37.4	2.4 (-)	4.9 (+)	44.5
	1993	15.8	14.0 (+)	0.3 (-)	30.3
SPD	1990	33.6	12.3 (-)	1.3 (+)	47.2
	1993	13.6	18.0 (+)	1.2 (+)	32.9
FDP	1990	25.8	4.1 (+)	*	29.9
	1993	30.9	3.6 (+)	0.4 (+)	34.9
GRU	1990	1.5	2.9 (+)	0.3 (-)	4.7
	1993	21.0	*	4.8 (+)	25.8
PDS	1990	77.2	0.1 (+)	0.2 (+)	77.5
	1993	70.3	8.7 (+)	0.9 (+)	79.9
WV	1990	2.0	0.7 (+)	0.6 (-)	3.3
	1993	9.6	4.3 (-)	12.7 (-)	26.5

Notes: significance level = .05; * = coeff. not sign.; aggregated data for municipalities, weighted by the number of persons entitled to vote in 1994; WV = *Wählervereinigungen*; GRU = Greens; index of fractionalization = 1 - (sum of the squares of voting shares). Local authority size is divided into quartiles in each Land.

The pattern in Brandenburg is more complex. First, only the PDS results are largely explained by the political factors (70 percent). The stability of the findings for the 1990 and 1993 local elections is comparable with that found in western Germany. Apart from this finding, however, the contrasting trends for the CDU and the SPD on one hand and the FDP and the Alliance 90/Greens on the other are remarkable. While the explanatory power of the model decreased for the local election results of the two large parties between 1990 and 1993, it increased for the two smaller ones. If one takes the regression coefficients into account, there are parallels between voting behavior at the local and the federal/Land levels for the PDS, and to a far lesser degree for the FDP and the Alliance 90/Greens as well. In contrast, local election results for the CDU and the SPD, particularly in 1993, do not correspond to the pattern in federal and Land elections.

The effect of local authority size on local elections is very similar in the three Länder examined here. Smaller parties benefit most from increasing city size, whereas the conservative WV perform best in rural areas. The 1990 Brandenburg results illustrate once again the fragility of local structures there.

In all three Länder the index of fractionalization has considerable effects on local election outcomes. However, it works in different ways in different places. In North Rhine-Westphalia the effect is as expected: the lower the index, the better large parties perform; the higher the index, the better small parties do. Almost by definition, a rising index value indicates success of various small parties, naturally at the overall expense of the large parties. Accordingly, the local election shares of the CDU and SPD have been shrinking since the local party system started factionalizing. The 1990 Brandenburg local election results fit into this pattern. Above and beyond this, the federal elections reveal the same relationships in all three Länder. The FDP and the Alliance 90/Greens benefit across the board from high fractionalization. A low level of fractionalization helps the CDU and the SPD.

The findings for local elections in Baden-Württemberg and Brandenburg (1993) are exactly the opposite. In these Länder, high levels of fractionalization had a large, positive influence on the voting shares of the CDU and SPD while the WV benefited from a low index value. Any plausible explanation offered for Baden-Württemberg must take account of the specific conditions of local elections in rural areas. In many smaller communities there are just a few voter group or citizen group tickets. Because the larger parties cooperate with these nonparty lists instead of running their own tickets, the index of fractionalization is extremely low. Accordingly, CDU and SPD local election results in larger towns and smaller cities are on average several percentage points higher that in rural communities. In large cities, though, there is greater fractionalization of the local party system, largely owing to the number of primarily left-alternative tickets, many of which do quite well. This development has hardly affected the SPD's share of the vote and, with small exceptions, only moderately decreased the CDU's support. Thus, in the final analysis, the fluctuations in the index of fractionalization reflect the strength of the WV in rural areas and small towns.

CONCLUSION

Compared to models of voting behavior at the federal and Land levels, models applied to local elections generally are less complex. It is widely agreed that one cause of a specifically "local" voting behavior is the existence of a particular attitude toward local politics. This is reflected in strong issue- or candidate-orientation or a preference for consociational forms of settling political conflict at the local level through consultation and consensus.

The empirical analysis of voting behavior in Baden-Württemberg, North Rhine-Westphalia, and Brandenburg provides further evidence of the structural and policy differences in the political debate in eastern and western Germany. Despite polarization at the federal and Land levels, the findings are similar: there are two basic patterns of voting behavior at the local level. There can be little doubt that local politics in North Rhine-Westphalia is structured along the lines of federal politics. The factors that determine politics at the federal and Land levels also determine the results of local elections. An examination of other contextual characteristics did not produce evidence to the contrary. In contrast, Baden-Württemberg has a dual system of local political competition. "Nonparty" tickets often run in rural areas and towns, whereas the federal parties dominate elections in the cities. This difference between the two Länder is not a result of sociostructural factors. In both Länder the relationship between voting behavior and social structure is the same in local and federal/Land elections, and their respective structures are essentially stable. The only question that remains unanswered is whether the two different patterns of local voting behavior are exclusively a result of the respective voting systems or whether these systems conceal different attitudes toward local politics. Given the data available, we cannot answer the question at this time.

The situation in Brandenburg appears to be still fluid. Against the background of a specifically eastern German form of federal and Land politics and generally a greater variability in election results, the results of the 1990 local elections resemble the situation in North Rhine-Westphalia: there is structural similarity between local and federal/Land elections. By contrast, the 1993 local elections tended toward the Baden-Württemberg model; federal and Land structures exert only partial influence because the WV play a considerable role in local elections in rural areas. Brandenburg's pattern could develop either way. On the basis of this analysis, we speculate that there is a greater possibility that a separate pattern will develop. If the western German experience is anything to go by, the relatively flexible provisions of the local electoral law and Brandenburg's predominantly rural/small town settlement pattern will encourage issue- and candidate-oriented elections at the local level.

The findings presented here emphasize the necessity of further research on voting behavior at all levels of government, particularly against the background of the current debate on the theory of democracy. The shape and spread of a specific attitude toward local politics, its relationship with regional political traditions, and its interaction with different electoral systems and elections cannot be established on the basis of aggregated data. Survey data will allow these questions to be answered at least at the level of the Länder.

NOTES

1. On the question of convergence in local voting behavior between the new and old Länder, see the author's analysis prepared for the Kommission für die Erforschung des sozialen und politischen Wandels in den neuen Bundesländern (KSPW) (Commission for Research on Social and Political Change in the Eastern Länder) (cf. Eith 1995).

2. The first factor of the factor analysis forms the horizontal axis of the system of coordinates and the second factor the vertical axis. The correlation between each party's share of the vote and the two factors serve as the coordinates to position each party.

3. The factor scores were estimated by regression analysis for each case and can thus function as variables. When used as predictors in a multivariate regression analysis, they have the advantage that they are uncorrelated.

4. The factor scores of the three (Baden-Württemberg, North Rhine-Westphalia) or four (Brandenburg) political factors (dimensions) were estimated for each case using regression analysis.

5. The index of fractionalization for each local authority is calculated as follows: 1 minus (sum of the squares of voting shares) (Rae 1968). If there are only a few parties at the local level, each with a large share of the vote, the index tends toward 0, if there are many each with a small share of the vote, the index tends toward 1.

6. Local authority size is divided into quartiles in each Land. Consequently, the cutoff figures for 1993 population (in Baden-Württemberg 1994) are not identical: Baden-Württemberg: 6,886/17,400/55,000; North Rhine-Westphalia: 32,600/89,700/300,000; Brandenburg: 1,542/11,100/32,000.

7. The three or four political factors were entered in the regression model in one single step and the rest of the characteristics stepwise. In this way the particular goodness of fit of each model can be measured.

APPENDIX A: DATA SOURCES

This analysis is based on the results of the following five local elections: Baden-Württemberg on 10/22/89 and 6/12/94; North Rhine-Westphalia on 10/16/94; and Brandenburg on 5/6/90 and 12/5/93. CDU, SPD, FDP, Alliance 90/Greens and PDS stood in all three Länder, as did the conservative WV, though only in local elections. In Brandenburg the WV includes Neues Forum, the Deutsche Forumspartei/NF, Demokratischer Aufbruch, the Bauernverband (1990), and independent citizens' tickets. In all three Länder the analysis is based on aggregated data for municipalities, compiled by the Office of Statistics. Because of this basis of aggregation, the number of cases used varies: Baden-Württemberg (N=1,110), North Rhine-Westphalia (N=396) and Brandenburg (N=1,700). Results in which one slate was elected unopposed were excluded. The data sets were weighted by the number of persons entitled to vote in 1994, without changing the number of cases. Although every effort was made to facilitate comparability, the corresponding coefficients for the three Länder are not directly comparable because of differences in the number of case studies. This must be taken into account in evaluating the results. The respective significance levels of the analyses are included in the interest of completeness, even though the data sets for the municipalities are complete in themselves and not random samples.

APPENDIX B: FACTOR ANALYSIS AND ELECTION RESULTS

A principal components analysis and a varimax rotation was applied to the results of the federal and Land elections in all three Länder. In Baden-Württemberg the three factors with an eigenvalue greater than 1 account for 88.3 percent of the total variance (54.4%, 19.1%, 14.8%), and in North Rhine-Westphalia for 94.3 percent (49.0%, 36.8%, 8.5%). The four factors for Brandenburg account for 81.4 percent of the total variance (39.3%, 20.7%, 13.2%, 8.2%). The KMO (Kaiser Meyer Olkin) measure is 0.77 (B-W), 0.72 (NRW) and 0.60 (Bran.).

APPENDIX C: FACTOR ANALYSIS WITH SOCIOSTRUCTURAL VARIABLES

In Baden-Württemberg and North Rhine-Westphalia a principal components analysis and a varimax rotation was performed on the available sociostructural variables. In Baden-Württemberg the five factors with an eigenvalue greater than 1 account for 82.1 percent of the total variance (37.6%, 18.9%, 11.9%, 7.8%, 5.8%). In North Rhine-Westphalia the three factors with an eigenvalue greater than 1 account for 75.9 percent of the total variance (52.3%, 15.2%, 8.4%). The KMO measure is 0.79 (B-W) and 0.85 (NRW).

Table 10. B.1. Factor Analysis: The Dimensions of Political Competition in Baden-Württemberg, North Rhine-Westphalia, and Brandenburg (rotated factor matrix)

		Factor 1	Factor 2	Factor 3	Factor 4
Baden - Württemberg (N = 1,110)					
SPD	BTW 1994	.971			
SPD	LTW 1988	.970			
SPD	BTW 1990	.944			
SPD	LTW 1992	.920			
CDU	LTW 1988	-.851	-.346		
CDU	BTW 1994	-.796	-.452	-.344	
CDU	LTW 1992	-.796	-.358	-.341	
CDU	BTW 1990	-.778	-.461	-.370	
GRU	BTW 1990		.945		
GRU	BTW 1994		.942		
GRU	LTW 1988		.923		
GRU	LTW 1992		.905		
PDS	BTW 1994	.345	.790		
FDP	LTW 1992			.893	
FDP	BTW 1994			.880	
FDP	BTW 1990			.859	
FDP	LTW 1988			.850	
North Rhine-Westphalia (N = 396)					
CDU	LTW 1990	.968			
CDU	LTW 1995	.966			
SPD	LTW 1990	-.952			
CDU	BTW 1990	.950			
CDU	BTW 1994	.949			
SPD	LTW 1995	-.938			
SPD	BTW 1990	-.928		-.355	
SPD	BTW 1994	-.910		-.393	
GRU	LTW 1995		.937		
GRU	BTW 1990		.928		
GRU	BTW 1994		.919	.325	
GRU	LTW 1990		.911		
PDS	BTW 1994	-.412	.812		
PDS	BTW 1990	-.396	.809		
FDP	LTW 1995			.917	
FDP	LTW 1990			.906	
FDP	BTW 1990		.309	.902	
FDP	BTW 1994	.374		.865	

		Factor 1	Factor 2	Factor 3	Factor 4
Brandenburg (N = 1,700)					
PDS	BTW 1994	.919			
PDS	LTW 1994	.918			
PDS	BTW 1990	.901	-.303		
PDS	LTW 1990	.901			
CDU	BTW 1990	-.857	-.361		
CDU	BTW 1994	-.793	-.492		
CDU	LTW 1990	-.791	-.415		-.305
CDU	LTW 1994	-.769	-.477		
SPD	BTW 1994		.924		
SPD	LTW 1990		.892		
SPD	BTW 1990		.881		
SPD	LTW 1994		.807		
FDP	LTW 1990			.828	
FDP	BTW 1990			.820	
FDP	BTW 1994			.791	
FDP	LTW 1994			.791	
GRU	BTW 1994				.861
GRU	LTW 1994				.852
GRU	BTW 1990	.577			.667
GRU	LTW 1990	.429			.643

Notes: Factor scores greater than .300; aggregated data for municipalities, weighted by the number of persons entitled to vote in 1994; LTW = Land elections (*Landtagswahlen*); BTW = federal elections (*Bundestagswahlen*).

11

Factors Explaining the Increase in PDS Support After Unification

Carsten Zelle

As in all of the Central and East European countries, the party that had ruled before the breakdown of communism somehow managed to reach the land of democratic party competition, even attracting significant portions of the vote in the former East Germany. The PDS (Party of Democratic Socialism), as the former SED (Socialist Unity Party) finally chose to label itself, received 16.4 percent of the vote in the first free elections of the then still existing GDR in March of 1990. This percentage shrank to an eastern German 11.1 percent in the first all-German federal (national) elections of the united country in December of 1990. Knowing that a large portion of the party's support came from what had been functionaries and beneficiaries of the socialist regime, politicians of the other parties as well as social scientists grudgingly came to view the party as a phenomenon one would have to live with for some time, yet also one that was unlikely to become more important.

Things appeared in a more dramatic light when it became clear that the party's electorate was not only a durable one, but also increased notably over the years. While surveys had indicated a moderate increase, the party's showing of 21.1 percent at the local elections in Brandenburg in late 1993 left analysts and the other parties puzzled–particularly so the Christian Democrats who finished only a close third in this election (20.6 percent). During the electoral marathon of what was called the "Super Election Year" of 1994, the PDS continued its string of relative successes in eastern Germany by repeatedly attracting around 20 percent of the vote in some of the new Länder. In the federal election of December 1994, the party received the support of 19.8 percent of the voters in the new Länder. In October of 1995, the party kept this strength in the Berlin state election. Despite the wide attention this result received, the 36.3 percent for the PDS in the eastern part of the city was similar to the 34.7 percent it had received in Berlin in the federal election held a year earlier. Thus, the party had demonstrated unmistakably that it was a factor that could not easily be discounted. At the same time, it became clear that the party would most likely remain an eastern German phenomenon. After attracting only 1.0 percent in the 1994 federal election in the old Länder, the party launched a large effort to improve its position in western Germany by focusing on the 1995 state election in Bremen–a traditional stronghold of communist parties during various episodes of the Federal Republic of Germany. When it gained only 2.4 percent of the vote in the May election in Bremen, it became obvious that there was little to gain for this party in the old Länder.

What accounts for the almost doubling of the party's share among the eastern electorate between the two federal elections of 1990 and 1994? As clearcut as the interpretation of the PDS as the party of the former regime had been right after unification, the growth of the party posed a number of riddles for social scientists. Depending on one's perspective, the electorate of the PDS after unification was portrayed as being driven by eastern identifications, by socialist ideology, by social values, by a mood of protest or by the problems of transformation–particularly unemployment and dependency of large segments of the population on a net of social welfare increasingly under attack in the united Germany.

In this chapter, I attempt to assess the relative weight these numerous factors have when trying to understand why support for the PDS increased in eastern Germany. In doing so, I focus on the demand side of electoral politics. Thus, I search for changes among voters that made them more likely to support the PDS. Changes on the part of the party, which might have made it more appealing to voters, are not investigated here (see Neugebauer and Stöss 1996).

EXPLANATIONS OF PDS SUPPORT

The following interpretations were proposed in the literature to help understand the electoral showings of the PDS. This list differs from the one recently proposed by Klein and Caballero (1996) in that its focus is mainly on political attitudes rather than on the personal situation of the individual, even though these are incorporated to some extent as well. Of the interpretations below, the first constituted the conventional wisdom after the 1990 elections, while the subsequent ones gained ground as the increase of the PDS vote became apparent.

Party of the Old Regime

This interpretation emerged immediately after the Volkskammer election of March 1990. Support for the SED-PDS was shown to come disproportionally from public employees with above-average levels of education. The interpretation of backward-oriented voting of former elites and functionaries was bolstered by the fact that the PDS had strongholds in cities, and particularly eastern Berlin, where agencies of the socialist government were based (see M.Jung 1990: 5-7; Roth 1990: 379). A key motive to vote for the PDS was said to be that these individuals were personal losers of German unification–not necessarily with regard to personal finances, but certainly in social status. This interpretation was in line with both the finding of exceptionally strong partisan attachments among supporters of the PDS (Neu 1994: 71) and the prognosis of poor electoral prospects for the party as a representative of status in a regime that had broken down (Kaase and Gibowski 1990: 25).

Accurate as this interpretation may be in the cross-section, some other factors are necessary for explaining why the party increased its share over the years. After all, the number of former functionaries cannot increase. Hence, some other change in attitudes, social position, or the like must have been responsible for this development. While the former functionaries may or may not have been subjected to this change in a particular way, it may constitute an explanation for the *increase* of PDS support, all-the-while former functionary status may continue to be a powerful explanatory variable in the cross-section.

Party of the East

This view holds that the PDS represents the internal division of German society into an eastern and a western section. The most obvious case in point for this interpretation is the lack of success for this party among western Germans. Winter (1996: 314-316) interprets the East-West division as a revitalization of the cleavage between center and periphery, which Lipset and Rokkan (1967) had described as resulting from the conflict over nation-building. A similar argument is made by Karl Schmitt in chapter 3 of this volume. Since indications are that self-identifications as "eastern Germans" are on the rise, this may help explain the growth of the PDS. Though it is explicitly backward-oriented and may even be accompanied by ideological elements, I consider eastern "nostalgia," be it complete or partial, as a special case of eastern identification (on the subject of nostalgia, see, e.g., Fritze 1995; Misselwitz 1996; in relation to the PDS vote, see Falter and Klein 1994, 1995; Klein and Caballero 1996; Neu 1995a).

Party of Socialist Ideology

Taking the label of the party seriously, it should represent the ideology of socialism, even if in a version it labels democratic. While survey data and electoral results had made it clear that the overwhelming majority of eastern Germans preferred the western system in the year of unification, support for socialism has increased since (see Westle 1994). To the extent that citizens not only adhere to certain goals strived for by socialism, but in fact want government and economy to be run according to this ideology, the party advocating the socialist ideology (even though an ambiguously revised version of it) could be expected to increase its electoral share. The pronounced self-placement of the PDS electorate on the left of the ideological spectrum (see Markus Klein in chapter 8 of this volume) could be taken as a case in point here.

Party of Socialist Values

According to this interpretation, the PDS and most of its electorate accept the judgment of history that socialism in its entirety is dead. Yet, while the means of socialist economy and government are no longer adhered to, some social goals continue to be cherished by large segments of the eastern electorate (see Veen and Zelle 1995). In particular, certain social values are said to be kept in high regard, even though socialist ideology is rejected. In fact, these values are at the center of a growing industry of literature on value differences between Germans in East and West. Neugebauer and Stöss (1996) interpret German unification as changing the balance on Lipset and Rokkan's conflict between workers and owners. Being materialized in the dispute over the relative weight of social justice as opposed to a free market in the contemporary German cleavage structure, the addition of the eastern German electorate strengthens the social justice pole. While not attracting support on the grounds of advocating an opposing ideology, in this view the PDS represents those for whom social justice heavily outweighs market freedom within the existing paradigm. If it could be demonstrated that this social pole had gained strength in eastern Germany, it would be easier to make sense out of the rise of the PDS.

Party of Problems with the Process of Transformation

While the two previous interpretations focus on long-standing attitudes of the eastern Germans, the PDS can also be viewed as a party perceived as fit to solve the political problems of the day. Particularly, strong urgency assigned to the problems of unemployment and of ensuring social welfare might motivate PDS support. Since these problems seem to be of particularly pressing character in eastern Germany, in this view the PDS could be viewed as representing East German interests vis-à-vis the process of transformation. In addition to the issue priorities, various aspects of the problem of unemployment—both at the individual and the societal level—might contribute to the understanding of party's expanded support base.

Party of Protest

When the interpretation is focused on either ideology, values, or issues, material policy proposals function as the main explanation. This is not the case when PDS support is viewed as indicating protest. It has become customary in Germany to assign the label "protest parties" to those that owe their support to negative attitudes toward established politics and policies rather than to policy proposals of positive content. The category protest vote may be particularly appropriate for the new voters the party attracted between 1990 and 1994 (see Neu 1995a: 173-174). Motivations for this protest may be general dissatisfaction with German politics and economics or dissatisfaction with the outcome of the unification process. In the latter case, it may also be interpreted in light of a conflict between subjective winners and losers of unification (see Neu 1995a: 203). The crucial point is that it is driven by political dissatisfaction with existing structures that cannot be traced to support for a substantive alternative.

Party of a Syndrome

Though most researchers emphasize one of the factors listed above, they also view PDS support as depending on a number of factors (most explicitly: Falter and Klein 1994: 34; Klein and Caballero 1996). In doing so, these factors can be viewed either as exhibiting the effects independently of each other, or as being so closely interrelated that they constitute a mind-set or eastern syndrome (this interpretation is hinted at in Neu 1995a, 203). If the latter is accurate, there is a type of voter who is characterized by most or all of the factors promoting PDS support. Thus, individuals would have to experience changes cutting so deeply that they stimulate adopting the eastern syndrome in order for them to change their party preference in favor of the PDS. In this view, the growth of the PDS signals the increased prominence of the eastern syndrome. Note that the model "party of the workers" is not on the list. At first sight, it is quite an amazing fact that a party in the socialist tradition has so little appeal to the working class as the PDS does (see Roth 1990: 376-380; and chapter 3 by Karl Schmitt in this volume).

The factors hypothesized to promote the rise of PDS support will be investigated from three perspectives. First, I will conduct aggregate analyses over time. Given the short time span since unification, this analysis is limited to inspection of the data points, not allowing for time series analyses. Second, I will conduct aggregate analysis in the cross-section comparing the relevant variables between the new Länder. Finally, I will address the question in a cross-sectional individual-level analysis. Special attention will be paid to the new PDS voters: what are their motives, and do they differ from the PDS standpatters?

DATA AND MEASUREMENT

Data sources are (1) surveys conducted by the Konrad Adenauer Foundation (KAS). These include at least 1,000 respondents in the East, and some of these are specifically designed to tap issues of relevance for the ongoing process of unification. The bulk of the individual-level analysis is performed with the help of merged spring and fall 1995 surveys, containing a total of 3,044 eastern German respondents with a total of 402 reporting a vote intention for the PDS. Except for correlation and regression analyses, these data were weighted to reflect the partisan and demographic distribution of the electorate; (2) survey results from other sources published by the respective researchers; and (3) statistics reported by the Federal Department of Statistics.

The variables for analysis are the following: The prime measure for the "party of the East"-hypothesis are self-identifications, which are tapped on two scales, running from 1 (no identification) to 7 (strong identification) in the KAS data. The variable "eastern-dominated identification" employed here is derived by subtracting German identifications from eastern identifications. It runs from -6 to +6. The results from other agencies are based on a forced-choice question asking respondents whether they think of themselves more as a German or more as an eastern German (Form A). Form B also included the option "more of a citizen of a region," the mention of which was not reported here. Unfortunately, researchers were forced to adapt their terminology to changing political conditions. Thus, the first surveys employed the category "citizen of the GDR," the ensuing ones "citizen of the former GDR" to tap eastern identifications. After 1992, only the category "eastern German" was used.

Socialist ideology as advocacy for a different organization of economy and government is mainly measured by the degree of agreement with the statement "a renewed socialism would be better for the future Germany than the current market system." Since the scales differed between the spring and fall KAS surveys, they were collapsed such that 3 indicated support for socialism, 1 indicated opposition, with 2 being the neutral position. In the longitudinal section, the statement reading "socialism makes sense in principle and can be implemented" is considered as well. By focusing on the ideology the party claims to represent, this variable is closely tuned to the analysis of the PDS.

The measurement of *support for social value orientations* is based on individual ratings of the general importance of certain goals. Thus, the goal "social justice" was set in relation to the goals "freedom" and "rule of law, democracy," which I interpret as representing the value cleavage identified by Neugebauer and Stöss. Thus, two scales result, ranging from +3 (social justice more important) to -3 (freedom or democracy, respectively, more important). Due to the high relevance of all these values in German society, the neutral center of the scale comprises most of the sample in both cases (in fall 1995 these were 59 and 57 percent, respectively). I interpret this as reflecting social reality rather than as a weakness of measurement (see chapter 8 by Markus Klein in this volume for a discussion of the different kinds of measurement issues in research of value orientations).

Issue priorities are necessary to test if the PDS represents the problems of the day. These were operationalized on the basis of individual importance (urgency) ratings as well. Both "unemployment" and "social welfare" were related to "environmental pollution" to tap interests of particular relevance for eastern Germans. The resulting scales range from +3 (unemployment or social welfare more important) to -3 (environment more important). In these cases most of the sample is located in the center category, too (62 percent in both cases in spring 1995). Unfortunately, in 1995, the issue variables are contained in the spring survey only.

Political dissatisfaction as the prime indicator for the "party of protest"-hypothesis is tapped through the question: "Generally speaking, how satisfied are you with democracy in Germany and the political system as whole?" The response "not satisfied" indicates political dissatisfaction, while the responses "satisfied" and "somewhat satisfied" are treated as satisfaction.

In addition, indicators of the respondents' *employment situation* are included in the analysis. In aggregate perspective the official unemployment rate is used together with public expectations regarding the future development of unemployment with the help of the question: "Do you think that in one year there will be more, equally as many, or fewer unemployed people in the Federal Republic?" In the 1990 and 1991 surveys, this question related to the GDR or to eastern Germany. In the individual-level analysis the unemployment rate is replaced by the fear that oneself or a member of one's family might be subjected to either total or partial joblessness.

VARIATION OVER TIME

For a factor to be responsible for changes in a party's vote share, it is reasonable to expect the two distributions to change in a parallel fashion over time. Thus, a first way to assess the relative importance of the factors hypothesized causal for the PDS increase is to monitor their development over time. Though the conclusions reached from this aggregate perspective can never be definite at the individual level, they may offer valuable hints. To the extent that one is willing to treat aggregate data as the kind of information that is truly important politically (Stimson 1991), knowing the distribution of certain variables and the degree of concomitant variation in the aggregate over time may even be more worthwhile than the focus on the individual. Due to paucity of data, rigorous analysis is impossible, however. The best I can do here is to ask which factors changed attitude positions among the eastern electorate such that they go with the increase of PDS support.

As it turns out, only a small number of these indicators changed in a steady fashion over the years. Most of them reached extremes some time between 1990 and 1994. Yet all of the factors potentially causing increased PDS support scored higher in 1994 than they had in 1990 (data shown in Table 11.1). Consider ideology and social values first. The percentage preferring a renewed socialism to the market economy increased from 14 to 21 between 1990 and 1994, with a high at 27 percent in 1993. As for value orientations, the stress on social justice in relation to freedom became somewhat more pronounced, increasing from 17 percent to 23 percent between 1990 and 1993. Note also that changes largely run in the opposite direction after 1993-94: Support for socialism in principle (not measured in 1990) decreased slightly between 1993 and 1995, as did the stress on social justice when related to rule of law and democracy (not measured in 1990), while it remained constant since 1993 when related to freedom. Despite this recent decline, support for socialist ideology and for social values in the eastern electorate was somewhat higher in 1994 than it had been in 1990.

This trend is even more obvious with regard to political issues: The percentage assigning unemployment a higher priority than environmental pollution doubled between 1990 and 1995, while it grew by a factor of five when social welfare was compared to environmental pollution. Simultaneously, dissatisfaction with the political system became more widespread, growing from 23 percent in 1991 to 34

Table 11.1. PDS Support and Factors Potentially Causing Its Growth in Eastern Germany, 1990-95

	1990	1991	1992	1993	1994	1995
1. PDS support						
% in federal election	11.1				19.8	
% in Land election	9.7-15.7				16.5-22.7	
% in surveys	9	9	13 (92/93)	14		Spring: 21 Fall: 20
2. Eastern identification						
a) EMNID (A)						
% mostly German			45		61	
% mostly eastern German			54		36	
b) IfD (90-92: A, 94: B)						
% mostly German	61		35 (Jan.) 40 (June)		34 (July) 45 (Dec)	
% mostly eastern German, '90-92: citizen of (former) GDR	32		60 (Jan.) 51 (June)		48 (July) 39 (Dec)	
c) KAS						
Mean "German" (7=high)			4.6			4.5
Mean "eastern German"			5.0			4.7
Eastern dominance (Ea.-Gm.)			.4 (92/93)			.2
3. Support for socialism						
% preferring renewed socialism to market system	14			27	21	23
% supporting socialism in principle				54		40
4. Value priorities						
% stressing social justice over freedom	17			23		23
% stressing social justice over the rule of law and democracy				32		27
5. Issue priorities						
% calling unemployment more urgent than pollution	17			26		36
% calling social welfare more urgent than pollution	6			22		30
6. Political dissatisfaction						
% not satisfied with democracy and political system		23		38	34	30
7. Unemployment						
% expecting unemployment to rise		41		66	33	56
Official unemployment rate (average per year)	7.3 (Dec.)	10.3	16.1	15.8	16.0	15.3 (95/1)

Sources: Election statistics, surveys conducted by the Konrad Adenauer Foundation (KAS) (weighted data) (1); *Der Spiegel*, No. 33/1994 (2a); Koch (1994), Noelle-Neumann (1992 and 1995) (2b); surveys conducted by the Konrad Adenauer Foundation (2c, 3, 4, 5, 6, 7; weighted data); Federal Department of Statistics (7). (A): only eastern German and German; (B) citizen of region included as additional option.

percent in 1994, after having reached a high at 38 percent in 1993. Possibly, either one of the trends may be related to the continuous increase in the unemployment rate from 7.3 percent in December 1990 to 16.0 percent in 1994. Yet, the percentage expecting unemployment to rise decreased between 1991 and 1994. This percentage was much higher in either 1993 and 1995, though.

Finally, consider eastern identifications. In 1990, 32 percent of eastern Germans thought of themselves primarily as "citizens of the GDR" while in 1994, 39 percent considered themselves "eastern Germans" (data reported by the Institut für Demoskopie [IfD] Allensbach). Thus, despite the expansion of the scale through a third category ("mostly citizen of region," selected by about 10 percent), the mention of the "eastern" category increased over this period. Of course this conclusion is valid only to the extent that one is willing to accept the references to the (former) GDR and to eastern Germany as equivalent. Be that as it may, a curvilinear development is what strikes the eye. In 1992, the percentage of "citizens of the former GDR" had been 60 in January and 51 in June. In July 1994 it was still at 48. The impression of a surge and decline phenomenon is corroborated by the results of the KAS and EMNID data, both of which report a decline in eastern identifications after 1992. In the case of the KAS data, the mean difference between eastern and German identification shrank slightly from .4 to .2 from 1992 to 1995.

How is this curvilinear development to be interpreted with regard to PDS support? Consider the change during 1994 in the Allensbach data in particular. It constitutes important–though sketchy–evidence for the notion of the PDS as the party of eastern identifications: While the percentage of eastern identifications decreased by 9 points between July and December 1994, the electoral share of the PDS remained largely constant between the European election of June 1994 (20.6 percent) and the federal election in December (19.8). While most probably of importance for the PDS, apparently the degree of eastern attachments does not translate directly into PDS support.

In sum, this first attempt to disentangle the causes for the increase in PDS support between 1990 and 1994 was unsuccessful. The data are in line with each one of the theoretical possibilities outlined above, including the "eastern syndrome." However, it is impossible to discriminate between these models on the basis of the evidence presented so far.

In passing, one might wonder why it is that these attitudes changed in the manner observed. A number of these trends can quite obviously be linked to changes in objective conditions, particularly the slow pace of the economic recovery and the high level of unemployment. As for identifications, ideology, and values, the line of interpretation hinted by Westle for identifications (1992: 25) and later elaborated for the ideology of socialism (1994) may be of additional value. According to this interpretation, latent attitudes present in eastern Germany were rendered less visible in 1990 due to unification euphoria. After the mood had cooled down, space opened for the latent attitudes to resurface. In any case, it is important to note that identifications, ideology, and values all appear to have taken a curvilinear course, having passed their high in the years 1992 and 1993 and declining ever since; the same is true for political dissatisfaction.

VARIATION ACROSS STATES

The strength of the PDS differs across the new Länder. In this section, I examine if these differences can be traced back to variation in the attitudes identified above. The relevant data are shown in Table 11.2, which lists the states' standings with regard to the respective variables, and in Table 11.3, which translates this information into state rankings. This latter table also contains Spearman correlations; these are reported for illustrative purposes rather than constituting rigorous hypothesis testing. With only five cases in the analysis, the bulk of coefficients remains way short of statistical significance.[1]

Still, the data suffice to demonstrate that there is a regional pattern to PDS support: The rankings of the party's shares at the 1994 Land and federal elections are correlated at .90, which is statistically significant at the .05 level. Moreover, the states in which the PDS is strongest also are the ones in which it had the largest gains (r=.60). This reflects the fact that the PDS consistently does best in the northernmost of the new Länder, Mecklenburg-Western Pomerania, while it has always been weakest in the southern states of Saxony and Thuringia.

What explains the cross-state variation? The PDS is strongest in those states where citizens are least satisfied with the political system (r=.90, significant at .05), most inclined to identify as eastern Germans (.72), and more likely to stress social values (.67 and .50). Judging from the correlation coefficients only, socialist ideology appears to play less of a role (.05). Yet, the population of Mecklenburg-Western Pomerania is the one which is by far most socialist of all the new Länder (at 33 percent), while the others cluster relatively closely together in this respect (between 17 and 22 percent). Thus, socialist ideology should not be discounted as a relevant factor even from this perspective of state-by-state comparison. On the other hand, issue priorities as well as indicators of the unemployment situation are only modestly related to the party's strength. What is more, the ranking of the increase in the unemployment rate is negatively related to PDS strength in the federal election (-.70). Indeed, Mecklenburg-Western Pomerania is the state that experienced the lowest increase in joblessness between 1990 and 1994.

When the differences in the increase of PDS support between the federal elections of 1990 and 1994 are related to these factors, the increase in unemployment continues to be negatively related to PDS support. Yet the overall unemployment rate in 1994 now appears as a potential predictor. Thus, states in which unemployment is high are the ones in which the PDS grew most notably, while it has little to do with the current strength of the party. The rankings of the remaining factors are not closely tied to the ranking of PDS increase, except for one of the value indicators: States in which the emphasis on "social justice" in comparison to "rule of law and democracy" is strongest are also the ones in which the PDS had the largest gains (r=.97).

Interesting as it may be, the quality of the data does not warrant digging more deeply into the state comparisons. Further regional disaggregation might provide a more solid data base. Yet, since most of the data are based on population surveys, smaller regional units would contain too few cases. Poor as the database may be,

Table 11.2. PDS Support and Factors Potentially Causing Its Growth in the New Länder

	MVP	Brand.	SA	Saxony	Thuringia
1. PDS support					
% in BT election '94	23.6	19.3	18.0	16.7	17.2
Change since 1990	+9.4	+8.3	+8.6	+7.7	+8.9
% in LT election '94	22.7	18.7	19.9	16.5	16.6
Change since 1990	+7.0	+5.3	+7.9	+6.3	+6.9
2. Eastern identification					
Mean difference "East Gn." - "German" (7-pnt.-scales)	.5	.4	.5	.1	.0
3. Support for socialism					
% preferring renewed socialism to market system	33	17	19	22	19
4. Value priorities					
% stressing social justice more than freedom	32	22	25	23	18
% stressing social justice more than rule of law and democracy	34	26	29	25	29
5. Issue priorities					
% unemployment more urgent than pollution	48	33	37	39	30
% social welfare more urgent than pollution	36	28	32	32	25
6. Political dissatisfaction					
% dissatisfied with democracy and political system	36	35	34	30	28
7. Unemployment					
% expecting unemployment to rise	30	43	35	28	34
% official unemployment rate	17.0	15.3	17.6	15.7	16.5
Change since 1991	+4.5	+5.0	+7.3	+6.6	+6.3

Notes: MVP = Mecklenburg Vorpommern, Brand. = Brandenburg, SA = Sachsen Anhalt; BT=*Bundestag*; LT=*Landtag*.
Sources: Election statistics (1), Konrad Adenauer Foundation (KAS), Fall 1995, N (East) = 2,000 (2, 4), KAS Fall 1994, N (East)= 1,513 (3, 6, 7), KAS Spring 1995, N (East) = 1,044 (5), weighted data, Federal Department of Statistics (7).

Table 11.3. PDS Support and Factors Potentially Causing Its Growth in the New Länder: Rankings

	MVP	Brand.	SA	Saxony	Thuringia	Spearman=s r with PDS federal	
						% (sig.)	increase (sig.)
1. PDS support							
%, BT election 1994	1	2	3	5	4		.60
Change since 1990	1	4	3	5	2	.60	
%, Land election 1994	1	3	2	5	4	.90*	.70
Change since 1990	2	5	1	4	3	.20	.60
2. Eastern identification	1	3	1	4	5	.72	.31
3. Support for socialism	1	5	3	2	3	.05	.36
4. Value priorities							
Social justice v. freedom	1	4	2	3	5	.50	.30
Social justice v. democracy	1	4	2	5	2	.67	.97*
5. Issue priorities							
Unemployment	1	4	3	2	5	.30	.10
Social welfare	1	4	2	2	5	.41	.21
6. Political dissatisfaction	1	2	3	4	5	.90*	.30
7. Unemployment							
Expectation	4	1	2	5	3	.40	.00
Official rate	2	5	1	4	3	.20	.60
Increase	5	4	1	2	3	-.70	-.50

Notes: * significant at .05 level. BT = *Bundestag*.
Sources: Election statistics (1), Konrad Adenauer Foundation (KAS), Fall 1995, N (East) = 2,000 (2, 4), KAS Fall 1994, N (East)= 1,513 (3, 6, 7), KAS Spring 1995, N (East) = 1,044 (5), weighted data, Federal Department of Statistics (7).

it allows for a few tentative conclusions: First, the increase in unemployment appears to be of no relevance for PDS support. Instead, the current level of unemployment plays a role in the intensity of the party's growth. Second, issue priorities appear unrelated to support for the PDS. This holds for both the current level of PDS support and the rate of increase. Given the fact that the stress on joblessness has increased notably over time, this finding is of particular relevance. Third, PDS support covaries with political dissatisfaction, eastern identifications, socialist ideology, and value orientations. Any interpretation focusing on these variables is in line with these results.

INDIVIDUAL-LEVEL VARIATION

So far, the analysis has achieved little in terms of reducing the field of explanatory hypotheses. Except for joblessness and issue priorities, both of which fared poorly in the state-by-state comparison, all the potential explanatory variables passed both types of aggregate investigation. I eventually turn to individual-level data, hoping to shed some more light on the nature of PDS support and its increase.

In a first step, I briefly examine an implication of the syndrome hypothesis. If the PDS vote indeed indicated a blend of identifications, ideology, values, and political dissatisfaction, possibly accompanied by problems on the job market and related issue concerns, these variables should be more than marginally related to each other in the cross-section. In fact, it should be possible to extract one single principal component to represent the syndrome dimension. A brief inspection of the Pearson correlations in Table 11.4 renders this interpretation somewhat dubious. Only in the cases of multiple indicators for the same concept (issue priorities and value orientations) do these coefficients exceed .25. The closest links exist between socialism, eastern identifications, and political dissatisfaction, ranging from .18 to .25. Also, the expectation that unemployment will increase is related to political dissatisfaction at .23, but it is related to the other variables at a considerable degree. Given that the remaining coefficients are even lower (though each in the expected direction and statistically significant), all these variables appear to lead a life of their own, even if partially related to other ones. A syndrome interpretation makes little sense in light of these data.

Table 11.4. Pearson Correlations Among the Explanatory Variables

	B	C	D	E	F	G	H	Fear job loss
A: Eastern dominance	.18	.18	.13	.07[a]	.12	.21	.11	.05
B: Socialism		.17	.13	.03[b]	.05[b]	.25	.09	.08
C: Social justice vs. freedom			.63	.14	.15	.15	.08	.10
D: Social justice vs. democracy				.14	.15	.14	.07	.09
E: Unemployment vs. pollution					.75	.07[a]	.06[b]	.10
F: Social welfare vs. pollution						.11	.06[b]	.12
G: Dissatisfaction							.23	.17
H: Expect unemployment increase								.13

Notes: All significant at .00, except [a] (p<.05) and [b] (n.s.).
Source: Cumulated eastern segments of the Spring and Fall Survey of the KAS. Total N = 3,044. Unweighted data. For E and F: Spring survey only (Total N=1,044).

This supports results reported elsewhere: eastern identifications turned out not to be closely tied to other political attitudes or to demographic variables (Zelle 1997). Not surprisingly, principal component analysis does not confirm the syndrome interpretation either. A first factor extracted from this data matrix accounts for 29 percent of the variance, followed by a second factor accounting for 18 percent (data not shown). Reducing the variables to one single dimension, as the syndrome hypothesis implied, cannot be justified given the relatively small distance between the first and second factors. Hence, the analysis here continues to treat the factors identified as separate variables, which are related to varying degrees, but which also are far from depicting the same underlying dimension.

Table 11.5. Correlates of PDS Support, 1995

	Pearson's r (sig.)	Beta weights (sig.)
1. Identification:	.21	.11
Prevalence of eastern identification	(.00)	(.00)
2. Ideology:	.29	.20
Socialism	(.00)	(.00)
3. Values:		
Social justice more than freedom	.13	.04
	(.00)	(.08)
Social justice more than democracy	.08	
	(.21)	
4. Issues:		
Jobs more than environment	.05	
	(.19)	
Social welfare more than environment	.06	
	(.12)	
5. Political dissatisfaction	.33	.23
	(.00)	(.00)
6. Unemployment:		
Expect unemployment to rise	.14	.04
	(.00)	(.03)
Fear of losing job	.04	
	(.12)	
	R²(adj.):	.17

Notes: Dependent variable: Vote intention PDS (2) vs. intention for other party (1). No party mentioned coded missing.
Source: Cumulated eastern segments of the Spring and Fall Survey of the KAS. Total N = 3,044, N PDS intention = 413, N other party = 1,708. Unweighted data. For 4.: Spring survey only (Total N=1,044, PDS intention =159, other parties =793).

Which of these individual factors explain support for the PDS? One of the potential factors can be rejected on the basis of a bivariate analysis: The stress an individual places on the issues of unemployment and social welfare in relation to environmental pollution is unrelated to PDS support (see Table 11.5). However, political dissatisfaction is most strongly linked to PDS support (.33), closely followed by attachment to the ideology of socialism (.29). Prevalence of eastern identification is third on the list (.21). Value orientations appear to be of lesser relevance. Valuing "social justice" more than "freedom" is related to the PDS vote at .13, while the confrontation between "social justice" and "rule of law, democracy" fails to yield a correlation at a statistically significant level. Unemployment, finally, leads to a mixed result: the expectation of rising unemployment enhances the probability of PDS support somewhat (.14), while the fear that oneself or a member of the family may lose a job is unrelated to PDS support.

Multiple regression analysis further clarifies these results. The set of explanatory factors is reduced to the three strong showings in the bivariate analysis: political dissatisfaction (beta .23), socialism (.20) and—at a distance—prevalence of eastern identifications (.11). Once ideology is in the equation, the weight of social values is reduced below the level of statistical significance, while the expectation of rising unemployment is so closely linked with political dissatisfaction that it adds little to the understanding of PDS support (.04), even though the coefficient remains within the boundaries of statistical significance ($p=.03$). Yielding an adjusted R^2 of .17, this equation can be considered a satisfactory, though by far not complete statistical explanation of PDS support. After all, the distribution of the dependent variable is heavily skewed. If the data are weighted such that the group of PDS supporters is as large as the electorate of the other parties, the adjusted R^2 rises to .23.[2]

Given the set of explanatory variables reduced to dissatisfaction, ideology, and identification, I decided to give the syndrome hypothesis one last chance. After all, these are the three variables that are most closely linked together in correlational analysis. Perhaps the data indicate that a large portion of PDS supporters is characterized by all three attitudes. It turns out that this is not the case: Only 20 percent of the PDS electorate simultaneously is dissatisfied with the political system, supports socialism, and feels attached more to eastern Germany than to the country as a whole. While notably larger than in the eastern electorate of other parties (3 percent), this percentage is too small to consider the PDS as representing a group of voters holding "typical" views on all three of these dimensions.

In sum, factors explaining PDS support at the individual level are political dissatisfaction, socialism, and to a lesser extent eastern identifications. Issue priorities and unemployment are not relevant; neither are value orientations once ideology is controlled for. There also are few, if any, indications that the explanatory variables should be considered tied to each other to form a "syndrome" of some kind. Since all three of the factors identified as predicting PDS support increased over time (see above), they are likely to have promoted the growth of the party's electorate between 1990 and 1994.

NEW VOTERS VERSUS STANDPATTERS

The reasons for the party's increase also can be addressed by investigating the newly converted voters. What were their motives join in to support the PDS? Do these motives differ from the motives of the PDS standpatters? In fact, it is plausible to expect differences. If the PDS of the year 1990 indeed was the party of the old functionaries, its growth is unlikely to stem from the same group. Rather, one might suspect that the party made inroads into groups previously more distanced to it and thus managed to increase its electoral share.

For these reasons, it makes sense to first compare the demographic composition of the two PDS electorates and then proceed to search for differences in motivations. In this analysis, respondents who report a vote intention for the party and say they have always voted for this party are treated as PDS standpatters. On the other hand, new voters of the PDS are those who either had been not eligible to vote, had abstained, or had voted for one of the other parties in one of the previous elections since unification. Table 11.6 contains the percentage the party received among a number of demographic groups, as well as the percentages for PDS standpatters and new PDS voters. In addition to the percentages, an index of disproportionality is included in the table. This index results when dividing the party's share within a group by the party's share in the sample.

It turns out that the PDS does equally well regardless of the respondent's gender. This holds for both types of voters. When considering age, however, a remarkable change is apparent. While those in the oldest bracket contribute the highest portion of stable PDS voters, they are least inclined to change to this party. Instead, the party drew its new voters disproportionally from the youngest respondents, and to a lesser extent from the middle category of the 30 to 44 year-olds. Apparently, the party's profile has changed during its process of growth. Interestingly, this produces an about even age distribution of the party's total electorate. With respect to education, the new PDS voters decrease the overrepresentation of the highly educated somewhat. Although these are drawn to the PDS in disproportionate percentages, new voters can be found among respondents holding an intermediate degree at about average frequency, while this group provides a below-average share of stable PDS voters. With respect to the respondent's occupation, the strong percentages of new voters among the youngest group are reflected in its disproportionate representation among those still in school or vocational training. The distribution of occupations evened out somewhat: White-collar employees newly joined the party at smaller rates than their contribution to the stable PDS electorate would predict. At the same time, the underrepresentation of the PDS in the working class is slightly weaker for new voters than it is in the case of the standpatters. The self-employed, who are unlikely to be stable voters of the PDS, contribute an average share to its new vote. In sum, the PDS electorate became younger, less educated, and less white-collar as a consequence of its growth.

Given these changes in sociodemographic profile, one may expect attitudinal differences between the old voters and the new voters as well. In particular, I expect the new voters to be drawn to the ideology of socialism to a lesser extent than the

Table 11.6. PDS Support in Sociodemographic Groups in Eastern Germany, 1995

	% PDS total	Dispro-portio-nality	Row Percentages				Sig. chi² (stable vs new)	Valid n
			% stable PDS	Disprop.	% PDS new	Disprop.		
Total	19.5		13.8		5.7			2,121
Gender								
Male	19.7	1.01	13.8	1.00	5.9	1.04	.77	1,053
Female	19.3	.99	13.8	1.00	5.5	.96		1,068
Age								
18-24	20.9	1.07	11.2	.81	9.7	1.70	.00	134
25-29	19.4	.99	13.8	1.00	5.6	.98		160
30-44	20.3	1.04	13.3	.96	7.1	1.25		581
45-59	19.0	.97	12.7	.92	6.3	1.11		575
60 and older	19.0	.97	15.7	1.14	3.3	.58		668
Education								
Lower	12.9	.66	9.3	.67	3.6	.63	.00	1,031
Intermediate	17.8	.91	11.9	.86	5.9	1.04		478
Higher	32.3	1.66	23.8	1.72	8.5	1.49		579
Profession								
In education	20.9	1.07	8.1	.59	12.8	2.25	.01	86
Blue-collar	11.9	.61	8.1	.59	3.9	.68		770
White-collar	25.9	1.33	19.5	1.41	6.4	1.12		1,072
Self-employed	13.9	.71	8.2	.59	5.7	1.00		122

Notes: The index of disproportionality indicates the degree of overrepresentation (or underrepresentation) of the party in a social segment. It is yielded by dividing the party's percentage in the group by the percentage in the sample.
Source: Cumulated eastern segments of the Spring and Fall Survey of the KAS. Total N = 3,044, N PDS intention = 413, N other party = 1,708. Unweighted data.

standpatters. This is because this ideology should be most pronounced among the older voters who are more likely to have socialized into it under the socialist system. Also, the older voters are more likely to have held functionary positions. With respect to social values I am hesitant to specify a hypothesis, since these values are not necessarily tied to the ideology of socialism. There is no reason to expect eastern identifications and political dissatisfaction to differ between these two groups. The correlations with a variable coded "1" for new PDS voters and "2" for PDS standpatters are contained in Table 11.7.

Table 11.7. PDS Standpatters versus PDS Newcomers: Correlations and Regression

	Pearson's r (sig.)	Beta weights (sig.)
1. Identification: Prevalence of eastern identification	.00	
2. Ideology: Socialism	.15 (.00)	.14 (.00)
3. Values: Social justice more than freedom	.00	
Social justice more than democracy	-.09 (.08)	
4. Issues: Jobs more than environment	.03 (.70)	
Social welfare more than environment	.00	
5. Political dissatisfaction	.07 (.13)	
6. Unemployment: Expect unemployment to rise	-.04 (.40)	
Fear of losing job	-.13 (.01)	-.12 (.02)
	R^2(adj.):	.03

Notes: Dependent variable: Always voted PDS (2), abstained, voted differently, or ineligible to vote in previous elections (1).
Source: Cumulated eastern segments of the Spring and Fall Survey of the KAS. Total N stable PDS = 292, new PDS voter = 121. Unweighted data. For 4.: Spring survey only (N stable PDS = 117, new PDS voter = 42.

Indeed, the new voters are markedly less likely to support the socialist ideology than the PDS standpatters. A correlation of .15 is quite impressive when keeping in mind that we are dealing with variation present within a party, not between two parties. The type of PDS support is unrelated to the other factors considered here, with one exception. This exception is that new voters are more likely to fear the loss of their own job or that of one their family members than old voters (r=-.13). Thus, the deteriorating job market reemerges as a potential predictor of the increase in PDS support after all. Both variables yield betas only slightly below the Pearson correlations when entered into a multiple regression. The R^2 of .03, while marginal by conventional standards, should also be viewed in light of the fact that we are dealing with within-party variance.

The conclusion from this part of the analysis is that the "second generation" of PDS voters is drawn to the party less by its ideological stance than the "first generation," but more on the grounds of its potential exposure to unemployment.

IDEOLOGY AND PROTEST

The previous analyses identified socialist ideology and political dissatisfaction as the two strongest predictors of PDS support. This leads to the question of whether a vote for the PDS should be considered primarily a signal of protest, or primarily as advocacy for a different societal order. Figure 11.1 illustrates four possible modes of thinking toward the political regime. It consists of the contrast between the combination of free market and Western democracy as it exists in the Federal Republic on one hand and socialist ideology on the other. Note that this is not to imply that socialism and democracy are opposites in principle. In fact, a large percentage of eastern Germans views these two ideas as compatible (see Westle 1994). Rather, it rests on the assumption that the political system of the Federal Republic will be considered incompatible with socialism as it existed in the GDR. Thus, an individual can support the ideology of socialism and, as a consequence, be dissatisfied with the political system of Germany. On the other hand, an individual can support both the free market ideology and the German political system (support). The remaining two modes of thinking constitute mixtures of these ideal types. Thus, ideological support for the market may be accompanied by political dissatisfaction to signal a mood of protest. Finally, a socialist by ideological orientation may still be supportive of the German political system if it works well in his or her judgment (tamed ideology).

Figure 11.1. Modes of Thinking About the Political Regime

	System evaluation	
Ideology	*Satisfied*	*Dissatisfied*
Free market society	Support	Protest opposition
Socialism	Tamed ideology	Ideological opposition

What category does the electorate of the PDS fall into? Are there differences between old and new voters? To investigate this question, the relevant variables were dichotomized in dissatisfied versus at least somewhat satisfied and socialist versus undecided or supporter of the free market system. Table 11.8 illustrates that only one quarter of the PDS electorate support the political regime in terms of both ideology and system evaluation. In contrast, two-thirds of the eastern electorate of other parties do so. Hence, the political thinking of the PDS electorate is very distinct from that of the majority of the eastern German electorate. Of the remainder in the PDS electorate, protest opposition slightly outnumbers ideological opposition (35 to 28 percent), and only a small segment (11 percent) supports socialism without being dissatisfied with the political system. Thus there is no majority position within the PDS electorate on this crucial question, and the message sent by PDS support is ambiguous, signaling ideological opposition and protest opposition at about the same frequency. The message is rendered even more unclear by the fact that an almost equally large percentage of the PDS electorate actually supports the political regime of the united Germany.

Old and new voters of the PDS differ in degree but not in kind in this regard. Still, the supporters constitute a significantly larger segment of the new voters than of the older voters (35 versus 22 percent), although the relation between protest opposition and ideological opposition is similar in the two groups.

Table 11.8. Protest of Ideology? The Composition of the PDS Electorate with Respect to Attitudes Toward the Political System (Eastern Germany, 1995)

	Column Percentages			
	Electorate of other parties	PDS Electorate	Stable PDS	PDS new
Support	67	26	22	35
Tamed ideology	10	11	12	7
Protest opposition	18	35	36	32
Ideological opposition	5	28	29	26

Sig. Chi^2 (stable vs. new): .03

Source: Cumulated eastern segments of the spring and fall surveys of the KAS. N stable PDS = 292; newly PDS = 121. Unweighted data.

SUMMARY AND CONCLUSION

This chapter investigated the factors underlying the remarkable increase of support for the PDS after unification. Starting with a longitudinal examination of the data, none of the hypothetical factors spelled out at the outset could be rejected: the growth of the PDS was accompanied by increases in eastern German identifications, support for the ideology of socialism, stress on values of social equality, perceived urgency of the issue of unemployment, political dissatisfaction, and unemployment. Hence, any of these variables could have caused the rise of the PDS–provided they bore a relationship to PDS support in the cross-section.

Consequently, the analysis turned to the cross-section. At the aggregate level, issue priorities and unemployment rates were not powerful explanatory variables. Against the backdrop, the bulk of the analysis rested on cross-sectional data on the individual level. First, it was established that the factors hypothesized to be causing the rise of the PDS were only weakly interrelated and thus could not be considered part of a "syndrome." The subsequent analysis treated these factors separately and thus identified political dissatisfaction, socialist ideology, and–to a lesser extent–identifications as eastern Germans ("Ostalgie") as the most important predictors of PDS support in the cross-section. Values, issues, and unemployment played less of a role. Given the fact that the development of all these factors paralleled the rise of the PDS, the variables selected in the cross-sectional analysis also are most likely to be responsible for the party's improved electoral standing in 1994. Hence, the growth of the PDS is likely to be the product of increased public dissatisfaction with the political system, increased support for the ideology of socialism, and increased frequency of identifications as eastern German.

Unfortunately, no two data sets containing the relevant variables in comparable operationalizations are available from the beginning and end of the period of interest. Therefore, it is not possible to assess in a more definite fashion the relative effects that trends in these variables may have on PDS support. All that can be concluded is that these three factors played a role in the expansion of the PDS.

Additional analyses produced results that add to this general picture. The new voters of the PDS are not only younger, less heavily white-collar, and slightly less educated than the old PDS electorate, they also are less ideological. Thus the merger of the old electorate with the new voters led to a set of voters that is less supportive of socialism than the traditional PDS electorate. A second point is that the new voters are more concerned about losing their jobs than the older ones. Unemployment thus is back in the explanation of the growth of PDS support. Given the somewhat mixed results with respect to the role of unemployment, future research will have to sort out the exact relationships in more detail.

Finally, I attempted to identify the message sent by PDS support. The party's electorate is divided roughly evenly into categories of protest opposition, ideological opposition, and regime support, while other parties' eastern electorate is overwhelmingly supportive of the political system and its ideological foundation. There are differences in degree between new and old PDS voters, with new voters being somewhat more supportive of the regime. Because there is no majority for any one mode of thinking toward the political regime among the PDS electorate, it cannot be interpreted as unambiguously signaling either protest or ideological opposition; in fact, it does both (cf. Falter and Klein 1994, 1995).

In this chapter, I attributed the increase in PDS support to attitudinal changes. This leads to the question of what drives these changes. Causes can be sought in the political realm as well as in the situation of individuals. Among the latter, deprivation experienced during the process of transformation appears to be a potentially powerful factor underlying these attitude changes, possibly among a former intelligentsia that had been excluded from elite positions in the GDR and once again finds its influence limited under the new system (Welzel 1997).

In light of the findings presented here, what are the future prospects for the party? All three attitudes identified as responsible for the party's growth–political dissatisfaction, socialist ideology, and eastern identifications–show signs of decline. Thus a continuation or even an acceleration of the party's growth appears unlikely. At the same time, none of these attitudes–with the possible exception of political dissatisfaction–is likely to be subject to quick changes. In particular, eastern identifications are unlikely to fade away soon (Zelle 1997). Similar arguments can be made for socialist ideology and, with reservations, for political dissatisfaction, which is partially dependent on the current evaluation of system performance. Given the assumed high stability of these attitudes in combination with signs of a slow decline for all of them, stagnation and a slow decrease in support appear to be the most likely outcomes regarding the future electoral fortunes of the PDS.

NOTES

1. Because it is not an independent state, East Berlin is not included.

2. Note that unlike the case in the analysis presented by Klein and Caballero, political dissatisfaction is an important predictor of the PDS vote in the multivariate analysis presented here. This is due to different methodological decisions, all of which are legitimate. Any of the following technical decisions are responsible for the differences in results: (1) Klein and Caballero measure ideology with the left-right scale, while support for socialism is used here. (2) In their path analytic model, Klein and Caballero specify political dissatisfaction as well as nostalgia as *effects* of ideology. As a result, even an indirect effect of the latter variables on the vote is rendered impossible to begin with. (3) Klein and Caballero apply tough standards the coefficients have to meet for entry into the model: beta has to be at a minimum of .1. At the same time, they employ a large number of variables (total of 16), some of which are interrelated. This makes it hard for a hypothesis not to be rejected by the data, and thus leaves only two direct predictors of the PDS vote (change in employment status and attachment to the PDS), as well as two predictors for PDS attachment (change in employment status again, and ideology). Though all the decisions Klein and Caballero took are legitimate, in my view the parsimonious beauty of the empirical solution they offer is due to these decisions and thus falls short of reflecting reality.

Part III

NEW DIRECTIONS:
THE IMPACT OF POLITICAL FACTORS
ON GERMAN ELECTIONS

12

Media Use, Interpersonal Communication, and Voting Behavior in Germany, 1990-95

Frank Brettschneider and Peter R. Schrott

INTRODUCTION

Although political communication has long constituted an important element of voting studies (Lazarsfeld, Berelson, and Gaudet 1944), there are few studies of political communication in German electoral behavior research (Klingemann and Voltmer 1989; Kaase 1986). A somewhat different situation can be detected in the area of media effects research. Since the 1930s, the importance attributed to mass media for election outcomes and voting behavior has waxed and waned. Studies conducted by Noelle-Neumann (1977) and Kepplinger (1980) renewed scholarly interest in the effects of mass media on political behavior by triggering an enormous controversy not only in the academic but also in the political world (Schulz and Schoenbach 1983; Kaase 1989a). However, a number of recent studies have established ambiguous effects of mass media on the vote.

Despite different approaches to, and findings about, the effects of mass media on political behavior and attitudes, few would argue that people get political information "first hand," that is, from direct contact with politicians. The more complex political structures, processes, and issues are, the more likely it is that the public has to rely on indirect observations. Mass media take on the function of providing this information. As Lippmann noted as long ago as 1922, mass media provide voters with information about the "world outside." In turn, this information forms "the pictures in our heads." Klingemann and Voltmer (1989) consequently (and accurately) describe media as the most important "bridge to the world of politics."

At the same time we find an indirect way of "reality observation" through interpersonal communication. The function of interpersonal communication, however, is less to gain original information on politics than to structure, organize, and clarify already obtained political information (Schenk 1994; Schmitt-Beck 1994b). Through interpersonal communication with other people in the social environment, a co-orientation with the opinions of others takes place. As a result, people share meanings of political information, thus facilitating opinion formation (Voltmer, Schabedoth, and Schrott 1995: 231).

Although Lazarsfeld, Berelson, and Gaudet attributed greater influence to interpersonal communication, mass communication is today perceived as being more dominant in the political process (see Gerhards 1991: 11; Klingemann 1986; Sarcinelli 1991). This increase in importance results from a decrease in primary group communication due to the dissolution of social structural contacts in which individuals live (Klingemann and Voltmer 1989). Moreover, interpersonal communication frequently is a means to obtain mediated information. This way, even those people who usually do not actively use media to gain information are exposed to information through their communication partners.

Thus, it is reasonable to assume that both the way people use these "media bridges" to the world of politics and interpersonal communication influence political behavior. In this context, German unification and the expansion of Germany by five new states (Länder) pose some interesting questions. First, the analysis of communication behavior and its impact on political participation (and hence the vote) are interesting because political attitudes in the new part of Germany must be based even less on direct experiences with politics than in the old Länder. Second, it is reasonable to expect a change in the communication behavior of East Germans between 1990 and 1995 due to a change of the media structure (i.e., ownerships and biases) in the eastern part of Germany (for details, see Brettschneider 1997). Finally, interpersonal communication is likely to be of much greater importance in the new states, because personal discussions were much more consequential in the former GDR due to the lack of the number and variety of media channels (Feige 1990). Therefore, for the election of 1990, interpersonal communication most likely had a compensating meaning in the East, while the relationship between interpersonal communication and mass media generally is seen as complementary in a democratic context (Chaffee 1986). In the East Germany of 1990, people had to deal with conflicting information provided partially by old (and distrusted) media.

With respect to elections, a stronger media impact can be expected in the new states because in 1990 long-term party identifications cannot possibly have been as strong and as frequent as in the old states, to say the least (see chapter 1 by Christopher J. Anderson and Carsten Zelle, chapter 3 by Karl Schmitt, and chapters 4 and 11 by Carsten Zelle in this volume). This means that the short-term influences of candidate evaluations and issue orientations should have had a greater meaning for the electorate there–as the research presented in chapter 6 by Hans Rattinger and Jürgen Krämer and chapter 5 by Angelika Vetter and Oscar W. Gabriel in this volume documents, although these differences do not appear to be overwhelming. In the present context, this is important because the media influence is stronger for these short-term orientations. Hence, we expect the impact of the media to more pronounced in the new states.

In the following analysis we attempt to answer five questions pertaining to the amount, the structure, and the consequences of individual interpersonal and mass communication:

1. How do people in East and West Germany use mass media? How often do they discuss politics? And did communication behavior change between 1990 and 1995?
2. Is it possible to detect certain types of media uses and interpersonal communication, and what are their distributions in East and West Germany?
3. Is there a relationship between political communication and voter turnout?
4. Is there a direct and measurable relationship between vote intention and political communication? What is the importance of media usage in a voting behavior model, and is it identical in East and West Germany?
5. Is there an impact of mass media and interpersonal communication on issue orientations and candidate evaluations?

After discussing the most important research findings about political communication and voting behavior, we will present our research design and analyze the relationship between political communication and voting behavior in Germany for 1990 and 1995.

ELECTORAL RESEARCH AND POLITICAL COMMUNICATION

Guided by the ideas of propaganda research that media directly affect attitudes and opinions of recipients (see Hovland, Janis, and Kelly 1953), Lazarsfeld et al. (1944) in their seminal study *The People's Choice* tried to establish a direct effect of media usage on voting behavior. However, after realizing that no such effect could be found, electoral behavior research and communication research split up and pursued different research paradigms in the years to come. It was not until the 1970s that new efforts were undertaken to find relationships between political communication, mass media, and elections.

After the publication of the Columbia group's analyses (Lazarsfeld, Berelson, and Gaudet 1944; Berelson, Lazarsfeld, and McPhee 1954), electoral researchers developed models that excluded direct media effects. While *The People's Choice* still assumed a two-step-flow of communication, political communication was completely absent in the model of *The American Voter* (Campbell et al. 1960). In the Michigan model the main determinant of voters' decisions is party identification—a long-term attachment to a party obtained primarily through the political socialization process in the family and reinforced by repeated voting for the same party. Aside from this long-term effect, there also are short-term effects of issue orientations and candidate evaluations.

For an issue to have any impact, the following conditions have to be fulfilled (Campbell et al. 1960): The issue must be of personal importance to the voter; the voter must have formed an opinion about this issue; finally, there must be a noticeable difference between the competing parties on this issue. Once a given issue fulfills these conditions, the voter calculates the distance between his or her issue positions and those of the parties. If this collides with the voter's party identification, there are several possibilities: The individual changes his or her party preference (issue vote); the voter changes his or her issue position (adaptation); the voter neglects the issue or projects his or her issue position onto the party, thinking that the party holds the same issue position.

Candidate evaluations consist of an affective part (sympathy) and a cognitive component (competence evaluation). But how do voters form an opinion on characters and competence of politicians if they do not have any direct contact with them? What issues do they perceive as being important, and how do they form issue orientations? The Michigan model simply assumes that voters obtain information on issues and candidates, but they do not explicitly say how this is done.

The "rational choice" approach by Downs (1957) rests on similar assumptions: that voters systematically search for information on parties and party positions on the issues, and that they compare those issue stands. Based on a cost benefit analysis, they finally vote for the party that promises the biggest benefit based on prior experiences and future expectations. This means that the voter knows about his or her own preferences, is able to order these preferences in a meaningful way, and finally behaves rationally. This approach requires political information on parties and candidates, and it further assumes that the voting decision is based on that information. However, few studies attempt to follow up on the problem of information gain. They mostly argue that although voters do not have time and resources to obtain perfect information about the candidates and party's positions on issues, they nevertheless are able (due to ideological shortcuts that relate parties and candidates with certain positions) to use "predictive labels" quickly and with little costs involved to arrive at a rational decision (see, e.g., Enelow and Hinich 1984).

COMMUNICATION RESEARCH AND ELECTIONS

After Klapper inaugurated the era of "minimal effects" in 1960, communication research turned away from studying electoral behavior. Nevertheless, media effects research yielded results that were important for behavioral research. The most prevalent approach in media research–the agenda-setting approach–argues that the importance of the media is not to influence attitudes, but rather to guide the recipient in which issue is important to think about (for a review on agenda setting, see Brettschneider 1994). "The press may not be successful much of the time in telling people what to think, but it is stunningly successful in telling its readers what to think about" (Cohen 1963: 13). According to this approach, mass media place emphasis on certain topics through the frequency and placement of their coverage. They therefore decide which problems are important (and, hence, need to be dealt with), and which are seen as unimportant. The media are more successful the less people perceive reality directly. The importance of an issue for the population is thus not based on reality itself, but rather on media coverage about this reality. This coverage, however, does not mirror reality but instead filters and distorts it (see Weaver 1984: 682).

This power of the media to shape public political discussions justifies the analysis of media effects on the vote decision. Furthermore, Iyengar and Kinder show that media ultimately even shape attitudes through this very agenda setting: "The power of the networks does not end with viewers' political agendas. ... By calling attention to some matters while ignoring others, television news influences the standards by which governments, presidents, policies, and candidates for public office are judged. Priming refers to changes in the standards that people use to make political evaluations" (Iyengar and Kinder 1987: 63).

Priming is based on the linkage of three arguments: (1) To evaluate candidates and issues, the voter does not take the complete information on these persons and topics into account because it would be too much effort. (2) Instead, voters rely only on information that is available at the time of evaluating candidates and issues. (3) Mass media determine which information is available. For example, if media coverage emphasizes national security topics, people are most likely to evaluate candidates based on national security policy aspects rather than on other political aspects. This is why parties and politicians are strongly interested to get "their" topics on the media agenda during electoral campaigns (Ansolabehere and Iyengar 1994; Pfetsch 1994; Reiser 1994).

In the German context, this means that apparently it is useful for the CDU (Christian Democrats) when the campaign coverage emphasizes economic and foreign policy issues. On the other hand, the SPD (Social Democrats) are most interested in social policy issues while the Greens hope that environmental topics will dominate the media coverage. Hence, mass media also have an impact on opinion formation and voting decisions even if they do not change attitudes that already exist. Often it suffices that they emphasize certain topics (Kepplinger et al. 1989: 75), and thus "activate" predispositions (Finkel and Schrott 1995).

As in agenda setting or priming, media coverage can also affect the perceptions of how opinions are distributed in society and thus have attitudinal and even behavioral effects without changing one single political attitude directly (Noelle-Neumann 1980; Donsbach 1987). However, in some situations even such direct effects can occur. Short-term effects are rare if the relevant attitudes are strongly imbedded in the individual's belief system. This is the case with party identification, values, and ideologies. Yet short-term effects are more common in the case of "tabula rasa" situations (Noelle-Neumann 1994: 568) as well as in the evaluation of politicians. "Tabula rasa" situations occur if an issue is new on the political agenda—that is, when there are no formed opinions. In such cases, the early coverage outlines and determines the subsequent discussion ("framing"). It also is probable that positive or negative links between issues and certain parties and politicians are built during this framing phase.

Attitudes about politicians are more variable than attitudes toward political issues. First, candidate evaluations are less closely linked with stable elements of the belief system than are issue orientations. Therefore a changing candidate evaluation does not affect basic beliefs. Second, it is easier to influence emotional components. As with candidate orientations, media coverage about candidates shows relatively strong changes. "Media darlings" quickly turn into "media victims." One example of this phenomenon was the media coverage of Chancellor

Helmut Kohl and his challenger Oskar Lafontaine during the election campaign of 1990. Schulz and Kindelmann (1993; also Kindelmann 1994) argue that a "clumsy chancellor" turned into a "statesman" during the German unification process. At the same time Lafontaine turned from a "resourceful and eloquent hope" simply into a "loser" and the amount of voters who wanted to see Kohl as the future chancellor (as opposed to Lafontaine) increased as well (Schmitt-Beck 1994a: 282).

Since there is little selective exposure in the case of negative coverage about persons (see Donsbach 1991), it is easier to change attitudes of politicians from good to bad ones. This is mainly done by visual coverage of television, while competence evaluations of politicians are based more on textual information of print media and of television (Kepplinger, Brosius, and Dahlem 1994a; Lodge, Steenbergen, and Brau 1995; Wagner 1983).

CAMPAIGN RESEARCH AS A COMMUNICATION LINK

Studies of political campaigns represent the strongest link between communication and electoral behavior research. They are of central importance because the examination of campaign effects can tell us much about voters' decision-making; about how new information presented during campaigns is processed by voters; which party strategies are being used; and how mass media cover the entire campaign. Journalists follow norms and rules in their news selection (Staab 1990). These rules are utilized by parties to get their issues on the media agenda. Although they are not always successful in doing so, it is nevertheless a very important part of any campaign strategy (Mathes and Freisens 1990; Popkin 1992).

Parties frequently stage events mainly to obtain media coverage. The goal of these "pseudo events" is to gain from their expected effects on the public (better images, agenda setting of own policies, getting rid of politically unwelcome topics). Aside from press conferences and news statements, typical pseudo events are party conventions which are more or less organized for the assembled journalists rather than for the participating party members (Kepplinger 1989: 10; see also Radunski 1980). During the election campaign of 1990, almost half of the media coverage in the most important daily prime-time news shows consisted of pseudo events (see Pfetsch 1994: 19; Schmitt-Beck and Pfetsch 1994).

However, the analysis of campaign effects also is important for our normative evaluation of the political process. Many scholars argue, for example, that the information presented during contemporary campaigns is deceptive, simplistic, and manipulates the electorate (Patterson 1989). Yet, despite the central importance of campaigns, there is a conspicuous absence of studies which explicitly investigate amount and types of campaign effects on voters. After the seminal work of the Columbia group around Lazarsfeld, more than twenty years passed until another study analyzed individual-level change over the full course of a campaign (see Patterson and McClure 1976; Patterson 1980). Since that time, researchers have attempted to study campaign effects, either through the individual's self reported "time of final decision" or exposure to campaigns (see the reviews in Graber 1993a and 1993b; Chaffee and Choe 1980). Further research emphases were on changes in public opinion (Farah and Klein 1989; Frankovic 1993; for West-Germany see Noelle-Neumann 1980) as well as on analyses of short-term changes in vote intentions or voter's evaluations of candidates (see Bartels 1993; Granberg and Holmberg 1988; Markus 1982; Schrott 1990a and 1990b).

Studying the full effect of a campaign, Finkel (1993) developed a model based on the Columbia group approach. According to his model, the main effect of campaigns is to "activate" certain fundamental attitudes and values already in place at the outset of the contest. In the American presidential election of 1980, changes in attitudes did take place during the campaign, but the effect of these changes was largely to strengthen the probability that individuals would vote in accordance with their initial predispositions. In a modified form this model was also tested for the German election of 1990 (Finkel and Schrott 1995). The results corroborated the American findings and showed that German campaigns also mainly reinforce voters' attitudes and bring them in line with their underlying political predispositions. Instead of manipulating individuals, campaigns seem to enhance the ability and the tendency of individuals to cast the vote based on more meaningful grounds, or on what Gelman and King (1993) have called the electorate's "enlightened preferences." Neither study, however, analyzed the actual media coverage. Instead, they assumed that changes in attitudes resulted from information obtained either through mass media channels or interpersonal communication.

DATA AND RESEARCH DESIGN

To fully study the impact of mass media on voting behavior a complex design is necessary. Data are needed (1) on the actual media content, (2) on media usage and perceptions of media content by the voters, (3) on the evaluations of issue salience, issue preferences, as well as on candidate evaluations and on performance in office, (4) on party identification, and (5) on voting behavior (Kepplinger, Brosius, and Dahlem 1994a).

Unfortunately, we do not have all of these data available. Data for secondary analysis, which would allow for tests of the relationship between mass media and voting behavior, are rather rare because there is little connection between communication researchers (who study media usage but not political attitudes) and political scientists (who study political attitudes and behavior but not media usage). The analyses presented below are based on two data sets which allow some preliminary analyses of the relationship between mass media and interpersonal communication on the one hand and political attitudes on the other hand.[1]

Our analysis of the relationship between political communication and voting behavior rests on the classical social-psychological model, also called the Michigan model (Campbell et al. 1960) (see Figure 12.1). As in the United States, large numbers of Germans hold relatively strong party identifications that can be

Figure 12.1. Voting Model

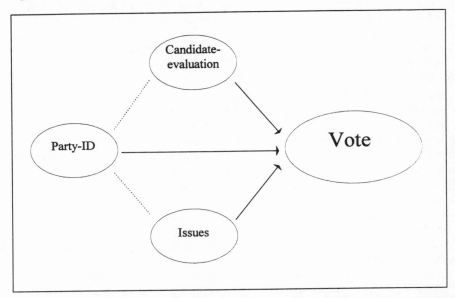

activated during the campaign (Finkel and Schrott 1995). Although scholars initially expressed considerable doubt regarding the applicability of the concept of party identification to the German context, by the early 1980s consensus seemed to emerge that there was more room and functional necessity for parties and attachment in the sense of the Michigan concept of party identification than used to be the case (Falter and Rattinger 1982; Baker, Dalton, and Hildebrandt 1981; Norpoth 1978).

Despite recent evidence of a decline in party identification in the Federal Republic, party line voting nevertheless remains high in Germany, and higher than in the United States (Klingemann and Wattenberg 1992). Assuming that party identification in the East was not at all or much less developed in 1990 than in 1995 despite some preexisting "quasi-party attachment" (Bluck and Kreikenbom 1993), its importance for the voting decision should also be weaker in 1990. We expect, however, that the voting pattern in the new Länder should be somewhat more stable in 1995 after two federal and several state elections (Dalton and Buerklin 1995).

Aside from party identification, we include evaluations about the two chancellor candidates (in 1990), and evaluations of government's and opposition-party's performance (in 1995) in the model. Although previous research suggests that candidate evaluations are not as important in the German electoral context as in the United States (Klingemann and Wattenberg 1992; Kaase 1994), it is possible that they have an independent influence on voting behavior in certain situations (Kepplinger, Brosius, and Dahlem 1994a). Candidate evaluation effects are especially plausible in 1990, when party identifications in the East were not as strongly developed yet, and the incumbent chancellor was challenged by a relatively well known figure. Furthermore, these evaluations are those factors most likely to change during a campaign, and which advertising and other campaign efforts are often designed to influence (Radunski 1980; Schulz and Kindelmann 1993).

Using the data sets mentioned above, however, poses a problem that exists throughout the analyses: Due to different survey formats and varying question wording, a comparison over time is very difficult. For example, given that evaluations of the two chancellor candidates were asked in 1990 but not in 1995, we had to use the evaluations of parties instead. Party evaluation scales ran from +5 to -5 and were formed into an index for government parties (CDU/CSU, FDP) minus the evaluation of opposition parties (SPD, B90/Greens, PDS).

Unfortunately, even the party identification measure turned out to be problematic. Because researchers assumed in 1990 that Easterners could not be attached to political parties in the original sense of the concept, no such question was asked in the 1990 survey. However, the survey asked respondents about the strength of their partisan attachment with regard to the party that the respondent was going to vote for. Using vote intention and this strength variable, we created a "party identification" variable similar to the variable for the respondents from the former Federal Republic. For our vote model (see below) this meant that the correlation between vote intention and party identification was very high (over .90). Therefore, to estimate our 1990 model we used the previous vote decision (federal election of 1987 for the old Länder and Volkskammer election 1990 for the new Länder) as a control variable instead of party identification.

Measuring issue orientations posed the biggest problem. Although we had ample questions asking attitudes about various political issues in 1990, no such questions were asked in the 1995 survey. Because it was one of our goals to compare voters over time and to show the development in East Germany, we decided to keep our models on a minimal level of comparison. Hence we included the only question asked in both surveys, namely that of satisfaction with democracy. This "pseudo issue" ranged from "very satisfied" with democracy (+2) to "very unsatisfied" (-2).[2]

Thus, we propose the following base models for 1990 and 1995:

1990: Vote = a + b1PREVOTE + b2SATDEM + b3DCAND + e

1995: Vote = a + b1PID + b2SATDEM + b3DREGOP + e
where
Vote = Vote Intention 1990 and 1995
PID = Party identification in 1995
PREVOTE = Previous Vote for 1990 (West Germany: federal election 1987; East Germany: Volkskammer election 1990)
DCAND = Difference in Evaluation of Chancellor Candidates 1990
DREGOP = Difference in Evaluation of Government and Opposition Parties 1995
SATDEM = Satisfaction with Democracy
a = Constant
e = error term
b1, b2, b3 = regression weights linking variables to the vote.

Our dependent variable is vote intention of the so-called *Zweitstimme* (the second vote), the individual's party preference in a national election. We differentiate between vote intention for one of the government parties (coded as +1) or for one of the opposition parties (coded as -1). Respondents abstaining from the election received a 0. Our independent variables represent standard measures of these concepts in German electoral research (for the exact question wording, see the Appendix to this chapter). Our difference variables CAND (evaluation of candidates) and REGOP (evaluation of parties) were measured on a scale from +10 (pro Chancellor Kohl and progovernment parties, respectively) to -10 (proopposition chancellor candidate Lafontaine and proopposition parties). The respondents were asked to rate candidates and parties from "thought very badly" (coded -5) of a candidate (or party) to "thought very much" (coded +5) of a candidate (or party). Party identification was coded from +5 (pro government parties) to -5 (opposition parties). As our main interest lies in communication effects, we first add such variables to our base model to test for direct effects on the vote above and beyond above postulated short-term factors.

When operationalizing interpersonal communication we again face the problem of comparability. In 1990 our "active" interpersonal communication variable (PERS) measured those respondents who were frequently involved in political discussions and at the same time rarely were in agreement with their discussion partners indicating persuasion processes.[3] In 1995 PERS was measured as those respondents who frequently discussed politics and who tried to persuade their communication partners (see the Appendix for question wordings). Our "passive" respondents (PASS) talked very little about politics, and if they talked at all they were rarely in disagreement (in 1990) or never tried to convince other people (in 1995). Thus, when it comes to interpersonal communication we cannot directly compare the magnitude of our coefficients. We can, however, compare the structural effects due to the somewhat similar underlying concepts, that is frequency of discussions and level of agreement (to keep things simple we decided to name our interpersonal communication variables identically).

Media exposure variables are measured as the amount of days per week reading the political part in a newspaper (a scale ranging from 0 to 6), and/or watching TV news (0 to 7 days). Adding media exposure and interpersonal communication yields the following model:

1990:   Vote = a   + b1PREVOTE + b2SATDEM + b3DCAND
                    + b4PRINT +b5TV + b6PASS + b7PERS + e

1995:   Vote = a   + b1PID + b2SATDEM + b3DREGOP
                    + b4PRINT +b5TV + b6PASS + b7PERS + e

where

Vote, PID, PREVOTE, DCAND, DREGOP, SATDEM are the same as in the base model, and

PRINT = reading the political section of newspaper
TV = watching TV news
PASS = respondents with little or no interpersonal communication
PERS = respondents with strong interpersonal communication and persuasion.

However, we do not assume a direct media effect on the vote. Neither do we assume a change in vote intention simply due to political discussions. From previous research we have learned that media exposure and interpersonal communication may exert substantial effects on short-term factors–that is, on candidate evaluations and on issue orientations. Hence, we expect the relationships depicted in Figure 12.2.

To test for such indirect communication effects on the vote, we analyze the effects of media exposure and interpersonal communication on political issue orientations and candidate evaluations separately by estimating regressions with those variables as dependent variables:

1990: SATDEM = a + b1PID + b2DCAND + b3 PRINT + b4 TV + b5PASS + b6PERS + e

DCAND = a + b1PID + b2 SATDEM + b3 PRINT + b4 TV + b5PASS + b6PERS + e

1995: SATDEM = a + b1PID + b2DREGOP + b3 PRINT + b4 TV + b5PASS + b6PERS + e

DREGOP = a + b1PID + b2 SATDEM + b3 PRINT + b4 TV + b5PASS + b6PERS + e

where all variables are coded as above.

Figure 12.2. Political Communication and Voting Intentions

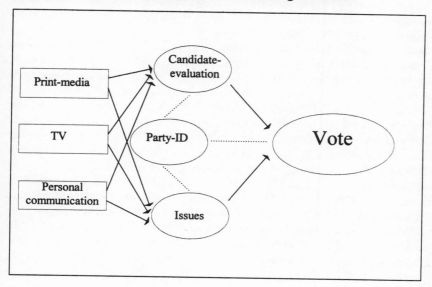

To study media and communication effects in a causal sense, we would need information about the actual content of political communication--either mediated through discussions or through direct media exposure. Because we do not have such detailed data, we follow arguments in previous research pointing to the relatively high convergence of political news coverage (especially during campaigns). Based on extensive research in agenda setting and news selection rationales by journalists, we would expect a potential media effect if voters follow campaign coverage closely. In this case, voters are likely to be exposed to somewhat similar information during such a period (Schrott and Meffert 1995). If media coverage operates similarly in quantity and bias (toward certain campaign topics), we would expect measurable media effects due to a differing media exposure. However, such effects can be interpreted only as correlations of assumed processes because causal analyses of such phenomena (as noted above) would need to control for the actual content of the campaign coverage, and would need panel data to show the actual changes due to political communication.

RESULTS

Media Exposure

In the Federal Republic of Germany almost all households own at least one TV set. Moreover, in 1995 80 percent (1990: 91 percent) in the new Länder and 71 percent (1990: 76 percent) in the old Länder subscribed to a daily newspaper (Berg and Kiefer 1996, 26). This remarkable abundance of media outlets in German households is mirrored by its media ratings. Media exposure is higher in the Federal Republic than in almost any other western industrialized nation (Brettschneider et al. 1994). This does not only hold for media exposure in general, but also for media usage of television news programs and (the political part of) newspapers. Table 12.1 gives an overview of (political) media usage in the old and the new parts of Germany with some remarkable findings. First, in 1990 as well as in 1995 East Germans were significantly more prone to read the political parts of their daily newspapers than were West Germans. However, the differences in 1995 were much smaller than after and around unification. The same was true for television news programs. The strong differences seen in 1990 are diminished by 1995. The differences in the levels of news exposure from 1990 to 1995 are most likely rooted in different question wordings (see Appendix) and should be treated with caution.

The heavier media usage in 1990 in the East is probably due to the extraordinary historical situation. The breakdown of the old system with all its accompanying social, economic, and political changes produced a greater need for interpretation and orientation. This, in turn, led to an increase in information seeking and political communication (Voltmer, Schabedoth, and Schrott 1995). Five years after unification, those communication differences seem to have disappeared. To examine whether this finding holds generally, information on newspaper reading and news watching were combined. Lazarsfeld, Berelson, and Gaudet (1944) put

Table 12.1. Media Consumption in Western and Eastern Germany, 1990 and 1995 (column percentages)

Print Media:
1990= filter question: Do you regularly or every now and then read a newspaper? If so, on how many days a week do you read reports about current affairs in Germany and other countries in ...?
1995= On how many days a week do you read reports about current affairs in Germany and other countries in a newspaper?

TV:
1990= I will now give you the names of several news programs on television. Please tell me for each how often you usually see them in a week. Tagesschau, Tagesthemen, Heute, Heute-Journal, SAT.1 Blick, RTL-aktuell, Aktuelle Kamera Am Abend, Aktuelle Kamera Zwo.
1995= On how many days a week do you normally watch news programs on television?

Print Media	1990		1995	
Reading about current affairs in a newspaper	Western Germany N= 1,332	Eastern Germany N= 685	Western Germany N= 1,006	Eastern Germany N= 1,018
Not at all	34.7	13.3	5.4	4.9
1 day a week	3.2	1.5	5.4	3.4
2 days a week	6.8	3.5	8.7	6.4
3 days a week	9.4	7.3	11.2	8.1
4 days a week	7.1	6.3	8.5	6.8
5 days a week	6.6	6.9	9.8	10.6
6 or 7 days a week	32.3	61.3	50.9	59.8
Eta	.29 ***		.09 ***	

TV	1990		1995	
Watching news programs on TV	Western Germany N= 1,340	Eastern Germany N= 692	Western Germany N= 1,006	Eastern Germany N= 1,021
Not at all	5.1	3.6	0.6	1.4
1 day a week	2.2	2.3	0.9	0.9
2 days a week	8.4	5.1	2.6	2.0
3 days a week	16.6	10.3	3.6	4.5
4 days a week	19.0	9.2	6.2	4.8
5 days a week	17.7	13.3	9.2	7.8
6 or 7 days a week	31.1	56.2	76.9	78.6
Eta	.18***		.00 n.s.	

*Notes:*** $p < .001$; n.s. = not significant.
Sources: CNEP 1990, KSPW 1995.

forward the "more and more" rule: People who frequently watch television also read the newspaper extensively. In the German case of the 1990s this rule holds only partially. Although there is a relationship between television watching and newspaper reading, this relationship is rather weak (as pointed out in Figures 12.3 and 12.4). Therefore we seek to develop typologies of media users who concentrate either on television or on newspapers, on both or on neither one.

Figures 12.3 and 12.4 show the results of cluster analyses that demonstrate the expected types of media users. The analyses were conducted separately for East and West Germany in 1990 and 1995. We combined those groups who were very similar with respect to their print and television usage, but very dissimilar to other groups: Media abstainers in 1990 practically never read a newspaper and watched television news only two days a week. Pure television users received their information solely from broadcast news and never read newspapers. Heavy print users read the political parts of a newspaper daily, but watched television news only twice a week. The general information seekers finally got their political information from print as well as from television news.

In 1990 these four types were similar in their structural behavior in East and West, but the sizes of the segments in the population were different. Again, East Germans used mass media more extensively than their western compatriots: The size of media abstainers and pure television users were significantly smaller in the new Länder, while the group of general information seekers was substantially larger.

In 1995 we found three noticeable changes: First, the group means on the y-axes were pushed upward, indicating that all groups showed a heavier television news exposure than in 1990. This, however, is most likely an artifact of a change in question wording. Second, the relatively small differences from 1990 (between East and West) with respect to the placement of the four groups almost entirely disappeared. Third, not only did the structural behavior of the individual groups converge, but the size of the group segments also grew similar. Another interesting point is the very large group of general information seekers (64 and 71 percent, respectively), while media abstainers and pure print media users represent only small groups with not more than 6 percent each.

In research on the United States, DeFleur and Ball-Rokeach (1989; similarly Robinson 1976; McLeod and McDonald 1985; McDonald and Reese 1987) differentiated between the active information seeker who chooses media sources and media content conscientiously and the casual observer who randomly receives media messages. Applied to our typologies, the pure print users and general information recipients could be counted as active information seekers. They read newspapers regularly, and it is very unlikely to receive political messages randomly through such a behavior. Exposure to broadcast news, in contrast, is often not goal oriented but rather habitualized behavior and part of the every day television ritual (Donsbach 1989). The pure television users can therefore be called casual observers. Substantively this group differentiation is important because purely television oriented people hold a different view of the political world. They perceive politics as being simple and entertaining, while active information seekers

Figure 12.3. Types of Media Consumption in Wester and Eastern Germany, 1990

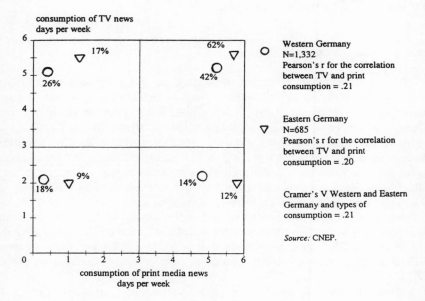

Figure 12.4. Types of Media Consumption in Wester and Eastern Germany, 1995

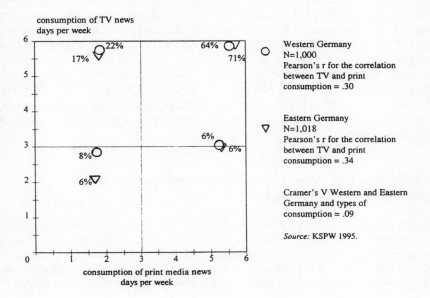

show a differentiated and complex thinking of politics (Schenk and Pfenning 1990: 422). Furthermore, newspaper readers are better able to argue their opinions than TV viewers (see Noelle-Neumann 1982: 37).

Interpersonal Communication

While exposure to mass communication could be seen as "audience activity" as postulated by Milbrath (1965), interpersonal communication represents a more active behavior. It actually bridges political involvement to political participation. Compared to other countries, Germans participate relatively frequently in various forms of interpersonal communication. Yet, at the beginning of the 1990s political discussions were more frequent in the East. This stands in contrast to West Germans in the early 1950s when a withdrawal of the citizenry to the private sphere took place. Thus, the massive societal changes led to a more political-minded activity in East Germany. However, such behavioral patterns did not last. Since 1990 the frequency of political discussions as well as the attempt to convince others has decreased continually (see Brettschneider et al. 1994: 545 and 578). Analyses of the CNEP and KSPW[4] data corroborate this trend: In 1995 there were no more differences between East and West concerning interpersonal communication (Table 12.2).

This convergence can also be seen when frequency of discussions is combined with the indicators "opinion disagreement" (1990) and "persuasion attempts" (1995). Figures 12.5 and 12.6 show how slight differences in placement and frequencies of the various types in 1990 practically had disappeared by 1995. The individual interpersonal communication types are not only defined by almost identical group means but also by identical sizes: The persuasive discussants (one quarter of the respondents in 1995) frequently discuss politics and try to convince others. They resemble what Lazarsfeld et al. called "opinion leaders." Passive discussants, too, frequently discuss politics (again about 25 percent of the respondents in 1995), but they do not attempt to convince others (1995) or are in disagreement (1990). This group can be compared to Lazarsfeld et al.'s "opinion followers." The passive respondents (about 50 percent of the population) do not participate in political discussions at all. They therefore do not try to convince anybody either.

The Relationship Between Mass Communication and Interpersonal Communication

Gumpert and Cathcart (1982: 26) criticize the treatment of interpersonal and mass communication as isolated phenomena. One of the few studies that tried to study both phenomena together is again Lazarsfeld et al.'s seminal Erie County study (1944). They found that opinion leaders use mass media more frequently and derived the two-step flow of communication hypothesis from their findings. Active

Table 12.2. Personal Communication in Western and Eastern Germany, 1990 and 1995 (column percentages)

Frequency of discussions:

1990= Apart from your spouse, with which person have you discussed political affairs most frequently over the last few months? How often do you talk about political affairs?

1995= As you know, some people are politically very active whereas other people often do not find the time or are simply not interested in politics. I will now read to you a couple of activities. Please tell me for each how often you perform the following activities.

Leading a political discussion?

Persuasive efforts/ difference of opinion:

1990= When you talk to this person about politics, how often would you say do you *differ* on the topic?

1995= How often do you try to win over friends to your political point of view?

	1990		1995	
Frequency of discussion Western Germany	Western Germany	Eastern Germany	Western Germany	Eastern Germany
	N= 1,340	N= 692	N= 1,012	N= 1,020
Never	37.2	29.3	25.9	24.7
Rarely	16.8	5.2	29.2	27.7
Sometimes	33.2	26.7	30.1	31.5
Often	12.8	38.7	14.8	16.1
Eta	.22 ***		.03 n.s.	

	1990		1995	
Persuasive efforts differing opinions	Western Germany	Eastern Germany	Western Germany	Eastern Germany
	N= 1,340	N= 692	N= 1,006	N= 1,020
Never	36.9	32.2	39.0	41.0
Rarely	23.4	23.1	31.3	32.8
Sometimes	29.5	32.1	23.2	19.1
Often	10.1	12.6	6.6	7.1
Eta	.06 n.s.		.03 n.s.	

Notes: *** $p < .001$; n.s. = not significant.
Sources: CNEP 1990, KSPW 1995.

Figure 12.5. Types of Personal Communication in Western and Eastern Germany, 1990

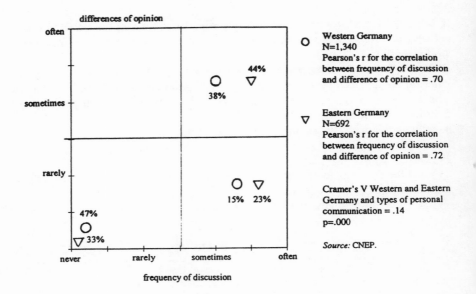

Figure 12.6. Types of Personal Communication in Western and Eastern Germany, 1995

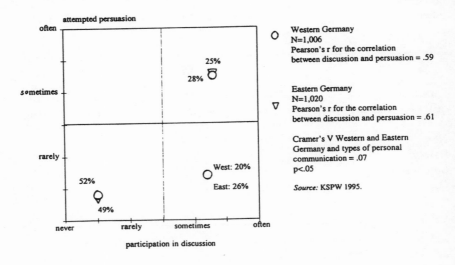

opinion leaders receive their political information from mass media and hand those informations, although filtered, over to the less active parts of the population. These opinion followers use mass media rarely and therefore get their information about the political "world outside" only indirectly through contacts with opinion leaders.

Because of the development and distribution of television, the hypothesis concerning opinion followers has essentially become obsolete (see Klingemann 1986). Table 12.3 supports previous findings and shows that not even 7 percent in 1990 and less than 3 percent in 1995 received their information solely from interpersonal communication. Instead, for a large segment of the population, mass media turns out to be the only "bridge" to the world of politics. In both parts of Germany, individuals who depend on mass media and never interpret mediated news in interpersonal communication mainly consist of the politically uninterested with little formal education and of retired persons (see Brettschneider and Schrott 1995).

Another sizable group are the "persuasive" media users. They seek information from mass media, they discuss politics with others, and they attempt to persuade others. Such individuals are highly educated and politically interested. The "communication addressees" possess two bridges to the world of politics–mass media and interpersonal communication. They do not, however, try to convince their discussion partners. Finally, there is the group of the "apathetic" who are not involved in political communication at all: In 1995, 5.9 percent of West Germans and 4 percent of East Germans belonged to that group. They are the least interested in politics and display the lowest levels of formal education.

Table 12.3. Types of Communication, 1990 and 1995 (total percentages for Western and Eastern Germany)

Types of media consumption

Types of personal communication	Media abstainers	Preferring TV	Preferring print	Using all media
Generally passive	"The apathetic"	"The TV addicts"	"The print addicts"	
	1990: 11.7/2.9 1995: 5.9/4.0	1990: 14.0/7.4 1995: 15.0/10.9	1990: 21.2/22.4 1995: 30.7/34.2	
Passive debaters	"The non media debaters"	"The communication addressees" 1990: 12.8/21.4 1995: 18.9/25.1		
Active debaters	1990: 6.9/6.0 1995: 2.4/1.6	"The persuasive media consumers" 1990: 33.3/40.0 1995: 27.0/24.3		

Notes: 1990: N western Germany = 1,332; N eastern Germany = 685. 1995: N western Germany = 994; N eastern Germany = 1,017.
Sources: CNEP 1990, KSPW 1995.

Political Communication and Voter Turnout

How does political communication influence elections? First, communication may have an impact on voting turnout; second, it may influence the actual voting behavior. To analyze the relationship between political communication and turnout, we use the communication groups described above as the basis for our analyses. The dependent variable, turnout, was measured in 1990 as the intention to vote later in the year, whereas in 1995 respondents were asked whether they had voted in 1994. Since the reported intentions as well as actual participation were higher than the actual turnout in both national elections (1990 and 1994), the variance in our dependent variable was relatively small (see Table 12.4).

A multiple classification analysis reveals that the six communication types have a significant and consistent effect on turnout in both years and for both parts of Germany. The apolitical were the least to turn out, and persuasive media users as well as communication addressees were the most likely to vote. The latter included those respondents who used mass media and participated in political discussion. Among those who were not involved in interpersonal communication, respondents using solely print media were more prone to vote than pure television users. These results corroborate earlier findings in the United States (O'Keefe and Mendelsohn 1978; for Germany see Brettschneider and Schrott 1995; Klingemann and Voltmer 1989).

Political Communication and the Voting Decision

To answer the second question concerning the relationship between political communication and voting behavior, we first analyzed the base model mentioned above. In both years our dependent variable was vote intention for one of the parties, coded 1 for government parties, -1 for opposition parties, and 0 for nonvoters. Table 12.5 shows the results of the base model.

As expected PREVOTE and PID have the strongest effect on voting intention, followed by candidate/party evaluation and satisfaction with democracy. Structurally the vote determinants in East and West resembled each other in 1990. However, the previous voting decision in the national election of 1987 was a much stronger predictor of the vote in the West than the Volkskammer election of 1990 in the East. Not surprisingly, voting decisions also are subject to short-term influences during times of profound transformation. Furthermore, quite a few parties simply disappeared or merged with other parties between the Volkskammer election and the national election later in the very same year. In 1995 the predictive gap between the two models narrowed substantially. Yet in both years satisfaction with democracy displayed some remarkable results: While voting behavior in the former Federal Republic was not influenced by this variable in either year, satisfaction with democracy certainly helped the governing parties in the East.[5]

Table 12.4. Voting Participation and Types of Communication in East and West Germany, 1990 and 1995

1990: The next general election will take place on December 2, as an all-German election. Will you vote in this election?
0 = no/don't know, 1 = yes.
1995: In the last general election in October of t year a lot of people abstained from voting. How about you; did you vote in the last election?
0 = no, 1 = yes.

	1990				1994			
	Western Germany		Eastern Germany		Western Germany		Eastern Germany	
	N = 1,277; x̄ = 0.86		N = 612; x̄ = 0.89		N = 913; x̄ = 0.89		N = 910; x̄ = 0.83	
Types of communication	x̄ (bi)	x̄ (multi)[1]	x̄ (bi)	x̄ (multi)[1]	x̄ (bi)	x̄ (multi)[1]	x̄ (bi)	x̄ (multi)[1]
The apathetic	0.68	0.69	0.87	0.89	0.71	0.73	0.65	0.68
The TV addicts	0.77	0.78	0.87	0.87	0.84	0.84	0.68	0.77
The print addicts	0.88	0.88	0.88	0.88	0.89	0.89	0.82	0.88
The nonmedia debaters	0.82	0.82	0.61	0.63	0.85	0.86	0.67	0.82
The communication addressees	0.95	0.94	0.91	0.91	0.92	0.91	0.84	0.95
The persuasive media consumers	0.92	0.91	0.93	0.93	0.94	0.94	0.93	0.92
Eta/Beta	0.24	0.22***	0.23	0.22***	0.17	0.16***	0.21	0.19***
R^2 including the covariates		0.07***		0.06***		0.04***		0.06***

Notes: [1] Mean controlling for the variables education, age, and sex. *** $p < .001$; significance of the main effects and the complete explained variance.
Sources: CNEP 1990, KSPW 1995.

Table 12.5. Regression Model of Vote Intention in Western and Eastern Germany, 1990 and 1995 (standard deviation in parentheses)

	Vote intention 1990		Vote intention 1995	
	Western Germany N=1,012	Eastern Germany N=570	Western Germany N=681	Eastern Germany N=699
Party identification (PID)	n.a.	n.a.	.169*** (.01)	.179*** (.01)
Last vote (PREVOTE)[1]	.480*** (.02)	.270*** (.04)	n.a.	n.a.
Candidate evaluation (ΔCAND)	.067*** (.00)	.056*** (.01)	n.a.	n.a.
Evaluation of government and opposition (ΔREGOP)	n.a.	n.a.	.099*** (.01)	.068*** (.01)
Satisfaction with democracy (SATDEM)	-.010 (.02)	.067** (.03)	-.022 (.02)	.055* (.02)
Constant	.020	-.249	-.119	-.107
R^2	.65	.30	.66	.57

Notes: [1] Western Germany: general election 1987, eastern Germany: Volkskammer election 1990. n.a. = not asked; * $p < .05$; ** $p < .01$, *** $p < .001$.
Sources: CNEP 1990, KSPW 1995.

The inclusion of media exposure and interpersonal communication does not increase the predictive power of the model. The results in Table 12.6 corroborate previous findings, which could not detect any (or only very minor) substantial direct effects of political communication on the vote. This does not mean, however, that political communication lacks any influence whatsoever. There might well be an indirect impact through short-term influences—that is, candidate evaluations and issues.

Political Communication and Satisfaction with Democracy

Due to a lack of data it was impossible to analyze traditional issues such as perception of the economy, stands on abortion, and the like. As outlined above, however, we could make use of a "pseudo issue" on satisfaction with democracy. This "pseudo issue" now serves as dependent variable. Besides our political communication variables party identification and candidate/party evaluations are included as control variables.

Table 12.6. Regression Model of Vote Intention in Western and Eastern Germany, 1990 and 1995: Basic Model and Political Communication (standard deviation in parentheses)

	Vote intention 1990		Vote intention 1995	
	Western Germany N=1,008	Eastern Germany N=565	Western Germany N=670	Eastern Germany N=695
Party identification (PID)	n.a.	n.a.	.167*** (.01)	.178*** (.01)
Last vote (PREVOTE)[1]	.480*** (.02)	.268*** (.04)	n.a.	n.a.
Candidate evaluation (ΔCAND)	.067*** (.00)	.056*** (.01)	n.a.	n.a.
Evaluation of government and opposition (ΔREGOP)	n.a.	n.a.	.103*** (.01)	.067*** (.01)
Satisfaction with democracy (SATDEM)	-.010 (.02)	.068** (.03)	-.026 (.02)	.057* (.02)
Media consumption				
Print media (PRESSE)	.000 (.01)	.002 (.02)	.003 (.01)	.004 (.01)
Television (TV)	.007 (.01)	-.010 (.02)	-.036 (.02)	.015 (.02)
Personal communication				
Passive (PASS)	.044 (.05)	-.011 (.09)	-.112 (.06)	.108 (.06)
Active debaters (PERS)	.037 (.05)	-.070 (.08)	-.035 (.06)	.031 (.06)
Constant	-.044	-.185	.135	-.277
R^2	.65	.30	.66	.58

Notes: [1] Western Germany: general election 1987, eastern Germany: Volkskammer election 1990. n.a. = not asked; * $p < .05$; ** $p < .01$, *** $p < .001$.
Sources: CNEP 1990, KSPW 1995.

When we look at Table 12.7, we find that political communication has only weak effects on the issue attitude. The model with the most predictive power shows an R^2 of .12 for the former Federal Republic in 1990. In 1995 this explained variance is reduced to 1 percent (7 and 3 percent, respectively, in the East).

Table 12.7. Regression Model of Satisfaction with Democracy in Western and Eastern Germany, 1990 and 1995 (standard deviation in parentheses)

	Vote intention 1990		Vote intention 1995	
	Western Germany N=1,278	Eastern Germany N=668	Western Germany N=966	Eastern Germany N=986
Party identification (PID)	-.008. (.01)	.060*** (.02)	.010 (.02)	.178 (.02)
Candidate evaluation (ΔCAND)	.071*** (.01)	.040*** (.01)	n.a.	n.a.
Evaluation of government and opposition (ΔREGOP)	n.a.	n.a.	.026 (.02)	.032** (.01)
Media consumption				
Print media (PRESSE)	.035** (.01)	-.009 (.02)	.005 (.02)	.056** (.02)
Television (TV)	.029 (.02)	.014 (.03)	.026 (.03)	-.006 (.03)
Personal communication				
Passive (PASS)	.123 (.08)	.010 (.13)	-.172* (.09)	.051 (.08)
Active debaters (PERS)	.007 (.08)	.289* (.12)	-.030 (.10)	-.133 (.09)
Constant	3.283	2.146	2.179	1.837
R^2	.12	.07	.01	.03

Notes: n.a. = not asked; * $p < .05$; ** $p < .01$, *** $p < .001$.
Sources: CNEP 1990, KSPW 1995.

The sources of the weak effect of political communication differed for the two parts of Germany in both years. In 1990, the frequency of reading newspapers was linked to satisfaction with democracy in the West, while East Germans who participated actively and persuasively in discussions were the more satisfied. Clearly, print media coverage of the unification process led West Germans to be more convinced of the democratic idea. Print media in the East did not exert such a system-stabilizing effect, but in 1990 most print media were still in the hands of the former communists and thus distrusted. Similarly, people in the East who debated politics (and the future democracy of Germany as a whole) were more satisfied with democracy than active West Germans for whom the idea as such was not novel.

The picture changed somewhat in 1995 insofar as East Germans are positively influenced by print media (which are now owned by West German publishers and probably more "trustworthy"), while in West Germany only the passive display a somewhat weaker satisfaction with democracy. Another question to tap political communication effects asked about the most important political issue facing the nation. In 1990 up to 4 and in 1995 up to 6 answers were coded. We assume that people who actively seek information from mass media and through interpersonal communication should be able to mention more problems than those for whom politics is not that important.

As Table 12.8 shows this is indeed the case, even after controlling for age, education, and gender. The apolitical mention the fewest number, and the persuasive discussant the greatest number, of political problems. When we compare users of print and broadcasting media, we find that newspaper readers show a stronger awareness when it comes to politics.

Political Communication and Evaluation of Candidates and Parties

How are evaluations of parties and candidates shaped by political communication? While candidate evaluations play a significant role for the voting decision in the United States (see Wattenberg 1991), this determinant is seen as a more minor factor in the German context (see Kaase 1994). Nevertheless there is also evidence for the importance of candidates in the German electoral process (see Norpoth 1977; Lass 1995; Kepplinger, Brosius, and Dahlem 1994a; Finkel and Schrott 1995). As mentioned above, these short-term factors are most likely to be affected by political communication processes because most people never meet a politician personally and instead have to rely on other sources for information about politicians.

Table 12.9 summarizes the results of our model. At a first glance, the fit is much higher than the fit for the satisfaction with democracy model. This is mainly due to the strong relationship between the short-term factors candidate/party evaluations and the long-term vote determinant party identification.

In 1990, the model for West Germany explains twice the variance of the model for the former GDR. Yet, neither media exposure nor interpersonal communication plays a statistically significant role in either analysis. Although insignificant, the signs of the regression coefficients suggest that newspaper reading in West Germany worked in favor of Lafontaine, while television news exposure was going toward supporting Chancellor Kohl. Other research found similar (and significant) effects (see Holtz-Bacha and Kaid 1993). Through content analyses Kepplinger, Brosius, and Dahlem (1994a), and Schönbach and Semetko (1994) found that TV news in the last few weeks prior to election day strongly favored Chancellor Kohl and hurt Lafontaine.

In 1995 the models for East and West Germany explain roughly the same amount of variance. Again we find a very weak relationship between political communication and the evaluation of government and opposition parties. In the

Table 12.8. Perception of Problems and Types of Communication in East and West Germany, 1990 and 1995 (bi- and multivariate group means and correlation coefficients)

1990: What are, in your opinion, the most important problems facing the nation? 0 = no answer; 4 = four answers.
1995: What are, in your opinion, the most important problems facing the nation? 0 = no answer; 6 = four answers.

	1990				1994			
	Western Germany		Eastern Germany		Western Germany		Eastern Germany	
	N = 1,277; x̄ = 2.81		N = 612; x̄ = 3.11		N = 942; x̄ = 3.75		N = 927; x̄ = 3.82	
Types of communication	x̄ (bi)	x̄ (multi)[1]	x̄ (bi)	x̄ (multi)[1]	x̄ (bi)	x̄ (multi)[1]	x̄ (bi)	x̄ (multi)[1]
The apathetic	2.36	2.36	2.75	2.80	3.40	3.38	3.23	3.25
The TV addicts	2.45	2.54	2.94	2.98	3.41	3.40	3.41	3.44
The print addicts	2.79	2.83	2.82	2.84	3.62	3.65	3.69	3.72
The nonmedia debaters	2.79	2.72	2.95	2.94	3.68	3.63	3.67	3.62
The communication addressees	2.91	2.89	3.29	3.27	4.00	3.99	3.79	3.78
The persuasive media consumers	3.08	3.03	3.26	3.24	3.98	3.96	4.31	3.26
Eta/Beta	0.24	0.21***	0.22	0.20***	0.17	0.16***	0.20	0.18***
R^2 including the covariates	0.08***		0.06***		0.03***		0.05***	

Notes: [1] Mean controlling for the variables education, age, and sex. *** p < .001; significance of the main effects and the complete explained variance.
Sources: CNEP 1990, KSPW 1995.

Table 12.9. Regression Models of Candidate, Government, and Opposition Evaluations in East and West Germany, 1990 and 1995 (standard deviation in parentheses)

	Evaluation of candidates 1990		Evaluation of government and opposition, 1995	
	Western Germany N=1,278	Eastern Germany N=668	Western Germany N=966	Eastern Germany N=986
Party identification (PID)	1.040***	.642***	.722***	.808***
	(.03)	(.05)	(.03)	(.03)
Satisfaction with democracy (SATDEM)	.897***	.437***	.116	.220**
	(.10)	(.13)	(.07)	(.08)
Media consumption				
Print media (PRESSE)	-.074	.007	.095*	.003
	(.04)	(.08)	(.04)	(.05)
Television (TV)	.108	.135	.079	.202
	(.06)	(.10)	(.07)	(.07)
Personal communication				
Passive (PASS)	.368	.377	.519***	.156
	(.29)	(.44)	(.18)	(.20)
Active debaters (PERS)	.280	-.273	-.300	-.279
	(.29)	(.41)	(.20)	(.23)
Constant	-3.096	-.423	-.584	-1.113
R^2	.50	.30	.46	.41

Notes: * p < .05; ** p < .01, *** p < .001.
Sources: CNEP 1990, KSPW 1995.

former Federal Republic only newspaper reading showed some effect favoring the government parties. The same holds for passive respondents. They are less interested in politics, and clearly favor the status quo—that is, the governing parties.

CONCLUSION

We started our analyses by asking how much mass media are used in the daily news-gathering processes, and how important personal political discussions are in the political process. We were particularly interested in differences between East and West Germans in political communication processes, and whether potential differences between the two groups have diminished from 1990 to 1995. Further research questions dealt with typologies of media exposure and how political communication is linked to voting behavior. The most important results of this chapter can be summarized as follows:

1. Mass media are used more extensively in the eastern German Länder than in the former West Germany. We attribute this to the greater need for a new political orientation in the East during times of momentous change. Nevertheless, the similarity of media exposure in both parts of Germany was stronger in 1995 than in 1990.

2. Based on its greater trustworthiness and reach, television is the main information source. For about 15 percent of Germans television newscasts are the only connection to politics. However, this information is based on a habitual television watching behavior and not an active information seeking.

3. We found no differences between East and West regarding interpersonal communication. For half of all Germans, politics is not a topic for discussion. About 25 percent not only talk politics frequently, but also try to persuade their communication partners.

4. About 50 percent of Germans use mass media as their only link to politics. For these individuals news content is not being interpreted and shaped through discussions. Their social co-orientation about the "world outside" is based solely on media reality.

5. Interpersonal (political) communication as well as print media usage is conducive to electoral participation while simply watching television news does not effect voting turnout.

6. Political communication (as measured in this study) does not have an independent effect on the vote (next to party identification, candidate evaluations, and satisfaction with democracy).

7. Surprisingly, we find only weak relationships between political communication and short-term factors (candidate evaluations and our "pseudo issue" satisfaction with democracy). Furthermore, we do not only find different effect patterns in East and West but also differences over time.

8. We find a strong relationship between political communication and the amount of societal problems named by an individual. According to these findings, people who participate heavily in political discussions and those reading newspapers are more aware of national problems.

Still, the question remains whether these findings are generalizable, or whether they are due to contextual factors. What lessons for further research do we draw from these findings? First, media effects, though not found to be very strong in this study, cannot be neglected in studies of electoral behavior. We would argue that there is a need for intensifying research activities that focus on the role media play in the German democracy. Second, more and better data are needed for understanding the complex web of relationships in the German case. Unfortunately, questions pertaining to political communication and political attitudes are only rarely asked in the same surveys. If German political science is to take the importance of media exposure and interpersonal communication for the political process seriously, the inclusion of communication variables in regularly conducted surveys is needed. These questionnaires should not only include (among political attitude questions) simple media usage questions but also gather information on how specific news content is selected by the respondent and on how trustworthy a given information source is. To achieve comparisons over time, it is necessary to develop a set of questions asked continuously (see a proposed "media demography" in Brettschneider and Schrott 1995).

Third, more interdisciplinary research is necessary, including a mix of different approaches and the linkage of different types of data. More cooperation between political scientists and communication researchers would be a first step in this direction. Survey data as well as data derived from content analysis could be matched. In a study on the 1990 election, Schrott and Meffert (1995) linked information from a content analysis of campaign coverage with a representative survey of German voters. Their primary results show significant effects of political campaign communication. Other analyses using content analytical data also demonstrate considerable communication effects (see Holtz-Bacha and Kaid 1993; Kepplinger, Brosius, and Dahlem 1994a). As mentioned above, to fully study the impact of mass media on voting behavior, data are needed on the actual media content, media usage, perceptions of media content by the voters, and on a variety of political attitudes influencing voting behavior (Kepplinger, Brosius, and Dahlem 1994a). As of now, however, Schönbach's (1987: 390) statement still holds: "Mass media and elections in . . . Germany still represent a puzzle with many missing pieces."

NOTES

We thank the primary investigators Max Kaase, Hans-Dieter Klingemann (both Wissenschaftszentrum Berlin), Franz Urban Pappi (University of Mannheim), Manfred Kuechler (Hunter College, New York), and Oscar W. Gabriel (University of Stuttgart) for making the data available. We are also grateful to Steven Finkel for helpful comments and criticism, and further appreciate the skillful research assistance of Mathias Lange and Edith Dietrich.

1. The first wave of the "Cross National Election Project" (CNEP) study of the 1990 German election (people aged 18 and over, N= 1,340 respondents in the former Federal Republic including West-Berlin, N= 692 respondents from the new German Länder–that is, the former GDR); (2) a KSPW survey conducted early in 1995 (people aged 16 and over, N=1,014 respondents from the former Federal Republic, and N=1,022 respondents from the former GDR).

2. We are well aware that satisfaction with democracy is not a "political issue." Deviating from its theoretical conceptionalization as indicator for regime orientations (Easton 1965) satisfaction with democracy, however, can also be seen (at least up to a certain degree) as an indicator for satisfaction with the performance of the governing parties (see some indications in Gabriel 1986: 234). Given that part of the changes in satisfaction with democracy are due to changes in the

performance of the political system, especially with respect to economic factors (Gabriel 1994a: 109), satisfaction with democracy can at least partly be used as indicator for satisfaction with governmental performance in one of the most important areas influencing the vote, that is economic performance. Although we are well aware that this procedure is questionable, the alternative would have been to skip issues altogether from our model. This, in turn, would have led to a model that only scarcely resembles the basic Michigan approach.

3. Our interpersonal communication variables were dummies (coded as 1 if conditions applied and 0 otherwise). We derived these variables through a cluster analysis (see Brettschneider and Schrott 1995).

4. CNEP: Comparative National Elections Project. KPSW: Kommission zur Erforschung des sozialen, politischen und wirtschaftlichen Wandels in den neuen Bundesländern (Research Commission on the Social, Political, and Economic Development in the New States).

5. It is plausible that this variable measured different ideas in the East and West: In the East it might well be that satisfaction with democracy really tapped the affection with the former GDR and its political order.

APPENDIX

Comparative National Elections Project 1990 Data

Newspapers
On how many days a week do you read about current affairs in Germany and other countries in . . . ? Reports about current affairs are read on . . . day(s) per week

TV News
I will now give you the names of several news programs on television. Please tell me for each how often you usually see it in a week.
Usually seen on:

Tagesschau	_ days	_ never
Tagesthemen	_ days	_ never
Heute	_ days	_ never
Heute-Journal	_ days	_ never
SAT 1 Blick	_ days	_ never
RTL-aktuell	_ days	_ never

Personal Communication
Most people are talking about their more important affairs with other people. Remember the last six months: Who have you been talking to about important affairs? When you talk to these people, how often do you talk to them about politics? (we chose the person that was talked to most often)

When you talk to those people (here: our chosen target person) about politics, how often would you say do you differ on the topic?

    often   sometimes   rarely   never

Party ID

Many people tend to identify with one party in the long run, even though they may vote differently at times. Do you identify with a special party? If so, which party do you, generally speaking, prefer?

SPD	_
CDU	_
CSU	_
FDP	_
GREENS	_
other party, viz. . . .	_
no	_

How strong would you say is your identification with this party; very strong, quite strong, moderate, quite weak, weak?

very strong	_
quite strong	_
moderate	_
quite weak	_
very weak	_

Voting Intention: Party List

In a German general election you have two votes: one for your constituency candidate and one for the candidate list of your preferred party. You find here a ballot paper similar to the one you will get at the general election. Which party do you intend to vote for with your party list vote? Party List Vote goes to . . .

Content with democracy

How about democracy in Germany? How content or discontent are you–all in all–with democracy as it is practiced in Germany?

very content	_
quite content	_
somewhat content	_
somewhat discontent	_
quite discontent	_
very discontent	_

Candidate Evaluation
The coming general election also decides whether Helmut Kohl or Oskar Lafontaine will be the new chancellor. Imagine a thermometer going from minus five to plus five with zero in the middle. Please signify on this thermometer what you think about the two candidates. Plus 5 here means that you like the candidate very much. Minus 5 means that you dislike him very much.
What do you think about Helmut Kohl?
What do you think about Oskar Lafontaine?

Perception of Problems
What are, in your opinion, the most important problems facing the country?
Open question; up to four answers were possible.

KSPW (Research Commission on the Social, Political, and Economic Development in the New States) 1995 Data

Newspapers
On how many days a week do you read about current affairs in Germany and other countries in ... ?
        Reports about current affairs are read on ... day(s) per week

TV News
On how many days a week do you normally watch news programs on television?
        on ... day(s) per week.
        less than once a week, viz. ....

Personal Communication
As you know, some people are politically very active whereas other people often do not find the time or are simply not interested in politics. Could you please tell us, how often you perform the following activities?

Leading a political discussion?
How often do you try to win over friends to your political point of view?

often	sometimes	rarely	never
–	–	–	–

Voting Intention: Party List
If there were a general election next Sunday, which party would you vote for?
        I would vote for ...   –
        I would not vote   –

Evaluation of government and opposition
What do you think, generally speaking, about the German political parties? Please signify your evaluation with the following scale. +5 means that you like a party very much, -5 means that you dislike it very much. The values in between are for finer gradations of your evaluation.
What do you think about: CDU/CSU, SPD, Bündnis 90/Greens, PDS?

Content with democracy
How content are you with democracy in Germany generally speaking?
        _ 1   _ 2   _ 3   _ 4   _ 5

Perception of Problems
What are, in your opinion, the most important problems facing the nation today? Open question, up to six answers were possible.

13

Candidate Characteristics and Electoral Performance: A Long-Term Analysis of the German Bundestag

Thomas D. Lancaster

Most research on electoral dynamics in the Federal Republic of Germany appropriately focuses on political parties because they are at the heart of German electoral politics (Dalton 1989; Dalton 1993a; Padgett 1989). However, the fact that individual candidates actually stand for election to the Bundestag is too frequently neglected. While individual candidates unquestionably ride the electoral fortunes or misfortunes of their political parties, some candidate characteristics systematically and significantly affect German electoral performance. This chapter thus argues that who runs, not just what party label a candidate possesses, is fundamentally important to a full understanding of German electoral dynamics. Thus, in studying candidate effects, this study deals with a similar subject as the one by Angelika Vetter and Oscar W. Gabriel in chapter 5 of this volume. Yet, unlike Vetter and Gabriel, who concentrate on the candidates for chancellor, I focus on the candidates for the Bundestag in the individual districts, searching for candidate effects on a level below that of most prominent politicians in Germany. Moreover, I focus on actual candidate characteristics as well on the actual electoral returns in first votes they receive, while Vetter and Gabriel analyze perceptions on the candidates and their implication for individual behavior.

The analysis begins by suggesting why previous research has neglected individual candidate characteristics. The proportional aspect of Germany's mixed electoral system with its party lists is at the core of this explanation. Second, it focuses attention on district (Wahlkreis) contests in order to assess effects of candidate characteristics. Third, following description of the data itself, three individual candidate characteristics are considered: gender, age, and incumbency status. With each, three different indicators of electoral performance are measured. Finally, these three characteristics and the three indicators of electoral performance are compared and their relative importance assessed. Given this volume's focus, the dynamic nature of the impact of candidate characteristics is emphasized throughout.

THE NEGLECT OF CANDIDATE EFFECTS

Candidate effects are generally not considered in most analyses of German electoral dynamics for several reasons. First, German voters tend to think in terms of party, especially at election time (Dalton 1989). Second, government formation following each election, and the necessary coalition building processes, is played out along party lines. In Germany's parliamentary democracy, who comes to power depends fundamentally upon dynamics within the party system. Third, and potentially the most important in terms of actual Bundestag representation, the Basic Law and German electoral laws strongly emphasize the role of parties.

The legal basis for party centrality is no better seen than in Germany's dual electoral system (Kaase 1984). Under this system created in 1949, voters are given two distinct choices.[1] The "first vote" is cast for a candidate who has been nominated in a local party meeting to be that party's candidate in a single member constituency (Wahlkreis). Much like in the United States and Britain, a simple plurality suffices to win a Bundestag seat. The voter's other choice comes in the selection of one of the competing party lists. These lists are different for each of Germany's Länder. State party conventions determine the names and the order of candidates on each Land party list (Roberts 1988).

This "second vote" is clearly the most important because it determines a party's overall electoral fortunes. These votes directly translate into parliamentary seats: the percentage of votes a party receives in the second vote determines the final allocation of total parliamentary seats, as long as it passes the 5 percent threshold.[2] For example, a party that receives 40 percent of the second vote is entitled to 40 percent of the Bundestag seats. While district seats are actually allocated first, it is the "second vote" that is used to fill the seats to which a party is entitled, even if the party did not do well in the district races. Furthermore, the electoral law reinforces a party's role in that changing the list's order or any form of preference voting is prohibited.

Intentionally or not, by analyzing aggregate electoral outcomes most studies of German elections emphasize the "second vote" in the country's mixed electoral system because it determines the final distribution of seats (Dalton 1993a). Concern over final distribution of Bundestag seats and relative party strength clearly justify such analysis. However, party lists and the importance Germany's mixed electoral system places on them obfuscates the effects of individual candidate characteristics. List systems strongly constrain the potential for any influence of candidate characteristics on vote choice. They channel the vote into an expression of party, not individual, preference. Not surprisingly, then, the only candidate characteristics initially thought to matter under such conditions are those projected by the images of candidates for chancellor (see Kaase 1994; Kepplinger et al. 1992; Schrott 1990b). Emphasis on scholarly analysis of the party vote is encouraged by other factors. Standardization of the vote intention question for comparative purposes, for example, totally neglects the impact of Germany's district vote (see Finkel and Schrott 1995). And, analysis of the Bundestag itself tends to place membership only within the parties' electoral context (Loewenberg 1967; Loewenberg and Patterson

1979) and with little emphasis on dynamic trends (Mueller 1983).[3] If the influence of individual candidate characteristics is to be understood, we must redirect our analysis to where they are least constrained in Germany's mixed electoral system--in the district races. This means taking an uncommon perspective on German electoral dynamics.[4]

DISTRICT ELECTIONS IN A MIXED SYSTEM

Table 13.1 reports the results of Germany's general elections in a way not normally considered. Aggregate results are reported here by party, for district races in Germany between 1949 and 1994 (Schindler 1984, 1988). The party strengths of district seat allocations can then be compared to the more traditional manner of viewing electoral results in Germany. Several important differences are apparent. CDU/CSU candidates tend to do better in district races than those from the SPD. The SPD has won a majority of the single member district seats in only three of Germany's thirteen general elections. Moreover, while relying heavily on party list results, SPD candidates do in fact frequently win election from district seats. Most important in terms of looking at German elections from a new perspective, the table shows that district contests in Bundestag elections differ considerably from outcomes of the entire mixed system. Significant differences can be found in a party's success in the district races and the final allocation of Bundestag seats. At the high end, in 1957 the CDU/CSU won 78.1 percent of all district seats but received only 54.3 percent of the Bundestag seats, a difference of 23.8 percentage points.

Table 13.1 also shows that district races tend to be won only by Germany's two largest parties: the CDU/CSU and the SPD. This is central to this chapter's consideration of individual candidate effects. As with other single member district systems such as Britain and the United States, this part of Germany's electoral system clearly disadvantages small parties. Following a "learning curve" from 1949 to 1957, it was not until the first all-German election in 1990 that anyone other than a CDU/CSU or SPD member won a plurality in a district. Since only candidates from Germany's major parties tend to compete successfully in district races, this chapter limits its analysis to the district candidates of the Christian Democratic parties and the Social Democratic Party.

MEASUREMENT OF INDIVIDUAL EFFECTS

Focusing on the district races only permits an assessment of the effects of individual candidates on electoral performance in Germany. This then requires data at the level of the individual candidate. Candidate characteristics of district candidates in German national elections are contained in an original data set complied by the author on all Bundestag candidates from 1949 to 1994. This chapter considers three individual characteristics as independent variables: gender,

Table 13.1. Comparison of District Races Won and Overall Party Representation and Strength in German Parliamentary Elections, 1949-94

	DISTRICTS Percent of Seats Won (actual number in parenthesis)				TOTAL Percent of Seats Won (party vote in parenthesis)			
	CDU[a]	SPD	Other	Total	CDU	SPD	FDP	Other
1949	47.5% (139)	39.7% (96)	12.8% (31)	242	34.6% (31.0)	32.6% (29.2)	12.9% (11.9)	19.9% (27.9)
1953	70.7% (171)	19.0% (46)	10.3% (25)	242	49.9% (45.2)	31.0% (28.8)	9.9% (9.5)	9.2% (16.5)
1957	78.1% (193)	19.0% (47)	2.8% (7)	247	54.3% (50.2)	34.0% (31.8)	8.2% (7.7)	3.5% (10.3)
1961	63.2% (156)	36.8% (91)	---	247	48.5% (45.4)	38.1% (36.2)	13.4% (12.8)	--- (5.6)
1965	62.1% (154)	37.9% (94)	---	248	49.4% (47.6)	40.7% 39.3)	9.9% (9.5)	--- (3.6)
1969	48.8% (121)	51.2% (127)	---	248	48.8% (46.1)	45.2% (42.7)	6.0% (5.8)	--- (5.4)
1972	38.7% (96)	61.3% (152)	---	248	45.4% (44.8)	46.4% (45.9)	8.2% (8.4)	--- (0.9)
1976	54.0% (134)	46.0% (114)	---	248	49.2% (48.6)	42.9% (42.6)	7.9% (7.9)	--- (0.9)
1980	48.6% (120)	51.4% (127)	---	248	45.5% (44.5)	43.7% (42.9)	10.7% (10.6)	--- (2.0)
1983	72.5% (179)	27.5% (68)	---	248	49.0% (48.8)	38.8% (38.2)	6.8% (6.9)	5.4% (6.1)
1987	67.7% (168)	31.9% (79)	---	248	44.9% (44.3)	37.4% (37.0)	9.3% (9.1)	8.5% (9.6)
1990	71.6% (235)	27.4% (90)	.3% (2)	328	48.2% (43.8)	36.1% (33.5)	11.9% (11.0)	3.8% (11.7)
1994	67.4% (221)	31.4% (103)	1.2% (4)	328	43.8% (41.5)	37.5% (36.4)	7.0% (6.9)	11.8% (15.2)

Notes: [a] includes CDU and CSU.

age, and incumbency status. Besides party affiliation, personal information such as name and date of birth are included in this data set. Gender was determined from the candidate's name and, if necessary, the German language endings of the person's profession. Photographs in Kürschners Volkshandbuch: Deutscher Bundestag also were consulted. Age was measured by subtracting a candidate's year of birth from the year in which a given election was held.

This study's dependent variable is a candidate's performance in each election in each district. The data set contains electoral information on each district in which the candidates ran. Information includes district number, the Land (German state) in which the district is located, and electoral results in that district for the current and previous election. The series of Kürschners handbooks also served as the source for who won a seat in the Bundestag, whether or not they were elected from a district or a party list, and incumbency status of the candidate. Reordering of the individual-level data by name rather than election year facilitated the determination of the type of incumbency (e.g., whether or not a particular candidate won the seat in the previous election, won a seat off the party list in the previous election, or was seeking to regain a previously lost seat, etc.). For this chapter's purposes, electoral performance is measured in three ways: the winning or losing of a district seat regardless of margin; increasing or decreasing the percentage of vote in that district received by the candidate's political party as compared to the previous election; and narrowing or widening the gap between that candidate's party and the other major party in terms of percentage of vote received in the current and previous election.

Finally, the robustness of the data set with its inclusion of district candidates in all thirteen of Germany's general elections permits consideration of trends across time in the relationships between candidate characteristics and electoral performance.[5] Such across-time comparison is an essential step toward a more complete understanding of the dynamics of German elections.

EFFECTS OF CANDIDATE CHARACTERISTICS

Gender as Candidate Characteristic

The scholarly and political communities' knowledge of the impact of candidate gender on electoral outcomes has been growing rapidly (Hunter and Denton 1984; Matland 1994; Norris et al. 1992; Rule 1987; Welch and Studlar 1986). In many German political parties, attention has heightened as to the number and placement of female candidates (Kolinsky 1991). Most of this has focused only on the party lists.[6] Or, it has been discussed in terms of the Bundestag as a whole (Anderson 1993b: 83-85). Less understood is gender's impact on district races.

Election as Success

Does a candidate's gender affect electoral success in Germany's single-member districts? Figure 13.1 presents strong evidence that it does. This figure shows the percentage of male and female candidates who won their respective district races between 1949 and 1990. While many more males than females stand as district candidates, we are not concerned with absolute numbers. Central to this analysis' focus on the effect of gender on electoral performance, Figure 13.1 shows that female candidates have consistently done worse over the years than male candidates in winning seats in Germany's Wahlkreise. If electoral victory is the standard, ceteris paribus, females do not make as strong district candidates as males.

One explanation of why female candidates don't fare well at the district level is that they are not given the same opportunities. An important opportunity for individual candidates is the chance to stand for a relatively secure or "safe" seat. In any democratic system, candidates prefer electoral security over higher probabilities of running in a losing effort. Female candidates may proportionately lose more frequently than men in Germany's single-member plurality races because they are disproportionately made their party's standard bearer in districts that have been closely contested historically. In other words, the relative lack of electoral success for female district candidates might be due to their having to run in contests where the chances for winning a Bundestag seat would be more difficult for anyone, regardless of gender or other characteristics. As Roberts (1988) describes, Wahlkreis candidates are selected at district party meetings. This more localized candidate-selection process may create a strong link between gender, who gets to stand in which district, and the perceived competitiveness of that candidate.

The hypothesis that female candidates tend to run disproportionately in unsafe districts was tested on the data set described above. Critical here, of course, is the operationalization of the concept "safe seat." District "safeness" was measured as a party's size of electoral victory in that district in the previous election. Three margins of victory were considered: a 5, 10, and 15 percent difference between the percentage of the vote received for the CDU/CSU and the SPD candidate.[7] Preliminary analysis demonstrated that the 5 percent difference revealed little. It was subsequently dropped from further consideration.

Table 13.2 reports the results of the testing of this hypothesis. The evidence supports the contention that female candidates are more likely to stand in contested seats. Both 10 and 15 percent operationalizations of seat safety reveal that candidate gender influences the type of district in which a person will stand for election. For example, with the more stringent "safe seat" definition of 15 percent, 61.1 percent of all female candidates between 1969 and 1990 ran in contested districts. In contrast, 52.7 percent of male candidates did so. This 8.4 percentage difference suggests candidate gender and a party's electoral support are systematically linked at the district level in Germany.

Cognizant of the interaction of individual candidate characteristics and political parties in Germany, Table 13.2 also shows that this relationship of gender and where a candidate runs exists for both the CDU/CSU and SPD. Regardless of which definition of a safe seat is used, Germany's two major political parties both more frequently grant men than women the chance to run in safe seats. Party differences can nevertheless be found. The SPD has run almost twice as many female candidates in district races and is slightly more likely than the CDU/CSU to permit them to run in safe seats.

Figure 13.1. Winning District Candidates to the German Bundestag, 1949-90

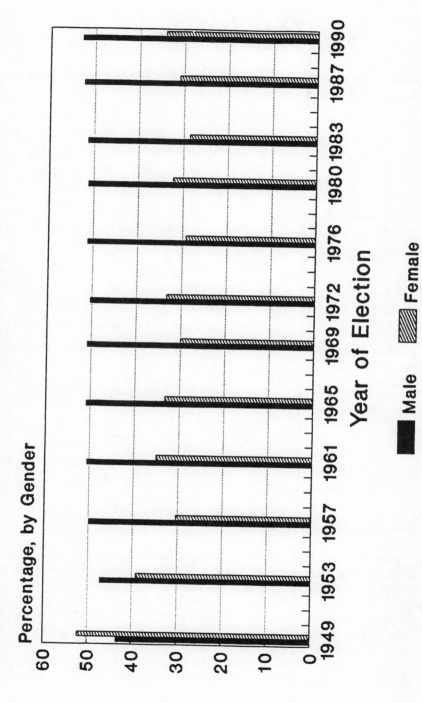

Table 13.2. Candidacy by Gender and Safeness of the Seat, 1969-90

		10% Safety		15% Safety	
		Male	Female	Male	Female
ALL CANDIDATES					
	Not Safe	36.2%	42.9%	52.7%	61.1%
		(1,156)	(120)	(1,681)	(171)
	Safe	63.8%	57.1%	47.3%	38.9%
		(2,036)	(160)	(1,511)	(109)
	Total	100.0%	100.0%	100.0%	100.0%
		(3,192)	(280)	(3,192)	(280)
CDU/CSU					
	Not Safe	36.5%	40.8%	52.8%	63.3%
		(598)	(40)	(864)	(62)
	Safe	63.5%	59.3%	47.2%	36.7%
		(1,040)	(58)	(774)	(36)
	Total	100.0%	100.0%	100.0%	100.0%
		(2,638)	(98)	(1,638)	(98)
SPD					
	Not Safe	35.9%	44.0%	52.6%	59.9%
		(558)	(80)	(817)	(109)
	Safe	64.1%	56.0%	47.4%	40.1%
		(996)	(102)	(737)	(73)
	Total	100.0%	100.0%	100.0%	100.0%
		(1,554)	(182)	(1,554)	(182)

Party Improvement as Success

Gender effects on where candidates stand for election suggest a second look at the concept "electoral success." A majority of Germany's district candidates are in fact double candidates—that is, they also appear on their party's Land list. For most candidates, but especially females, election to the Bundestag depends more upon one's position on the party list.[8] District candidacy is frequently service to one's party; a realistic appraisal of a district's history of results shifts a candidate's hope for Bundestag membership to the party list. As a consequence, winning a district seat may be too narrow a definition of electoral success. Given this analysis's focus on district races, measures of electoral success should be inclusive enough to capture the incentive structures for individual candidates engaging in what otherwise might be viewed as wasted effort. Consistent with this logic, district candidacy might be considered successful if the party's performance over the previous election improves, even if they lose the Wahlkreis seat. A second measure of electoral success might thus be an increase in the number of votes cast for the candidate's party over the previous general election. With this new operationalization of our dependent variable, we return to questions of the influence of candidate characteristics.

Table 13.3 reports the testing of the hypothesis that gender affects improvement in party performance. While not supporting the basic relationship, the table shows that party suppresses this relationship. Even though the CDU/CSU has fielded almost half the number of female district candidates as the SPD, when they do so, it improves the party's district fortunes. From 1969 to 1990, 37.8 percent of the female CDU/CSU candidates improved the number of votes cast for the party over the previous election. Only 31.2 percent of their male counterparts similarly helped the party. This 6.6 percentage difference suggests that gender as a candidate characteristic influences electoral outcomes in Germany. Female candidates improve the CDU/CSU's change in votes received while males do so for the SPD.

Relative Party Improvement

Besides actually winning the district or improving the number of votes cast for a party, a third measure of electoral performance also reveals the influence of candidate characteristics. As mentioned earlier, almost all district contests in Germany are in fact races between the two largest parties only. Even though most of Germany's major parties and many minor ones field candidates, in all but a few districts has the race been anything other than one between SPD and CDU/CSU candidates. Electoral performance might also be thought of as the improvement over the previous election's result of the relative performance of the two major parties. In other words, improvement of the CDU/CSU's electoral performance by 1 percent might not be considered a success if the SPD gained 6 percent over the previous election, even if a CDU/CSU candidate won the district. Beyond questions of who actually wins the Wahlkreis seat, electoral performance is often a relative concept. We thus operationalize it here as relative to the other major party.

Table 13.4 reports the empirical relationship between candidate gender and relative party performance in Germany from 1969 to 1990. A strong pattern also exists with this third measure: female candidates improved their party's relative performance more frequently than male candidates, 55.4 percent compared to 45.0 percent, respectively. Table 13.4 further shows that the influence of this candidate characteristic on the change in the difference between the votes garnered for their party and Germany's other major party is concentrated in the CDU/CSU. While the Christian Democrats are much less likely to field district candidates, when they do female candidates more frequently improve their party's relative performance: 53.1 percent compared to 32.7 percent--a difference of 20.4 percent.

Table 13.3. Gender and Electoral Effects: Improvement in Terms of District Party Performance Over Previous Election, 1969-90

	Major Parties Combined		CDU/CSU		SPD	
	Male	Female	Male	Female	Male	Female
Improved	38.5%	36.8%	31.2%	37.8%	46.2%	36.3%
	(1,229)	(103)	(511)	(37)	(718)	(66)
Worsened	61.5%	63.2%	68.8%	62.2%	53.8%	63.7%
	(1,963)	(177)	(1,127)	(61)	(836)	(116)
Total	100.0%	100.0%	100.0%	100.0%	100.0%	100.0%
	(3,192)	(280)	(1,736)	(98)	(1,554)	(182)

Table 13.4. Gender and Electoral Results: Change from Previous Election of Difference in Support for the Major Parties, 1969-90

	Major Parties Combined		CDU/CSU		SPD	
	Male	Female	Male	Female	Male	Female
Better	45.0%	55.4%	32.7%	53.1%	58.0%	56.6%
	(1,436)	(155)	(535)	(52)	(901)	(103)
Worse	55.0%	44.6%	67.3%	46.9%	42.0%	43.4%
	(1,756)	(125)	(1,103)	(46)	(653)	(79)
Total	100.0%	100.0%	100.0%	100.0%	100.0%	100.0%
	(3,192)	(280)	(1,638)	(98)	(1,554)	(182)

To conclude consideration of this initial candidate characteristic, analysis of three difference operationalizations of electoral performance at the district level strongly suggests that gender does have a systematic influence on German electoral dynamics. Gender matters if winning the seat is the criterion: since the Federal Republic's early years male candidates have consistently won district seats more frequently than female candidates. This finding, however, only partly reveals the effects of candidate gender. Other, lesser known, patterns exist. First, female candidates are less likely to be given the opportunity to run in safe districts. Second, when they do run they generally improve the party's electoral performance, particularly for the CDU/CSU. And third, the CSU/CSU significantly gains from fielding female candidates in terms of improvement from the previous election of the difference in the number of votes cast in the district for that party and the SPD. Germany's Christian Democrats present fewer electoral opportunities for female candidates but, when they do, the party appears to be amply rewarded.

AGE AS CANDIDATE CHARACTERISTIC

As with gender, age is a candidate characteristic that many believe affects electoral politics. In Germany, a plausible hypothesis is that age is positively associated with electoral success at the district level. Such a hypothesized relationship is generally based on the known effect of age on party list position. How candidate age works at the district level is less well understood. The following analysis thus considers, in a manner parallel to that of gender, the influence of candidate age on three different measures of electoral outcomes: the winning of the district seat; the improvement of party performance over the previous election results from that same district; and change in a party's district electoral performance relative to Germany's other major political party.

Election as Success

As mentioned earlier, the effect of age on German electoral dynamics was measured by subtracting a district candidates' year of birth from the year an election was held. This interval range of candidate age necessitated the use of correlation analysis. A variable for winning the district was thus created: values of 1 were assigned to winning candidates and 0 to those who lost the plurality vote. Actual age and this won/lost district variable were then correlated for all district candidates between 1969 and 1990. A coefficient of .130 suggests that candidate age does have a moderate effect on the likelihood of winning a Wahlkreis seat in Germany. Ceteris paribus, the chance of winning a seat is increased by 13 percent for each year of age. And, while this relationship holds for both major parties, age affects electoral success more for SPD candidates (.137) than for those representing the CDU/CSU (.103).

Table 13.5 expounds upon the dynamic nature of these findings. The table's first column highlights over time the nature of this relationship between age and electoral success relationship. A candidate's age has consistently influenced district electoral success. While not as strong as the effect on list position in Germany's mixed electoral system nor as clear a pattern as gender's influence on winning a district seat, a candidate's age clearly affects the outcomes of Germany's district races. Again, taken together, this influence is primarily due to age's consistent importance for SPD candidates. The evidence suggests for CDU/CSU candidates other factors offset age in effecting the likelihood of victory in a district.

Unlike gender, a candidate's age does not appear to correlate with seat safety. A dichotomized (0-1) classification of a contested/safe district revealed no pattern regardless of concept operationalization: a 5, 10, or 15 percent level of difference between the electoral support of the two major parties in that district in the previous election. Nor does political party appear to interact significantly with age; while no relationship emerged for the CDU/CSU candidates, only slight correlations existed for the SPD candidates with the 10 percent (-.057) and 15 percent (-.056) measure of a safe seat.

Table 13.5. Age and District Candidacy to the Bundestag, 1953-94

	Successful District Candidates	Average Age District Cand. Succ.	Unsucc.	District Winners, by party		Average Age Winners Only	
				CDU/CSU	SPD	CDU/CSU	SPD
1953	.206	52.4	48.7	.084	.154	52.6	51.7
1957	.115	52.1	49.9	.043	.055	52.4	50.8
1961	.110	52.6	50.3	-.007	.119	53.5	51.0
1965	.102	50.9	48.9	.039	.130	51.0	50.7
1969	.115	49.3	47.1	.075	.162	50.0	48.6
1972	.087	46.4	44.9	.053	.167	46.9	46.1
1976	.117	47.2	45.3	-.001	.225	46.5	48.1
1980	.116	47.5	45.7	.055	.178	47.5	47.5
1983	.165	49.5	47.0	.095	.207	49.2	50.2
1987	.220	51.3	48.0	.194	.154	51.9	49.9
1990	.125	50.3	48.4	-.048	.146	50.5	50.0
1994	.122	50.7	48.8	.065	.198	50.2	51.6

Party Improvement: Absolute and Relative

Like gender, age influences one's chances of winning a district seat in the Bundestag. Also like gender, a candidate's age influences in a somewhat unexpected manner other aspects of German electoral dynamics at the district level. While not as strong as gender's impact, the older a candidate the worse his or her performance is in terms of electoral support.

Candidate age correlates with party performance compared to the previous election at a -.078 level for all candidates, -.069 for CDU/CSU members, and -.064 for SPD candidates, with all correlations statistically significant. Essentially the same relationship also exists for candidate age and improvement in relative party performance--indicated by a statistically significant correlation of -.055. Controlling for political party produced weaker and statistically insignificant coefficients. Age thus has a positive effect on a candidate's likelihood on winning a district seat but it negatively influences both measures of electoral support.

In sum, age does affect Germany's electoral dynamics. It influences the likelihood of a candidate winning a district seat to the Bundestag, especially for SPD candidates. Unlike gender, however, age is not strongly related to who stands for election in safe seats. And when all district candidates between 1969 and 1990 are considered, age has a slight negative effect on both absolute and relative party performance. This finding may, however, be a consequence of the fact that older candidates are more likely to rely on the party lists to return to the Bundestag. Such a logic questions if age can be separated from other candidate characteristics, such as the role incumbency plays in German electoral politics.

INCUMBENCY ADVANTAGES

Although not a physical trait like gender and age, candidate incumbency is one individual characteristic generally considered to be of fundamental importance in all representative democracies (Somit et al. 1994). In terms of comparative analysis, however, Germany's mixed election system introduces a conceptual problem: What is "district incumbency"?

For this analysis, the incumbent in a district is considered the holder of the parliamentary seat from that constituency at the time of the election. While straightforward enough, Germany's double electoral system potentially makes such a definition appear rigid. Such a classification means that sometimes a candidate will be considered a district nonincumbent despite Bundestag membership, having been elected in the previous election from the party list. Furthermore, double candidates frequently run in the same district for several elections. This creates a possible scenario in which a person wins a district one time, loses it the next election but still wins on the party list, and then retakes the district seat in a third general election. Despite continuous parliamentary service, this analysis classifies such a candidate as a losing district incumbent in the second election and as a winning district nonincumbent in the third.[9]

Table 13.6 acknowledges the concept of incumbency's complex nature in Germany.[10] A broader measure of incumbency that includes both holders of district and list seats in the Bundestag suggests that the two parts of Germany's double electoral system remain in fact essentially separate. This table shows that most district incumbents win in their districts and most list incumbents return to the Bundestag given their party list position. While fully recognizing the sense of security double candidacy presents, especially to district incumbents, measuring district incumbency as the current holder of the district seat captures the predominate pattern of election and reelection to district seats in Germany. It also remains loyal to the measurement of incumbency in other countries.[11]

Election as Success

Table 13.6 clearly shows that incumbency strongly affects one's likelihood of winning a seat in the Bundestag. 91.0 percent of all district incumbents won reelection from the same district in general elections from 1969 to 1990. In sharp contrast only 7.3 percent of the nonincumbents won district seats and only 11.4 percent of list incumbents did so. Furthermore, while 9.0 percent of the district incumbents actually lost their district seat, only 2.0 percent failed to gain a seat in the Bundestag since most district incumbents were also on their party lists. Most important in terms of this chapter's focus, incumbency strongly predicts the likelihood of reelection from a district.[12] In addition, the existence of double candidacy virtually assures district incumbents election to the Bundestag, one way or another.

Not reported in Table 13.6, adherence to the more stringent definition of district incumbent (classifying list incumbents as nonincumbents in the districts) and returning to our analysis of only the district races, the 91.0 percent success rate of reelection to the district (1,229 of 1,351) compares to a 33.1 percent district election rate for nonincumbents (379 of 1,145). Party differences reflect the CDU/CSU's overall advantage in district races as reported in Table 13.1: between 1969 and 1990 94.5 percent of CDU/CSU incumbents won district seats compared to 86.6 percent of SPD incumbents. A similar party difference exists with the number of nonincumbents that did not win a district seat: 62.1 percent for the CDU/CSU compared to 71.0 percent for the SPD. Thus, while district incumbency matters for both major parties in Germany, its influence is stronger for the CDU/CSU candidates.

The explanation given earlier that women candidates tend to lose district races more frequently than men because they must compete in more competitive constituencies suggests a similar explanation for the high number of incumbent victories. Surprisingly, this is not the case with district incumbents. At neither the 5, 10, or 15 percent operationalization of seat safety did being a district incumbent make one more or less likely to stand in a contested or safe seat. And this cannot be entirely explained by the fact that district incumbents are frequently double candidates. Double candidacy in fact is used as an electoral safety net more frequently by nonincumbents: 80.8 percent of nonincumbent district candidates were double candidates compared to 61.5 percent for district incumbents. Controlling for the safety of the seat does not significantly lessen the strength of this relationship.

Table 13.6. Incumbency Effects on Gaining a Seat in the German Bundestag, 1969-90

	District Incumbent	List Incumbent	Non-Incumbent
District	91.0% (1,229)	11.4% (125)	7.3% (379)
List seat	7.0% (95)	82.6% (908)	7.4% (382)
Lost	2.0% (27)	6.0% (66)	85.3% (4,424)
Total	100.0% (1,351)	100.0% (1,099)	100.0% (5,185)

In sum, incumbency status goes a long way toward explaining electoral victory in district races to the German Bundestag. Comparatively speaking, this is not surprising. However, the fact that seat safety does not help explain this suggests that beyond simply winning or losing, other incumbency-related patterns are not so obvious. This is certainly true regarding incumbency's effects on party performance and change in relative party strength.

Party Improvement: Absolute and Relative

District incumbency affects German party performance, as measured by the difference between the percentage of the district vote received in a given election and the previous election. The effect, however, is negative. As shown in Table 13.7, German voters appear to possess a slight tendency to vote for nonincumbents at the district level. Nonincumbents tend to fare better in terms of change in electoral support than incumbents. Between 1969 and 1990, the party vote for district incumbents improved in 32.4 percent of the district races compared to nonincumbents' 39.9 percent. And, consistent with an anti-incumbent explanation, this loss of electoral support is much stronger among CDU/CSU incumbents. This party difference is logically consistent since, as seen in Table 13.1, the CDU/CSU tends to hold more district seats. Despite variation within parties, anti-incumbent voting systematically surfaces in Germany's district races.

Anti-incumbent voting in Germany's district races is even stronger when electoral support is operationalized as party improvement relative to the other major party. Table 13.8 shows that there is a 13 percent difference in electoral improvement for district incumbents and nonincumbents. Nonincumbents are more likely to improve relative party performance even if they still lose the seat. This second measure of electoral performance reveals as well that incumbents do worse than nonincumbents in improving party support. And this appears the case with both major parties although slightly stronger for the SPD.

Table 13.7. Incumbency and Electoral Effects: Improvement in Terms of District Party Performance Over Previous Election, 1969-90

Major Parties Combined		CDU/CSU		SPD	
	District Incumbent	Non-Incumbent	District Incumbent	Non-Incumbent	District Incumbent	Non-Incumbent
Improved	32.4% (437)	39.9% (457)	23.4% (175)	32.8% (173)	43.4% (262)	46.0% (284)
Worsened	67.6% (914)	60.1% (688)	76.6% (572)	67.2% (355)	56.6% (342)	54.0% (333)
Total	100.0% (1,351)	100.0% (1,145)	100.0% (747)	100.0% (528)	100.0% (604)	100.0% (617)

Table 13.8. Incumbency and Electoral Results: Change from Previous Election of Difference in Support for the Major Parties, 1969-90

	Major Parties Combined		CDU/CSU		SPD	
	District Incumbent	Non-Incumbent	District Incumbent	Non-Incumbent	District Incumbent	Non-Incumbent
Better	37.0% (500)	50.0% (572)	26.5% (198)	35.2% (186)	50.0% (302)	62.6% (386)
Worse	63.0% (851)	50.0% (573)	73.5% (549)	64.8% (342)	50.0% (302)	37.4% (231)
Total	100.0% (1,351)	100.0% (1,145)	100.0% (747)	100.0% (528)	100.0% (604)	100.0% (617)

To conclude, incumbency as a candidate characteristic is extremely important in district races to the Bundestag. As in most plurality systems, Germany's district incumbents overwhelmingly fare better than nonincumbents in winning district seats. The possibility of being a double candidate in Germany grants even greater electoral protection to many candidates. Another pattern, however, is less well known. Incumbency has a negative component in German electoral dynamics. District incumbency tends to whittle away at the parties' electoral successes. In carrying their party banner, district incumbents tend to lose votes more than nonincumbents. This occurs both in terms of absolute party support and votes cast relative to the other major party. Incumbency as a candidate characteristic clearly matters in terms of capturing Bundestag seats, but it also carries some less understood negative consequences at the district level.

A COMPARATIVE ASSESSMENT

Up to this point this chapter has focused individually on gender, age, and incumbency as three different candidate characteristics. To varying degrees, each was found to affect German elections at the district level. The analysis has thus far only considered the separate effect of each characteristic on electoral outcomes. We conclude with a test of the relative strength of these three candidate characteristics as well as the overall explanatory power of the three different measures of electoral performance.

In order to compare the effects of these three candidate characteristic variables, variable values were recoded. In terms of the dependent variables, values were assigned as 1=candidate won the district and 0=candidate lost the district for any given election. A similar 1-0 coding was assigned to the other two dependent variable measures--improvement/loss in party support from the previous election and improvement/loss in relative party support. The independent variables of gender, age, and incumbency were given the values of male=1, female=0, age as actual age (year of election minus candidate's year of birth), district incumbent=1, and nonincumbent=0.

The three candidate characteristic variables were then included in a series of three multivariate models. Each of these three regression models contained as its dependent variable one of the three measures of electoral performance considered above. The estimated model of *winning candidates* took the following form:

$$\text{Winner} = .2469 + .0696 \text{ Gender} + .0005 \text{ Age} + .5696 \text{ Incumbent}$$
$$(.053) \quad (.030) \quad\quad\quad (.001) \quad\quad\quad (.017)$$

Standard errors in parentheses below each estimate indicate that all coefficients except age are statistically significant at the .05 level or better.

Overall, this model's estimated parameters are consistent with the previously discussed bivariate analysis. Males and incumbents are more likely to win district seats than females or nonincumbents, while age appears to have only a very slight influence. Again reminding us of this assessment's proper context, the size of the y-intercept's parameter suggests that many factors other than candidate characteristics are required to explain electoral outcomes in Germany's district elections. Despite the commonly understood notion that candidate success depends upon broader party success, this model additionally suggests that candidate characteristics also have a systematic influence.

Besides statistically controlling for the independent influences of the other candidate characteristics, such multivariate analysis also permits comparison of the three explanatory variables themselves. Together these three candidate characteristics explain 36.3 percent (adjusted R^2) of the variation in the win/loss dependent variable. Standardized coefficients, however, suggest that much of this explanatory power of who wins the district rests with incumbency status: incumbency (.5928), gender (.0375), and age (.0092). In Germany, incumbency is clearly the single most important candidate characteristics in explaining the winning of district seats.

Such findings are not unexpected. More interesting, and in a manner consistent with the bivariate work reported earlier, such multivariate analysis shows that incumbency status, being a male candidate, and age has a *negative* effect on actual electoral results (again, defined as improvement from the previous election in the difference between the two major parties in that district).

$$\text{Result} = .6304 - .0764 \text{ Gender} - .0014 \text{ Age} - .1127 \text{ Incumbent}$$
$$(.068) \quad (.038) \quad\quad\quad (.001) \quad\quad\quad (.022)$$

The explanatory power of this model (adjusted $R^2 = .0177$) and the large y-intercept coefficient reinforces this chapter's assumptions that many factors other than candidate characteristics help explain electoral performance in Germany's party-oriented political system. It is nevertheless interesting to notice here that certain candidate characteristics consistently affect the parties' electoral support. Specifically, male, older, and incumbent candidates tend to cost their party votes relative to Germany's other major party from one election to the next; in contrast, female, younger, and incumbent candidates are associated with stronger relative party performance. While winning the district seat is not the issue here, candidate characteristics in Germany do appear to influence elections in Germany, albeit in ways less visible and frequently less understood.[13]

CONCLUSION

Most research on the outcomes of German elections neglect the impact of candidate characteristics. This is easily justified. Political parties dominate German electoral dynamics. The country's mixed electoral system gives greater weight to the lists over the single-member constituencies. Moreover, the parliamentary foundation with its emphasis on "chancellor democracy" and coalition building makes German politics less individualistic and more collective oriented than, say, the United States. Relatively stable voting patterns also reinforce the scholarly emphasis on studying political parties rather than candidate characteristics.

Calls for better understanding the influence of candidate characteristics on German election outcomes are also contained in this body of literature. Analytically, we are beginning to see where and why candidate characteristics have a "window of opportunity." Students of German electoral behavior are increasingly coming to understand that Germany's two-vote system presents more opportunities for both individualistic and regional influences to impact electoral outcomes than other countries' traditional party list system, that patterns in German voting behavior are changing (Dalton 1989; Dalton and Rohrschneider 1990), that Germans are "splitting" their two votes in the mixed electoral system at an increasing rate (Dalton 1989; Klingemann and Wattenberg 1990, 1992; Zelle 1995b), that short term changes occur in voting intentions, and that campaigns influence electoral behavior in Germany. All of these suggest that while the political parties' role in the dynamics of German elections remains central other systematic influences are also present.

This analysis suggested that a different perspective than that normally taken in the study of German electoral dynamics assists in seeing such lesser known patterns. The research reported here took such a nontraditional look. First, instead of analyzing the results of Germany's elections at a highly aggregated level or at the level of the individual voter through consideration of public opinion data, this work analyzed German election data with the candidate as the unit of analysis. Second, this chapter focused only on Wahlkreis races. Unlike a great deal of other work on German electoral behavior, the research reported here did not concern itself with the final party distribution as determined by the second vote in Germany's mixed electoral system. By focusing on the district races only, it sought to isolate factors other than political party that impact electoral outcomes.

Despite coming from a different empirical perspective, this chapter's results are intended to add to a common understanding of Germany electoral dynamics. The very research design employed here is grounded on the assumption that political parties are fundamental to electoral outcomes in Germany. Beyond that, however, this analysis has shown that individual candidate characteristics systematically influence German electoral performance. Specifically, we found that candidate incumbency, gender, and, to a lesser degree, age influences electoral performance in terms of the actual winning of the district context, change the support a candidate's party receives, and its electoral outcomes relative to Germany's other major political party. While individual district candidates clearly ride the electoral fortunes of their political parties, the type of candidate also affects German electoral dynamics.

NOTES

I would like to acknowledge the assistance of the Emory University Research Committee, whose funding facilitated the initial collection of the data.

1. In the 1949 election only, voters were given a single vote to cast either for a district candidate or for a party list. Beginning in 1953, German voters began using the present two-vote system.

2. As made well known by the PDS (Party of Democratic Socialism) in the 1994 election, the German election law actually states either 5 percent *or* at least three district seats. By winning four district seats in 1994, the PDS was allocated the seventeen seats it was proportionally entitled to despite not reaching the 5 percent threshold. Also, in 1990 both the Greens and the PDS won Bundestag seats as a consequence of the Constitutional Court's decision that in that one election the 5 percent rule should apply to either the western or eastern part of the newly reunited country.

3. Anderson (1993a: 3-4) states it succinctly: "Those studies that are available on the Bundestag generally focus on objective socio-demographic characteristics of its members at particular points in time (cf. Kaack 1967, 1969, 1971, 1988; Mueller 1983), or they seek to investigate the functioning of the legislature as a parliamentary body, on occasion with the help of surveys of, or about, Bundestag deputies (cf. Loewenberg 1967; Loewenberg and Patterson 1979; Herzog et al. 1990). However, there have been few studies which analyze the composition of the Bundestag over time and few which explore the consequences of Germany's electoral system for the distribution of Bundestag members with particular social or political characteristics."

4. Anderson (1993a) does consider district races, but not only in an aggregate analysis.

5. As part of an ongoing project, analysis of some elections will not be considered in this chapter.

6. The Christian Democrats even recently adopted this quota system.

7. Anderson (1993a: 13) operationalizes a safe seat "as a seat where the member receives 55 percent or more of the vote." One problem with this definition, however, is that election results from the same election are used to determine what is a safe seat. The selection processes, of course, precedes the election itself.

8. For more details, see Lancaster (1994).

9. Research also needs to help clarify incumbency in terms of mass and elite attitudes. To what extent do Bundestag members elected from party lists live, maintain offices, and think of themselves as representing a particular district? The degree to which the legalistic definition of district incumbency utilized in this chapter admittedly misses the psychological and even representative nature of parliamentary incumbency unquestionably merits additional investigation.

10. District races in Germany's eastern Länder are not included in this analysis. Conceptual issues of incumbency are particularly complex there, particularly as to how analysis should consider service to earlier legislatures, such as the Volkskammer.

11. At least two other classifications exist. One is of district incumbents who chose to run in another constituency, one in which they were not the incumbent. From 1969 to 1990 I found seven incumbents who fit this category. Of these seven, two won a seat from this new district, four lost but still gained a parliamentary seat from a party list, and only one failed to win any seat. A second category includes district incumbents who chose not to stand as a candidate in any district, opting instead to run as a list candidate only. Between 1969 and 1990, this occurred ten times, almost always as a person was bringing his or her long Bundestag career to a conclusion. Of these ten, seven won a Bundestag seat from the list system. Given this chapter's focus on district incumbency and the conceptual problem these two categories introduce, both were excluded from the analysis.

12. As might be expected, district incumbents' losses in their constituencies tended to occur in elections with greater interparty volatility. Between 1969 and 1990, ninety-five district incumbents lost the district but still won on a party list and twenty-seven completely failed to gain reentry into the Bundestag. By specific election, in 1972, four district incumbents won party list seats and ten won no seat (of a total 175 district incumbents). These same figures were twenty-three and two, respectively, (193 total) in 1976, nine and four in 1980, forty-one and nine (222 total) in 1983, ten and two (206 total) in 1987, and eight and zero (186 total) in 1990.

13. Similar results were also found in estimation of a model of a party's electoral improvement over the previous election. Age and incumbency were again both negative and statistically significant while the overall model explained only about 1 percent of the variation in the dependent variable. In this model, however, gender was positive and not statistically significant.

14

Political Parties and the Changing Framework of German Electoral Competition

Susan E. Scarrow

Most of the preceding chapters have examined the dimensions and implications of electoral change at the individual level. Many of them only implicitly have acknowledged the importance of the institutional framework within which this competition has occurred. Yet this framework deserves closer scrutiny, because in Germany, as elsewhere, it is a crucial ingredient of electoral politics. Electoral competition always occurs within an institutional framework that selectively privileges some contestants. These unequal advantages are produced by electoral systems, which affect voters' strategic calculations, the translation of votes into seats, the dynamics of coalition bargaining, and even intraparty relationships. They are derived from constitutional structures and legislative rules, such as those which make it more or less easy for small parties to exercise influence (Duverger 1954/1951; Sartori 1976; Laver and Schofield 1990; Taagepera and Shugart 1989; Lijphart 1994). They also are conferred by legal structures that regulate relations between parties and society, and between parties and the state (Müller 1993). Of the latter, laws on party finance may be particularly important (Naßmacher 1989a). In the German context, these aspects of the framework of electoral competition clearly have shaped the development of parties' organizations and electoral strategies (Poguntke 1995). It is just as clear that they have shaped individual electoral behavior by limiting voters' choices and by boosting the prospects of particular competitors.

It is important to remember that these institutions are not purely exogenous variables, forced upon parties by tradition or by outside powers. Instead, parties have been the creators as well as the objects of their institutional environment. Indeed, efforts to reshape institutional incentives and constraints have been a recurring feature of German party competition. The choices voters have made reflect both the success, and the failure, of partisan efforts to shape key rules.

Perhaps because of the relative stability of German electoral laws over the past half century, most accounts of German electoral behavior treat the institutional framework as a constant, largely ignored, instead of seeing it as an essential part of electoral contests (for a recent exception see chapter 10 by Ulrich Eith in this volume, who takes advantage of the state-by-state variation in local elections laws by employing them as explanatory variable). However, to truly understand the dynamics of German electoral competition, it is not sufficient to examine how parties and voters behave at election times. It is also necessary to examine how the parties have acted between elections to try to shape the circumstances under which the next elections would be fought. Examining the evolution of the institutional dimension is particularly appropriate in a book like the present one, which examines not just a single election, but rather half a century of developments in German electoral politics.

This chapter thus shifts away from this book's primary focus on the German electorate to examine other key aspects of electoral politics—party competition and cooperation—to shape institutional rules. The following examination focuses on party interactions in writing and revising two key elements of the electoral environment: electoral system rules and laws governing public subsidies for political parties. The first of these areas has been largely stable since 1956; the second has been subject to constant revision. The accounts below consider the reasons for this difference, and discuss the extent to which the dominant parties have worked together to shape a system that is biased in their favor.

PARTY INTERESTS AND STRUCTURAL CHANGE

Political scientists have made much greater efforts to assess the impact of electoral systems and other structures of electoral competition than to understand the processes through which such structures are created and reshaped. But although such institutions are notoriously resistant to deliberate reform efforts (Shepsle 1989: 143-144; March and Olsen 1989), they clearly do change. The challenge for those who investigate such changes is to show how existing political configurations constrain the evolution of institutional parameters. In the German case, one of the key questions is why a polity long dominated by two big party blocks should not have deviated from what has been diagnosed as a more general "trend toward proportionality" (Lijphart 1994: 56). In other words, why did the big parties fail to consolidate their electoral advantage by instituting more majoritarian reforms? To understand the sources of, and limits on, this impulse toward proportionality, it is necessary to examine the political context in which decisions have been made.

As other chapters in this book document, German electoral competition repeatedly has divided parties of the right from parties of the left, and these divisions have been reflected in most governing alliances. Although grand coalitions occasionally have formed at both the state and federal levels, German parties never have campaigned for big party cooperation as the preferred electoral outcome. This suggests that competition to shape the framework of electoral competition is likely to reflect similar lines of conflict between the big parties of the left and right. However, the configuration of government coalitions does not necessarily determine the shape of legislative coalitions on particular issues (Laver and Schofield 1990: 66-67). This is most evident when government is conducted by a minority coalition, but in Germany it long has been the case that much legislation is adopted with supramajority coalitions. Such cooperation has been most visible in periods when the government has required opposition party support in the Bundesrat (the upper house of parliament), but it has not been confined to these periods or to issues which require supramajorities (von Beyme 1991: 272-276). Furthermore, German parliamentary tradition supports the adoption of legislation by alliances that differ significantly from the formal executive coalitions.

If formal coalition agreements do not create uniform expectations about what partnerships will shape or constrain institutional reforms, considering how parties benefit from specific proposals may provide better guidance. Indeed, scholars who study electoral reform repeatedly have found that parties' perceived interests are more useful than their avowed principles as guides for predicting party positions in debates on structural reform (cf. Nohlen 1984; Bogdanor 1987; Tsebelis 1990: 223-231; Brady and Mo 1992; Bawn 1993).

Thus it becomes important to inquire how parties define their interests, and how existing institutions shape their assessments of what is feasible and desirable (cf. March and Olsen 1989: 162-163). One important unanswered question is whether parties always calculate benefits exclusively in terms of the most imminent election, or whether their positions sometimes also reflect expectations about longer-term effects of reform. But even this question may miss the mark, because it treats parties as unitary actors. In fact, politicians from a single party may have different positions on reform depending on what they view as the party's top priority (for instance, preserving individual careers, or maximizing the party's policy influence) (Lehoucq 1995: 27). To the extent that internal bargaining affects positions in interparty struggles over system reforms, the definition of party interest cannot be inferred a priori by outside observers (Bredthauer 1973: 111; Shugart 1992).

As this discussion suggests, invoking partisan self-interest may be insufficient for explaining the roles played by German parties in shaping the framework of their own competition. Instead, it is also necessary to investigate how parties have defined their interests when expectations about short-term and long-term benefits differed, and when apparent payoffs were likely to be unevenly distributed within the parties. The reform areas examined in the following accounts have this characteristic of producing payoffs which differ both in terms of outcomes and predictability. Electoral system reforms are necessarily zero-sum changes, and the likely results of these changes usually can be predicted with some confidence. In contrast, reforms to party subsidies may benefit all parties, although the biggest beneficiaries of these reforms may be hard to estimate in advance. These differences may foster very different dynamics of party competition in these two policy areas.

Each section that follows investigates the most important changes, and attempted changes, to the German electoral system and party finance laws since 1949. Each case considers the circumstances which put institutional reform on the agenda, and looks at the bargaining and interest (re)definitions which generated or undermined legislative majorities in favor of institutional redesign. They also examine the extent to which parties have been able to deploy resources other than legislative seats as effective weapons in battles over institutional design. These studies suggest that short-term payoffs are the most important determinant of the dynamics of bargaining over institutional reform. Parties repeatedly have failed to support reforms which are likely to be in their long-term interest if these conflict with short-term consideration; conversely, they have supported other reforms which bring short-term rewards, but which are likely to impose long-term costs.

REVISING THE ELECTORAL LAW

The legislative battles with the most direct implications for electoral competition are those concerning the electoral law itself. Primarily because of the intensity of initial disagreements about the shape of West Germany's federal electoral system, the first two federal elections were contested under temporary laws. This made electoral system design a priority for much of the 1950s. After a permanent electoral law was adopted, electoral reform remained on the agenda. However, in the absence of external pressures, such as the need for a functional electoral law, parties were never again able to unite behind major reforms.

From the First to the Second Electoral Law, 1949-53

Unlike its Weimar predecessor, the 1949 Basic Law did not specify the shape of the electoral system. Instead, the Parliamentary Council, which drafted the Basic Law, passed a provisional electoral law for the 1949 federal election. This step ensured that the first elected parliament would have to reconsider the question.

From 1945 onward, the main issue in German electoral system debates was how much to use electoral laws to combat party system fragmentation. In the Parliamentary Council the Christian Democratic Union, and to a lesser extent the Christian Social Union, strongly advocated majoritarian systems because they would narrow the party system. The two parties initially proposed a federal electoral system that was primarily based on plurality contests in single-member districts (Golay 1958: 139; Lange 1975: 344-348; Jesse 1985: 90-97). This position was at times supported by the small German Party (DP), which opposed proportional plans unless they allowed parties to present joint lists. However, a CDU-CSU-DP coalition lacked a majority in the Parliamentary Council. Eventually the Free Democratic Party united with the Social Democratic Party and the remaining small parties (the Communist Party–KPD, and the Center Party–Z) to enact an effectively proportional system which combined district and list seats (for details, see Table 14.1).

The plan originally adopted by the Parliamentary Council made no provision for excluding small parties. However, the state minister-presidents insisted on adding the requirement that parties must win at least 5 percent of a state's vote before its state-list candidates were eligible to receive seats (Golay 1958: 138-147; Lange 1975: 360-400). Despite the addition of this hurdle, eleven parties won seats in the 1949 federal election. Subsequently even more parties began to compete in state-level contests as party licensing requirements were lifted. Thus, the outcome of the first election strengthened the arguments of those advocating a more majoritarian electoral law.

The first government, a coalition of the CDU, CSU, FDP, and DP, was slow to propose a permanent electoral law, apparently because CDU ministers hoped (in vain) to win SPD support for a single-member district system (Jesse 1985: 98). When the cabinet finally did offer a proposal, it recommended moving to a system which was less proportional, and which distributed district seats using preference votes. The latter aspect favored CDU and CSU candidates, who were the obvious second choices for supporters of small, antisocialist, parties. This proposal was strongly opposed by the SPD, by some FDP legislators, and by most of the smallest parliamentary parties. It did not even enjoy full support in the CDU, because some legislators from this party remained committed to a pure single-member-district/plurality system. Furthermore, on its initial reading the proposal was rejected by the Bundesrat because CDU-led governments in North Rhine-Westphalia and Schleswig-Holstein were unwilling to support it over the objections of their smaller coalition partners, the Center Party and Alliance of Expellees (BHE), respectively. The federal government at first maintained that this vote was no obstacle because the constitution did not give the Bundesrat an absolute veto on bills affecting federal electoral law. This contention angered many CDU-led state governments who defiantly defended states' rights to block such legislation. Given this intraparty conflict, and given the federal government's narrow majority in the Bundestag, the CDU/CSU modified its proposals in hopes of splitting the FDP vote and winning support from one or more of the smallest parties.

The final Bundestag debates about the new electoral law, only three months before the deadline for the 1953 elections, focused on two proposals which divided the partners in the center-right coalition. The CDU and CSU bill, which had the support of the small DP, proposed modifying the 1949 system by adding the requirement of absolute majorities for district seats (with double ballots), and by separating the distribution of list and district seats (thus reducing the proportionality of outcomes). In contrast, the FDP plan merely proposed to modify the 1949 proportional system by adding separate ballots for district contests and party lists. The latter change, which imitated a practice already in use in Bavaria, was thought to favor the FDP by enabling voters to influence district-level contests even if they cast their list vote for a party (like the FDP) that had little chance of winning district seats.

Because the SPD supported the FDP plan, the parliament was almost equally split on the issue. This gave the parliament's smallest parties a decisive role. The KPD supported the FDP's plan, but if this plan were to overcome unanimous opposition from the CDU and CSU, it also would need the backing of the Center Party and the Bavarian Party (BP). Contrary to Bawn's assertion (1993: 975),

Table 14.1. German Federal Electoral Law: Major Revisions, 1949-97

YEAR	SUPPORT ON FINAL READING	CATALYST FOR REVISION	MAIN PROVISIONS
1949	For: SPD, FDP, Z, KPD Against: CDU, CSU, DP	n.a.	*Compensatory Member System *400 seats (60% single member districts; 40% state lists). *Voter has single vote. *d'Hondt formula for list seats; district results considered. *Possibility of surplus seats. *Threshold: 5% or 1 district seat, calculated for each state. *Validity: for 1949 only.
1953	For: CDU, SPD, FDP Against: CSU, Z/BP, DP, KPD	1949 Law valid for one election only.	*Compensatory Member System *484 seats (50% single member districts; 50% state lists). *Voter has district vote and party list vote. *d'Hondt formula for list seats; district results considered. *Possibility of surplus seats. *Threshold: 5% nationwide or 1 direct seat. *Validity: for 1953 only.
1956	For: CDU, SPD, FDP, GB/BHE Against: CSU, DP	1953 Law valid for one election only.	Same as 1953 except permanent validity and: *Threshold: 5% nationwide or 3 direct seats. (The base number of Bundestag seats was raised to 494 with accession of Saarland in 1956, and to 496 in 1964)
1985	For: CDU, CSU, SPD, FDP	FDP Pressure on coalition partners.	Same as 1956 except: *Hare-Niemeyer formula to distribute list seats.
1990	For: CDU, CSU, FDP	German Unification & BVerfG ruling on appeal by Greens, PDS, & Republikaner	Same as 1985 except: *Base number of Bundestag seats raised to 656 *Temporary provisions for 1990 election only, including separate 5% thresholds for eastern and western Germany (as required by BVerfG ruling).

Sources: Schindler (1986:20-27; 1994:23-29).

small-party opposition to a single-member-district system was by no means a foregone conclusion, even though the smallest parties undeniably had benefitted from proportional representation in 1949. The Center Party and Bavarian Party could bargain with both camps because they had regional strongholds and could thus hope to win district seats alone, or through pacts with larger partners. (The latter type of bargain explains why the small DP supported the CDU's plan.) Up until the last minute the CDU unsuccessfully wooed these two small parties with promises of electoral pacts. In the end, the FDP and SPD secured the support of the two small parties for the decisive second-reading vote by agreeing to reduce the electoral hurdle to 3 percent in at least one state. This was a big concession by the FDP, which originally proposed that the 1953 law should raise the threshold to 5 percent calculated on a nationwide, not state-level, basis. The deal with the small parties gave the FDP plan a narrow majority on its second reading, and led to the defeat of the CDU/CSU proposal at the same stage.

This second-reading vote made clear that the next election would be fought under a proportional system, and it thus put pressure on the CDU to conciliate its most probable post-election coalition partner, the FDP. At this point the CDU offered to support the FDP's plan if it reintroduced the original idea of a 5 percent nationwide threshold. The FDP willingly accepted this deal. The SPD publicly deplored this change, but it, too, supported the FDP bill on its final reading. In contrast, the CSU and DP voted against the new measure to show their disappointment at not getting a more majoritarian electoral system (Jesse 1985: 97-100; 223-225; FAZ 1953c: 3; FAZ 1953d: 1; FAZ 1953a: 3; FAZ 1953b: 3).

Three of the small parties that were outmaneuvered by the FDP took their fight for survival to the Constitutional Court. The parties' right to use this channel in electoral law cases already had been established by a 1952 ruling (BVerfG 1952: 1, 208-261). The Court quickly agreed with the Gesamtdeutsche Volkspartei (All-German People's Party, GVP) that the new law's ballot access provisions should be loosened (BVerfG 1953: 3, 19-34). However, it did not use the occasion to overturn its 1952 ruling, which held that an electoral threshold was a constitutionally permissible addition to a proportional representation system as long as the hurdle did not exceed 5 percent (BVerfG 1952: 1, 208-261; FAZ 1953e: 1). In these rulings, as in most subsequent electoral law decisions, challenger parties were able to win only minor concessions by appealing to the Constitutional Court to overturn legislation which was evidently designed to hurt small parties.

Thus, the second electoral law was instituted with an electoral threshold that was relatively high compared to 1949, and even compared to what the Bundestag had endorsed on the bill's first reading. The FDP was particularly responsible for this increase in the threshold. It and other small parties used their position in state-level coalitions to exercise a disproportionate influence over national-level bargaining, but the smallest parties were unable to maintain their gains, or to enlist the additional protection of the Constitutional Court. Partly because of this failure, the parliament elected under the second electoral law was reduced from eleven to six parties; moreover, two of these parties (Z and DP) owed their positions to electoral agreements with the CDU and/or FDP.

The Permanent Electoral Law, 1953-57

Like its predecessor, the second electoral law was valid for only a single election, so electoral reform automatically entered the legislative agenda after the 1953 election. The renewed debate took place under much different conditions, because the CDU/CSU now held a narrow absolute majority of Bundestag seats. Despite this, Chancellor Konrad Adenauer chose to form a much broader government which included all the nonsocialist parties (except the tiny Center Party). Given that passage of a permanent electoral law required only a simple majority, conditions after 1953 seemed to favor passage of arrangements more to the liking of the CDU and CSU. However, splits within these parties prevented them from agreeing in the definition of party preferences. Furthermore, CDU interests at the state-level dictated against imposing the majoritarian rules that would have benefitted the party at the federal level.

In the second legislative period, unlike the first, the cabinet could not agree on a common proposal for electoral reform. Instead, coalition members tabled a variety of plans. As in 1953, one group of CDU/CSU parliamentarians sponsored a bill to introduce a single-member district/plurality system. A bigger CDU/CSU and DP group subsequently backed a system (called the "ditch system") which would have significantly reduced proportionality in another way, by increasing the proportion of district seats, and by ignoring the results of district contests in the distribution of list seats. In contrast, both the FDP and SPD tabled proposals which retained the full proportionality of the two previous electoral laws.

CDU/CSU support for the "ditch system" directly challenged the parliamentary aspirations of their several small coalition partners. Indeed, this may have been the point. Throughout the second session, CDU/CSU leaders invoked the threat of electoral reform whenever the FDP balked at the chancellor's handling of treaties and constitutional amendments which required supramajority votes (such as the Saarland treaty and constitutional change to permit German rearmament). The small parties repeatedly succumbed to this electoral blackmail. However, they failed to win reciprocal guarantees that the larger parties would safeguard their interests in the new electoral law (Kitzinger 1960: 26; Lange 1975: 602-630; Kaack 1971: 222-224).

The tactic of using electoral reform as a Damoclean sword finally failed in early 1956, when the FDP reacted angrily to the CDU/CSU "ditch system" proposal. At this point the federal coalition wobbled, and the FDP in North Rhine-Westphalia withdrew from its coalition with the CDU in favor of an alliance with the SPD. This switch gave opponents of the ditch system sufficient Bundesrat votes to block unwanted electoral reforms. It also made an impression on CDU leaders who did not want to lose the FDP as a potential state or federal coalition partner. The CDU leadership quickly backed away from the "ditch system" in favor of a proportional representation plan already endorsed by the FDP. As a result, the permanent law adopted in 1956 was virtually identical to its temporary predecessor, except that it further tightened entry requirements for the smallest parties (see Table 14.1). In 1956, as in 1953, it was the small FDP which was most directly responsible for raising the electoral threshold, because FDP leaders hoped that their party would emerge as the sole small party–and sole small coalition partner–after the 1957 elections (Jesse 1985: 226).

Although CDU support for the FDP plan did not come quickly enough to stop a majority of FDP representatives from withdrawing from the federal coalition, the electoral system bargain held (Kitzinger 1960: 15). The new proportional electoral law was adopted with the support of the CDU, FDP, SPD, and GB/BHE (All German Bloc/Alliance of Expellees), while the CSU and DP maintained their opposition and called for a more majoritarian system (Lange 1975: 689-709).

The Bavarian Party and the All-German People's Party once again appealed to the Constitutional Court to overturn key provisions of the new law. Both parties tried to convince the Court that the countrywide 5 percent hurdle, and the new alternative threshold of three district seats, made it overly difficult for new parties, or for regionally based parties, to qualify for list seats. The small parties were unable to persuade the Court to act as their protector, and the higher hurdles remained in place (FAZ 1957: 1; BVerfG 1957: 6, 84-99, 99-103).

Thus, in 1956, as in 1953, the alliances struck in bargaining over the electoral system cut across coalition partnerships. In the negotiations that led up to passage of the legislation that is the basis of contemporary German electoral law, the parties neither defined their interests exclusively in terms of the interests of their parliamentary allies, nor did they assess proposed systems solely in terms of their probable effects on "big" or "small" parties. Although the smallest parties played a crucial role at one stage of the bargaining process, they ultimately were excluded from the deal and were, as a result, effectively excluded from the parliament.

THE FAILURE OF MAJORITARIAN REFORMS, 1961-69

After the 1957 federal election, the number of parliamentary parties dropped to four, with the CDU and CSU sitting as a single parliamentary group. Although the election gave the CDU/CSU a large majority in both the Bundestag and Bundesrat, the parties did not use this position to try to consolidate power by introducing a more majoritarian electoral system. However, their interest in electoral reform revived after the 1961 election deprived them of an absolute majority.

The CDU first revisited the idea of majoritarian reforms during coalition negotiations with the FDP in 1961. It renewed the discussion in 1962, after the FDP withdrew from the federal coalition in the wake of the *Spiegel* affair. At this point Chancellor Adenauer authorized coalition negotiations with the SPD; a central condition in these talks was that the SPD must agree to institute a single-member-district electoral system (Lücke 1968: 36). In the course of the following conversations, SPD leaders signaled that they would consider abandoning the party's long-held preference for proportional systems. This shift was facilitated by the changing voting patterns, evident in 1961, which made it more likely that the

SPD could win a two-party contest fought under plurality rules. The tentative discussions collapsed as soon as the FDP renegotiated its coalition with the CDU/CSU. Nevertheless, this episode did make clear that both the SPD and the CDU now recognized that large party interests might be served by introducing a more majoritarian electoral system.

Thus, when the SPD and CDU/CSU finally formed the grand coalition government in 1966, it was not surprising that their coalition agreement included a strong commitment to consider majoritarian reforms. During the subsequent three years, the grand coalition government used its supramajorities in the Bundestag and Bundesrat to pass many previously unfeasible reforms. They did not, however, make much headway on electoral reform, even though the subject occupied a prominent place on the political agenda and was the subject of much debate both within the parties and within the scholarly community (see, for instance, party reports on electoral reform, reprinted in Lücke 1968: 94-171; also Bredthauer 1973).

In this period, the CDU and CSU remained the strongest proponents of a more majoritarian electoral system. The SPD's electoral reform commission tentatively endorsed the switch to a less proportional system, but the party's national and local leaders never fully supported the idea of abandoning a known system in favor of one whose precise results were uncertain. Such doubts were heightened by a 1968 study commissioned by the SPD, which concluded that a single-member-district system was likely to confine the SPD to a permanent second place within a two-party system (Jesse 1985: 35-36). This was a considerably worse position than second place in a three-party system, as SPD leaders knew from their own experience in state legislatures. Furthermore, just as state-level coalition considerations influenced CDU decisions in 1956, in 1968 SPD reluctance to back electoral reform stemmed in part from fear of losing FDP support at the state level. Finally, the SPD's hesitancy on the issue arose from calculations about possible alliances after the 1969 election: whatever the decision on electoral reform, the FDP was likely to play a critical role in postelection coalition negotiations, because the grand coalition partners had agreed early on that electoral reform would go into effect only after the 1969 election (Jesse 1985: 125). In other words, the SPD's short-term and state-level coalition interests kept it from supporting radical reforms which might have benefitted the party in the long term—just as some had predicted even before the grand coalition formed (cf. Raschke 1965: 80).

Had the outcome of the 1969 federal election once again led to the formation of a grand coalition, and particularly had the far-right National Democratic Party entered the parliament at this time, Germany might well have adopted an electoral system that more distinctly favored its large parties. In the event, however, prospects for abandoning proportional representation vanished in 1969 after the FDP resumed its role as coalition-maker. Since then, there have been no serious debates about major electoral reforms. However, this has not entirely ended efforts to tinker with the electoral system. Three minor changes deserve mention here.

Amending Distribution Rules, 1982-97

The first of these reforms was adopted in 1985, when all the parliamentary parties voted to alter the formula for calculating the distribution of list seats. This minor, but at the time controversial, change from the d'Hondt to the Hare/Niemeyer formula slightly improved the chances for small parties at the cost of larger parties. In early 1982 the SPD/FDP coalition first introduced legislation to this effect as a concession to the FDP. The revised formula was not adopted before the breakup of the left-liberal coalition, but the FDP persuaded its new coalition partner to back this change. The measure passed with all-party support (Jesse 1985: 218-219; Deutscher Bundestag 1985: 8942).

A second change affected only the electoral system used in the 1990 "unification" election. The original election plans, developed by CDU-led governments in West and East Germany, called for the retention of the existing nationwide 5 percent threshold. As a way to help smaller parties, particularly those in the East, it made a one-time concession that permitted parties which were not contestants in the same states to link their lists for purposes of passing the 5 percent hurdle. Immediately before the 1990 elections, three small parties which expected to be hurt by the threshold asked the Constitutional Court to overturn these aspects of the electoral law. The parties-the Greens, the Party of Democratic Socialism (PDS-the reformed Communist Party), and the far-right Republikaner-all shared the trait of being well-organized in only one of the two parts of united Germany. They claimed that the electoral law unfairly discriminated against small parties, which had had little time to build up support in new territories, and that the possibility of electoral alliances gave large parties unfair opportunities to help their favorite smaller parties. The Court upheld their complaint, and ruled that the 5 percent threshold should be applied separately in East and West for the 1990 election only (BVerfG 1990: 82, 322-352, 353-383; Anderson 1993b: 75-76).

The third of the recent debates about electoral reform began in the mid-1990s in response to complaints about the size of the Bundestag, which grew from a base of 496 to 656 seats after German unification. In 1995, CDU and SPD leaders strongly supported proposals to reduce the size of the parliament. The CSU and Greens more reluctantly endorsed the idea, while the FDP strongly opposed it. Some FDP legislators even hinted that such a reform would constitute grounds for breaking up the coalition.

The FDP's opposition to the plan apparently stemmed from its determination to retain parliamentary seats. In the early 1990s the party lost almost all of its seats in state parliaments; as a result, the FDP's would-be officeholders increasingly pinned their hopes on party success in the federal legislature. While the FDP's primary concern was to keep as large a delegation as possible, it and other parties also voiced concern about the method for making any reductions. The SPD originally proposed eliminating more list than district seats; this was sympathetically received by the CDU leadership, although some CDU parliamentarians favored eliminating more district than list seats-which would greatly increase the size of district seats (*Die Welt* 1995: 2). The PDS, which entered the 1994 parliament on the basis of its district victories, charged that shrinking the parliament in this way was a thinly disguised attempt to eliminate the PDS from the Bundestag by making it more difficult for small parties to win district seats. The plausibility of this charge was increased by the fact that the CSU called for a simultaneous increase (to five or even six) in the number of district seats that parties with under 5 percent of the total vote must win in order to qualify for list seats (Günsche 1995: 2). At the same time, there were two renewed judicial efforts to alter the existing electoral laws.

The first of these was an appeal by the SPD government in Lower Saxony asking the Constitutional Court to block the distribution of surplus seats on the grounds that they made some votes count more than others. The CDU, the main beneficiary of surplus seats, was the primary target of this appeal, but elimination of surplus seats might also hurt the PDS. The second appeal was brought by a group of law professors, who wanted the Court to invalidate the three-seat alternative to crossing the 5 percent threshold. The Court rejected both of these appeals. Indeed, in the 1997 ruling unanimously upholding the three-seat rule, as in the 1990 ruling on the dual electoral threshold, the contemporary Court showed itself to be more sympathetic to small-party claims than were some of its predecessors of the 1950s (FAZ 1997:1-2).

Debate on parliamentary consolidation was postponed until after a Bundestag commission released a report on the matter, in mid-1997. This report recommended only a modest reduction of thirty list and thirty district seats. Despite broad support for this comparatively small reduction, there is no guarantee that the ultimate legislation will exactly conform to this proposal. As in previous episodes of reform, the extent of changes that hurt smaller parties depends on the importance of these parties as coalition partners at the state and federal level. Up to now, the FDP has exerted an extremely strong influence over the shape of electoral reforms (as in many other policy areas). In the mid-1990s the FDP lost its pivotal role as coalition partner in many states, and its position at the federal level was also increasingly vulnerable. How the SPD and CDU/CSU choose to treat FDP (and PDS) interests in renewed reform debates is likely to reveal much about how the big parties assess the smaller parties' prospects of survival.

As the episodes recounted in this section make clear, competition to shape German electoral institutions has been dominated by short-term interests. This was most visible in the 1960s, when the large parties failed to implement a system that would have favored them over small competitors. Yet this is not the entire story, for although it has been fairly easy to gauge the likely effects of proposed electoral reforms, parties never have defined their interests entirely in terms of what they would lose or gain from the reform itself. They also have considered how the reforms might affect political bargaining at other levels and on other issues.

REVISING THE FRAMEWORK OF PARTY SUBSIDIES

As in debates on electoral reform, confrontation between the CDU/CSU and SPD was very pronounced in the 1950s and early 1960s in debates on party subsidies.

However, in contrast to the area of electoral reform, the biggest parties overcame their earlier conflicts in the area of party finance by the mid-1960s. Ever since, they have worked together to find mutually beneficial solutions to their funding problems. In contrast to experiences with electoral reform, the big parties' cooperation in this area has been reined in not by considerations of coalition politics, but by the efforts of small parties unable to enter into coalition bargains.

Authorization to provide public funds for parties is derived indirectly from the Basic Law's recognition of parties' obligation to "participate in forming the political will of the people." The same article also stipulates that parties "shall publicly account for the sources of their funds." In the event, however, the constitutional injunction to enact financial disclosure procedures went unheeded for more than fifteen years because the governing parties had no interest in revealing the names of their donors. In the meantime, however, the parliament found time to pass other laws which more directly benefitted party finances.

Tax Subsidies, 1954-58

In the 1950s, the initial struggles over political finance pitted the SPD against the CDU and CSU. The SPD's objections to party subsidies had strategic as well as historical and constitutional foundations: traditionally only the SPD had funded itself primarily from a large dues-paying membership, whereas parties of the center and right had relied heavily on contributions from business donors. The SPD thus led the opposition in 1954, when the Bundestag passed its first measure to indirectly subsidize party fund-raising efforts by adding political contributions to the list of charitable and other donations that could be deducted from individual and corporate income tax. The SPD attempted to delete this provision from the broader tax reform package, but the move was defeated despite support from most of the FDP and even from some trade unionists within the CDU (Heidenheimer 1957: 381; *Frankfurter Rundschau* 1957: 1).

In the absence of a Parties Law, it was unclear which groups were affected by this tax code revision. As initially implemented, the deduction was automatic only for donations made to parties represented in state or federal legislatures. The Gesamtdeutsche Volkspartei, a party without any Bundestag seats, appealed this interpretation to the Constitutional Court. In a 1957 decision that set the pattern for many future battles over subsidy legislation, the Court showed that it was much more sympathetic to small parties' claims in this area than in the area of electoral system design. The Court ruled that donations to nonlegislative parties must be granted the same tax status as donations to other parties (BVerfG 1957: 6, 273-281).

The immediate impact of this decision was limited because the Court had invalidated the broader principle of tax deductibility for political contributions within a year. The case that precipitated this ruling was brought by the SPD-led state government of Hesse (supported by two other SPD-led states) and was apparently intended to prod the Court into ruling that the government must introduce the constitutionally prescribed financial disclosure legislation (FAZ 1958: 1). In the event, the Court did not pronounce on the absence of a Parties Law, but it did uphold the SPD's specific challenge by overturning the existing tax legislation on the grounds that it unequally favored parties with richer donors. Importantly, however, the Court also opened the way for future subsidy legislation by making clear that the constitution permitted public subsidies for parties' electioneering activities (BVerfG 1958: 8, 51-71).

Subsidies for Parliamentary Parties, 1959-66

This new judgement hurt the nonsocialist parties, which saw an immediate drop in their contributions. They responded by acting on the Court's hint and introducing direct subsidies to parties. In 1959 the governing CDU/CSU inserted into the annual budget a very modest subsidy (DM5 million) for the parliamentary parties' "political education work." The subsidy was distributed proportionally to party strength in the Bundestag. During the 1961 coalition negotiations, the FDP successfully pressed for an increase in these subsidies and for a new payment format: as of 1963, 20 percent of the subsidies was split equally among the four parliamentary parties (a change that benefitted the CSU as well as the FDP), while the rest continued to be distributed in proportion to parliamentary strength (Kaack 1971: 384). The coalition partners increased the subsidies again in the 1963 and 1964 budgets.

At first, the SPD voiced opposition to these subsidies, and in 1964 the party went so far as to make a very public gesture of refusing to spend the monies for party purposes; instead, it used them to purchase educational materials and services for schools (SPD 1965: 183-195). In 1965, the SPD-governed state of Hesse appealed to the Constitutional Court to overturn the subsidies, arguing that it was unconstitutional to pay public funds for general party purposes. Yet, by the time this appeal was heard, the SPD's position already had begun to shift, and in deliberations before the court the party's representative endorsed the constitutionality of public subsidies for party work as long as the payments were made within the framework of a Parties Law (BVerfG 1966: 20, 57-119).

Not surprisingly, it was the parties which were too small to gain parliamentary representation which most strongly opposed the initial subsidies. In 1960 the Gesamtdeutscher Block/Bund der Heimatentrechteten (GB/BHE or All-German Bloc/Federation of Expellees) unsuccessfully appealed to the Constitutional Court, complaining that subsidies which were restricted only to parliamentary parties violated constitutional guarantees of equal treatment (BVerfG 1961: 12, 276-280). In 1962 the party renewed its appeal, and in 1964 the Bavarian Party lodged a similar complaint. In its 1966 rulings on these suits, and on the Hessian government's broader complaint against all subsidies, the Court agreed with the plaintiffs on the most important points. The Court clarified its 1958 tax-law decision and agreed with the SPD charge that general public subsidies for parties were unconstitutional. However, the decision also made clear that public support for parties' electioneering activities would be an acceptable alternative. Because it declared the existing system of subsidies unconstitutional, the Court rejected the small parties' demands to be included in these payment schemes, but it did indicate that future subsidies would have to include parties which did not cross the 5 percent electoral threshold (BVerfG 1966: 20, 57-119; 119-144).

The 1967 Parties Law and Campaign Subsidies

The parties lost little time in implementing a new system of subsidies which met the constitutional requirement of funding only parties' campaign activities. The SPD, which by now had dropped its opposition to public subsidies, actively supported this all-party initiative. Under the new system, a total of DM2.50 per eligible voter was divided proportionally among all parties which received at least 2.5 percent of the overall vote in federal elections (see Table 14.2). This system of campaign financing was incorporated within the long-awaited Parties Law, a section of which finally stipulated how parties were supposed to report the sources of their funds.

The 1967 law did not end the pattern of small-party opposition to subsidy systems designed by and for the largest parliamentary parties. The Nationaldemokratische Partei Deutschlands (National Democratic Party or NPD) immediately but unsuccessfully appealed against the establishment of any type of subsidy, on the grounds that these hampered citizens' freedom in forming their own political views (BVerfG 1967: 22, 42-50). In addition, the NPD, the Europäische Föderalistische Partei (European Federal Party), and the Bayerische Staatspartei (Bavarian State Party)—none of which were represented in the Bundestag —successfully appealed to the Constitutional Court to nullify some of the new law's provisions. The Court agreed with them that the new system of party finance, like that overturned in 1966, unfairly excluded very small competitors. The Court held that only a threshold of no higher than one half of one percent (0.5 percent) would be acceptable (BVerfG 1969: 24, 300). The parliamentary parties then revised the public finance system in line with this judgment.

Thus, passage of the Parties Law marked a crucial turning point in the dynamics of competition to shape the system of public subsidies. Up to this point, the SPD could claim the moral high ground by opposing subsidies and highlighting its own status as a membership-financed party. Once it collaborated to implement the 1967 Parties Law, the SPD lost its distinctiveness on this issue and also became increasingly dependent on fickle public revenues. In the 1970s and 1980s, the SPD built up high debts partly because its campaign budgets were based on overly optimistic predictions about party votes (and therefore public subsidies) in upcoming elections. In turn, these debts predisposed the SPD to cooperate with other parties whenever opportunities to increase total subsidies arose (Wewer 1990: 258-261). Meanwhile, very small parties continued to turn to the courts to defend their interests.

Table 14.2. Laws Affecting German Party Finance: Major Revisions, 1949-97

YEAR	SUPPORT ON FINAL READING[1]	CATALYST FOR REVISION	MAIN PROVISIONS
1954	*For:* CDU, CSU, FDP, DP[2] *Against:* SPD, FDP, GB/BHE[3]	n.a.	Tax Law *Donations to political parties are tax deductible up to 5% of income for individuals or 2% of revenues for businesses. Declared unconstitutional by BVerfG in 1958 in response to appeal by SPD-led state of Hesse.
1966	*For:* CDU, CSU, SPD, FDP	BVerfG decisions in cases brought by state of Hesse, NPD, DP/BHE	Parties Law *Funds are for electioneering only. *Total funds of DM2.50/eligible voter. *Distributed proportionally to party vote in federal election. *Parties receiving at least 2.5% of federal vote benefit, as do parties without state lists which win 10% of vote in a district. *Partial prepayment of funds ahead of election. *Party donations tax deductible up to DM600/individual. *Parties must publish the names of individuals or corporations giving more than DM20,000/year.
1969	*For:* CDU, CSU, SPD, FDP	BVerfG decision in case brought by NPD, Europa-Partei	Parties Law, Same as 1966 except: *Parties receiving at least 0.5% of federal vote benefit.
1974	*For:* CDU, CSU, SPD, FDP	High debts hurting all parties.	Same as 1969 except: *Total funds of DM3.50/eligible voter.
1979	*For:* CDU, CSU, SPD, FDP	BVerfG decision in case brought by individual candidate.	Same as 1974 except: *Independent candidates receiving at least 10% of district vote benefit.

Year	Vote	Cause	Provisions
1983	*For*: CDU, CSU, SPD, FDP *Against*: Greens	Finance scandals affecting all parties.	Same as 1979 except: *Total funds of DM5.00/eligible voter. *Party donations tax deductible up to 5% of income per individual or up to 2% of payroll for corporations. *Equalization formula: compensation for parties which benefit less from tax deduction because donors give less relative to party's electoral size.
1988	*For*: CDU, CSU, SPD, FDP *Against*: Greens	BVerfG decision in case brought by Greens.	Same as 1983 except: *Party donations tax deductible up to DM60,000. *Parties must publish names of donors giving over DM40,000. *Equalization formula recalculated to help parties with big memberships. *Annual base payment of up to 6% of total fund to parties receiving at least 2% of nationwide vote.
1993	*For*: CDU, CSU, SPD, FDP *Against*: Greens, PDS (& some SPD)	BverfG decision in case brought by Greens.	*Funds no longer restricted to electioneering. *Equalization fund abolished. *Base payment abolished. *Party donations tax deductible up to DM6,000/individual. *Donations from firms are no longer tax deductible. *Parties must publish names of donors giving over DM20,000. *Total funds limited (to approx. DM230 million plus inflation). *Distribution to parties according to formula that considers number of votes plus ability to attract donations. *No party may receive more than 50% of its total budget from public funds.

Notes: 1. In some cases, a few individuals did not vote with their parliamentary group. 2. Voted against SPD amendment to eliminate deduction from tax code. 3. Voted for SPD amendment on final reading to eliminate deduction from tax code. SPD + 15 CDU/CSU + 9 FDP + 12 GB/BHE + 1 DP + 2 unaffiliated; 19 abstentions.
Sources: Schindler (1983: 89–91; 1986: 112–114; 1994: 129–131); *FAZ* (1993a & b).

Revising the Parties Law, 1974-94

The topic of public subsidies generated little partisan controversy during the 1970s. In 1974 all parliamentary parties cooperated to increase overall subsidy levels, and in 1979 they further boosted their revenues by creating a similarly well-financed scheme to cover the (far cheaper) campaigns of parties competing in elections to the European Parliament. However, by the early 1980s revelations about illegal and improper party finance practices had made the subject much more politically sensitive.

Despite increased public attentiveness to questions of party finance, the established parliamentary parties found it difficult to gain competitive advantage from the issue, because all were touched by the financing scandals. Instead, they had incentives to cooperate in passing legislation to address the problems that came to light. As a result, even though the 1983 reform of party finance legislation was produced in a period of shifting coalitions and bitter partisan confrontation, its provisions were the result of negotiations among all the established parties. For instance, the SPD agreed to institute high levels of tax deductibility for political donations, a change which disproportionately aided the CDU, CSU, and FDP. In return, and as a concession to the Constitutional Court's 1958 ruling on tax advantages for political parties, the new legislation established an "equalization" fund intended to compensate parties (like the SPD) whose supporters generally had more modest means and gave smaller donations, and who were thus likely to benefit least from favorable tax treatment for political contributions (Naßmacher 1989b: 36; Landfried 1990: 48). In addition, the new law helped all the parties by increasing the overall amount of the subsidies.

The 1983 reforms were not adopted unanimously. They were vociferously opposed by the Greens, who entered the Bundestag in 1983 on a platform of opposition to politics as usual. The Greens immediately used the well-proven judicial recourse of small parties, asking the Constitutional Court to reconsider the admissibility of a wide range of party subsidy provisions. The Court disagreed with the party's broadest charges and upheld public funding for the party-linked political education foundations. However, it did demand modifications to the new provisions on tax-deductibility for political contributions (BVerfG 1986: 73, 1-39, 40-117).

This decision prompted CDU, CSU, SPD, and FDP treasurers to draft a new package of party finance reforms. The new legislation not only addressed problems raised by the Court, but also "corrected" the 1983 equalization formula, which—contrary to the intent of the original big-party deal—had not helped the SPD (Landfried 1990: 55-56). In addition, the 1988 legislation tilted the distribution of funds slightly in favor of small—but not very small—parties by setting aside 6 percent of the subsidy total for parties winning at least 2 percent of the vote in the previous federal election (the *Sockelbeitrag* or threshold contribution). Finally, the new legislation doubled the level at which donor names must be publicized (Landfried 1990: 64-70).

As in 1983, the 1988 reforms had the support of all the parliamentary parties except the Greens, and as in 1983, the Greens appealed to the Constitutional Court to undo measures which the party could not block in the legislature. This time the party's complaints found a much more sympathetic audience. In its 1992 judgment, the Court ruled against much of the existing political finance framework, even to the extent of overturning its own earlier decisions. For instance, the Court relaxed a restriction imposed by its 1966 ruling, which had held that public subsidies must be used exclusively for campaign activities. In most other respects, however, the 1992 judgment tightened previous rulings and provided detailed guidelines for constitutionally acceptable subsidy legislation. It found the equalization formula unconstitutional and stipulated that new legislation must restrict subsidy payments to no more than half of each party's income, must limit the tax-deductibility of political contributions to levels which "average" citizens could afford, and must return the threshold for public reporting of donations to the lower rate of DM20,000. In keeping with its judgments from the 1960s, the Court also ruled that the *Sockelbeitrag* was unconstitutional because it delinked parties from the support of members and/or voters (BVerfG 1992: 85, 264-328).

In January 1994, at the beginning of a year which was crowded with local, state, and federal elections, the Bundestag adopted the sixth revision to the party finance section of the Parties Law. In accordance with the Court's instructions, the new law coupled the distribution of subsidies to parties' relative success in state and federal elections, and to their absolute success in fund-raising through small contributions (whether in the form of donations or of membership dues). The legislation departed from the Court's recommendations by establishing a payment system which favored smaller parties by overweighing the payment for the first 5 million votes in a federal election—a departure from equality that makes the new legislation once again vulnerable to judicial appeal (FAZ 1993b: 3).

ELECTORAL COMPETITION AND COMPETITION TO SHAPE INSTITUTIONS

Why have traditional electoral rivals cooperated on party finance but not on major aspects of electoral reform? The answer is not just a matter of timing—that electoral reform was an issue in the 1950s, a period when big-party rivalry was greatest. In fact, cooperation on party subsidies began in the 1960s, at almost the same time that big-party cooperation on electoral reform collapsed. Instead, the explanation seems to lie in the nature of the benefits that each type of cooperation would provide, both in the certainty of the payoff, and in the discreetness of the reward. CDU, CSU, and SPD proponents of more majoritarian electoral systems believed that such systems would produce a long-term increase in the number of legislative seats held by each of the largest parties, just as proponents of party subsidies believed that these would remedy shortfalls in the parties' budgets. Although it seemed that the big parties would profit in both instances, the rewards of electoral reform would have been distributed much less evenly than the public subsidies: whereas even a second-place party profits from increased revenues, only one party at a time can take advantage of a system that increases the likelihood of single-party government. Thus, although in Germany the largest parties might have benefitted equally in the *long term* from electoral system changes, uncertainty about the timing of the payoff inhibited cooperation.

Short-term calculation of interest also may have played a role in either facilitating or inhibiting cooperation. In the case of electoral reform, CDU and SPD fear of alienating the FDP blocked shifts to a system in which the FDP might have been obsolete, but only in the long term. In the case of subsidies, the reverse effect may have been at work: cooperation occurred because the short-term rewards of joint action were positive-sum, even though the long-term benefits of cooperation were likely to be distributed disproportionately. In fact, Wewer argues that the SPD's support for subsidies in 1967 was short-sighted, because these subsidies enabled the opposition CDU to regain its strength in the 1970s by constructing a professional bureaucracy and building a contributing membership (Wewer 1990: 261) In sum, whereas short-term coalition considerations always have made the CDU/CSU and SPD reluctant to cooperate in passing electoral reforms which would provide forseeable long-term benefits, in cases of political finance laws short-term calculations have had exactly the opposite effect of encouraging cooperation despite possible long-term costs.

Finally, it is important to note that an exclusive focus on bargaining between parliamentary parties would overlook an important component of these struggles to reshape the framework of electoral competition. As the third columns in Tables 14.1 and 14.2 show, small parties inside and outside the legislature have acted as vital catalysts in many episodes of institutional reform, often using appeals to the Constitutional Court to circumvent legislative bargains. Because the Constitutional Court granted standing even to parties which were not represented in legislatures, small parties gained an ability to shape legislation that far exceeded their electoral success. Although small parties' complaints were largely unsuccessful in stopping the electoral law changes which hastened their marginalization, complaints filed by the losers in legislative struggles repeatedly provided the occasion for rulings overturning existing party finance arrangements. Even apparently positive-sum changes, like across-the-board increases in party subsidies, have not been immune from such attacks. The wider implication of this is clear: to the extent that they are able to move institutional reform struggles from the legislative to the judicial arena, parties which lack "blackmail potential" under Sartori's definition (1976: 122-123), and which are "politically irrelevant" according to Panebianco's calculations (1988: 214), may nevertheless play important roles in episodes of institutional redesign. Because competition has not been confined to the legislative and electoral arenas, the largest parties have not been in complete control of the outcomes even when they have cooperated.

THE IMPACT OF INSTITUTIONAL REFORM

Contemporary German politics would look very different if the reforms–and the failed reforms–described above had taken a different turn. Of these, the effects of the electoral system decisions are perhaps easiest to judge. The successive increase in entry thresholds, and the Constitutional Court's rejection of most complaints filed by small parties, contributed to–but were not the sole cause of–the rapid consolidation of the German party system in the 1950s. Conversely, however, the retention of a proportional system in the 1960s facilitated the re-expansion of the party system in the 1980s and 1990s, and Court rulings in the 1990s have defended small parties' political access. Were a single-member-district system now in use, German electoral politics would look much different than it does today: most notably, the regionally strong PDS would send a few delegates to the Bundestag, but probably neither the Greens nor the FDP would be represented. Recent shifts in electoral behavior, discussed in other chapters in this volume, also would have produced much different effects under a single-member-district system. For instance, parties would have less need to be concerned about declining turnout in a winner-take-all system, while disaffected voters would find it more difficult to register a protest without "wasting" their vote (see also Anderson 1993a on other likely effects that can be attributed to the electoral system choice). Even some of the details of the electoral reform decisions have observable effects on contemporary political competition. Perhaps the most ironic of these is the increasing likelihood that the FDP will lose its parliamentary seats because of the party's 1953 success in making the 5 percent electoral threshold a nationwide, not state-by-state, figure.

It is harder to assess how changes in party finance laws have affected electoral competition. On one hand, public subsidies have benefitted the largest parties by helping them build up strong organizations that fight elections and project a strong, year-round, presence. As early as 1971, Heino Kaack argued that the established parties needed this "crutch" of state subsidies because they faced strong popular distrust, a diagnosis which still seems applicable today (Kaack 1971: 692). More recently, Gordon Smith has argued in a similar vein that state subsidies are essential for helping the established parties fend off their new challengers, because these funds enable the parties to create professional campaign organizations (Smith 1993: 88). Yet it is not only established parties which have benefitted from party finance legislation. In the 1980s and 1990s public funds were particularly important to fledgling parties of the far right, whose small electoral totals earned them public subsidies which dramatically increased their revenues. While public financial support was not responsible for the appeal of these parties, it certainly contributed to their visibility and to their attempts to project organizational coherence.

The preceding analysis serves as a reminder of the extent to which party actions–and inactions–have modified the impact of changes in electoral behavior. Even outside election periods, partisan struggles to reshape the institutions of electoral competition have shaped, and have been shaped by, the dynamics of this competition itself. The dominant patterns of German electoral competition–rivalry between the CDU/CSU and SPD, and the key role of the FDP as coalition-maker–have been particularly evident in the critical efforts to modify the electoral system. The large parties repeatedly proved unwilling to cooperate in tailoring election formulas so as to ensure their long-term domination of the party system. Instead, in 1953, 1956, and 1969 both CDU and SPD eventually rejected proposals to adopt a single-member-district system because they needed the FDP as a potential or actual partner in federal *and* state coalitions. The net result has been an electoral system that has remained basically unchanged since 1949, even though all the current legislative parties would have reason to prefer different systems.

In the area of party finance, however, there is ample support for the diagnosis that contemporary German parties often cooperate in cartel fashion to promote common structural interests (Katz and Mair 1995). Since the mid-1960s, CDU, CSU, SPD, and FDP regularly have cooperated in what they all have viewed as a positive-sum game of expanding public subsidies for political parties. Such cooperation even has been evident in some realms of electoral law reform, where established parliamentary parties–including the FDP–consistently have cooperated to the disadvantage of smaller rivals and would-be rivals. These collusionary patterns are troubling, for they suggest an antidemocratic situation in which citizens are unable use elections to influence policy outcomes. To the extent that supposed electoral rivals work together to the disadvantage of other possible rivals, their behavior may hasten some of the developments noted elsewhere in this book, such as the apparent weakening of ties between voters and the parties (see, e.g., Carsten Zelle's discussion a "political frustration" approach to explain the decline in party identification in chapter 4). Cooperation on matters such as the structure of public subsidies or electoral laws also might enable the established parties to buffer themselves from the impact of changes in citizens' electoral behavior. In either case, whether partisan interaction takes the form of cooperation or competition, the electoral framework, and parties' roles in shaping it, clearly are central to the unfolding story of stability and change in German elections.

BIBLIOGRAPHY

Abramson, Paul R., and John H. Aldrich. 1982. "The Decline of Electoral Participation in America." *American Political Science Review* 76:502-521.

Abramson, Paul R., Susan Ellis, and Ronald Inglehart. 1997. "Research in Context: Measuring Value Change." *Political Behavior* 19 (1): 41-59.

Anderson, Christopher J. 1993a. "The Composition of the German Bundestag since 1949: Long-Term Trends and Institutional Effects." *Historical Social Research* 18:3-25.

Anderson, Christopher J. 1993b. "Political Elites and Electoral Rules: The Composition of the Bundestag, 1949-1990." In *The Domestic Politics of German Unification*, ed. Christopher Anderson, Karl Kaltenthaler, and Wolfgang Luthardt. Boulder, CO: Lynne Rienner Publishers.

Anderson, Christopher J. 1996. "Political Action and Social Integration." *American Politics Quarterly* 24 (1):105-124.

Anderson, Christopher J., and Daniel S. Ward. 1996. "Barometer Elections in Comparative Perspective." *Electoral Studies* 15:447-460.

Anderson, Christopher, and Carsten Zelle. 1995. "Helmut Kohl and the CDU Victory." *German Politics and Society* 13:12-35.

Ansolabehere, Stephen, and Shanto Iyengar. 1994. "Riding the Wave and Claiming Ownership Over Issues. The Joint Effects of Advertising and News Coverage in Campaigns." *Public Opinion Quarterly* 58:335-357.

Armingeon, Klaus. 1994. "Gründe und Folgen geringer Wahlbeteiligung." *Kölner Zeitschrift für Soziologie und Sozialpsychologie* 46:43-64.

Asher, Herbert. 1976. *Causal Modelling*. Beverly Hills, CA: Sage.

Baker, Kendall, Russell J. Dalton, and Kai Hildebrandt. 1981. *Germany Transformed: Political Culture and the New Politics.* Cambridge, MA: Harvard University Press.

Barnes, Samuel H, Max Kaase et al., eds. 1979. *Political Action. Mass Participation in Five Western Democracies.* Beverly Hills, CA: Sage.

Bartels, Larry M. 1993. "Messages Received: The Political Impact of Media Exposure." *American Political Science Review* 87:267-285.

Bawn, Kathleen. 1993. "The Logic of Institutional Preferences: German Electoral Law as a Social Choice Outcome." *American Journal of Political Science* 37:965-989.

Bean, Clive, and Elim Papadakis. 1994a. "Polarized Priorities or Flexible Alternatives? Dimensionality in Inglehart's Materialism-Postmaterialism Scale." *International Journal of Public Opinion Research* 6:264-288.

Bean, Clive, and Elim Papadakis. 1994b. "Polarized Priorities *and* Flexible Alternatives: Response to Inglehart and Hellevik." *International Journal of Public Opinion Research* 6:295-297.

Bennett, Stephen E. 1991. "Left Behind: Exploring Declining Turnout Among Noncollege Young Whites, 1964-1988." *Social Science Quarterly* 72:314-333.

Berelson, Bernard R., Paul F. Lazarsfeld, and William N. MacPhee. 1954. *Voting: A Study of Opinion Formation in a Presidential Campaign.* Chicago: University of Chicago Press.

Berg, Klaus, and Marie-Luise Kiefer, eds. 1996. *Massenkommunikation V. Eine Langzeituntersuchung zur Mediennutzung und Medienbewertung 1964-1995.* Baden-Baden: Nomos.

Berger, Manfred, Wolfgang Gibowski, Matthias Jung, Dieter Roth, and Wolfgang Schulte. 1990. "Sieg ohne Glanz: Eine Analyse der Bundestagswahl 1987." In *Wahlen und Wähler. Analysen aus Anlaß der Bundestagswahl 1987,* ed. Max Kaase and Hans-Dieter Klingemann. Opladen: Westdeutscher Verlag.

Berger, Manfred, Wolfgang Gibowski, Dieter Roth, and Wolfgang Schulte. 1977. "Die Bundestagswahl 1976: Politik und Sozialstruktur." *Zeitschrift für Parlamentsfragen* 8:197-231.

Berger, Manfred, Wolfgang Gibowski, Dieter Roth, and Wolfgang Schulte. 1983. "Stabilität und Wechsel: Eine Analyse der Bundestagswahl 1980." In *Wahlen und politisches System. Analysen aus Anlaß der Bundestagswahl 1980,* ed. Max Kaase and Hans-Dieter Klingemann. Opladen: Westdeutscher Verlag.

Berger, Manfred, Wolfgang Gibowski, Dieter Roth, and Wolfgang Schulte. 1986. "Legitimierung des Regierungswechsels. Eine Analyse der Bundestagswahl 1983." In *Wahlen und politischer Prozeß. Analysen aus Anlaß der Bundestagswahl 1983,* ed. Hans-Dieter Klingemann and Max Kaase. Opladen: Westdeutscher Verlag.

Beyme, Klaus von. 1991. *Das politische System der Bundesrepublik Deutschland nach der Vereinigung*. Munich: Piper.

Blücher, Viggo Graf. 1962. *Der Prozeß der Meinungsbildung: Dargestellt am Beispiel der Bundestagswahl 1961. Ergebnisse von Emnid-Untersuchungen während und nach der Legislaturperiode des 3. Deutschen Bundestags*, 2d. ed. Bielefeld: Emnid.

Bluck, Carsten, and Henry Kreikenbom. 1991. "Die Wähler der DDR: Nur issue-orientiert oder auch parteigebunden?" *Zeitschrift für Parlamentsfragen* 22:495-502.

Bluck, Carsten, and Henry Kreikenbom. 1993. "Quasiparteibindung und Issues." In *Wahlen in Zeiten des Umbruchs*, ed. Oscar W. Gabriel and Klaus G. Troitzsch. Frankfurt/Main: Lang.

Bogdanor, Vernon. 1987. "Electoral Reform and British Politics." *Electoral Studies* 6:115-121.

Böhme, Rolf. 1994. *Je mehr wir haben, desto mehr haben wir zuwenig*. Bonn: Dietz.

Brady, David, and Jongryn Mo. 1992. "Electoral Systems and Institutional Choice." *Comparative Political Studies* 24:405-429.

Bredthauer, Rüdiger. 1973. *Das Wahlsystem als Objekt von Politik und Wissenschaft: Die Wahlsystemdiskussion in der BRD 1967/68 als politische und wissenschaftliche Auseinandersetzung*. Meisenheim am Glan: Verlag Anton Hain.

Brettschneider, Frank. 1994. "Agenda Setting. Forschungsstand und politische Konsequenzen." In *Politik und Medien. Analysen zur Entwicklung der politischen Kommunikation*, ed. Michael Jäckel and Peter Winterhoff-Spurk. Berlin: Vistas.

Brettschneider, Frank. 1997. "Massenmedien und politische Kommunikation." In *Handbuch Politisches System der Bundesrepublik Deutschland*, ed. Oscar W. Gabriel and Everhard Holtmann. Munich: Oldenbourg.

Brettschneider, Frank, Katja Ahlstich, Bettina Klett, and Angelika Vetter. 1994. "Daten zu Gesellschaft, Wirtschaft und Politik in den EG-Mitgliedsstaaten." In *Die EU-Staaten im Vergleich. Strukturen, Prozesse, Politikinhalte. 2d ed*, ed. Oscar W. Gabriel and Frank Brettschneider. Opladen: Westdeutscher Verlag.

Brettschneider, Frank, and Peter R. Schrott. 1995. *Kommunikationsverhalten und Mediennutzung*. Contribution to the KSPW-Project "Wandel politischer Orientierungen und Verhaltensmuster in Deutschland seit dem Beitritt der fünf neuen Länder." Berlin: KSPW.

Brinkmann, Heinz U. 1988. "Wahlverhalten der 'neuen Mittelschicht' in der Bundesrepublik Deutschland." *Aus Politik und Zeitgeschichte* (B 30-31):19-32

Brody, Richard A. 1978. "The Puzzle of Political Participation in America." In *The New American Political System*, ed. Anthony King. Washington DC: American Enterprise Institute.

Budge, Ian, Ivor Crewe, and Dennis Farlie, eds. 1976. *Party Identification and Beyond. Representations of Voting and Party Competition.* New York: John Wiley & Sons.

Bürklin, Wilhelm.1988. *Wahlverhalten und Wertewandel.* Opladen: Leske & Budrich.

Bürklin, Wilhelm, Markus Klein, and Achim Ruß. 1994. "Dimensionen des Wertewandels. Eine empirische Längsschnittanalyse zur Dimensionalität und der Wandlungsdynamik gesellschaftlicher Wertorientierungen." *Politische Vierteljahresschrift* 35:579-606.

Bürklin, Wilhelm, Markus Klein, and Achim Ruß. 1996. "Postmaterieller oder anthropozentrischer Wertewandel? Eine Erwiderung auf Ronald Inglehart und Hans-Dieter Klingemann." *Politische Vierteljahresschrift* 37:517-536.

Burnham, Walter D. 1987. "Elections as Democratic Institutions." In *Elections in America,* ed. Kay L. Schlozman. Boston: Allen and Unwin.

BverfG (Bundesverfassungsgericht). Various years 1952-1992. *Entscheidungen.* Tübingen: J. C. B. Mohr.

Campbell, Angus, Philip E. Converse, Warren E. Miller, and Donald E. Stokes. 1960. *The American Voter.* New York: John Wiley & Sons.

Campbell, Angus, Gerald Gurin, and Warren E. Miller. 1954. *The Voter Decides.* Evanston, IL: Row and Petersen.

Chaffee, Steven H.. 1986. "Mass Media and Interpersonal Channels: Competitive, Convergent, or Complementary?" In *Inter/Media. Interpersonal Communication in a Media World.* 3d ed., ed. Gary Gumpert and Robert Cathcart. New York: Oxford University Press.

Chaffee, Steven H., and Sun Yuel Choe. 1980. "Time of Decision and Media Use During the Ford-Carter Campaign." *Public Opinion Quarterly* 44:53-69.

Clarke, Harold D., and Nitish Dutt. 1991. "Measuring Value Change in Western Industrialized Societies: The Impact of Unemployment." *American Political Science Review* 85:905-920.

Clarke, Harold D., Nitish Dutt, and Jonathan Rapkin. 1997. "Conversations in Context: The (Mis)measurement of Value Change in Advanced Industrial Societies." *Political Behavior* 19 (1): 19-39.

Cohen, Bernard C. 1963. *The Press and Foreign Policy.* Princeton, NJ: Princeton University Press.

Conradt, David P. 1993. *The German Polity.* 5th ed. New York: Longman.

Converse, Philip E. 1964. "The Nature of Belief Systems in Mass Publics." In *Ideology and Discontent,* ed. David E. Apter. Glencoe, IL: The Free Press.

Converse, Philip E. 1970. "Attitudes and Non-Attitudes: Continuation of a Dialogue." In *The Quantitative Analysis of Social Problems*, ed. Edward R. Tufte. Reading, MA: Addison-Wesley.

Converse, Philip E. 1976. *The Dynamics of Party Support. Cohort Analyzing Party Identification.* Beverly Hills, CA: Sage.

Crewe, Ivor. 1981. "Electoral Participation." In *Democracy at the Polls*, ed. David Butler, Howard R. Penniman, and Austin Ranney. Beverly Hills, CA: Sage.

Czarnecki, Thomas. 1992. *Kommunales Wahlverhalten. Die Existenz und Bedeutsamkeit kommunaler Determinanten für das Wahlverhalten. Eine empirische Untersuchung am Beispiel Rheinland-Pfalz.* Munich: Minerva.

Dahrendorf, Ralf. 1957. *Soziale Klassen und Klassenkonflikt in der industriellen Gesellschaft.* Stuttgart: Enke Verlag.

Dalton, Russell J. 1984. "Cognitive Mobilization and Partisan Dealignment in Advanced Industrial Democracies." *Journal of Politics* 46:264-284.

Dalton, Russell J. 1988. *Citizen Politics in Western Democracies. Public Opinion and Political Parties in the United States, Great Britain, West Germany, and France.* Chatham, NJ: Chatham House Publishers.

Dalton, Russell J. 1989. "The German Voter: Dealignment or Realignment?" in *Developments in West German Politics*, ed. Gordon Smith et al. London: Macmillan.

Dalton, Russell J., ed. 1992. *Germany Votes 1990: Unification and the New German Party System.* Oxford: Berg Publishers.

Dalton, Russell J. 1993a. *Politics in Germany.* 2d. ed. New York: HarperCollins.

Dalton, Russell J., ed. 1993b. *The New Germany Votes: Unification and the Creation of a German Party System.* Providence: Berg.

Dalton, Russell J. 1996. *Citizen Politics in Western Democracies. Public Opinion and Political Parties in the United States, Great Britain, West Germany, and France.* 2nd ed. Chatham, NJ: Chatham House Publishers.

Dalton, Russell J., and Wilhelm Bürklin. 1995. "The Two German Electorates: The Social Bases of the Vote in 1990 and 1994." *German Politics and Society* 13:79-99.

Dalton, Russell J., Scott C. Flanagan, and Paul A. Beck, eds. 1984. *Electoral Change in Advanced Industrial Democracies: Realignment or Dealignment?* Princeton, NJ: Princeton University Press.

Dalton, Russell J., and Robert Rohrschneider. 1990. "Wählerwandel und Abschwächung der Parteineigungen von 1972 bis 1987." In *Wahlen und Wähler. Analysen aus Anlaß der Bundestagswahl 1987*, ed. Max Kaase, and Hans-Dieter Klingemann. Opladen: Westdeutscher Verlag.

Dalton, Russell J., and Martin Wattenberg. 1993. "The Not So Simple Act of Voting." In *Political Science. The State of the Discipline II*, ed. Ada W. Finifter. Washington, DC: The American Political Science Association.

DeFleur, Melvin L., and Sandra J. Ball-Rokeach. 1989. *Theories of Mass Communication. 5th ed.* New York: Longman.

van Deth, Jan W., and Peter A.T.M. Geurts. 1989. "Value Orientation, Left-Right Placement and Voting." *European Journal of Political Research* 17:17-34.

Deutscher Bundestag. 1985. *Protokoll zu den Verhandlungen.*

Die Welt. 1995. "Die FDP will keinen Sessel in Bonn räumen," 3 June:2.

Dinkel, Reiner H. 1989. "Landtagswahlen unter dem Einfluß der Bundespolitik: Die Erfahrungen der letzten Legislaturperioden." In *Wahlen und politische Einstellungen in der Bundesrepublik Deutschland,* eds. Jürgen W. Falter, Hans Rattinger, and Klaus G. Troitzsch. Frankfurt/Main: Lang.

Dittrich, Karl. 1991. "Sozialstrukturelle Bestimmgründe der Wahlentscheidung." In *Wählerverhalten im Wandel. Bestimmungsgründe und politisch-kulturelle Trends am Beispiel der Bundestagswahl 1987,* ed. Hans-Joachim Veen and Elisabeth Noelle-Neumann. Paderborn: Schöningh.

Dittrich, Karl, and Lars Norby Johansen. 1983. "Voting Turnout in Europe. 1945-1978: Myths and Realities." In *Western European Party Systems: Continuity and Change,* ed. Hans Daalder and Peter Mair. London: Sage.

Donsbach, Wolfgang. 1987. "Die Theorie der Schweigespirale." In *Medienwirkungsforschung,* ed. Michael Schenk. Tübingen: J.C.B. Mohr.

Donsbach, Wolfgang. 1989. "Selektive Zuwendung zu Medieninhalten. Einflußfaktoren auf die Auswahlentscheidungen der Rezipienten." In *Massenkommunikation. Theorien, Methoden, Befunde,* ed. Max Kaase and Winfried Schulz. Opladen: Westdeutscher Verlag.

Donsbach, Wolfgang. 1991. *Medienwirkung trotz Selektion. Einflußfaktoren auf die Zuwendung zu Zeitungsinhalten.* Cologne: Böhlau.

Downs, Anthony. 1957. *An Economic Theory of Democracy.* New York: Harper and Row.

Duverger, Maurice. 1954/1951. *Political Parties.* Trans. Barbara and Robert North. New York: John Wiley & Sons.

Easton, David. 1965. *A Systems Analysis of Political Life.* New York: John Wiley & Sons.

Eilfort, Michael. 1994. *Die Nichtwähler–Wahlenthaltung als Form des Wahlverhaltens.* Paderborn: Schöningh.

Eith, Ulrich. 1995. *Interdependenzen von kommunalem Wahlverhalten und dem Wahlverhalten bei Bundes- und Landtagswahlen.* Paper presented at the KPSW conference, 28-30 September, Dresden.

Eith, Ulrich. 1997. *Wählerverhalten in Sachsen-Anhalt. Zur Bedeutung sozialstruktureller Einflußfaktoren auf die Wahlentscheidungen 1990 und 1994.* Berlin: Duncker & Humblot.

Eltermann, Ludolf K. 1978. "Zur Wahrnehmung von Kanzlerkandidaten. Imageprofilierung im Wechselspiel von Identifikation und Projektion." In *Wählerverhalten in der Bundesrepublik Deutschland,* ed. Dieter Oberndörfer. Berlin: Duncker & Humblot.

Eltermann, Ludolf K. 1980. *Kanzler und Oppositionsführer in der Wählergunst.* Stuttgart: Bonn Aktuell.

Emmert, Thomas. 1991. *Konfliktlinien, Sozialismus und Wahlverhalten. Ein sozialstruktureller Erklärungsversuch der Volkskammerwahl am 18. März 1990 in der DDR.* Masters Thesis: University of Heidelberg.

Enelow, James M., and Melvin J. Hinich. 1984. *The Spatial Theory of Voting.* Cambridge: Cambridge University Press.

Etzioni, Amitai. 1993. *The Spirit of Community: Rights, Responsibilities, and the Communitarian Agenda.* New York: Crown.

Falter, Jürgen W. 1977. "Einmal mehr. Läßt sich das Konzept der Parteiidentifikation auf deutsche Verhältnisse übertragen?" *Politische Vierteljahresschrift* 18:476-500.

Falter, Jürgen W. 1981. "Kontinuität und Neubeginn. Die Bundestagswahl 1949 zwischen Weimar und Bonn." *Politische Vierteljahresschrift* 22:236-263.

Falter, Jürgen W., and Markus Klein. 1994. "Die Wähler der PDS bei der Bundestagswahl 1994. Zwischen Ideologie, Nostalgie und Protest." *Aus Politik und Zeitgeschichte* (B51-52):22-34.

Falter, Jürgen W., and Markus Klein. 1995. "Zwischen Ideologie, Nostalgie und Protest: Die Wähler der PDS bei der Bundestagswahl 1994." In *Parteiendemokratie zwischen Kontinuität und Wandel. Die deutschen Parteien nach den Wahlen 1994,* ed. Gerhard Hirscher. Munich: Hanns-Seidel-Foundation.

Falter, Jürgen W., and Hans Rattinger. 1982. "Parties, Candidates and Issues in the German Federal Election of 1980: An Application of Normal Vote Analysis." *Electoral Studies* 1:65-94.

Falter, Jürgen W., and Hans Rattinger. 1983. "Parteien, Kandidaten und politische Streitfragen bei der Bundestagswahl 1980: Möglichkeiten und Grenzen der Normal-Vote-Analyse." In *Wahlen und politisches System. Analysen aus Anlaß der Bundestagswahl 1980,* ed. Max Kaase and Hans-Dieter Klingemann. Opladen: Westdeutscher Verlag.

Falter, Jürgen W., and Hans Rattinger 1986. "Die Bundestagswahl 1983: Eine Normalwahlanalyse." In *Wahlen und politischer Prozess. Analysen aus Anlaß der Bundestagswahl 1983*, ed. Hans-Dieter Klingemann and Max Kaase. Opladen: Westdeutscher Verlag.

Falter, Jürgen W., and Hans Rattinger. 1997. "Die deutschen Parteien im Urteil der öffentlichen Meinung 1977-1994." In *Parteiendemokratie in Deutschland*, ed. Oscar W. Gabriel, Oskar Niedermayer, and Richard Stöss. Bonn: Westdeutscher Verlag.

Falter, Jürgen W., and Siegfried Schumann. 1993. "Nichtwahl und Protestwahl: Zwei Seiten einer Medaille." *Aus Politik und Zeitgeschichte* (B11):36-49

Falter, Jürgen W., and Siegfried Schumann. 1994. "Der Nichtwähler–das unbekannte Wesen." In *Wahlen und Wähler. Analysen aus Anlaß der Bundestagswahl 1990*, ed. Hans-Dieter Klingemann and Max Kaase. Opladen: Westdeutscher Verlag.

Falter, Jürgen W., Siegfried Schumann, and Jürgen R. Winkler 1990. "Erklärungsmodelle von Wählerverhalten." *Aus Politik und Zeitgeschichte.*(B37-38):3-13.

Farah, Barbara G., and Eckart Klein. 1989. "Public Opinion Trends." In *The Election of 1988: Reports and Interpretations*, ed. Gerald M. Pomper. Chatham, NJ: Chatham House Publishers.

Faul, Erwin. 1965. "Sozialstruktur und Wahlbeteiligung." In *Wahlhandbuch 1965, Teil 3: Wahlergebnisse*, ed. Fritz Sänger and Klaus Liepelt. Frankfurt/Main: Europäische Verlagsanstalt.

FAZ (Frankfurter Allgemeine Zeitung). 1953a. "Adenauer schaltet sich erneut ein," 19 June: 3

FAZ. 1953b. "Die Erst- und Zweit-Stimme bei den Wahlen," 27 June: 3

FAZ. 1953c. "Gleiche Aussichten für Onnen und Scharnberg," 16 June: 3.

FAZ. 1953d. "Kompromißvorschlag zum Wahlgesetz," 17 June:1

FAZ. 1953e. "Teilerfolg der Gesamtdeutschen Volkspartei," 3 Aug:1

FAZ. 1953f. "Das Verfassungsgericht gegen Splitterparteien," 24 June:1.

FAZ. 1957. "Das Verfassungsgericht gegen Splitterparteien," 24 June:1

FAZ. 1958. "Die Parteispenden vor dem Verfassungsgericht," 14 May:1

FAZ. 1993a. "SPD will Parteienfinanzierungs-Entwurf trotz erheblicher Vorbehalte zustimmen," 11 Nov.:2.

FAZ. 1993b. "Parteienfinanzierung neu beschlossen," 13 Nov.:3.

FAZ. 1997. "Karlsruhe weist Klagen gegen Wahlrecht zurück," 11 April:1-2.

Feige, Andreas. 1990. "Gesellschaftliche Reflexionsprozesse und Massenkommunikation am Beispiel der DDR. Zur Funktion öffentlicher Kommunikation und besonders der Masenmedien vor und während der Massendemonstrationen im Herbst 1989." *Publizistik* 35:387-397.

Feist, Ursula. 1994. *Die Macht der Nichtwähler-Wie die Wähler den Volksparteien davonlaufen.* Munich: Knaur.

Feldman, Stanley. 1982. "Economic Self-Interest and Political Behavior." *American Journal of Political Science* 26:446-466.

Feldman, Stanley. 1983. "Economic Individualism and American Public Opinion." *American Politics Quarterly* 11:3-29.

Finkel, Steven E.. 1993. "Reexamining the 'Minimal Effects' Model in Recent Presidential Campaigns." *Journal of Politics* 55:1-21.

Finkel, Steven E., and Peter R. Schrott. 1995. "Campaign Effects on Voter Choice in the German Election of 1990." *British Journal of Political Science* 25:349-377.

Fiorina, Morris P. 1981. *Retrospective Voting in American National Elections.* New Haven, CT: Yale University Press.

Flanagan, Scott C. 1982a. "Changing Values in Advanced Industrial Societies: Inglehart´s Silent Revolution from the Perspective of Japanese Findings." *Comparative Political Studies* 14:403-444.

Flanagan, Scott C. 1982b. "Measuring Value Change in Advanced Industrial Societies. A Rejoinder to Inglehart." *Comparative Political Studies* 15:99-128.

Forschungsgruppe Wahlen. 1994a. *Bundestagswahl 1994: Eine Analyse der Wahl zum 13. Deutschen Bundestag am 16. Oktober 1994.* Mannheim: Forschungsgruppe Wahlen e.V.

Forschungsgruppe Wahlen. 1994b. "Gesamtdeutsche Bestätigung für die Bonner Regierungskoalition. Eine Analyse der Bundestagswahl 1990." In *Wahlen und Wähler. Analysen aus Anlass der Bundestagswahl 1990,* ed. Hans-Dieter Klingemann and Max Kaase. Opladen: Westdeutscher Verlag.

Frankfurter Rundschau. 1957. "Parteifinanzierung steuerlich abzugsfähig," 17 Nov.:1.

Frankovic, Kathleen. 1993. "Public Opinion in the 1992 Campaign." In *The Election of 1992,* ed. Gerald M. Pomper. Chatham, NJ: Chatham House Publishers.

Friedrichs, Jürgen. 1968. *Werte und soziales Handeln. Ein Beitrag zur soziologischen Theorie.* Tübingen: Mohr.

Fritze, Lothar. 1995. "Irritationen im deutsch-deutschen Vereinigungsprozeß." *Aus Politik und Zeitgeschichte* (B27):3-9.

Fuchs, Dieter, and Hans-Dieter Klingemann. 1990. "The Left-Right Scheme." In *Continuities in Political Action,* ed. M. Kent Jennings and Jan van Deth. New York: De Gruyter.

Fuchs, Dieter, and Robert Rohrschneider. 1998. "The Electoral Process in Unified Germany." *West European Politics,* forthcoming.

Gabriel, Oscar W. 1986. *Politische Kultur, Postmaterialismus und Materialismus in der Bundesrepublik Deutschland.* Opladen: Westdeutscher Verlag.

Gabriel, Oscar W. 1991. "Das lokale Parteiensystem zwischen Wettbewerbs- und Konsensdemokratie. Eine empirische Analyse am Beispiel von 49 Städten in Rheinland-Pfalz." In *Parteien und politische Traditionen in der Bundesrepublik Deutschland,* ed. Dieter Oberndörfer and Karl Schmitt. Berlin: Duncker und Humblot.

Gabriel, Oscar W. 1993: "Institutionenvertrauen im vereinigten Deutschland." *Aus Politik und Zeitgeschichte* (B43):3-12.

Gabriel, Oscar W. 1994a. "Die Bürger, die Parteien und die Demokratie in Westeuropa. Anmerkungen und Analysen zum Problem der Politikverdrossenheit." In *Die schwierigen Bürger,* ed. Gerd Hepp, Siegfried Schiele, and Uwe Uffelmann. Schwalbach: Wochenschau Verlag.

Gabriel, Oscar W. 1994b. "Politische Einstellungen und politische Kultur." In *Die EU-Staaten im Vergleich. Strukturen, Prozesse, Politikinhalte.* 2d ed, ed. Oscar W. Gabriel and Frank Brettschneider. Opladen: Westdeutscher Verlag.

Gabriel, Oscar W., and Frank Brettschneider. 1994. "Soziale Konflikte und Wählerverhalten: Die erste gesamtdeutsche Bundestagswahl im Kontext der längerfristigen Entwicklung des Parteiensystems der Bundesrepublik Deutschland." In *Wahlen und politische Einstellungen im vereinigten Deutschland,* ed. Hans Rattinger, Oscar W. Gabriel, and Wolfgang Jagodzinski. Frankfurt/Main: Lang.

Gabriel, Oscar W., Peter Haungs, and Matthias Zender. 1984. *Opposition in Großstadtparlamenten.* Melle: Knoth.

Gehring, Uwe W., and Jürgen Winkler. 1997. "Parteiidentifikation, Kandidaten- und Issueorientierungen als Determinanten des Wahlverhaltens in Ost- und Westdeutschland." In *Politische Orientierungen und Verhaltensweisen im vereinigten Deutschland,* ed. Oscar W. Gabriel. Opladen: Leske & Budrich.

Geiger, Theodor. 1967. *Die soziale Schichtung des deutschen Volkes.* Stuttgart: Enke Verlag.

Gelman, Andrew, and Gary King. 1993. "Why Are American Presidential Election Campaign Polls So Variable When Votes Are So Predictable?" *British Journal of Political Science* 23:409-451.

Gerhards, Jürgen. 1991. *Die Macht der Massenmedien und die Demokratie: Empirische Befunde. FS III 91-108.* Berlin: WZB.

Glastetter, Werner, Günter Högemann, and Ralf Marquardt. 1991. *Die wirtschaftliche Entwicklung in der Bundesrepublik Deutschland 1950-1989.* Frankfurt/Main: Campus.

Gluchowski, Peter. 1978. "Parteiidentifikationen im politischen System der Bundesrepublik Deutschland. Zum Problem der empirischen Überprüfung eines Konzepts unter variierten Systembedingungen." In *Wählerverhalten in der Bundesrepublik Deutschland,* ed. Dieter Oberndörfer. Berlin: Duncker und Humblot.

Gluchowski, Peter. 1983. "Wahlerfahrung und Parteiidentifikation. Zur Einbindung von Wählern in das Parteiensystem der Bundesrepublik." In *Wahlen und politisches System. Analysen aus Anlass der Bundestagswahl 1980,* ed. Max Kaase and Hans-Dieter Klingemann. Opladen: Westdeutscher Verlag.

Gluchowski, Peter. 1987. "Lebensstile und Wandel der Wählerschaft in der Bundesrepublik." *Aus Politik und Zeitgeschichte* (B12):18-32.

Gluchowski, Peter, and Hans-Joachim Veen. Forthcoming. "Entwicklung der Anhängerschaften der deutschen Parteien. Eine Langfristbetrachtung von 1953 bis 1997." *Zeitschrift für Parlamentsfragen.*

Gluchowski, Peter, and Carsten Zelle. 1992. "Demokratisierung in Ostdeutschland. Aspekte der politischen Kultur in der Periode des Systemwechsels." In *Regimewechsel. Demokratisierung und politische Kultur in Ost- und Mitteleuropa,* ed. Peter Gerlich, Fritz Plasser, and Peter A. Ulram. Vienna: Böhlau.

Gluchowski, Peter, and Carsten Zelle. 1993. "Vom Optimismus zum Realismus. Ostdeutschland auf dem Weg in das bundesrepublikanische politische System." In *Transformation oder Stagnation? Aktuelle politische Trends in Osteuropa,* ed. Fritz Plasser and Peter A. Ulram. Vienna: Signum.

Golay, John Ford. 1958. *The Founding of the Federal Republic of Germany.* Chicago: University of Chicago Press.

Golzem, Friederike, and Klaus Liepelt. 1976. "Wahlenthaltung als Regulativ: Die sporadischen Nichtwähler." In *Transfer 2, Wahlforschung: Sonden im politischen Alltag.* Opladen: Westdeutscher Verlag.

Graber, Doris A.. 1993a. *Mass Media and American Politics.* Washington, DC: Congressional Quarterly Press.

Graber, Doris A.. 1993b. "Political Communication: Scope, Progress, Promise." In *Political Science: The State of the Discipline II,* ed. Ada W. Finifter. Washington, DC: American Political Science Association.

Granberg, Donald, and Sören Holmberg. 1988. *The Political System Matters.* Cambridge: Cambridge University Press.

Gumpert, Gary, and Robert Cathcart. 1982. "The Interpersonal and Media Connection." In *Inter/Media. Interpersonal Communication in a Media World,* ed. Gary Gumpert and Robert Cathcart. New York: Oxford University Press.

Günsche, Karl-Ludwig. 1995. "Ältestenrat stimmt der Parlamentsreform zu." *Die Welt.* 23 June:2.

Gunzert, Rudolf. 1965. "Gründe der Stimmenthaltung." In *Wahlhandbuch 1965. Teil 3: Wahlergebnisse,* ed. Sänger, Fritz and Klaus Liepelt. Frankfurt/Main: Europäische Verlagsanstalt.

Heidenheimer, Arnold. 1957. "German Party Finance: The CDU." *American Political Science Review* 51:369-385.

Hermann, Dieter, and Raymund Werle. 1983. "Kommunalwahlen im Kontext der Systemebenen." *Politische Vierteljahresschrift* 24:385-405.

Herzog, Dietrich, Hilke Rebenstorf, Camilla Werner, and Bernhard Weßels. 1990. *Abgeordnete und Bürger. Ergebnisse einer Befragung der Mitglieder des 11. Deutschen Bundestages und der Bevölkerung.* Opladen: Westdeutscher Verlag.

Hibbs, Douglas A. 1982. "On the Demand for Economic Outcomes: Macroeconomic Performance and Mass Political Support in the United States, Great Britain, and Germany." *Journal of Politics* 44:426-462.

Hoffman-Jaberg, Birgit, and Dieter Roth. 1994. "Die Nichtwähler. Politische Normalität oder wachsende Distanz zu den Parteien." In *Das Superwahljahr. Deutschland vor unkalkulierbaren Regierungsmehrheiten,* ed. Wilhelm Bürklin and Dieter Roth. Cologne: Bund Verlag.

Holtz-Bacha, Christina, and Lynda Lee Kaid, ed. 1993. *Die Massenmedien im Wahlkampf. Untersuchungen aus dem Wahljahr 1990.* Opladen: Westdeutscher Verlag.

Hovland, Carl I., Irving L. Janis, and Harold H. Kelley. 1953. *Communication and Persuasion.* New Haven, CT: Yale University Press.

Huber, John D. 1989. "Values and Partisanship in Left-Right Orientations: Measuring Ideology." *European Journal of Political Research* 17:599-621.

Hunter, Alfred A., and Margaret A. Denton. 1984. "Do Female Candidates Lose Votes? The Experience of Female Candidates in the 1979 and 1980 Canadian General Elections." *Canadian Review of Sociology and Anthropology* 21:395-406.

Infas. 1994. *Politogramm Report Wahlen Bundestagswahl 1994: Wahl zum 13. Deutschen Bundestag am 16. Oktober 1994.* Bonn: Infas.

Inglehart, Ronald. 1971. "The Silent Revolution in Europe: Intergenerational Change in Post-Industrial Societies." *American Political Science Review* 65:991-1017.

Inglehart, Ronald. 1977. *The Silent Revolution: Changing Values and Political Styles Among Western Publics.* Princeton, NJ: Princeton University Press.

Inglehart, Ronald. 1985. "Aggregate Stability and Individual Level Flux in Mass Belief Systems: The Level of Analysis Paradox." *American Political Science Review* 79:97-116.

Inglehart, Ronald. 1987. "Value Change in Industrial Societies." *American Political Science Review* 81:1289-1303.

Inglehart, Ronald. 1989. *Kultureller Umbruch. Wertwandel in der westlichen Welt.* Frankfurt/Main: Campus.

Inglehart, Ronald. 1990. *Culture Shift in Advanced Industrial Society.* Princeton, NJ: Princeton University Press.

Inglehart, Ronald. 1994. "Polarized Priorities or Flexible Alternatives? Dimensionality in Inglehart's Materialism-Postmaterialism Scale. A Comment." *International Journal of Public Opinion Research* 6:289-292.

Inglehart, Ronald, and Paul R. Abramson. 1994. "Economic Security and Value Change." *American Political Science Review* 88:336-354.

Inglehart, Ronald, and Hans-Dieter Klingemann. 1976. "Party Identification, Ideological Preference and the Left-Right Dimension among Western Mass Publics." In *Party Identification and Beyond,* ed. Ian Budge, Ivor Crewe, and Dennis Farlie. London: John Wiley and Sons.

Inglehart, Ronald, and Hans-Dieter Klingemann. 1996. "Dimensionen des Wertewandels. Theoretische und methodische Reflexionen anläßlich einer neuerlichen Kritik." *Politische Vierteljahresschrift* 37:319-340.

Iyengar, Shanto, and Donald R. Kinder. 1987. *News That Matters.* Chicago: University of Chicago Press.

Jagodzinski, Wolfgang, and Steffen M. Kühnel. 1990. "Zur Schätzung der relativen Effekte von Issueorientierung, Kandidatenpräferenz und langfristiger Parteibindung auf die Wahlabsicht." In *Wahlen, Parteieliten, politische Einstellungen. Neuere Forschungsergebnisse,* ed. Karl Schmitt. Frankfurt/Main: Lang.

Jagodzinski, Wolfgang, and Steffen M. Kühnel. 1994. "Bedeutungsinvarianz und Bedeutungwandel der politischen Richtungsbegriffe 'links' und 'rechts'." In *Wahlen und politische Einstellungen im vereingten Deutschland,* ed. Hans Rattinger, Oscar W. Gabriel, and Wolfgang Jagodzinski. Frankfurt/Main: Lang.

Jagodzinski, Wolfgang, and Markus Quandt. 1997. "Wahlverhalten und Religion im Lichte der Individualisierungsthese: Anmerkungen zu dem Beitrag von Schnell und Kohler." *Kölner Zeitschrift für Soziologie und Sozialpsychologie* 49 (forthcoming).

Jesse, Eckhard. 1985. *Wahlrecht zwischen Kontinuität und Reform.* Dhsseldorf: Droste Verlag.

Jung, Helmut. 1982. *Wirtschaftliche Einstellungen und Wahlverhalten in der Bundesrepublik Deutschland. Eine Quer- und Längsschnittanalyse von 1971 bis 1976.* Paderborn: Schöningh.

Jung, Helmut. 1985. "Ökonomische Variablen und ihre politischen Folgen: Ein kritischer Literaturbericht." In *Wirtschaftlicher Wandel, religiöser Wandel und Wertwandel. Folgen für das politische Verhalten in der Bundesrepublik*, ed. Dieter Oberndörfer, Hans Rattinger, and Karl Schmitt. Berlin: Duncker & Humblot.

Jung, Matthias. 1990. "Parteiensystem und Wahlen in der DDR. Eine Analyse der Volkskammerwahl vom 18. März 1990 und der Kommunalwahlen vom 6. Mai 1990." *Aus Politik und Zeitgeschichte* (B27):3-15.

Kaack, Heino. 1967. *Zwischen Verhältniswahl und Mehrheitswahl.* Opladen: Leske Verlag.

Kaack, Heino. 1969. *Wahlkreisgeographie und Kandidatenauslese.* Opladen: Westdeutscher Verlag.

Kaack, Heino. 1971. *Geschichte und Struktur des deutschen Parteiensystems.* Opladen: Westdeutscher Verlag.

Kaack, Heino. 1988. "Die Soziale Zusammensetzung des Deutschen Bundestages." In *US-Kongress und Deutscher Bundestag*, ed. Uwe Thaysen, Roger Davidson, and Robert G. Livingston. Opladen: Westdeutscher Verlag.

Kaase, Max. 1970. "Determinanten des Wahlverhaltens bei der Bundestagswahl 1969." *Politische Vierteljahresschrift* 11:46-110.

Kaase, Max. 1984. "Personalized Proportional Representation: The 'Model' of the West German Electoral System." In *Choosing an Electoral System*, ed. Arend Lijphart and Bernard Grofman. New York: Praeger.

Kaase, Max. 1986. "Massenkommunikation und politischer Prozeß." In *Politische Wissenschaft und politische Ordnung. Analysen zur Theorie und Empirie demokratischer Regierungsweise. Festschrift zum 65. Geburtstag von Rudolf Wildenmann*, ed. Max Kaase. Opladen: Westdeutscher Verlag.

Kaase, Max. 1989a. "Fernsehen, gesellschaftlicher Wandel und politischer Prozeß." In *Massenkommunikation. Theorien, Methoden, Befunde*, ed. Max Kaase and Winfried Schulz. Opladen: Westdeutscher Verlag.

Kaase, Max. 1989b. "Mass Participation." In *Continuities in Political Action*, ed. M. Kent Jennings and Jan W. van Deth. New York: Walter de Gruyter.

Kaase, Max. 1994. "Is There Personalization in Politics? Candidates and Voting Behaviour in Germany." *International Political Science Review* 15:211-230.

Kaase, Max, and Wolfgang G. Gibowski. 1990. "Deutschland im Übergang: Parteien und Wähler vor der Bundestagswahl 1990." *Aus Politik und Zeitgeschichte* (B37-38):14-26.

Kaase, Max, and Hans-Dieter Klingemann, eds. 1990. *Wahlen und Wähler: Analysen aus Anlaß der Bundestagswahl 1987*. Opladen: Westdeutscher Verlag.

Kaase, Max, and Hans-Dieter Klingemann 1994a. "Electoral Research in the Federal Republic of Germany." *European Journal of Political Research* 25:343-366.

Kaase, Max, and Hans-Dieter Klingemann. 1994b. "Der mühsame Weg zur Entwicklung von Parteiorientierungen in einer 'neuen' Demokratie: Das Beispiel der früheren DDR." In *Wahlen und Wähler: Analysen aus Anlaß der Bundestagswahl 1990*, ed. Hans-Dieter Klingemann and Max Kaase. Opladen: Westdeutscher Verlag.

Katz, Richard, and Peter Mair. 1995. "Changing Models of Party Organization and Party Democracy: The Emergence of the Cartel Party." *Party Politics* 1:5-28.

Kepplinger, Hans Mathias. 1980. "Optische Kommentierung in der Fernsehberichterstattung über den Bundestagswahlkampf 1976." In *Politikfeld-Analysen 1979*, ed. Thomas Ellwein. Opladen: Westdeutscher Verlag.

Kepplinger, Hans Mathias. 1989. "Theorien der Nachrichtenauswahl als Theorien der Realität." *Aus Politik und Zeitgeschichte* (B15):1-16.

Kepplinger, Hans Mathias, and Hans-Bernd Brosius. 1990. "Der Einfluss der Parteibindung und der Fernsehberichterstattung auf die Wahlabsichten der Bevölkerung." In *Wahlen und Wähler. Analysen aus Anlass der Bundestagswahl 1987*, ed. Max Kaase and Hans Dieter Klingemann. Opladen: Westdeutscher Verlag.

Kepplinger, Hans Mathias, Hans-Bernd Brosius, and Stefan Dahlem. 1994a. *Wie das Fernsehen die Wahlen beeinflußt. Theoretische Modelle und empirische Analysen.* Munich: Verlag Reinhard Fischer.

Kepplinger, Hans Mathias, Hans-Bernd Brosius, and Stefan Dahlem. 1994b. "Charakter oder Sachkompetenz von Politikern: Woran orientieren sich die Wähler?" In *Wahlen und Wähler. Analysen aus Anlaß der Bundestagswahl 1990*, ed. Hans-Dieter Klingemann and Max Kaase. Opladen: Westdeutscher Verlag.

Kepplinger, Hans Mathias, Stefan Dahlem, and Hans-Bernd Brosius. 1992. "Helmut Kohl und Oskar Lafontaine im Fernsehen: Ein Experiment mit Teilnehmern in den alten und neuen Bundesländern." In *Die Massenmedien im Wahlkampf: Untersuchungen aus demWahljahr 1990*, ed. Christina Holtz-Bacha and Lynda Lee Kaid. Opladen: Westdeutscher Verlag.

Kepplinger, Hans Mathias, Klaus Gotto, Hans-Bernd Brosius, and Dietmar Haak. 1989. *Der Einfluß der Fernsehnachrichten auf die politische Meinungsbildung.* Freiburg: Alber.

Kevenhörster, Paul. 1983. "Kommunalwahlen: Instrument bürgerlicher Einflußnahme auf die Politik?" In *Bürgerbeteiligung und kommunale Demokratie*, ed. Oscar W. Gabriel. Munich: Minerva.

Key, V.O. 1952. *Politics, Parties and Pressure Groups.* 3rd ed. New York: Crowell.

Kiewiet, D. Roderick. 1983. *Macroeconomics and Micropolitics.* Chicago: University of Chicago Press.

Kindelmann, Klaus. 1994. *Kanzlerkandidaten in den Medien. Eine Analyse des Wahljahres 1990*. Opladen: Westdeutscher Verlag.

Kinder, Donald R., and D. Roderick Kiewiet. 1981. "Sociotropic Politics." *British Journal of Political Science* 11:129-161.

Kirchgässner, Gebhard. 1986. "Economic Conditions and the Popularity of West German Parties: A Survey." *European Journal of Political Research* 14:421-439.

Kirchgässner, Gebhard. 1991. "On the Relation Between Voting Intention and the Perception of the General Economic Situation: An Empirical Analysis for the FRG, 1972-1986." *European Journal of Political Economy* 7:497-526.

Kirchheimer, Otto. 1965. "Der Wandel des westeuropäischen Parteiensystems." *Politische Vierteljahresschrift* 8:20-41.

Kitschelt, Herbert. 1994. *The Transformation of European Social Democracy*. New York: Cambridge University Press.

Kitschelt, Herbert in collaboration with Anthony J. McGann. 1995. *The Radical Right in Western Europe. A Comparative Analysis*. Ann Arbor: University of Michigan Press.

Kitzinger, U. W. 1960. *German Electoral Politics*. Oxford: Clarendon Press.

Klages, Helmut. 1985. *Wertorientierungen im Wandel: Rückblick, Gegenwartsanalysen, Prognosen*. 2d ed. Frankfurt/Main: Campus.

Klages, Helmut. 1992. "Die gegenwärtige Situation der Wert- und Wertwandels-forschung–Probleme und Perspektiven." In *Werte und Wandel. Ergebnisse und Methoden einer Forschungstradition*, ed. Helmut Klages, Hans Jürgen Hippler, and Willi Herbert. Frankfurt/Main: Campus.

Klapper, Joseph T. 1960. *The Effects of Mass Communication*. New York: The Free Press.

Klein, Markus. 1995. "Wieviel Platz bleibt im Prokrustesbett? Wertewandel in der Bundesrepublik Deutschland zwischen 1973 und 1992 gemessen anhand des Inglehart-Index." *Kölner Zeitschrift für Soziologie und Sozialpsychologie* 47:207-230

Klein, Markus, and Claudio Caballero. 1996. "Rhckwärtsgewandt in die Zukunft. Die Wähler der PDS bei der Bundestagswahl 1994." *Politische Vierteljahresschrift* 37:229-247.

Kleinhenz, Thomas. 1995. *Die Nichtwähler: Ursachen der sinkenden Wahlbeteiligung in Deutschland*. Opladen: Westdeutscher Verlag.

Kleppner, Paul. 1982. *Who voted? The Dynamics of Electoral Turnout 1870-1980*. New York: Praeger.

Klingemann, Hans-Dieter. 1979. "Measuring Ideological Conceptualizations." In *Political Action: Mass Participation in Five Western Democracies*, ed. Samuel H. Barnes and Max Kaase. Beverly Hills, CA: Sage.

Klingemann, Hans-Dieter. 1982. "Fakten oder Programmatik?" *Politische Vierteljahresschrift* 23:214-224.

Klingemann, Hans-Dieter. 1985. "West Germany." In *Electoral Change in Western Democracies. Patterns and Sources of Electoral Volatility*, ed. Ivor Crewe and David Denver. London: Croom Helm.

Klingemann, Hans-Dieter. 1986. "Massenkommunikation, interpersonale Kommunikation und politische Einstellungen. Zur Kritik der These vom 'Zwei-Stufen Fluß' der politischen Kommunikation." In *Politische Wissenschaft und politische Ordnung. Analysen zur Theorie und Empirie demokratischer Regierungsweise. Festschrift zum 65. Geburtstag von Rudolf Wildenmann*, ed. Max Kaase. Opladen: Westdeutscher Verlag.

Klingemann, Hans-Dieter, and Max Kaase, ed. 1994. *Wahlen und Wähler. Analysen aus Anlaß der Bundestagswahl 1994*. Opladen: Westdeutscher Verlag.

Klingemann, Hans-Dieter, and Jacob Steinwede. 1993. "Traditionelle Kerngruppenbindung der Wähler in der Bundesrepublik: Stabilität oder Veränderung in den achtziger Jahren?" In *Wohlfahrtsstaat, Sozialstruktur und Verfassungsanalyse*, ed. Hans-Dieter Klingemann and Wolfgang Luthardt. Opladen: Westdeutscher Verlag.

Klingemann, Hans-Dieter, and Charles Lewis Taylor. 1977. "Affektive Parteiorientierung, Kanzlerkandidaten und Issues. Einstellungskomponenten der Wahlentscheidung bei Bundestagswahlen in Deutschland." *Politische Vierteljahresschrift* 18:301-347

Klingemann, Hans-Dieter, Hans-Joachim Veen, Peter Gluchowski, Bernhard Weßels, and Carsten Zelle. 1998. *Nichtwähler-Wechselwähler-Parteibindungen*. Bonn (forthcoming)

Klingemann, Hans-Dieter, and Katrin Voltmer. 1989. "Massenmedien als Brücke zur Welt der Politik. Nachrichtennutzung und politische Beteiligungsbereitschaft." In *Massenkommunikation. Theorien, Methoden, Befunde*, ed. Max Kaase and Winfried Schulz. Opladen: Westdeutscher Verlag.

Klingemann, Hans-Dieter, and Martin P. Wattenberg. 1990. "Zerfall und Entwicklung von Parteiensystemen: Ein Vergleich der Vorstellungsbilder von den politischen Parteien in den Vereinigten Staaten von Amerika und der Bundesrepublik Deutschland." In *Wahlen und Wähler. Analysen aus Anlaß der Bundestagswahl 1987*, ed. Max Kaase, and Hans-Dieter Klingemann. Opladen: Westdeutscher Verlag.

Klingemann, Hans-Dieter, and Martin P. Wattenberg. 1992. "Decaying Versus Developing Party Systems: A Comparison of Party Images in the United States and West Germany." *British Journal of Political Science* 22:131-149.

Kluckhohn, Clyde. 1951. "Values and Value Orientations in the Theory of Action. An Exploration in Definition and Classification." In *Toward a General Theory of Action*, ed. Talcott Parsons and Edward Shils. Cambridge, MA: Harvard University Press.

Kolinsky, Eva. 1991. "Political Participation and Parliamentary Careers: Women's Quotas in West Germany." *West European Politics* 14:56-72.

Köser, Helmut. 1991. "Der Gemeinderat in Baden-Württemberg. Sozialprofil, Rekrutierung, Politikverständnis." In *Kommunalpolitik in Baden-Württemberg,* ed. Theodor Pfizer and Hans-Georg Wehling. 2nd ed. Stuttgart: Kohlhammer.

Kramer, Gerald H. 1983. "The Ecological Fallacy Revisited: Aggregate- versus Individual-Level Findings on Economics and Elections, and Sociotropic Voting." *American Political Science Review* 77:92-111.

Küchler, Manfred. 1986. "Wahl- und Surveyforschung." In *Politikwissenschaft in der Bundesrepublik Deutschland. Sonderheft 17 der Politischen Vierteljahresschrift,* ed. Klaus von Beyme. Opladen: Westdeutscher Verlag.

Lancaster, Thomas D. 1994. "Incumbency Advantage, German Style: An Analysis of 'Double' Candidates in a Two Vote Electoral System." Paper presented at the Annual Meeting of the Midwest Political Science Association, Chicago.

Lancaster, Thomas D., and Rebecca Davis. 1992. "European Electoral Structures and Women's Political Participation: A Comparative Study in the Federal Republic of Germany." Paper presented at the Midwest Political Science Association Annual Meeting, Chicago.

Lancaster, Thomas D., and W. David Patterson. 1990. "Comparative Pork Barrel Politics: Perceptions from the West German Bundestag." *Comparative Political Studies* 22:458-477.

Landfried, Christine. 1990. *Parteifinanzen und politische Macht.* Baden-Baden: Nomos Verlagsgesellschaft.

Lange, Erhard. 1975. *Wahlrecht und Innenpolitik.* Meisenheim am Glan: Verlag Anton Hain.

Lass, Jürgen. 1995. *Vorstellungsbilder über Kanzlerkandidaten. Zur Diskussion um die Personalisierung von Politik.* Opladen: Deutscher Universitäts-Verlag

Laver, Michael, and Norman Schofield. 1990. *Multiparty Government:The Politics of Coalition in Europe.* Oxford: Oxford University Press.

Lavies, Ralf-Rainer. 1973. *Nichtwählen als Kategorie des Wahlverhaltens.* Düsseldorf: Droste.

Lazarsfeld, Paul. F., Bernard Berelson, and Hazel Gaudet. 1944. *The People's Choice.* New York: Columbia University Press.

Lazarsfeld, Paul F., Bernard Berelson, and Hazel Gaudet. 1968. *The People's Choice.* 3rd ed. New York: Columbia Unversity Press.

Lehoucq, Fabrice. 1995. "Institutional Change and Political Conflict: Evaluating Alternative Explanations of Electoral Reform in Costa Rica." *Electoral Studies* 14:23-45

Leighley, Jan E., and Jonathan Nagler. 1992. "Individual and Systemic Influences on Turnout: Who Votes? 1984." *Journal of Politics* 54:718-740.

Leithner, Christian. 1993. "Economic Conditions and the Vote: A Contingent Rather Than Categorial Influence." *British Journal of Political Science* 23:339-372.

Lepsius, M. Rainer. 1966. "Parteiensystem und Sozialstruktur: Zum Problem der Demokratisierung der deutschen Gesellschaft." In *Wirtschaft, Geschichte und Wirtschaftsgeschichte*, ed. Wilhelm Abel and Knut Borchardt. Stuttgart: G. Fischer.

Lepsius, M. Rainer. 1973. "Parteiensystem und Sozialstruktur: zum Problem der Demokratisierung der deutschen Gesellschaft." In *Deutsche Parteien vor 1918*, ed. Gerhard A. Ritter. Cologne: Kiepenheuer & Witsch.

Lewis-Beck, Michael S. 1988. *Economics and Elections: The Major Western Democracies.* Ann Arbor: University of Michigan Press.

Lewis-Beck, Michael S., and Brad Lockerbie. 1989. "Economics, Votes, Protests: Western European Cases." *Comparative Political Studies* 22:155-177.

Lücke, Paul. 1968. *Ist Bonn doch Weimar?* Frankfurt/Main: Verlag Ullstein.

Lijphart, Arend. 1994. *Electoral Systems and Party Systems.* Oxford: Oxford University Press.

Lippmann, Walter. 1922. *Public Opinion.* London: Allen & Unwin.

Lipset, Seymour M. 1960. *Political Man.* New York: Doubleday.

Lipset, Seymour M. 1972. "Ideology and No End: The Controversy Till Now." *Encounter* 39(6):17-24.

Lipset, Seymour M. 1981. *Political Man. The Social Basis of Politics.* 2d ed. Baltimore: The Johns Hopkins University Press.

Lipset, Seymour M., and Stein Rokkan. 1967. "Cleavage Structures, Party Systems, and Voter Alignments: An Introduction." In *Party Systems and Voter Alignments: Cross-National Perspectives,* ed. Seymour M. Lipset and Stein Rokkan. New York: Free Press.

Lockerbie, Brad. 1993. "Economic Dissatisfaction and Political Alienation in Western Europe." *European Journal of Political Research* 23:281-293.

Lodge, Milton, Marco R. Steenbergen, and Shawn Brau. 1995. "The Responsive Voter: Campaign Information and the Dynamics of Candidate Evaluation." *American Political Science Review* 89:309-326.

Loewenberg, Gerhard. 1967. *Parliament in the German Political System.* Ithaca, NY: Cornell University Press.

Loewenberg, Gerhard and Samuel Patterson. 1979. *Comparing Legislatures.* Boston: Little, Brown.

Löffler, Berthold, and Walter Rogg. 1991. "Kommunalwahlen und kommunales Wahlverhalten." In *Kommunalpolitik in Baden-Württemberg 2d ed.* ed. Theodor Pfizer and Hans-Georg Wehling. 2d ed. Stuttgart: Kohlhammer.

Maag, Gisela. 1991. *Gesellschaftliche Werte. Strukturen, Stabilität und Funktion.* Opladen: Westdeutscher Verlag.

MacKuen, Michael, Robert S. Erikson, James A. Stimson. 1989. "Macropartisanship." *American Political Science Review* 83:1125-1142.

March, James G., and Johan P. Olsen. 1989. *Rediscovering Institutions: The Organizational Bases of Politics.* New York: Free Press.

Marciniak, Friedhelm. 1978. *Wahlverhalten in Nordrhein-Westfalen 1948-1970. Eine statistisch-ökologische Analyse.* Cologne: Böhlau.

Markus, Gregory B. 1982. "Political Attitudes During an Election Year: A Report on the 1980 NES Panel Study." *American Political Science Review* 76:538-560.

Markus, Gregory B. 1988. "The Impact of Personal and National Economic Conditions on the Presidential Vote: A Pooled Cross-Sectional Analysis." *American Journal of Political Science* 32:135-154.

Marsh, Alan. 1975. "The Silent Revolution, Value Priorities and the Quality of Life in Britain." *American Political Science Review* 69:21-30.

Maslow, Abraham H. 1954. *Motivation and Personality.* New York: Harper and Row.

Mathes, Rainer, and Uwe Freisens. 1990. "Kommunikationsstrategien der Parteien und ihr Erfolg. Eine Analyse der aktuellen Berichterstattung in den Nachrichtenmagazinen der öffentlich-rechtlichen und privaten Rundfunkanstalten im Bundestagswahlkampf 1987." *In Wahlen und Wähler. Analysen aus Anlaß der Bundestagswahl 1987,* ed. Max Kaase and Hans-Dieter Klingemann. Opladen: Westdeutscher Verlag.

Matland, Richard E. 1994. "Putting Scandinavian Equality to the Test: An Experimental Evaluation of Gender Stereotyping of Political Candidates in a Sample of Norwegian Voters." *British Journal of Political Science* 24:66-85.

Mayer, Hans-Ludwig. 1991. "Wählerverhalten bei der Bundestagswahl 1990 nach Geschlecht und Alter." In *Wirtschaft und Statistik,* ed. Statistisches Bundesamt. Wiesbaden: Statistisches Bundesamt.

McDonald, Daniel G., and Stephen D. Reese. 1987. "Television News and Audience Selectivity." *Journalism Quarterly* 64:763-768.

McLeod, Jack M., and Daniel G. McDonald. 1985. "Beyond Simple Exposure. Media Orientations and Their Impact on Political Processes." *Communication Research* 12:3-33.

Meier, Artur. 1990. "Abschied von der sozialistischen Ständegesellschaft." *Aus Politik und Zeitgeschichte* (B16-17):3 - 14.

Metje, Matthias. 1994. *Wählerschaft und Sozialstruktur im Generationenwechsel.* Wiesbaden: Deutscher Universitäts-Verlag.

Meulemann, Heiner. 1985. "Säkularisierung und Politik, Wertewandel und Wertstruktur in der Bundesrepublik Deutschland." *Politische Vierteljahresschrift* 26:29-51.

Mielke, Gerd, and Ulrich Eith. 1994. *Honoratioren oder Parteisoldaten? Eine Untersuchung der Gemeinderatskandidaten bei der Kommunalwahl 1989 in Freiburg.* Bochum: Brockmeyer.

Milbrath, Lester W. 1965. *Political Participation. How and Why Do People Get Involved in Politics?* Chicago: Rand McNally.

Miller, Warren E. 1992. "The Puzzle Transformed: Explaining Declining Turnout." *Political Behavior* 14:1-43.

Miller, Warren E. 1995. "An Organizational History of the Intellectual Origins of the American National Election Studies." *European Journal of Political Research* 25:247-265.

Misselwitz, Hans-J. 1996. *Nicht länger mit dem Gesicht nach Westen. Das neue Selbstbewußtsein der Ostdeutschen.* Bonn: Dietz.

Moreau, Patrick, and Viola Neu. 1994. *Die PDS zwischen Linksextremismus und Linkspopulismus.* St. Augustin: Konrad-Adenauer-Stiftung (Interne Studien Nr. 76).

Mueller, Emil Peter. 1983. *Soziale Strukturen im X. Deutschen Bundestag.* Cologne: Deutscher Instituts-Verlag.

Müller, Wolfgang. 1993. "The Relevance of the State for Party System Change," *Journal of Theoretical Politics* 5:419-454.

Müller-Schneider, Thomas. 1994. *Schichten und Erlebnismilieus. Der Wandel der Milieustruktur in der Bundesrepublik Deutschland.* Wiesbaden: Deutscher Universitäts Verlag.

Naßmacher, Karl-Heinz. 1979. "Zerfall einer liberalen Subkultur - Kontinuität und Wandel des Parteiensystems in der Region Oldenburg." In *Vom Milieu zur Volkspartei: Funktionen und Wandlungen der Parteien im kommunalen und regionalen Bereich*, ed. Herbert Kühr. Königstein: Hain Verlag.

Naßmacher, Karl-Heinz. 1989a. "Structure and Impact of Public Subsidies to Political Parties in Europe: The Examples of Austria, Italy, Sweden and West Germany." In *Comparative Political Finance in the 1980s*, ed. Herbert Alexander. Cambridge: Cambridge University Press.

Naßmacher, Karl-Heinz. 1989b. "Parteienfinanzierung als verfassungspolitisches Problem." *Aus Politik und Zeitgeschichte* (B11): 27-38.

Neu, Viola. 1994. "Sympathisantenpotentiale und Wählerhochburgen. " In Patrick Moreau and Viola Neu, *Die PDS zwischen Linksextremismus und Linkspopulismus*. Sankt Augustin: Konrad-Adenauer-Stiftung (Internal Studies 76/1994).

Neu, Viola. 1995a. "Die PDS im deutschen Parteiensystem: Wähler und Sympathisanten." In Jürgen P. Lang, Patrick Moreau, and Viola Neu, *Auferstanden aus Ruinen . . . ? Die PDS nach dem Superwahljahr 1994*. Sankt Augustin: Konrad-Adenauer-Stiftung. (Internal Studies 111/1995).

Neu, Viola. 1995b. "Die PDS nach dem Super-Wahljahr: Zwischen Aufbruch und Stagnation?" *Civis* 2/1995:35-45.

Neugebauer, Gero, and Richard Stöss. 1996. *Die PDS. Geschichte. Organisation. Wähler. Konkurrenten.* Opladen: Leske & Budrich.

Niclauß, Karlheinz. 1988. *Kanzlerdemokratie: Bonner Regierungspraxis von Konrad Adenauer bis Helmut Kohl*. Stuttgart: Metzler.

Nie, Norman H., Sidney Verba, and John R. Petrocik. 1976. *The Changing American Voter*. Cambridge, MA: Harvard University Press.

Niedermayer, Oskar. 1992. "Vergleichende Umfrageforschung." In *Vergleichende Politikwissenschaft*, ed. Dirk Berg-Schlosser and Ferdinand Müller-Rommel. 2nd Ed. Opladen: Leske und Budrich.

Noelle-Neumann, Elisabeth. 1977. "Das doppelte Meinungsklima. Der Einfluß des Fernsehens im Wahlkampf 1976." In *Wahlsoziologie heute. Analysen aus Anlaß der Bundestagswahl 1976,* ed. Max Kaase. Opladen: Westdeutscher Verlag.

Noelle-Neumann, Elisabeth. 1980. *Die Schweigespirale. Öffentliche Meinung - unsere soziale Haut.* Munich: Piper.

Noelle-Neumann, Elisabeth. 1982. "Fernsehen und Lesen. Ein Werkstatt-Bericht." *Gutenberg-Jahrbuch* 57:35-46.

Noelle-Neumann, Elisabeth. 1994. "Wirkung der Massenmedien auf die Meinungsbildung." In *Publizistik. Massenkommunikation,* ed. Elisabeth Noelle-Neumann, Winfried Schulz, and Jürgen Wilke. Frankfurt/Main: Fischer Taschenbuch Verlag.

Nohlen, Dieter. 1984. "Changes and Choices in Electoral Systems." In *Choosing and Electoral System: Issues and Alternatives*, ed. Arend Lijphart and Bernard Grofman. New York: Praeger.

Norpoth, Helmut. 1977. "Kanzlerkandidaten. Wie sie vom Wähler bewertet werden und seine Wahlentscheidung beeinflussen." *Politische Vierteljahresschrift* 18:551-572.

Norpoth, Helmut. 1978. "Party Identification in West Germany. Tracing an Elusive Concept." *Comparative Political Studies* 11:36-61.

Norris, Pippa, Elizabeth Vallance, and Joni Lovenduski. 1992. "Do Candidates Make a Difference? Gender, Race, Ideology and Incumbency." *Parliamentary Affairs* 45:496-517.

Oberndörfer, Dieter, ed. 1978. *Wählerverhalten in der Bundesrepublik: Studien zu ausgewählten Problemen der Wahlforschung aus Anlaß der Bundestagswahl 1976.* Berlin: Duncker & Humblot.

Oberndörfer, Dieter, and Gerd Mielke. 1990. *Stabilität und Wandel in der westdeutschen Wählerschaft. Das Verhältnis von Sozialstruktur und Wahlverhalten im Zeitraum von 1976 bis 1987.* Freiburg: Arnold Bergstraesser Institut.

Oberndörfer, Dieter, Gerd Mielke, and Ulrich Eith. 1994. "In den Siegesbechern der Parteien finden sich Wermutstropfen." *Frankfurter Rundschau* No. 24:16.

Oberndörfer, Dieter, and Karl Schmitt, ed. 1991. *Parteien und politische Traditionen in der Bundesrepublik Deutschland.* Berlin: Duncker und Humblot.

O'Keefe, Garrett J., and Harold Mendelsohn. 1978. "Nonvoting. The Media's Role." In *Deviance and Mass Media, Vol. 2,* ed. Charles Winick. Beverly Hills, CA: Sage.

Padgett, Stephen. 1989. "The Party System." In *Developments in West German Politics,* ed. Gordon Smith et al. London: Macmillan.

Padgett, Stephen, ed. 1993. *Parties and Party Systems in the New Germany.* Aldershot: Dartmouth.

Panebianco, Angelo. 1988. *Political Parties: Organization and Power.* New York: Cambridge University Press.

Pappi, Franz U. 1973. "Parteiensystem und Sozialstruktur in der Bundesrepublik." *Politische Vierteljahresschrift* 14:191-213.

Pappi, Fanz U. 1976. "Sozialstruktur und Bundestagswahlen aus kommunalpolitischer Sicht." *Kommunales Wahlverhalten.* Bonn: Eichholz.

Pappi, Franz U. 1977. "Sozialstruktur, gesellschaftliche Wertorientierungen und Wahlabsicht. Ergebnisse eines Zeitvergleichs des deutschen Elektorats 1953 und 1976." In *Wahlsoziologie heute: Analysen aus Anlaß der Bundestagswahl 1976,* ed. Max Kaase. *Sonderheft der Politischen Vierteljahresschrift* 18:195-229.

Pappi, Franz U. 1985. "Die konfessionell-religiöse Konfliktlinie in der deutschen Wähler-schaft: Entstehung, Stabilität und Wandel.ä In *Wirtschaftlicher Wandel, religiöser Wandel und Wertwandel. Folgen für das politische Verhalten in der Bundesrepublik,* ed. Dieter Oberndörfer, Hans Rattinger, and Karl Schmitt. Berlin: Duncker & Humblot.

Pappi, Franz U. 1990. "Klassenstruktur und Wahlverhalten." In *Wahlen und Wähler: Analysen aus Anlaß der Bundestagswahl 1987,* ed. Max Kaase and Hans-Dieter Klingemann. Opladen: Westdeutscher Verlag.

Pappi, Franz U. 1991. "Wahrgenommenes Parteiensystem und Wahlentscheidung in Ost- und Westdeutschland." *Aus Politik und Zeitgeschichte* (B44):15-26.

Pappi, Franz U., and Edward O. Laumann. 1974. "Gesellschaftliche Wertorientierungen und politisches Verhalten." *Zeitschrift für Soziologie* 3:157-188.

Parsons, Talcott. 1980. "Über den Begriff 'Commitments'." In *Zur Theorie der sozialen Interaktionsmedien,* ed. Talcott Parsons. Opladen: Westdeutscher Verlag.

Patterson, Thomas E. 1980. *The Mass Media Election. How Americans Choose Their Presidents.* New York: Praeger.

Patterson, Thomas E. 1989. "The Press and Its Missed Assignment." In *The Elections of 1988,* ed. M. Nelson. Washington: Congressional Quarterly Press.

Patterson, Thomas E., and Robert D. McClure. 1976. *The Unseeing Eye. The Myth of Television Power in National Elections.* New York: Putnam.

Pfetsch, Barbara. 1994. "Themenkarrieren und politische Kommunikation. Zum Verhältnis von Politik und Medien bei der Entstehung der politischen Agenda." *Aus Politik und Zeitgeschichte* (B39):11-20.

Poguntke, Thomas. 1995. "Parties in a Legalistic Culture: The Case of Germany." In *How Parties Organize,* ed. Richard Katz and Peter Mair. London: Sage Publications.

Popkin, Samuel. 1992. *The Reasoning Voter: Communication and Persuasion in Presidential Campaigns.* Chicago: University of Chicago Press.

Powell, G. Bingham Jr., and Guy D. Whitten. 1993. "A Cross-National Analysis of Economic Voting: Taking Account of the Political Context." *American Journal of Political Science* 37:391-414.

Przeworski, Adam. 1991. *Democracy and the Market. Political and Economic Reforms in Eastern Europe and Latin America.* New York: Cambridge University Press.

Radtke, Günter D. 1972. *Stimmenthaltung bei politischen Wahlen in der Bundesrepublik Deutschland.* Meisenheim am Glan: Verlag Anton Hain.

Radunski, Peter. 1980. *Wahlkämpfe: Moderne Wahlkampfführung als Politische Kommunikation.* Munich: Olzog.

Rae, Douglas. 1968. "A Note on the Fractionalisation of Some European Party Sytems." *Comparative Political Studies* 1:413-418.

Raschke, Joachim. 1965. *Wahlen und Wahlrecht.* Berlin: Colloquium Verlag.

Rattinger, Hans. 1980. *Wirtschaftliche Konjunktur und politische Wahlen in der Bundesrepublik Deutschland.* Berlin: Dunker & Humblot.

Rattinger, Hans. 1983. "Arbeitslosigkeit, Apathie und Protestpotential: Zu den Auswirkungen der Arbeitsmarktlage auf das Wahlverhalten bei der Bundestagswahl 1980." In *Wahlen und politisches System. Analysen aus Anlaß der Bundestagswahl 1980*, ed. Max Kaase, and Hans-Dieter Klingemann. Opladen: Westdeutscher Verlag.

Rattinger, Hans. 1985. "Allgemeine und persönliche wirtschaftliche Lage als Bestimmungsfaktoren politischen Verhaltens bei der Bundestagswahl 1983." In *Wirtschaftlicher Wandel, religiöser Wandel, Wertwandel: Folgen für das politische Verhalten in der Bundesrepublik Deutschland*, ed. Dieter Oberndörfer, Hans Rattinger, and Karl Schmitt. Berlin: Duncker & Humblot.

Rattinger, Hans. 1986. "Collective and Individual Economic Judgments and Voting in West Germany, 1961-1984." *European Journal of Political Research* 14:393-419.

Rattinger, Hans. 1991. "Unemployment and Elections in West Germany." In *Economics and Politics: The Calculus of Support*, ed. Helmut Norpoth, Michael S. Lewis-Beck, and Jean-Dominique Lafay. Ann Arbor: University of Michigan Press.

Rattinger, Hans. 1993. "Abkehr von den Parteien? Dimensionen der Parteiverdrossenheit." *Aus Politik und Zeitgeschichte* (B11):24-35.

Rattinger, Hans. 1994a. "Parteineigungen, Sachfragen- und Kandidatenorientierung in Ost- und Westdeutschland 1990-1992." In *Wahlen und politische Einstellungen im vereinigten Deutschland*, ed. Hans Rattinger, Oscar W. Gabriel, and Wolfgang Jagodzinski. Frankfurt/Main: Lang.

Rattinger, Hans. 1994b. "Demographie und Politik in Deutschland: Befunde der repräsentativen Wahlstatistik 1953-1980." In *Wahlen und Wähler. Analysen aus Anlaß der Bundestagswahl 1990*, ed. Hans-Dieter Klingemann and Max Kaase. Opladen: Westdeutscher Verlag.

Rattinger, Hans. 1994c. "Parteiidentifikationen in Ost- und Westdeutschland nach der Vereinigung." In *Politische Kultur in Ost- und Westdeutschland*, ed. Oskar Niedermayer and Klaus von Beyme. Berlin: Akademie-Verlag.

Rattinger, Hans, and Zoltán Juhász. 1990. "Wirtschaftslage und Zufriedenheit mit dem politischen System in der Bundesrepublik Deutschland 1972-1987." *Wahlen, Parteieliten, politische Einstellungen: Neuere Forschungsergebnisse*, ed. Karl Schmitt. Frankfurt/Main: Lang.

Rattinger, Hans, and Jürgen Krämer. 1995. "Wahlbeteiligung und Wahlnorm in der Bundesrepublik Deutschland: Eine Kausalanalyse." *Politische Vierteljahresschrift* 36: 267-285.

Rattinger, Hans, and Walter Puschner. 1981. "Ökonomie und Politik in der Bundesrepublik Deutschland. Wirtschaftslage und Wahlverhalten 1953-1980." *Politische Vierteljahresschrift* 22:264-286.

Reiser, Stefan. 1994. "Politik und Massenmedien im Wahlkampf. Thematisierungsstrategien und Wahlkampfmanagement." *Media Perspektiven* (7):341-348.

348   *Bibliography*

Reiter, Howard L. 1979. "Why is Turnout Down?" *Public Opinion Quarterly* 43:297-311.

Roberts, Geoffrey. 1988. "The German Federal Republic: The Two-Lane Route to Bonn." In *Candidate Selection in Comparative Perspective: The Secret Garden of Politics,* ed. Michael Gallagher and Michael Marsh. London: Sage.

Robinson, Michael J. 1976. "Public Affairs Television and the Growth of Political Malaise: The Case of 'The Selling of the Pentagon'." *American Political Science Review* 70:409-432.

Rockeach, Milton. 1973. *The Nature of Human Values.* New York: Free Press.

Rose, Richard, and Ian McAllister. 1986. *Voters Begin to Choose. From Closed Class to Open Elections in Britain.* London: Sage.

Roth, Dieter. 1990. "Die Wahlen zur Volkskammer der DDR. Der Versuch einer Erklärung." *Politische Vierteljahresschrift* 31:369-393.

Roth, Dieter. 1992. "Sinkende Wahlbeteiligung-eher Normalisierung oder Krisensymptom." In *Protestwähler und Wahlverweigerer,* ed. Karl Starzacher, Konrad Schacht, Bernd Friedrich and Thomas Leif. Cologne: Bund.

Roth, Dieter. 1994. "Was bewegt die Wähler?" *Aus Politik und Zeitgeschichte* (B11):3-13.

Rudzio, Wolfgang. 1987. *Das politische System der Bundesrepublik Deutschland,* 2d ed. Opladen: UTB.

Rule, Wilma. 1987. "Electoral Systems, Contextual Factors and Women's Opportunity for Election to Parliament in Twenty-Three Democracies." *Western Political Quarterly* 40:477-498.

Sarcinelli, Ulrich. 1987. *Symbolische Politik. Zur Bedeutung sympolischer Politik in der Wahlkampfkommunikation.* Opladen: Westdeutscher Verlag.

Sarcinelli, Ulrich. 1991. "Massenmedien und Politikvermittlung-eine Problem- und Forschungsskizze." *Rundfunk und Fernsehen* 39:469-486.

Sartori, Giovanni. 1976. *Parties and Party Systems: A Framework for Analysis.* Cambridge: Cambridge University Press.

Schenk, Michael. 1994. "Meinungsbildung im Alltag-Zum Einfluß von Meinungsfhhrern und sozialen Netzwerken." In *Politik und Medien. Analysen zur Entwicklung der politischen Kommunikation,* ed. Michael Jäckel and Peter Winterhoff-Spurk. Berlin: Vistas.

Schenk, Michael, and Uwe Pfenning. 1990. "Politische Massenkommunikation: Wirkung trotz geringer Beteiligung? Neue Strategien der Persuasion." *Politische Vierteljahresschrift* 31:420-435.

Schindler, Peter. 1983. *Datenhandbuch zur Geschichte des Deutschen Bundestages 1949 bis 1982.* Baden-Baden: Nomos.

Schindler, Peter. 1984. *Datenhandbuch zur Geschichte des Deutschen Bundestages 1949 bis 1982*. Baden-Baden: Nomos.

Schindler, Peter. 1986. *Datenhandbuch zur Geschichte des Deutschen Bundestages 1980 bis 1984*. Baden-Baden: Nomos.

Schindler, Peter. 1988. *Datenhandbuch zur Geschichte des Deutschen Bundestages 1980 bis 1987*. Baden-Baden: Nomos.

Schindler, Peter. 1994. *Datenhandbuch zur Geschichte des Deutschen Bundestages 1983 bis 1991*. Baden-Baden: Nomos.

Schmitt, Karl. 1985. "Religiöse Bestimmungsfaktoren des Wahlverhaltens: Entkonfessionalisierung mit Verspätung?" In *Wirtschaftlicher Wandel, religiöser Wandel und Wertwandel. Folgen für das politische Verhalten in der Bundesrepublik,* ed. Dieter Oberndörfer, Hans Rattinger, and Karl Schmitt. Berlin: Duncker & Humblot.

Schmitt, Karl. 1989. *Konfession und Wahlverhalten in der Bundesrepublik Deutschland.* Berlin: Duncker & Humblot.

Schmitt, Karl. 1993. "Politische Landschaften im Umbruch. Das Gebiet der ehemaligen DDR 1928-1990." In *Wahlen in Zeiten des Umbruchs,* ed. Oscar W. Gabriel and Klaus G. Troitzsch. Frankfurt/Main: Lang.

Schmitt, Karl. 1994. "Im Osten nichts Neues? Das Kernland der deutschen Arbeiterbewegung und die Zukunft der politischen Linken." In *Das Superwahljahr. Deutschland vor unkalkulierbaren Regierungsmehrheiten?,* ed. Wilhelm Bürklin and Dieter Roth. Cologne: Bund-Verlag.

Schmitt, Karl. 1995. "Die Landtagswahlen 1994 im Osten Deutschlands. Früchte des Föderalismus: Personalisierung und Regionalisierung." *Zeitschrift für Parlamentsfragen* 26:261-295.

Schmitt-Beck, Rüdiger. 1994a. "Eine 'vierte Gewalt'? Medieneinfluß im Superwahljahr 1994." In *Das Superwahljahr. Deutschland vor unkalkulierbaren Regierungsmehrheiten?* ed. Wilhelm Bürklin and Dieter Roth. Cologne: Bund-Verlag.

Schmitt-Beck, Rüdiger. 1994b. "Intermediation Environments of West German and East German Voters: Interpersonal Communication and Mass Communication During the First All-German Election Campaign." *European Journal of Communication* 9:381-419.

Schmitt-Beck, Rüdiger, and Barbara Pfetsch. 1994. "Politische Akteure und die Medien der Massenkommunikation. Zur Generierung von Öffentlichkeit in Wahlkämpfen." In *Öffentlichkeit, öffentliche Meinung, soziale Bewegungen,* ed. Friedhelm Neidhardt. Opladen: Westdeutscher Verlag.

Schönbach, Klaus. 1987. "The Role of Mass Media in West German Election Campaigns." *Legislative Studies Quarterly* 12:373-394.

Schönbach, Klaus, and Holli A. Semetko. 1994. "Medienberichterstattung und Parteienwerbung im Bundestagswahlkampf 1990. Ergebnisse aus Inhaltsanalysen und Befragungen." *Media Perspektiven* 7:328-340.

Schoof, Peter. 1980. *Wahlbeteiligung und Sozialstruktur in der Bundesrepublik.* Frankfurt/Main: Haag und Herchen.

Schrott, Peter. 1990a. "Electoral Consequences of 'Winning' Televised Campaign Debates." *Public Opinion Quarterly* 54:567-585.

Schrott, Peter. 1990b. "Wahlkampfdebatten im Fernsehen von 1972 bis 1987: Politikerstrategien und Wählerreaktion." In *Wahlen und Wähler: Analysen aus Anlaß der Bundestagswahl 1987,* ed. Max Kaase and Hans-Dieter Klingemann. Opladen: Westdeutscher Verlag.

Schrott, Peter R., and Michael F. Meffert. 1995. *Media Usage and Campaign Effects: Candidate Evaluations and Issues.* Paper presented at the Annual Meeting of the American Political Science Association, Chicago, August 31 - September 3, 1995.

Schultze, Rainer-Olaf. 1991. "Wählerverhalten und Parteiensystem." In *Wahlverhalten,* ed. Hans-Georg Wehling. Stuttgart: Kohlhammer.

Schultze, Rainer-Olaf. 1994. "Aus Anlaß des Superwahljahres: Nachdenken über Konzepte und Ergebnisse der Wahlsoziologie." *Zeitschrift für Parlamentsfragen* 25:472-493.

Schulz, Winfried, and Klaus Kindelmann. 1993. "Die Entwicklung der Images von Kohl und Lafontaine im Wahljahr 1990. Ein Vergleich der Wählerurteile mit den Urteilen ausgewählter Leitmedien." In *Die Massenmedien im Wahlkampf: Untersuchungen aus dem Wahljahr 1990,* ed. Christina Holtz-Bacha and Lynda Lee Kaid. Opladen: Westdeutscher Verlag.

Schulz, Winfried, and Klaus Schönbach ed. 1983. *Massenmedien und Wahlen. Mass Media and Elections: International Research Perspectives.* Munich: Ölschläger.

Schulz, Wolfram. 1990. *Kontinuität oder Wandel? Parteieigung und Sozialstruktur in der Bundesrepublik von 1963 bis 1985* (Berlin Working Papers and Reports on Social Science Research, Nr. 54). Berlin: Zentralinstitut für Sozialwissenschaftliche Forschung.

Shaffer, Stephen D. 1981. "A Multivariate Explanation of Decreasing Turnout in Presidential Elections 1960-1976." *American Journal of Political Science* 25:68-95.

Shepsle, Kenneth. 1989. "Studying Institutions: Some Lessons from the Rational Choice Approach." *Journal of Theoretical Politics* 1:131-147.

Shively, W. Phillips. 1979. "The Development of Party Idenfication among Adults: Exploration of a Functional Model." *American Political Science Review* 73:1039-1054.

Shugart, Matthew. 1992. "Leaders, Rank and File, and Constituents: Electoral Reform in Colombia and Venezuela." *Electoral Studies* 11:21-45.

Silver, Brian D., Barbara A. Anderson, and Paul R. Abramson. 1986. "Who Overreports Voting?" *American Political Science Review* 80:613-624.

Singer, Otto. 1992. "The Politics and Economics of German Unification: From Currency Union to Economic Dichotomy." *German Politics* 1:78-94.

Smith, Gordon. 1993. "Dimensions of Change in the German Party System." In *Parties and Party Systems in the New Germany*, ed. Stephen Padgett. Aldershot: Dartmouth.

Smith, Gordon, William Paterson, Peter H. Merkl, and Stephen Padgett, ed. 1992. *Developments in German Politics*. Durham, NC: Duke University Press.

Smyser, W.R. 1993. *The German Economy: Colossus at the Crossroads*. 2d ed. New York: St. Martin's Press.

Sniderman, Paul M., and Richard A. Brody. 1977. "Coping: The Ethics of Self-Reliance." *American Journal of Political Science* 21:501-521.

Somit, Albert et al. 1994. *The Victorious Incumbent: A Threat to Democracy*. Aldershot: Dartmouth.

SPD. 1965. *Jahrbuch 1964/65*. Bonn: Neuer Vorwärts Verlag.

Staab, Joachim Friedrich. 1990. *Nachrichtenwert-Theorie. Formale Struktur und empirischer Gehalt*. Freiburg: Alber.

Statistisches Bundesamt [Federal Statistics Agency], ed. 1954. *Statistisches Jahrbuch für die Bundesrepublik Deutschland 1954*. Wiesbaden: Kohlhammer.

Statistisches Bundesamt [Federal Statistics Agency], ed. 1994. *Datenreport 1994*. Bonn: Bundeszentrale für Politische Bildung.

Steiner, Jürg. 1969. *Bürger und Politik*. Meisenheim am Glan: Anton Hain.

Stimson, James A. 1991. *Public Opinion in America. Moods, Cycles, and Swings*. Boulder, CO: Westview.

Taagepera, Rein, and Matthew Shugart. 1989. *Seats and Votes*. New Haven, CT: Yale University Press.

Teixeira, Ruy A. 1987. *Turnout Decline in the United States 1960-1984*. New York: Greenwood Press.

Teixeira, Ruy A. 1992. *The Disappearing American Voter*. Washington, DC: Brookings.

Tsebelis, George. 1990. *Nested Games. Rational Choice in Comparative Politics*. Berkeley: University of California Press.

Veen, Hans-Joachim. 1991. "Einführung–Wählergesellschaft im Umbruch." In *Wähler-verhalten im Wandel: Bestimmungsgründe und politisch-kulturelle Trends am Beispiel der Bundestagswahl 1987*, ed. Hans-Joachim Veen and Elisabeth Noelle-Neumann. Paderborn: Schöningh.

Veen, Hans-Joachim, and Peter Gluchowski. 1994. "Die Anhängerschaften der Parteien vor und nach der Einheit - eine Langfristbetrachtung von 1953 bis 1993." *Zeitschrift für Parlamentsfragen* 25:165-186.

Veen, Hans-Joachim, and Elisabeth Noelle-Neumann, eds. 1991. *Wählerverhalten im Wandel: Bestimmungsgrhnde und politisch-kulturelle Trends am Beispiel der Bundestagswahl 1987*. Paderborn: Schöningh.

Veen, Hans-Joachim, and Carsten Zelle. 1995. "National Identity and Political Priorities in Eastern and Western Germany." *German Politics* 4:1-26.

Verba, Sidney, and Norman H. Nie. 1972. *Participation in America: Political Democracy and Social Equality*. New York: Harper & Row.

Verba, Sidney, Norman H. Nie, and Jae-on Kim. 1978. *Participation and Political Equality. A Seven-Nation-Comparison*. Cambridge, MA: Harvard University Press.

Vester, Michael, Peter v. Oertzen, Heiko Geiling, Thomas Hermann, and Dagmar Müller. 1993. *Soziale Milieus im gesellschaftlichen Strukturwandel. Zwischen Integration und Ausgrenzung*. Cologne: Bund Verlag.

Voltmer, Katrin, Eva Schabedoth, and Peter R. Schrott. 1995. "Individuelle Teilnahme an politischer Kommunikation. Zur Bedeutung von interpersonaler und massenmedialer Kommunikation im Prozeß der deutschen Vereinigung." In *Zwischen Wende und Wiedervereinigung. Analysen zur politischen Kultur in West- und Ost-Berlin 1990*, ed. Hans-Dieter Klingemann, Lutz Erbring, and Niels Diederich. Opladen: Westdeutscher Verlag.

Wagner, Joseph. 1983. "Media Do Make a Difference: The Differential Impact of Mass Media in the 1976 Presidential Race." *American Journal of Political Science* 27:407-430.

Wattenberg, Martin. 1984. *The Decline of American Political Parties, 1952-1984*. Cambridge, MA: Harvard University Press.

Wattenberg, Martin P. 1991. *The Rise of Candidate-Centered Politics*. Cambridge, MA: Harvard University Press.

Wattenberg, Martin P. 1994. *The Decline of American Political Parties 1952-1992*. Cambridge, MA: Harvard University Press.

Weatherford, M. Stephen. 1986. "Economic Determinants of Voting." *Research in Micropolitics: A Research Annual*, ed. Samuel Long. Greenwich, CT: JAI Press.

Weaver, David H. 1984. "Media Agenda-Setting and Public Opinion: Is There a Link?" In *Communication Yearbook 8*, ed. Robert N. Bostrom and B. H. Westley. Beverly Hills, CA: Sage.

Weege, Wilhelm. 1992. "Klasse, Elite, Establishment, Fhhrungsgruppen. Ein gberblick hber die politik- und sozialwissenschaftliche Diskussion." In *Die politische Klasse in Deutschland. Eliten auf dem Prüfstand,* ed. Thomas Leif, Hans-Josef Legrand, and Ansgar Klein. Bonn: Bouvier.

Wehling, Hans-Georg. 1991. "Zur Geschichte der kommunalen Selbstverwaltung im deutschen Südwesten." In *Kommunalpolitik in Baden-Württemberg* 2d ed. ed Theodor Pfizer and Hans-Georg Wehling. Stuttgart: Kohlhammer.

Welch, Susan, and Donley T. Studlar. 1986. "British Public Opinion Toward Women in Politics: A Comparative Perspective." *Western Political Quarterly* 39:138-154.

Welch, Susan, and Donley T. Studlar. 1990. "Multi-Member Districts and the Representation of Women: Evidence from Britain and the United States." *Journal of Politics* 52:391-412.

Welzel, Christian. 1997. *Demokratischer Elitenwandel. Die Erneuerung der ostdeutschen Elite aus demokratie-soziologischer Sicht.* Opladen: Leske & Budrich.

Wenzel, Heinz-Dieter. 1993. "Economic and Fiscal Aspects of German Reunification and Lessons for European Integration." In *Ungarn im neuen Europa: Integration, Transformation, Markteintrittsstrategien*, ed. Johann Engelhard. Wiesbaden: Gabler.

Wernicke, Immo H. 1976. *Die Bedingungen politischer Partizipation.* Meisenheim am Glan: Anton Hain.

Weßels, Bernhard. 1994. "Gruppenbindung und rationale Faktoren als Determinanten der Wahlentscheidung in Ost- und Westdeutschland." In *Wahlen und Wähler. Analysen aus Anlaß der Bundestagswahl 1990,* ed. Hans-Dieter Klingemann and Max Kaase. Opladen: Westdeutscher Verlag.

Westle, Bettina. 1992. "Untersthtzung des politischen Systems des vereinten Deutschland." In *Blickpunkt Gesellschaft 2. Einstellungen und Verhalten der Bundesbhrger in Ost und West,* ed. Peter Ph. Mohler and Wolfgang Bandilla. Opladen: Westdeutscher Verlag.

Westle, Bettina. 1994. "Demokratie und Sozialismus. Politische Ordnungsvorstellungen im vereinigten Deutschland zwischen Ideologie, Protest und Nostalgie." *Kölner Zeitschrift für Soziologie und Sozialpsychologie* 46:571-596.

Wewer, Göttrik. 1990. "Unfähig zu strategischem Denken? Sozialdemokraten und staatliche Parteienfinanzierung." In *Parteifinanzierung und politischer Wettbewerb*, ed. Göttrik Wewer. Opladen: Westdeutscher Verlag.

Wilamowitz-Moellendorff, Ulrich von. 1993. "Der Wandel ideologischer Orientierungs-muster zwischen 1971 und 1991 am Beispiel des Links-Rechts-Schemas." *ZA-Information* 32:42-71.

Winkler, Heinrich August. 1993. *Weimar 1918-1933. Die Geschichte der ersten deutschen Demokratie.* München: Beck.

354   Bibliography

Winkler, Jürgen. 1995. *Sozialstruktur, politische Tradtionen und Liberalismus. Eine empirische Längsschnittanalyse zur Wahlentwicklung in Deutschland 1871-1933.* Opladen: Westdeutscher Verlag.

Winter, Thomas von. 1996. "Wählerverhalten in den östlichen Bundesländern: Wahlsoziologische Erklärungsmodelle auf dem Prhfstand. *Zeitschrift für Parlamentsfragen* 27:298-316.

Wolfinger, Raymond E., and Steven J. Rosenstone. 1980. *Who Votes?* New Haven, CT: Yale University Press.

Woyke. Wichard. 1994. *Stichwort: Wahlen. Wähler - Parteien - Wahlverfahren.* 8th ed. Bonn: Bundeszentrale für politische Bildung.

Wright, William E. 1971. "Comparative Political Party Models." In *A Comparative Study of Party Organization* ed. William E. Wright. Columbia, OH: Bobbs Merrill.

Zapf, Wolfgang, Sigrid Breuer, Jürgen Hampel, Peter Krause, Hans-Michael Mohr, and Erich Wiegand. 1987. *Individualisierung und Sicherheit. Untersuchungen zur Lebensqualität in der Bundesrepublik Deutschland.* Munich: Beck.

Zelle, Carsten. 1994. "Steigt die Zahl der Wechselwähler? Trends des Wahlverhaltens und der Parteiidentifikation." In *Wahlen und politische Einstellungen im vereinigten Deutschland,* ed. Hans Rattinger, Wolfgang Jagodzinski, and Oscar W. Gabriel. Frankfurt/Main: Lang.

Zelle, Carsten. 1995a. *Der Wechselwähler. Eine Gegenüberstellung politischer und sozialer Erklärungsansansätze des Wählerwandels in Deutschland und in den USA.* Opladen: Westdeutscher Verlag.

Zelle, Carsten. 1995b. "Social Dealignment vs. Political Frustration: Contrasting Explanations of the Floating Vote in Germany." *European Journal of Political Research* 27:319-345.

Zelle, Carsten. 1995c. "Candidates, Issues and Party Choice in the Federal Election of 1994." *German Politics* 4:54-74.

Zelle, Carsten. 1997. *Ostalgie? National and Regional Identifications in Germany after Unification.* Birmingham: Institute for German Studies. (IGS Discussion Paper Series No. 97/10).

Zelle, Carsten. 1998. "Modernisierung, Personalisierung, Unzufriedenheit: Erklärungsversuche der Wechselwahl bei der Bundestagswahl 1994." In *Wahlen und Wähler. Analysen aus Anlaß der Bundestagswahl 1994*, ed. Max Kaase and Hans-Dieter Klingemann. Opladen: Westdeutscher Verlag.

Zohlnhöfer, Werner. 1965. "Parteiidentifizierung in der Bundesrepublik und in den Vereinigten Staaten." In *Zur Soziologie der Wahl. Sonderheft 9 der Kölner Zeitschrift für Soziologie und Sozialpsychologie,* ed. Erwin K. Scheuch and Rudolf Wildenmann. Cologne: Westdeutscher Verlag.

INDEX

ABOUT THE CONTRIBUTORS

CHRISTOPHER J. ANDERSON is Assistant Professor of Political Science at the State University of New York at Binghamton. Author of *Blaming the Government: Citizens and the Economy in Five European Democracies* (1995), his interests have centered around the interaction of the economy, political institutions, and political behavior in democracies. His research has been published in such journals as the *American Political Science Review*, *British Journal of Political Science*, *Comparative Political Studies*, *Electoral Studies*, and *European Journal of Political Research*.

FRANK BRETTSCHNEIDER is Assistant Professor in the Department of Political Science at the University of Stuttgart. His research focuses on public opinion, electoral behavior, media effects, and comparative politics. He recently published a monograph on public opinion and policy outcomes in Germany, and is the co-editor of a volume on the European Union, entitled *Die EU-Staaten im Vergleich* (1994). He also has published a number of journal articles on rational voting and election outcomes.

ULRICH EITH is Assistant Professor of Political Science at the University of Freiburg. Author of *Wählerverhalten in Sachsen-Anhalt. Zur Bedeutung sozialstruktureller Einfluß-faktoren auf die Wahlentscheidungen 1990 und 1994* (1997), a study of the impact of social strata on voting behavior in East Germany, his research has focused on party systems, political attitudes, voting behavior, right-wing extremism, and local politics.

OSCAR W. GABRIEL is Professor and Chair of the Department of Political Science at the University of Stuttgart. He has written and edited numerous books and articles on political behavior, local politics, and political systems. Recent examples include *Die EU Staaten im Vergleich* (1994), *Politische Orientierungen und Verhaltensweisen im vereinigten Deutschland* (1997), *Handbuch Politisches System der Bundesrepublik* (1997), and *Urban Democracy* (1998).

PETER M. GLUCHOWSKI is Head of the Social Research Division of the Konrad Adenauer Foundation in St. Augustin near Bonn. He is author of numerous publications on voting behavior and lifestyle research.

WOLFGANG JAGODZINSKI is Professor of Sociology, Director of the Central Archive for Empirical Social Research, and Director of the Institute for Applied Social Research at the University of Cologne. His research on comparative political sociology, value change, and voting behavior has appeared in journals such as the *American Political Science Review* and *Comparative Political Studies.*

MARKUS KLEIN is Assistant Professor at the Central Archive for Empirical Social Research at the University of Cologne. He has published several articles on value change and electoral behavior and is coauthor of *Wahlen und Wählerverhalten*, 2d. ed (1998), a textbook on theories of voting behavior. He currently works on conjoint analysis.

THOMAS KLEINHENZ is a business consultant in Munich. He is author of *Die Nichtwähler: Ursachen der sinkenden Wahlbeteiligung in Deutschland* (1995) as well as of a number of articles on electoral participation in Germany, and has coauthored several works on political transformation in eastern Germany and eastern Europe.

STEFFEN M. KÜHNEL is Professor of Empirical Social Research at the University of Giessen. His interests are in political sociology, rational choice theory and its applications in the social sciences, as well as statistical models for multivariate data analysis. He is coauthor of *Analyse von Tabellen und kategorialen Daten*, a German textbook on categorical data analysis. Most recently he has conducted a study about the relationship between environmental attitudes and traffic mode decisions.

JÜRGEN KRÄMER is a Doctoral Student at the University of Bamberg. His most recent work is "The Proximity and the Directional Theories of Issue Voting: Comparative Results for the USA and Germany," in *European Journal of Political Research* (32, 1997) (with Hans Rattinger).

THOMAS D. LANCASTER is Associate Professor of Political Science at Emory University in Atlanta. His research and teaching interests include comparative politics, with a specialization in western and southern European politics, comparative electoral behavior, and the logic of comparative political inquiry. His most recent works include contributing to *Western European Government and Politics* (1997) and coauthoring "Toward a Methodology for the Comparative Study of Political Corruption" in *Crime, Law, and Social Change* (27, 1997).

HANS RATTINGER is Professor of Political Science at the University of Bamberg. Professor Rattinger is author, co-author, and editor of twelve books on German elections, including *Wirtschaftliche Konjunktur und Politische Wahlen in der Bundesrepublik Deutschland* (1980) and has published a number of articles in journals such as *European Journal of Political Research, Electoral Studies, Public Opinion Quarterly, German Politics*, and *Journal of Common Market Studies.*

SUSAN E. SCARROW is Associate Professor of Political Science at the University of Houston. She is the author of *Parties and their Members* (1996) and coeditor of "The Politics of Anti-Party Sentiment," a special issue of the *European Journal of Political Research.* She also has published many articles and book chapters on party organization and party politics in Germany and elsewhere.

KARL SCHMITT is Professor of Political Science at the University of Jena. Mainly known for his work on religion, social structure, and political behavior, he is also author and editor of several books on German elections and politics, including *Konfession und Wahlverhalten in der Bundesrepublik Deutschland* (1989).

PETER R. SCHROTT is Director of the Department of Text Analysis, Media Analysis, and Coding at the Center for Survey Research and Methodology (ZUMA), University of Mannheim. He is interested in electoral behavior, political communication, public opinion, and research methodology. Coauthor of *The Joint Press Conference*, a book on American presidential televised debates, he has published a number of articles in journals such as *Political Behavior, Public Opinion Quarterly*, and the *British Journal of Political Science*.

ANGELIKA VETTER is Research Assistant in the Department of Political Science at the University of Stuttgart. Her most recent monograph dealt with questions of reliability and validity in measuring political efficacy. She is also working on research projects focusing on local politics, political culture, voting behavior, and political candidates. Her most recent work is an article written with Frank Brettschneider about media effects on internal and external efficacy.

ULRICH VON WILAMOWITZ-MOELLENDORFF is Research Fellow in the Social Research Division of the Konrad Adenauer Foundation. He has published articles and book chapters on voting behavior, attitudes toward European Unification, and regional development.

CARSTEN ZELLE was Assistant Professor at the Department of Political Science at the University of Potsdam. He is the author of *Der Wechselwähler* (1995) as well as a number of articles on electoral behavior, political culture, and political parties in such journals as *European Journal of Political Research, German Politics and Society*, and *German Politics*.

ISBN 0-275-96254-7

EAN

9 780275 962548

90000>

HARDCOVER BAR CODE